AMERICAN COLONIAL HISTORY

North America and the Caribbean, circa 1720. Map by Bill Nelson.

AMERICAN COLONIAL HISTORY

Clashing Cultures and Faiths

Thomas S. Kidd

Yale

UNIVERSITY

PRESS

New Haven & London

Published with assistance from the foundation established in memory of Calvin Chapin of the Class of 1788, Yale College.

Yale University Press books may be purchased in quantity for educational, business, or promotional use. For information, please e-mail sales.press@yale.edu (U.S. office) or sales@yaleup.co.uk (U.K. office).

Set in Electra type by Integrated Publishing Solutions, Grand Rapids, Michigan.

ISBN 978-0-300-18732-8 (paperback : alk. paper)

Library of Congress Control Number: 2015951238

A catalogue record for this book is available from the British Library.

Printed and bound by CPI Group (UK) Ltd, Croydon, CR0 4YY

10 9 8 7 6 5 4 3 2 1

CONTENTS

Each chapter is followed by three to four representative documents

related to the chapter's topic

Introduction

About 850 miles west of Jamestown, Virginia, a little south of the confluence of the Missouri and Mississippi rivers, stands the site of the city of Cahokia. Nine hundred years ago it was the largest city in the region that would become the United States. Cahokia was at least as big as London and Rome during the same period. By the twelfth century C.E., about twenty thousand people lived at Cahokia, which contained 120 ceremonial mounds, some of immense scope. The city spread over five square miles.

Earlier settlements, including a smaller one at Cahokia, had dotted the rich Mississippi river bottoms in the area before the eleventh century, but something changed dramatically to create the new city. The catalyst may have come from a spectacular astronomical phenomenon, a supernova. On July 4, 1054, people around the globe observed what appeared as a daytime star, four times as bright as Venus, resulting from the explosion of a star in its death throes. This kind of brilliant eruption is exceedingly rare—the last observed supernova in the Milky Way happened in 1604.

From China to America, observers noted and etched the phenomenon. At Chaco Canyon, in present-day New Mexico, an artist painted an image of the supernova on sandstone cliffs.[1] The residents of Chaco Canyon also began construction around 1054 on a large new kiva, a below-ground ceremonial building frequently seen at southwestern Indian dwellings.

Around the time of the supernova, the old village at Cahokia virtually vanished. Inhabitants replaced it with a larger complex of houses, plazas, and earthen pyramids. The city surrounded a vast grand plaza, topped at its north end by an astounding clay pyramid, which by the year 1200 towered a hundred feet over the plaza below, making it the third largest structure of its kind in the

New World, surpassed only by two pyramids in Mexico. One of these was the Pyramid of the Sun at Teotihuacán, a much older city, which at its height in the fifth century C.E. was one of the largest in the world, with perhaps 150,000 residents.

Cahokia's rapid ascent was led by powerful rulers and created deep social divides. The mounds there have yielded evidence of ritual burial and human sacrifice. One burial temple held the skeleton of a man who was interred on top of a blanket adorned with some twenty thousand shell beads. Close to his body lay four men who had been dismembered. In another nearby pit lay the carefully positioned bodies of fifty-three young women, all of whom presumably died during the same event. Other Cahokia-area excavations have produced hundreds of bodies that display signs of ceremonial killings. Archaeologists have surmised that these people may have fallen victim to rituals surrounding the death of a ruler, perhaps so he could have servants or companions to accompany him into the next life. Or perhaps elites meant to communicate that lowly Cahokians lived only at the rulers' will.

The silent testimonies of these bodies point us to both social and spiritual beliefs at Cahokia. The spiritual world inspired rituals, and influenced even the positioning of mounds and buildings, many of which aligned with vernal and autumnal equinoxes. Many Native Americans were profoundly religious, even if their faith was not as focused on doctrines as that of many Europeans, who would begin arriving in the Americas some three hundred years after Cahokia's heyday.

Things changed often in Native Americans' worlds prior to Columbus. Just as quickly as the city of Cahokia rose, it fell. By the mid-1300s the great complex was essentially abandoned. Cahokia's elite mound builders were probably victims of their own success, as their urban concentration made it difficult to supply the town's needs. Warfare, disease, and political controversy may have also contributed to Cahokia's demise. In any case, when Europeans began visiting the area in the seventeenth century, the Illini Indians living there did not know much about great Cahokia, its presence signaled only by overgrown mounds dotting the landscape. The mounds were "the works of their forefathers," some Illini told Revolutionary War leader George Rogers Clark, ancestors who were "formerly as numerous as the trees in the woods." Adding to a long list of European-American misnomers, French settlers called the ruined city "Cahokia," after one of the Illini's major clans.[2]

Religion indisputably inspired the first European settlement at Cahokia, which arrived with French Catholic missionaries in 1699. The Seminary of Foreign

Missions, based in Quebec (some 1,200 miles to the northeast) charged several missionaries to establish a station in the heart of the continent, hopefully even beyond the lands of the Illini. But instead the French priests created a settlement at Cahokia, founding the Mission of the Holy Family. By the 1720s, French and Illini villages adjoined the seminarians' residence, and French officials in the Illinois country granted the seminarians a vast tract of land amounting to one hundred square miles. Still, a 1723 census registered the presence of only twelve inhabitants of the French village. It did not count the priests, nor Indian or African slaves, of which there were probably a few by the early 1730s, as reflected by the construction of slave quarters. The missionaries owned these enslaved people. The Cahokia Indians' numbers ran well over a thousand, but despite the Europeans' small number, the French and their livestock had transformed their patterns of land use, leading to resentment against the new European settlers and their priests.[3]

Few Cahokia Indians converted at the mission, and anger against the French grew. In spring 1733 the priests and French laypeople fled from the mission under the cover of darkness, having heard that the Indians intended to surprise and kill them. (Only three years earlier, local Indians had done this at Natchez, farther down the Mississippi, killing more than two hundred French men, women, and children, and capturing some three hundred black slaves.) Nothing came of the Cahokia panic, but French officials did require the Cahokia Indians to settle further from the French village. They went nine miles away, to the base of the largest Cahokia mound ("Monks Mound," named later for a group of Trappist monks who farmed it in the early nineteenth century.) There the French established a new mission station for them.

Resentment over land did not just sour French and Cahokian relations; they embittered Fox and Cahokian Indians toward one another, too. This feud culminated in a devastating Fox raid on Cahokia in 1752. Christianized Cahokias were attending a Corpus Christi feast at the nearby Fort de Chartres when the attack came. Many Cahokias died or were taken captive. The raid set the stage for the eventual extinction of the Cahokias, who merged with the Peorias. The U.S. government would relocate the Peorias to Oklahoma following the Civil War.

War and diplomacy imposed a new—if largely nominal—order on Cahokia in 1763. The east bank of the Mississippi became British. The French loss in the Seven Years' War, and its concluding peace agreement at Paris in 1763, assigned eastern North America to the British. Under the terms of a secret treaty struck in

1762, France agreed to cede its lands west of the Mississippi (the "Louisiana territory") to Spain. French residents in the area felt they had entered a "political twilight zone," but some figured that French settlements on the west side of the river were a safer choice, even if they formally stood under Spanish control. With this in mind, French traders established a tiny settlement, La Ville de St. Louis des Illinois sur le Mississippi—or just "St. Louis"—in 1764. Soon Catholics began meeting in a tent chapel, which they used whenever itinerant priests crossed the wide river into Spain's American territory to shepherd the faithful.[4]

No one foresaw the Louisiana territory's 1803 sale to a nation that did not yet exist, or St. Louis's emergence as that nation's fourth largest city by 1900. Few remembered its eleventh-century predecessor across the river, either.

From July 4, 1054—the day of the supernova—to July 4, 1776, North America was in constant motion. Changes in settlements, alliances, culture, and environment were the norm. For America's people, nothing was inevitable or expected, from Columbus's arrival in 1492 to the American Revolution in 1776. Until January 1776, American independence seemed improbable, and few ever gave it a second thought. That is especially the case when you view early America's history from the banks of the Mississippi at Cahokia and St. Louis. The Revolution seemed hardly a consideration there. Even England was not a major consideration, at least until the Treaty of Paris redrew the continent's territorial boundaries in 1763 (with no consultation of most people who actually lived in places like the Illinois country). Yet that treaty remains as good a time as any to mark the end of the colonial era.

Even in the years leading up to 1776, there are other ways of looking at North America's history than the crisis of the British empire that led to the creation of the United States. For example, in 1776, Franciscan priests commissioned by the College of San Fernando in Mexico City founded a presidio and Mission San Francisco de Asís in Alta California, at the northern end of a string of missions that ran south to Mission San Diego (1769). In the coming decades, thousands of California Indians would receive baptism and enter the mission communities. Many would also leave, much to the priests' chagrin. They fled out of frustration and fear. Hundreds of Indians—about a third of the Christian adherents—abandoned Mission San Francisco in 1795, when an epidemic ravaged it, killing another quarter of the native inhabitants. The setting sun of George Washington's presidency was not much on their mind.[5]

Yet for Americans' memory of the colonial past, there is an appropriate concern with the background to the Revolution of 1776. How, in all the varied experiences of Indians, Africans, and Europeans, was the stage set for a sufficient union of American colonists to try to liberate themselves from British rule? *American Colonial History* will seek to answer that question, even if the everyday lives of those living in North America's colonies and the Caribbean reflected almost no concern over that issue, especially until 1763.

The story of America's colonial history is one of clashing and mixing people, meeting under unexpected circumstances in places from Boston to San Francisco to Havana, Cuba. Those already in America, the Indians, found the new arrivals an unwelcome but unavoidable contender for power and trade. Africans and Europeans also brought disease and dislocation to Native American people in ways that no group fully understood. Africans, who composed by far the largest of the groups who immigrated to the Americas in the colonial era, typically came involuntarily as slaves. They found themselves living, working, and dying on new European farms and plantations, but a fraction of Africans found avenues for advancement, prosperity, and freedom. Europeans came for business opportunities, for the chance to own land, and many of them came inspired by religious convictions and the prospect of practicing their vision of full biblical faith in peace, or at least peace for those who accepted that religious vision.

Two major themes organize *American Colonial History*: religion and conflict. The conditions that brought these disparate peoples together almost guaranteed cultural clashes. All of the groups—Indians, Africans, and Europeans—had deep traditions of often-brutal violence among and between their own neighbors before 1492. They extended those traditions of conflict in the destabilized New World. (The "New World" was every bit as new for the Indians as it was for Europeans and Africans, even though they did not cross an ocean to get there.)

Many Europeans, Native Americans, and Africans engaged in war, torture, and enslavement, before and after the arrival of the New World, practices that most observers today would regard as inhumane and intolerable. Though some of the details of that behavior may be disturbing, this book tries neither to avoid the violence of the cultural clashes, nor to make excuses for the actions of any group. Europeans do carry a disproportionate share of the blame for the violence and dislocation: they initiated colonization, they financed and executed much of slavery's development in the Atlantic world, they unintentionally introduced the most virulent diseases that ravaged the New World, and they possessed disproportionate power and resources for war-making.

Many in early America interpreted their interactions with their rivals, including violence and enslavement, through the lens of religion and spiritual beliefs. Although individuals varied as to the depth of their religious commitments, all peoples of Native America, Europe, and Africa brought spiritual practices and convictions with them into the colonial arena. Religion in colonial America could inspire everything from exploration to genocidal conquest, idyllic communes to generations of spite, and the dehumanization of entire peoples to advocacy for human rights.

For people in colonial America, religion was not only the path of salvation in the next life, it was a primary way of making sense of what was happening to them in the present life. It inspired groups like the Puritans to come to the New World; it drove the Spanish and French to commission evangelists among Native Americans; it offered Native Americans and Africans a measure of power in a world spinning out of control. The Europeans, most of them at least nominally Christian, sent missionaries to the front lines of empire. Some must have encouraged missions cynically, out of a desire to bolster imperial authority. Others did so out of a conviction that in Jesus, the people of the New World would find true spiritual succor into eternity. But perhaps the most common way religion functioned was to *explain*—explain the uncertain and often violent environment in which Americans found themselves between Columbus's voyages and the end of the Seven Years' War.

My hope is that readers of *American Colonial History* will come away with a distinct sense of how pervasive religion was in colonial America, and of the varied functions that religion served in the era, functions that were variously inspiring and appalling. The first two centuries of the American colonial story were indeed "barbarous years," as historian Bernard Bailyn has put it, although colonial Americans before 1689 (England's Glorious Revolution) hardly had an exclusive title to conflict and grotesque violence. Much of the story of colonial America, then, is bleak. Not that heroism was absent, but the same figures who sacrificed much to seek opportunity, or to live according the dictates of their conscience, could also brutally deny opportunity and the rights of conscience to others. Growing institutional and cultural stability did mark the period from 1689 to 1763, but patterns of conflict—often with religious roots—persisted both in settled eastern areas and in the expanding colonial west. The greatest military clash of the colonial era, the Seven Years' War, encapsulated many of themes of this book: violence rooted in imperial and economic rivalry was explained in religious terms (Catholic versus Protestant power), and intra-European clashes left Native Americans to make difficult decisions about alliances and the elusive possibilities of neutrality. The decisive political outcome of the Seven Years' War—the expulsion of the French from eastern North America—stabilized the British colonies in the short term. But it left a vacuum in which yet more conflict, this time between British colonists and London-based authorities, would erupt into war and revolution in 1775.

My book depends on decades of excellent work produced by historians of colonial America, including the English, French, and Spanish empires, African American culture and slavery, and Native American history, before and after the arrival of Europeans and Africans. I hope that my notes adequately reflect my debt to these historians and other scholars, and that the chapters may serve as launching points for deeper research for readers wanting to know more.

ACKNOWLEDGMENTS

It has been a great pleasure to work with my Yale University Press editor, Sarah Miller, and the rest of the Yale team who helped bring this book to fruition. Thanks to my Baylor assistants, Tim Grundmeier, Paul Gutacker, and Grace Pak, for their assiduous work; to my friend and literary agent Giles Anderson; and to my colleagues in Baylor's history department and at Baylor's Institute for Studies of Religion. As always, I am so thankful for my wife, Ruby, and for my boys, who make all my work worth it.

NATIVE AMERICANS AND THE
EUROPEAN ENCOUNTER

Some 15,000 years ago, an ancient North American Indian dropped—or lost, or threw away—a blue-gray piece of carved stone that had served as a cutting tool. It fell along what would become a creek bank in a place later claimed by the Spanish, the Comanches, Mexico, the Republic of Texas, and finally, the state of Texas and the United States of America. Fifteen millennia later, archaeologists dug up the stone tool, along with a trove of more than 19,000 other artifacts, at central Texas's Buttermilk Creek site. This discovery pushed back the dates of the earliest known settlements in North America by two thousand years. The Buttermilk Creek settlement tells us that "Americans"—meaning people who lived in what would become known as the Americas—have existed for a very long time. Maybe they came millennia earlier than the ancestors of those who migrated to Buttermilk Creek. In any case, human history in the Americas far predated Columbus's arrival.[1]

✦ ✦ ✦

Well before the Buttermilk Creek resident dropped his tool, the first wave of Paleo-Indians began crossing a land bridge from present-day Siberia to Alaska which ice age conditions had exposed. These Indians were "hunter-gatherers" who traveled in groups of fewer than fifty or so, pursuing game in their wanderings. They established seasonal camps at convenient locations, near watering holes that might supply the Indians and their quarry alike. The quarry they pursued were reminiscent of some modern species, only much bigger: seven-foot-long beavers, and bison with antlers as big as a modern Texas longhorn's. Mammoths, almost the size of elephants, were twelve-foot-tall, ten-ton behemoths. Some Paleo-Indians may have had to compete for game with predators like the saber-tooth cat. Although the ancient Indians hunted smaller species, too, they especially coveted the bigger animals. A mammoth kill could give them meat for months, because they could dry the animal's flesh. Some even developed refrigeration techniques, such as filling a mammoth or mastodon's intestines with meat—like big sausages—and depositing them at the bottom of a chilly body of water, marking the spot and going back as needed.

With this rich bounty of animals and wide open spaces, Paleo-Indians quickly spread through North and South America. Some of the earliest known settlements are quite far south, as far as current-day Peru. Some Siberian migrants may have actually moved south by canoe, along the Pacific coast. In any case, the spread of ancient Indians corresponded with the mass extinction of most of their giant prey. We do not know for sure why this extinction happened, but it seems likely that the new human presence, as well as a pattern of global warming, contributed to the great beasts' demise. Gone were the mammoths and giant bison, and over time the Indians came to focus on smaller animals as well as other food sources such as nuts and berries. This transition heralded the coming of the Archaic culture of Indians, which lasted until roughly 1000 B.C.E.

Archaic Indians living close to water sources depended on fish, mussels, and oysters for sustenance, sometimes leaving startling evidence of how much they manipulated the environment to catch their prey. More than a century ago, Boston subway workers began excavating thousands of sharpened stakes below Boylston Street in the Back Bay neighborhood. This two-acre area, uncovered during a century of subway and office construction, revealed a four-thousand-year-old series of fish traps. Native fishermen would build brush fences parallel to the shore. High tide waters would go over the fences, but as the tide receded these fences would trap a number of fish, which the fishermen harvested. The fences also proved a good habitat for oysters. Silting in the Back Bay helped preserve the stakes, but one can imagine similar techniques ancient Americans might have used in other tidal areas.[2]

Across North and Central America, Native Americans molded the landscape, using controlled burns to clear hunting lands, building traps, and constructing ceremonial mounds, some of which matched the pyramids of ancient Egypt as architectural feats. The Olmec people of the southern Gulf of Mexico coastal plain (now in the Mexican states of Veracruz and Tabasco) erected impressive platformed cities, including San Lorenzo, which around 1500 B.C.E. became the first complex, large-scale town in Central or North America. The center of the town sat on an enormous terrace built from some three million cubic yards of rock hewn from mountains fifty miles from San Lorenzo. Even more striking were the huge stone monuments placed all over San Lorenzo, featuring huge, lumpy heads with exaggerated lips, or spirit entities such as the "were-jaguar," an Olmec deity. San Lorenzo fell or went into decline around 1200, but the Olmecs created an even larger center nearby at La Venta, with a one-hundred-foot-high clay mound. La Venta has yielded four massive head carvings, each weighing several tons and featuring helmets that look a bit like the leather head-gear worn by football players in early twentieth-century America. The heads presumably honored Olmec royalty.[3]

As remarkable as these Central American sites were, early mounds built in the lower Mississippi River valley probably predated them by a couple thousand years. Native Americans in present-day Louisiana created earthen mounds that radiocarbon testing has dated to about 3500–3000 B.C.E., which means they are older than the Giza pyramids in Egypt. We do not know exactly how the earliest Americans used these mounds, whether as living spaces, ceremonial sites, or both.

The most stunning accomplishment of lower Mississippi mound-building, however, began around 1400 B.C.E., about the same time as San Lorenzo. At Poverty Point, in northeastern Louisiana, residents built a bird-shaped earthen mound, which today stands seventy-two feet high, overlooking the floodplain of the Mississippi Delta. Because it is not built from stone, the mound does not strike visitors to Poverty Point as all that unusual. Indeed, no one recognized what the Poverty Point complex was until aerial photographs in the 1950s revealed a complex pattern of six long, C-shaped ridges flanking a number of mounds. The longer you reflect on the abrupt hill jutting up from the flat delta landscape, the more you begin to appreciate the scale of the project. Scholars estimate that building it required workers to dig and carry a stunning 27 million large baskets of dirt. Given the mammoth scale of the bird mound and other features, archaeologists once assumed that it took the residents of Poverty Point hundreds of years to build the mounds, including the bird mound. Recent analysis of soil erosion, however, has revealed just the opposite: the hunter-gatherers somehow managed to erect the bird mound in less than ninety days, which would have required the labor of at least three thousand workers. But even that number of workers seems impossibly low, if the mound went up that fast. How and why the mound builders—"the Da Vincis of Dirt," as archaeologists have called them—accomplished this feat remains a mystery.[4]

The mound-builders' impact on their surroundings was dramatic; less dramatic but more significant was the turn to agricultural crops, including the "Three Sisters": squash, beans, and corn. Mayan and Olmec peoples began to cultivate native species of maize, or corn, by the middle of the third century B.C.E., and it spread through North America after that. In the second century B.C.E., evidence of large-scale field clearing for maize began to appear among the Olmec. By the opening of the second millennium C.E., maize accounted for more than 50 percent of the food eaten by commoners in many areas. It suffused not only their diets but their mental worlds. Ears of corn became common symbols in Olmec carvings, in which rulers' headdresses often featured an ear of maize emblazoning the front. Corn came to play a key role in some Native American creation narratives. At Acoma Pueblo in present-day New Mexico, parents of newborn children ritually exchanged gifts with medicine men, who blessed the infant with a spotless ear of corn. Iroquois shamans sometimes wore cornhusk masks when seeking to cure sickness.[5]

The advent of agriculture helps explain the coming of centralized towns (pueblos) among the Hohokam and Anasazi people of the American southwest. They developed elaborate irrigation systems to cultivate maize and other plants in their relatively arid climate. In northwestern New Mexico, the Anasazi built the "great houses" of Chaco Canyon, a major center of trade and religious ceremonies. Trade goods at Chaco Canyon reflect an expansive network that stretched to the Pacific and into the Mayan regions of central America; archaeologists have discovered traces of Mayan cacao (chocolate) in drinking vessels there. The building of Pueblo Bonito, the largest of Chaco Canyon's houses, required some 30,000 tons of sandstone blocks spread over almost two acres. It contained about 650 rooms and stood four stories high. Pueblo Bonito was divided by a central wall aligned to run perfectly north–south, and on each side of the wall stood a great kiva, a ceremonial chamber. As was common for important buildings, the layout accommodated the position of the sun on its solstices.

Two hundred years before a similar decline transpired at Cahokia, the Anasazi center at Chaco Canyon fell into disuse after about 1150 C.E., probably due to drought, soil exhaustion, and resulting political turmoil. One of the new settlements to rise following the demise of Chaco Canyon was Acoma Pueblo, about a hundred miles to the south. Founded around 1300, Acoma is probably the oldest continuously inhabited settlement within what would become the United States.[6]

A French traveler among Canada's Wendats in the early seventeenth century was cooking one evening when he threw some fish bones into the fire. The Indians "scolded me well," he recalled, "and took them out quickly, saying that I did wrong and that I should be responsible for their failure to catch any more, because there were spirits of a sort, or the spirits of the fish themselves whose bones were burnt, which would warn the other fish not to allow themselves to be caught, since their bones also would be burnt."

The Wendats believed the same things about deer, moose, and other game. One day, the French traveler was about to burn a squirrel skin—how else was one to dispose of animal refuse?—but the Indians stopped him and told him to go outside the lodge to dispose of it. Otherwise, they said, the fish nets in the lodge would "tell the fish. I said to them that the nets could see nothing; they replied that they could, and also that they could hear and eat. 'Then give them some of your *sagamité* [porridge],' I said. One of them replied to me: 'It is the fish that feed them, not we.'"[7]

Native Americans lived in a world that was more pervasively religious—or spiritual—than Europeans did. Most Native languages did not even have a word for religion. That concept, in western use, can imply a set of beliefs or practices set apart from the rest of life. Separating the sacred and mundane did not make sense in the mental world of Native Americans.

Regional differences mattered, of course, but there were also spiritual commonalities one could find across Indian communities in early North America. The physical world was teeming with spiritual forces. Fish nets might communicate with fish. Humans were not so different from the plants and animals surrounding them, nor from sky, earth, fire, and water. Humans were elemental and sentient, as were their surroundings.

Sensible people would account for spirit beings by honoring and appeasing them. Many early Native American communities depended upon hunting for sustenance, as illustrated by the ever-present arrowheads and other projectile points found in traces of the earliest Indian settlements. But one did not flippantly kill animals; Native Americans engaged in rituals to recognize and honor the spirits that governed the hunt and animated their prey. When the Micmacs of Nova Scotia butchered beavers, for example, they tried not to let a single drop of blood fall to the ground.

Blood mattered. From the Great Lakes to central America, some hunters ritually cut themselves before going out, believing that the shedding of their own blood would bring favor from resident spirits. Hunters treated carcasses with care, believing that callous behavior would earn them poor catches in the future. Some speculate that the reason archaeologists find so many intact spear- and arrowheads at old Native American settlements is (aside from the relative hardiness of flint and other rock-hewn materials) that hunters may have sacrificed some of the weapons that killed game in the hunt.

Childbearing and fertility impinged in surprising ways on the hunt. Micmacs forbade menstruating women from eating beaver meat, lest they offend the beaver's spirit. Some Indians excluded pregnant women from hunting grounds, fearing that their mere presence would scatter game. Some prohibited infertile women from lingering when bears were being processed, cooked, and eaten.

Although one can distinguish between the practices of Native American religions and those of Christianity and Judaism, one should also not overstate the differences. Mosaic law had required the ancient Israelites to sequester menstruating women, too, and offered many guidelines on the proper preparation of food. The Bible suggests that we live in a physical world surrounded by "powers and principalities" of both good and evil. Native Americans believed in a multiplicity of spirits and gods, but often believed in a primary spiritual being, one reminiscent of the monotheistic God. Algonquian Indians of New England revered Cautantowwit, their leading deity, as the giver (and withholder) of corn, and believed that the souls of good people went to live in his home after they died. Many buried the dead in a fetal position facing southwest, the presumed direction of Cautantowwit's land.[8]

But the Native American notion of "god" or "gods" was more flexible than the monotheistic view. For Algonquins, signs in nature reflected flashes of *manitou,* or spiritual power. English observers often translated *manitou* as "God." Roger Williams, the founder of Providence, Rhode Island, and a relatively sympathetic observer of native culture, remarked that "there is a general custom amongst them, at the apprehension of any excellency in men, women, birds, beasts, fish, &c. to cry out *Manitoo,* that is, it is a God."[9]

Native Americans also took dreams seriously. Many European Christians did, too, but the world revealed to Indians in dreams seemed more real than the waking world. They sought out shamans to help them interpret dreams; they instigated visions by long fasts and the use of plants with psychoactive properties. Jesuit martyr Jean de Brébeuf was stunned by how literally the Wendats took guidance from dreams. "They look upon their dreams as ordinances and irrevocable decrees. . . . [A dream] is the Mercury in their journeys, their domestic economy in their families. The dream often presides in their councils; traffic, fishing, and hunting are undertaken usually under its sanction. . . . It prescribes their feasts, their dances, their songs, their games—in a word, the dream does everything and is in truth the principal God of the Hurons [Wendats]."[10]

Pre-Columbian burial sites can offer clues, like the Algonquins buried facing southwest, regarding early Native American beliefs about life after death. Some of the Mississippian mounds, as we have seen, functioned partly as places of internment. One of the earliest North American burial mounds archaeologists have found, however, was far to the northeast, along the Quebec-Labrador border. There, in a grave carbon dated to 5300 B.C.E., a teenager was buried with hunting tools, a harpoon and other items that the youth might have been expected to take into the afterlife. The funereal pit also contained a shovel fashioned from a caribou antler.[11]

Hundreds of miles up the Mississippi from Cahokia, Indians of eastern Iowa and southern Wisconsin built a mysterious series of "effigy mounds." These constructions probably ended around the time that the building of Cahokia began in earnest, in the mid-eleventh century C.E. One of the most famous collections is at Effigy Mounds National Monument, at a river bluff in eastern Iowa. This site contains about two hundred mounds, including twenty-six in the form of animal effigies. Ten of those are the "Marching Bears," symmetrically spaced in a head-to-tail lineup. Observers once assumed that these were burial mounds, but most of the mounds contain no skeletons or other funereal deposits. Therefore, the mounds must have had tribal and ceremonial importance; some have suggested that the mounds served as conduits of spiritual power and healing. The Marching Bears may also have astronomical significance, as well, since they seem to shadow the Big Dipper as it moves around Polaris, the North Star. It is easy to surmise that these symbolic constructions held religious meaning; it is difficult to articulate exactly what that meaning was.[12]

From the era of European contact, we at least have written descriptions of many Native American ceremonies, but mostly from European perspectives. (A lack of written languages generally leaves knowledge of pre-Columbian native societies to archaeologists and anthropologists.) In spite of their biases, these European sources still offer windows into Indian ceremonies and religious practices. In Ontario, Jean Brébeuf witnessed a remarkable Wendat reburial rite in 1636, their Feast of the Dead. Wendats opened the coffins of relatives initially buried on scaffolds. The bodies of some who had died fairly long ago had decomposed mostly to skin and bones. More recently deceased corpses, Brébeuf noted, stank and teemed with worms, yet the families carefully prepared these bodies for final burial like the others. They cleaned and scraped the bones of any remaining skin and flesh, disassembled the skeleton, and placed it in a beaver skin bag.

This second burial was meant to usher one of the person's souls (everyone had two souls, the Wendats believed) skyward to the village of souls, where the female moon spirit Aataentsic presided. The other soul lingered near the deceased person's bones, although some were reborn into infant Wendats. Families held feasts in honor of the dead, accompanied by singing, chanting, and mourning. Then, in the spring of that year, around planting time, hundreds of Wendats from around the region gathered at a central ossuary pit, about ten feet deep and twenty-four feet in diameter. The Indians built a large scaffold surrounding the pit. After displaying the bone bags and funereal gifts at the scaffold, the Wendats deposited them into the common grave. Once the ossuary was nearly full, women placed corn on top of the bones.[13]

For Wendats and the five million or so other Native Americans living north of the Rio Grande in the decades preceding 1492, death came often through war, accidents, and infant mortality. Diseases, such as encephalitis and polio, were significant causes of death, of course, but not in the desolating way they would be after the coming of the Europeans. The epidemic diseases brought by Europeans are perhaps the single most important factor determining the fate of North America after 1492.

The diseases had devastating effects on Europeans, too, especially in the Black Death of the fourteenth century. Contact with unfamiliar peoples may have spread that epidemic, as bubonic plague seems to have originated in Asia and spread among traders on the Silk Road. By the middle of the fourteenth century, the horrific malady had probably killed one hundred million people, or a third of Europe's population.

Europeans also contracted new diseases as they began to colonize the west coast of sub-Saharan Africa in the fifteenth century. Malaria and yellow fever proved especially deadly. As Europeans and Africans crossed the Atlantic in ever-greater numbers, those illnesses added to the woes of Native American populations.

Because Native American peoples developed in relative isolation over long periods of time, they experienced different, relatively innocuous disease climates that did not prepare them for the microbiological onslaught precipitated by the Europeans. Virtually no one had the adaptive immunity that came with surviving a bout of European maladies such as smallpox. The epidemics unleashed unfathomable destruction, reminding Christian observers of biblical plagues. John Winthrop wrote in 1634 that "For the natives, they are neere all dead of small Poxe, so as the Lord hathe cleared our title to what we possess."[14]

Catastrophic epidemics played out over and over as Native Americans encountered European sailors and traders, who carried strains of disease, including the bubonic plague, the flu, and smallpox. Kiowa Indians told a story about Saynday, a trickster hero, meeting a stranger clothed in black clothes who looked at first glance like a preacher or missionary.

"Who are you?" Saynday asked.

"I'm smallpox," the stranger replied.

"Where do you come from and what do you do and why are you here?"

"I come from far away, across the Eastern Ocean. I am one with the white men . . . I bring death. My breath causes children to wither like young plants in the spring snow. I bring destruction. No matter how beautiful a woman is, once she has looked at me she becomes ugly as death. And to men I bring not death alone but the destruction of their children and the blighting of their wives. The strongest warriors go down before me. No people who have looked at me will ever be the same."[15]

The initial waves of disease often killed roughly half of the Native Americans affected. The epidemics kept ravaging the same populations, however, and also spread as contact moved through the Americas. More isolated Indians of the Pacific Northwest, the upper Midwest, and the Texas panhandle suffered epidemics well into the nineteenth century. The Mandans, who lived along the Missouri River in North Dakota, had already endured major disease outbreaks in the eighteenth century before another wave of smallpox came in 1837. Because of that epidemic, the Mandans went from about 2,000 people to less than 150.[16]

Medical explanations for the catastrophic results of European–Native American contact are important but somewhat elusive. There could have been genetic reasons for a lack of resistance to some of the diseases, but the science behind such explanations remains in flux. A lack of adapted immunity, which some Europeans gained by surviving childhood diseases, makes sense in some instances, such as smallpox. But other maladies like the flu, pneumonia, or diarrhea can repeatedly infect the same person. Some Indians would presumably have adapted to some of the diseases after the first epidemic hit their group, yet they continued to die in great numbers in episodic waves of sickness.

Native Americans also became more susceptible to disease as they contended with the adverse conditions of displacement and conquest. Few Europeans ever *intended* to sicken Indians as a policy of empire (though we will see attempts to do so during the Seven Years' War), but the Europeans certainly contributed to a social environment more conducive to the outbreaks. Archaeological evidence at pre-Columbian Native American settlements such as Chaco Canyon repeatedly suggest soil depletion as an explanation for decline. If hunger and malnutrition occasionally preceded European contact, they became more pressing problems after 1492. Malnutrition, in turn, adversely affects the immune system. It was no coincidence, then, that the 1837 smallpox outbreak among the Mandans was preceded by famine conditions and extreme cold that forced them to spend most of their time crowded together in their lodge houses.[17]

The context of disease mattered. Europeans also suffered from disease in America, especially when put into biologically stressful, malnourished situations

Tres Zapotes Colossal Head 1 (Monument A),
Veracruz, Mexico (Museum). Photograph copyright
2009 by HPJD, Wikimedia Commons.

similar to those of beleaguered native peoples. The most obvious example comes from the Jamestown colony, where perhaps 80 percent of all English settlers died in the first fifteen years of settlement, due to disease (especially scurvy and dysentery), malnutrition, and periodic violence between the English and local Indians. American armies in the Revolution and Civil War also struggled terribly with poor supplies, malnutrition, and concomitant outbreaks of disease, including smallpox.

Columbus inaugurated the "Age of Discovery," although he was hardly the first explorer to come to America. The earliest explorers, as we have seen, came from Asia across the Bering Strait (and perhaps by other Pacific routes) many thousands of years before Columbus. Norse explorers came to far northeastern North America around 1000 C.E., too. Their icy outpost at Vinland, Newfoundland, did not survive.

The Norsemen hugged the icy north Atlantic coast; five centuries later Columbus crossed the warm equatorial waters of the Atlantic looking for China. He died knowing that he had never quite discovered the trading centers there. Yet he also thought, in spite of their earthly disappointments, that his voyages possessed transcendent significance of biblical proportions. "God made me messenger of the new heaven and the new earth of which he spoke in the Apocalypse of St. John after having spoken of it through the mouth of Isaiah; and he showed me where to find it," the Genoese sailor reflected. Perhaps the East Indies were not his God-ordained destination after all.[18]

Columbus might well have envisioned 1492 as a year of apocalyptic significance. The year opened with the surrender of Muslim Granada, in southern Spain, concluding the long *Reconquista*, the struggle to subdue the Muslim-controlled territories of the Iberian peninsula. On January 2, Columbus's patrons, Queen Isabella and King Ferdinand, took the Muslim Nasrids' palaces in an elaborate ceremony, the Muslim ruler Muhammad XI having agreed to relinquish Granada some months earlier. Then, at the height of summer, Spain expelled its remaining Jewish families who had refused to convert to Christianity, many of them leaving from the port of Palos. Just days later, Columbus's ships, the *Pinta*, *Niña*, and *Santa María*, sailed west from the same town.

Columbus wrote admiringly of Spain's monarchs, "who love and promote the Christian faith, and are enemies to the doctrine of Mahomet [the Prophet Muhammad], and of all idolatry and heresy." They had sent him to the East Indies and its people "to learn their disposition, and the proper method of converting them to our holy faith; and furthermore, directed that I should not proceed by land to the East, as is customary, but by a Westerly route. . . . So, after having expelled the Jews from your dominions . . . ennobled me that thenceforth I might call myself Don, and be High Admiral of the Sea."[19]

Concern for the fate of the Holy Land, and crusading efforts to dislodge Muslims from Jerusalem, stirred the imaginations of European Catholics. Columbus's voyages not only might bring the gospel to the unexplored lands across the Atlantic, but also might represent the opening of a new eastern front against the Muslim powers, Europe's Christians believed. Similarly, apocalyptic writers expected that a mass conversion of the Jews would precede the millennial reign of Christ on earth. The expulsion of non-converts could convince wavering Jews to affirm Jesus as messiah.

Columbus anticipated that the riches of the New World might help fund the monarchs' campaigns against Jerusalem. On the day after Christmas in 1492, he wrote in his journal that he hoped the Spanish would find so much gold that it would supply everything they needed for a decisive crusade to liberate the Holy Sepulcher (the reputed site of Jesus's burial and resurrection). He recalled a pleasant conversation in which he had discussed this prospect with Isabella and Ferdinand.

These end-times ambitions help explain why Columbus bothered to com-

Aerial image of the earthworks at the Poverty Point site, West Carroll Parish, Louisiana, 1960. Aerial photograph CTK-2BB-125. Copyright 1960 by the USDA Agricultural Stabilization and Conservation Service, Wikimedia Commons.

pile his *Libro de las Profecias* (*Book of Prophecies*) around 1501. In it, he cobbled together a host of prophetic writings from the Bible and other sources, all of which pointed to the providential significance of his explorations, as well as the coming restoration of the Holy Sepulcher to Christian control. Columbus's studies suggested to him that once Christians conquered Jerusalem, the stage would be set for Christ's return. He figured that this consummation of divine history might come within 155 years.

If religious inspiration prompted Columbus's voyages, so did a bad miscalculation about the length of the western route to Asia. Contrary to common misconceptions today about Columbus's era, most European experts at that time did not believe that the world was flat; they did not expect Columbus's ships to fall off the edge of the world. Indeed, since ancient Greece, some scholars already knew that the world was a sphere, and they had calculated with surprising accuracy the globe's circumference. Columbus was in a minority of those who believed that east Asia was much closer to Europe than it actually was. As a result of his erroneous calculations, Columbus figured that the East Indies were about 3,500 miles west of Europe. When he hit land at 3,000 miles west, he assumed he was somewhere near China or Japan. He persisted in that mistaken assumption until his death in 1506.

Columbus landed first in the Bahamas, and then established a settlement on the island he named Hispaniola (present-day Haiti and Dominican Republic). He named the place La Navidad, because he landed there on Christmas Day. Before the twelve days of Christmas were up, Columbus was back on the *Niña*, getting ready for the trip home. His account of the first voyage caused a sensation in Europe, and he made three more trips to the New World during his life.

When Columbus came to Hispaniola in 1492, hundreds of thousands of natives (Tainos) lived there, in addition to many others on nearby islands. Because Columbus commissioned Father Ramón Pané to study the Tainos' religious practices, we know quite a lot about them. They called their deities *zemis*, and the two primary deities were Yúcahu—sovereign over the cassava plant and the salty waters of the Gulf—and his mother Atabey, who lorded over fresh water and childbirth. Cassava, a root crop, was the center of the Tainos' extensive agricultural regime. It took the place typically occupied by maize in Native Americans' belief systems. Tainos acknowledged many other zemis, including the spirits of the dead and spirits resident in the natural environment.[20]

The Tainos carved figures of zemis and used them in rituals. Pané observed that they used the hallucinogenic plant *cohoba* to facilitate communication with a zemi, and that they would "pray to it and to please it and to ask and find out from the aforesaid zemi good and bad things and also to ask it for riches." Leading men would assemble, and a lord would often relate a cohoba-induced vision, saying that he had "spoken with the zemi and that they will achieve victory, or their enemies will flee, or there will be a great loss of life, or wars or hunger or another such thing, according to what he, who is drunk, may relate of what he remembers. You may judge in what state his brain may be," Pané commented, "for they say they think they see the houses turn upside down, with their foundations in the air, and the men walk on foot toward the heavens."[21]

The Spanish settlers who came to Hispaniola in the decade after Columbus suffered terribly from disease and malnutrition, with probably two-thirds of them perishing. But the Tainos suffered even more. Within half a century, their numbers plummeted from roughly 300,000 to about 500 survivors, well over a 99 percent decline. Columbus also inaugurated native enslavement, taking dozens of captives for export to Europe on his first visit, and then sanctioning a shipload of 550 Indians for forcible export to Spain in 1495. The Spanish monarchs reportedly balked at the slave trade in Indians, but only because Columbus did not have clear legal title to enslave those whom the king and queen now considered their subjects.[22]

Before the coming of Europeans, Native Americans lived in a world in flux. Settlements and societies rose, moved, fought, and fell. Yet 1492 remains a fundamental juncture of disruption, beginning a process of massive decline among Native Americans and the emergence of European power in the Americas. Paleo-Indians, and the residents of places like the Buttermilk Creek settlement, had begun forging an American New World many millennia ago; now the disease and death accompanying the Europeans were ravaging and recreating America again.

JESUIT MISSIONARY PAUL LE JEUNE ON THE
HURON/WENDAT FEAST OF THE DEAD (1636)

From Edna Kenton, ed., *The Indians of North America*, taken from Reuben Thwaites, ed., *The Jesuit Relations and Allied Documents* (New York, 1927), 1: 303–8.

. . . many think we have two souls, both of them being divisible and material, and yet both reasonable; the one separates itself from the body at death, yet remains in the Cemetery until the feast of the Dead, — after which it either changes into a Turtledove, or, according to the most common belief, it goes away at once to the village of souls. The other is, as it were, bound to the body, and informs, so to speak, the corpse; it remains in the ditch of the dead after the feast, and never leaves it, unless some one bears it again as a child. He pointed out to me, as a proof of this metempsychosis, the perfect resemblance some have to persons deceased. A fine Philosophy, indeed. Such as it is, it shows why they call the bones of the dead, *Atisken*, "the souls."

A day or two before setting out for the feast, they carried all these souls into one of the largest Cabins of the Village, where one portion was hung to the poles of the Cabin, and the other portion spread out through it; the Captain entertained them, and made them a magnificent feast in the name of a deceased Captain, whose name he bore. I was at this feast of souls, and noticed at it four peculiar things. First, the presents which the relatives made for the feast, and which consisted of robes, Porcelain collars, and kettles, were strung on poles along the Cabin on both sides. Secondly, the Captain sang the song of the deceased Captain, in accordance with the desire the latter had expressed, before his death, to have it sung on this occasion. Thirdly, all the guests had the liberty of sharing with one another whatever good things they had, and even of taking these home with them, contrary to the usual custom of feasts. Fourthly, at the end of the feast, by way of compliment to him who had entertained them, they imitated the cry of souls, and went out of the Cabin, crying *haéé, haé*.

The master of the feast, and even *Anenkhiondic*, chief Captain of the whole Country, sent several pressing invitations to us. You might have said that the feast would not have been a success without us. I sent two of our Fathers, several days beforehand, to see the preparations, and to learn with certainty the day of the feast. *Anenkhiondic* gave them a very hearty welcome, and on their departure conducted them himself a quarter of a league thence, where the pit was,

Part of the Serpent Mound (Portsmouth, Ohio). Photograph copyright 1940 by the
Department of Agriculture, U.S. National Archives, Wikimedia Commons.

and showed them, with great demonstrations of regard, all the preparations for
the feast.

The feast was to take place on the Saturday of Pentecost but some affairs that
intervened, and the uncertainty of the weather, caused it to be postponed until
Monday. The seven or eight days before the feast were spent in assembling the
souls, as well as the Strangers who had been invited; meanwhile from morning
until night the living were continually making presents to the youth, in consideration of the dead. On one side the women were shooting with the bow for a
prize — a Porcupine girdle, or a collar or string of Porcelain beads; elsewhere in
the Village, the young men were shooting at a stick to see who could hit it. The
prize for this victory was an ax, some knives, or even a Beaver robe. From day to
day the souls arrived. It is very interesting to see these processions, sometimes
of two or three hundred persons; each one brings his souls, that is, his bones,
done up in parcels on his back, under a handsome robe, in the way I have
described. Some had arranged their parcels in the form of a man, ornamented
with Porcelain collars, and elegant bands of long red fur. On setting out from
the Village, the whole band cried out *haéé, haé,* and repeated this cry of the
souls by the way. This cry they say relieves them greatly; otherwise the burden,

although of souls, would weigh very heavily on their backs, and cause them a backache all the rest of their lives. They go short journeys; our Village was three days in going four leagues to reach *Ossossané*, which we call la Rochelle, where the ceremonies were to take place. As soon as they arrive near a Village they cry again *haéé, haé*. The whole Village comes to meet them; plenty of gifts are given on such an occasion. Each has his rendezvous in one of the Cabins, all know where they are to lodge their souls, so it is done without confusion. At the same time, the Captains hold a Council, to discuss how long the band shall sojourn in the Village.

All the souls of eight or nine Villages had reached la Rochelle by the Saturday of Pentecost; but the fear of bad weather compelled them, as I have said, to postpone the ceremony until Monday. We were lodged a quarter of a league away, at the old Village, in a Cabin where there were fully a hundred souls hung to and fixed upon the poles, some of which smelled a little stronger than musk.

On Monday, about noon, they came to inform us that we should hold ourselves in readiness, for they were going to begin the ceremony; they took down at the same time, the packages of souls; and the relatives again unfolded them to say their last adieus; the tears flowed afresh. I admired the tenderness of one woman toward her father and children; she is the daughter of a Chief who died at an advanced age, and was once very influential in the Country; she combed his hair and handled his bones, one after the other, with as much affection as if she would have desired to restore life to him; she put beside him his *Atsatonewai*, that is, his package of Council sticks, which are all the books and papers of the Country. As for her little children, she put on their arms bracelets of Porcelain and glass beads, and bathed their bones with her tears; they could scarcely tear her away from these, but they insisted, and it was necessary to depart immediately. The one who bore the body of this old Captain walked at the head; the men followed, and then the women, walking in this order until they reached the pit.

Let me describe the arrangement of this place. It was about the size of the place Royale at Paris. There was in the middle of it a great pit, about ten feet deep and five brasses wide. All around it was a scaffold, a sort of staging very well made, nine to ten brasses in width, and from nine to ten feet high; above this staging there were a number of poles laid across, and well arranged, with cross-poles to which these packages of souls were hung and bound. The whole bodies, as they were to be put in the bottom of the pit, had been the preceding day placed under the scaffold, stretched upon bark or mats fastened to stakes about the height of a man, on the borders of the pit.

The whole Company arrived with their corpses about an hour after Midday, and divided themselves into different cantons, according to their families and Villages, and laid on the ground their parcels of souls, almost as they do earthen pots at the Village Fairs. They unfolded also their parcels of robes, and all the presents they had brought, and hung them upon poles, which were from 5 to 600 toises in extent; so there were as many as twelve hundred presents which remained thus on exhibition two full hours, to give Strangers time to see the wealth and magnificence of the Country. I did not find the Company so numerous as I had expected; if there were two thousand persons, that was about all. About three o'clock, each one put away his various articles, and folded up his robes.

Meanwhile, each Captain by command gave the signal; and all, at once, loaded with their packages of souls, running as if to the assault of a town, ascended the Stage by means of ladders hung all round it, and hung them to the cross poles, each Village having its own department. That done, all the ladders were taken away; but a few Chiefs remained there and spent the rest of the afternoon, until seven o'clock, in announcing the presents which were made in the name of the dead to certain specified persons.

"This," said they, "is what such and such a dead man gives to such and such a relative." About five or six o'clock, they lined the bottom and sides of the pit with fine large new robes, each of ten Beaver skins, in such a way that they extended more than a foot out of it. As they were preparing the robes which were to be employed for this purpose, some went down to the bottom and brought up handfuls of sand. I asked what this ceremony meant, and learned that they have a belief that this sand renders them successful at play. . . .

At seven o'clock, they let down the whole bodies into the pit. We had the greatest difficulty in getting near; nothing has ever better pictured for me the confusion there is among the damned. On all sides you could have seen them letting down half-decayed bodies; and on all sides was heard a horrible din of confused voices of persons, who spoke and did not listen; ten or twelve were in the pit and were arranging the bodies all around it, one after another. They put in the very middle of the pit three large kettles, which could only be of use for souls; one had a large hole through it, another had no handle, and the third was of scarcely more value. I saw very few Porcelain collars; it is true, they put many on the bodies. This was all that was done on this day.

All the people passed the night on the spot; they lighted many fires, and slung their kettles. We withdrew for the night to the old Village, with the resolve to return the next morning, at daybreak, when they were to throw the bones into the pit; but we could hardly arrive in time, although we made great haste, on account of an accident that happened. One of the souls, which was not securely tied, or was perhaps too heavy for the cord that fastened it, fell of itself into the pit; the noise awakened the Company, who immediately ran and mounted in a crowd upon the scaffold, and emptied indiscriminately each package into the pit, keeping, however, the robes in which they were enveloped. We had only set out from the Village at that time, but the noise was so great that it seemed almost as if we were there. As we drew near, we saw nothing less than a picture of Hell. The large space was quite full of fires and flames, and the air resounded in all directions with the confused voices of these Barbarians; the noise ceased, however, for some time, and they began to sing, — but in voices so sorrowful and lugubrious that it represented to us the horrible sadness and the abyss of despair into which these unhappy souls are forever plunged.

Nearly all the souls were thrown in when we arrived, for it was done almost in the turning of a hand; each one had made haste, thinking there would not be enough room for all the souls; we saw, however, enough of it to judge of the rest. There were five or six in the pit, arranging the bones with poles. The pit was full, within about two feet; they turned back over the bones the robes which bordered the edge of the pit, and covered the remaining space with mats and bark. Then they heaped the pit with sand, poles, and wooden stakes, which they threw in without order. Some women brought to it some dishes of corn; and that day, and the following days, several Cabins of the Village provided nets quite full of it, which were thrown upon the pit.

We have fifteen or twenty Christians interred with these Infidels; we said for their souls a *De profundis*, with a strong hope that, if divine goodness does not stop the course of its blessings upon these Peoples, this feast will cease, or will only be for Christians, and will take place with ceremonies as sacred as the ones we saw are foolish and useless; they are even now beginning to be a burden to them, on account of the excesses and superfluous expenses connected with them.

The whole morning was passed in giving presents; and the greater part of the robes in which the souls had been wrapped were cut into pieces, and thrown from the height of the Stage into the midst of the crowd for any one who could get them. . . .

EPIDEMICS AMONG NEW ENGLAND'S INDIANS (1637)

From Thomas Morton, *The New English Canaan* (Boston, 1883), 132–34.

. . . in short time after the hand of God fell heavily upon them, with such a mortall stroake that they died on heapes as they lay in their houses; and the living, that were able to shift for themselves, would runne away and let them dy, and let their Carkases ly above the ground without buriall. For in a place where many inhabited, there hath been but one left a live to tell what became of the rest; the livinge being (as it seemes) not able to bury the dead, they were left for Crows, Kites and vermin to pray upon. And the bones and skulls upon the severall places of their habitations made such a spectacle after my coming into those partes, that, as I travailed in that Forrest nere the Massachussets, it seemd to mee a new found Golgatha.

But otherwise, it is the custome of those Indian people to bury their dead ceremoniously and carefully, and then to abandon that place, because they have no desire the place should put them in the minde of mortality: and this mortality was not ended when the Brownists of New Plimmouth were setled at Patuxet in New England: and by all likelyhood the sicknesse that these Indians died of was the Plague, as by conference with them since my arrivall and habitation in those partes, I have learned. And by this meanes there is as yet but a small number of Salvages in New England, to that which hath beene in former time, and the place is made so much the more fitt for the English Nation to inhabit in, and erect in it Temples to the glory of God.

CHRISTOPHER COLUMBUS'S OBSERVATIONS ON THE ISLAND OF HISPANIOLA (1493)

From R. H. Major, trans. and ed., *Select Letters of Christopher Columbus*, 2d ed. (London, 1870), 5–9.

Española is a wonder. Its mountains and plains, and meadows and fields, are so beautiful and rich for planting and sowing, and rearing cattle of all kinds, and for building towns and villages. The harbours on the coast, and the number and size and wholesomeness of the rivers, most of them bearing gold, surpass anything that would be believed by one who had not seen them. There is a great difference between the trees, fruits, and plants of this island and those of *Juana*. In this island there are many spices and extensive mines of gold and other metals. The inhabitants of this and of all the other islands I have found or gained intelligence of, both men and women, go as naked as they were born, with the exception that some of the women cover one part only with a single leaf of grass or with a piece of cotton made for that purpose. They have neither iron nor steel nor arms, nor are they competent to use them; not that they are not well-formed and of handsome stature, but because they are timid to a surprising degree. Their only arms are reeds, cut in the seeding time, to which they fasten small sharpened sticks, and even these they dare not use; for on several occasions it has happened that I have sent ashore two or three men to some village to hold a parley, and the people have come out in countless numbers, but as soon as they saw our men approach, would flee with such precipitation that a father would not even stop to protect his son; and this not because any harm had been done to any of them, for from the first, wherever I went and got speech with them, I gave them of all that I had, such as cloth and many other things, without receiving anything in return, but they are, as I have described, incurably timid. It is true that when they are reassured and thrown off this fear they are guileless, and so liberal of all they have that no one would believe it who had not seen it. They never refuse anything that they possess when it is asked of them; on the contrary, they offer it themselves, and they exhibit so much loving kindness that they would even give their hearts; and, whether it be something of value or of little worth that is offered to them, they are satisfied. I forbade that worthless things, such as pieces of broken porringers and broken glass, and ends of straps, should be given to them; although, when they succeeded in obtaining them, they thought they possessed the finest jewel in the world. . . .

I gave away a thousand good and pretty articles which I had brought with me in order to win their affection; and that they might be led to become Christians, and be well inclined to love and serve their Highnesses and the whole Spanish nation, and that they might aid us by giving us things of which we stand in need, but which they possess in abundance. They are not acquainted with any kind of worship, and are not idolaters; but believe that all power and, indeed, all good things are in heaven; and they are firmly convinced that I, with my vessels and crews, came from heaven, and with this belief received me at every place at which I touched, after they had overcome their apprehension. And this does not spring from ignorance, for they are very intelligent, and navigate all these seas, and relate everything to us, so that it is astonishing what a good account they are able to give of everything; but they have never seen men with clothes on, nor vessels like ours. On my reaching the Indies, I took by force, in the first island that I discovered, some of these natives, that they might learn our language and give me information in regard to what existed in these parts; and it so happened that they soon understood us and we them, either by words or signs, and they have been very serviceable to us. They are still with me, and, from repeated conversations that I have had with them, I find that they still believe that I come from heaven. And they were the first to say this wherever I went, and the others ran from house to house and to the neighbouring villages, crying with a loud voice: "Come, come, and see the people from heaven!" And thus they all, men as well as women, after their minds were at rest about us, came, both large and small, and brought us something to eat and drink, which they gave us with extraordinary kindness.

THE SPANISH EMPIRE IN AMERICA

In 1607, the English founded Jamestown in Virginia. That same year, about 1,800 miles to the southwest, the Spanish governor of New Mexico founded La Villa Real de la Santa Fé de San Francisco de Asís at the foot of the Sangre de Christo ("blood of Christ") mountains. Shortened to Santa Fé ("holy faith"), the town became the capital of the Kingdom of New Mexico in 1610. By 1630 there were about 250 Spaniards living there, but the colonists held around 700 mestizos (people of mixed Spanish and Indian descent) and Indians "in service" on farms and on government projects, so perhaps more than 1,000 people lived in and around the capital.[1]

Many Pueblos in the area resented their rough treatment by the Spanish, but the Europeans kept them in fear with firearms (harquebuses). "If this were not the case," wrote Fray Alonso de Benavides, "the Indians would often be inclined to murder the Spaniards." Benavides observed that the Pueblos were routinely "divided into the two factions of warriors and sorcerers. The warriors have attempted to bring everyone under their command and authority in opposition to the sorcerers. And the sorcerers have tried to sway everyone to their side, making it rain, preparing the land for good seeding, and doing other things that the warriors jeered at. Because of all this, there were continuous civil wars among these people, so bad that they killed each other and laid waste to entire pueblos. The devil, of course, had his usual harvest."[2]

Spanish Franciscan missionaries must have found the tension between warriors and sorcerers strangely familiar. From its founding, priests and politicians were at odds about the purposes of New Mexico. Was it a holy sanctuary, or a money-making enterprise? Fray Isidoro Ordonez lambasted the colony's governor for abusing Indians and employing them without pay in the construction of the villa's new government buildings. If the governor did not put a stop to this, the friar warned, Ordonez would excommunicate him. When the governor questioned Ordonez's credentials as the colony's official prelate, Ordonez followed through on his threat and removed the governor from the church's good graces. The next time he tried to attend mass, the governor found that the priest had removed his ceremonial front-row chair and pitched it into the street. As the crisis escalated, Ordonez had the governor arrested and imprisoned in a convent at a nearby village. "Let no one argue with vain words," Ordonez thundered, "that I do not have the same power and authority that the Pope in Rome has, or that if his Holiness were [here] in New Mexico he could do more than I."[3]

Regardless of these difficulties, Fray Alonso de Benavides reported in 1630 that many Pueblos had become model Christian converts. When the priests rang the bell for mass, the Indians assembled "as well scrubbed and neat as can be." When they knelt to pray, they did so with such sincerity that one might guess that they had been Christians all their lives. They sang as choir members, made confession, and learned the catechism. They loved and submitted to the priests, Benavides assured himself.[4]

But signs suggested that the Franciscans' evangelization of the Pueblos was not going as well as they had hoped. As Spanish labor abuses continued, the Pueblos also faced periodic conflicts with Apaches and other nomadic tribes in the region. The priests discovered that the converts returned to their traditional religious practices with disturbing frequency. Worse, Spanish officials sometimes looked away as they did so. The Franciscans particularly despised the Pueblos' ritual dances, which the priests saw as demonic orgies. One of the governors, however, told the priests in 1660 that he had seen the dances. They were innocuous festivals that "signified nothing," he insisted.[5]

The Pueblos watched as the politicians and priests squabbled. Offending converts received whippings from the priests for instances of syncretism. Years of drought led to famine. Sometimes desperate Pueblos ate cow hides, but as herds died off, they could not even fill their bellies with leather. Disease set into the weakened populations. Between 1638 and 1680, the region's Pueblo population dropped from roughly 40,000 to 17,000. The arrival of Jesus's missionaries may have brought spiritual comfort to some, but in the earthly realm, the coming of the Spanish kingdom brought little but misery.[6]

Spanish America came before English America. Each step of Spanish colonization came roughly a century before that of the English, in spite of the coincidence of Santa Fé's and Jamestown's founding. The English were aware of the presence of Spanish colonies from Peru to New Mexico to Florida, and mindful of the Catholic threat that those colonies represented to them.

As the Spanish developed mines, ranches, and plantations on the Caribbean islands in the early sixteenth century, the precipitous decline of the Tainos pushed explorers into the Central American mainland to find more conscripts for labor. In 1519, two years after Martin Luther inaugurated the Protestant Reformation in Germany, Hernán Cortés entered Mexico and began to plan a confrontation with the great Aztec emperor Montezuma. Cortés had already acquired a number of farms and gold mines during the conquest of Cuba. Claiming Mexico for Christ and the Spanish king, Cortés fought a series of battles that he narrated in tales that read like Old Testament accounts of the Israelites fighting the Canaanites. Reporting native armies of improbable numbers (over one hundred thousand), Cortés's army, he said, fought against incredible odds. But "it truly seemed that God was fighting for us," and they killed legions and received few casualties of their own. "As we were carrying the banner of the Cross and were fighting for our Faith and in the service of Your Sacred Majesty," he told the king, God gave them the victory. Cortés explained that "as Christians we were obliged to wage war against the enemies of our faith; and thereby we would win glory in the next world."[7]

Cortés and his men finally came to Montezuma's great city of Tenochtitlán. In 1519, this was easily the largest city in the Americas, with about two hundred thousand residents. It was larger than any town in Spain, and about the same size as Paris. The city featured a two-hundred-foot-tall stone pyramid devoted to the Aztec gods of war and rain. The Aztecs practiced rituals of human sacrifice there.

As Cortés and his men approached the wooden drawbridge leading into the lake-encircled city, Montezuma and the Aztecs greeted them in an elaborate ceremony. Cortés dismounted from his horse to embrace the emperor, but his attendants signaled for him to stand back—no one touched Montezuma without invitation to do so. Nevertheless, Cortés and Montezuma exchanged gift necklaces. Cortés said that Montezuma declared the Spanish to be the descendants (or perhaps spirits) of a great lord who came "from where the sun rises." He supposedly acknowledged the Spanish king as their rightful lord, and promised that the Aztecs would obey him. This was likely an unwitting—or witting—Spanish misinterpretation of Montezuma's pronouncements of respect and hospitality.[8]

Reminiscent (again) of Old Testament scenes of the cleansing of pagan temples, Cortés purged the idols at the great pyramid, shattering them on the steps and placing icons of the Virgin Mary and other saints where the idols had stood. Montezuma was indignant and predicted that this rash act would precipitate an uprising. The Aztecs "believed that those idols gave them all their worldly goods, and that if they were allowed to be ill treated, they would become angry and give them nothing and take the fruit from the earth leaving the people to die of hunger." Cortés countered that the Aztecs needed to understand that there was only one true God, and that they should worship him alone.[9]

Cortés soon apprehended and imprisoned Montezuma, precipitating an Aztec backlash that drove the Spanish from Tenochtitlán. In 1521, however, the Spanish, along with Indian allies including the Tlaxcaltecs, returned and conquered the city, which had suffered an outbreak of smallpox during the intervening time and lost much if its population. A Spanish historian recorded how the "pustules that covered people caused great desolation; very many people died of them, and many just starved to death; starvation reigned, and no one took care of others any longer." The Spanish and their allies razed much of the vulnerable city, killing and wounding perhaps another one hundred thousand. They especially targeted the Aztec priests, throwing them to their war dogs and burning their sacred texts.[10]

These scenes of conquest played out repeatedly in other parts of the Caribbean, Mexico, and Peru. Spanish settlement came slowly to North America, however. The relatively sedentary farming Indians of Mexico and Peru made ideal colonial targets; northern Indians had fewer and smaller towns or cultivated fields. Still, stories of gold and silver drew Spanish explorers into Florida and north of the Rio Grande.

One of the most remarkable stories of Spanish exploration came from an expedition on the Gulf Coast of Florida in 1528. The Spanish troops suffered relentless attacks from Appalachee Indians, and escaped on barges along the coast. The barges foundered off the Texas shoreline, and eventually only four invaders survived out of three hundred who had started in Florida. These four became slaves among the Karankawa Indians. One of the remaining explorers, Alvar Núñez Cabeza de Vaca, wrote an extraordinary account of the journey that followed, which ultimately took them across Texas and New Mexico to the Pacific.

The key to Cabeza de Vaca and his companions' survival was the Indians' conviction that the men possessed healing powers. The Avavares, who lived northwest of Corpus Christi Bay, pressed them to heal their sick. Cabeza de Vaca complied, making the sign of the cross, blowing on the patient, and saying a Pater Noster and an Ave Maria (standard Catholic prayers). According to Cabeza de Vaca, these prayers worked, somewhat to the travelers' amazement and to the delight of the Indians. He recounted how he came upon one man who was not just sick but dead, with eyes rolled up into his head and no pulse. Cabeza de Vaca prayed for the man, who soon stood up and was "entirely well."

He wrote that this "caused great astonishment and consternation, and in all the land no one talked of anything else."[11]

The Avavares were keenly aware of competing spiritual power between their old world and that of the Spanish. They hoped that the castaways could combat malevolent forces among them. They related a tale of a being they called "Mala Cosa," or Evil Thing, who had tormented them some fifteen years earlier. He was short of stature and wore a European-style beard. In spite of his size, he would seize anyone he wished and, using a flint knife, would cut three gashes into their side. Then Mala Cosa would pull out the person's intestines, cut out a section, and throw it into the fire. Some of the Indians showed the incredulous travelers their scars from where Mala Cosa had slashed them. Cabeza de Vaca told them that if they became Christians, they would no longer have to fear Mala Cosa. He would not dare come among them if they believed in Jesus.[12]

As Cabeza de Vaca's party moved through northwestern Mexico, he regretted the sights of devastation wrought by conquistadors, finding local Native Americans fearful of any contacts with the Spanish. Promising more amicable relations, Cabeza de Vaca told the king that "if [Native Americans] are to be brought to be Christians and into obedience of Your Imperial Majesty, [they] must be led by good treatment." Cabeza de Vaca was not the only Spaniard to hold such views, but native societies typically endured a great deal of upheaval and desolation before a gentler imperial approach came into play.[13]

Once he returned to Spain, Cabeza de Vaca approached Hernando de Soto, whom the crown had tasked with the exploration of Florida, about a possible partnership. Since Cabeza de Vaca had become uncomfortable with the standard model of conquest, he did not accompany Soto into Florida in 1539. Soto did bring at least six hundred men, including several priests, and hundreds of sets of iron collars and chains to use on Indian captives. His army cut a path of destruction through the American southeast. Resistant Indians faced summary execution, dismemberment, and burning at the stake. Perhaps the most lethal tactic, however, was unintentional: Soto brought several hundred pigs with him for food. Pigs can carry a variety of diseases, from anthrax to tuberculosis. These pigs may have contributed as much as Soto's men to the subsequent demographic collapse among native people. The number of Caddos along the Texas-Arkansas border probably dropped from about 200,000 to around 8,500 in the century and a half after Soto's expedition.[14]

The profound disruptions inaugurated by Soto and his pigs so decimated prominent Indian groups of the southeast that two centuries later, its Native American world was entirely refashioned. The eastern woodlands became a "shatter zone" disrupted by waves of disease, European traders, and new commerce in Indian slaves and deerskins. By 1700, the southeast saw the emergence of "coalescent" native societies that would play a prominent role in Indian-American diplomacy and war. These new societies included the Cherokees, Creeks, Choctaws, and Catawbas.[15]

As they did with Cabeza de Vaca, Indians in Soto's path pled with his army to heal the sick and bring rain to parched lands. After crossing "Rio Grande"—the Mississippi River—Soto responded to such requests from the Casqui Indians of eastern Arkansas by erecting a tall cross and instructing them that "in the heavens above there was One who had the power to make them whole, and do whatever they could ask of Him, whose servant he was; that this great Lord made the sky and the earth, and man after His image; that he had suffered on the tree of the true cross to save the human race, and risen from the grave on the third day . . . and that, having ascended into heaven, He was there with open arms to receive all that would be converted to Him." Having positioned the cross at the highest point in the Indian town, he and his men knelt before it, and enjoined the Indians to do likewise. Soto said that "from that time thenceforth they should thus worship the Lord."[16]

When Soto died in 1542, his second-in-command, Luis de Moscoso, determined to hide his death from the Indians, "for Soto had given them to understand that the Christians were immortal." Weighing the body down with sand, they sunk Soto into the waters of the Mississippi. When an Indian leader inquired as to Soto's whereabouts, Moscoso "told him that he had ascended into the skies, as he had done on many other occasions; but as he would have to be detained there some time," Soto had left Moscoso in charge.[17]

Even among the Spanish, some were not so convinced about Soto's eternal fate. Dissenting Spanish Catholic priest Bartolomé de las Casas even speculated that after the horrors of the expedition, Soto died without confessing his sins and thus was no doubt "buried in hell." As a young man, Las Casas had seen parades in his native Seville welcoming Christopher Columbus back from his first voyage to the Indies in 1493. The explorer showed off seven Tainos he brought with him, as well as other New World novelties, including parrots and a bouncing rubber ball. The sights of the parade and Columbus's effusive description of the new lands inspired Las Casas and other Spaniards to join in colonization efforts, so Las Casas went with his father to Hispaniola in 1502. Las Casas served as a *doctrinero*, a lay religious teacher, and went on to receive an *encomienda* of Indian workers. Once he was ordained, Las Casas went as a chaplain on an expedition to Cuba, where, as he recalled, he saw the Spanish wreak "terrible havoc and devastation," with Taino parents sent to the mines, children starved to death, and many Indians murdered in cold blood. He personally owned several Indian slaves who had been taken as war captives.[18]

Influenced by small numbers of priests who had begun to criticize Spanish abuses of the Indians, Las Casas repented of his own complicity in violence and took up their cause. Las Casas did not necessarily denounce slavery per se at this point, proposing that the Spanish might import Africans as slaves instead of oppressing the native Caribbean population. Although he came to register similar concerns about enslaving Africans as he did about Indian slavery, Las Casas himself owned several enslaved Africans into the 1540s. In any case, his advocacy on behalf of Indians earned him powerful enemies, but also won the ear of powerful friends, not least Pope Paul III. The pope issued a 1537 edict, *Sublimis Deus*, which referred to the Indians' abusers as the devil's "lackeys," and greedy swindlers who "enslave [Indians], burdening them with so many afflictions such as they scarcely impose on the brute animals that serve them." The pope demanded that Catholics stop indiscriminately enslaving native peoples, and work instead toward drawing them to the Christian faith. Although the proclamation hardly ended all abuses and enslavement, it did give pause to Spanish emperor Charles V, who sought to mitigate Spanish practices in the New World.[19]

In the early 1540s, Las Casas wrote an influential indictment of Spanish imperialism, *An Account, Much Abbreviated, of the Destruction of the Indies* (*Brevísima relación de la destruición de las Indias*). The account was polemical and took an idyllic view of the Indians of the Caribbean and their Edenic existence prior to Columbus's coming. God had created them a "simple people, altogether without subtlety, malice, or duplicity, excellent in obedience . . . the most humble, most patient, meekest and most pacific . . . the most delicate, slender, and tender of complexion and the least able to withstand hard labor." (Las Casas did not dwell on evidence that Indians warred with one another prior to European contact.) In his Christian humanist appeal to the natives' basic rights, Las Casas lamented how Spaniards, like ravenous wolves among gentle sheep, came among them to do nothing "but dismember, slay, perturb, afflict, torment, and destroy the Indians." *The Destruction of the Indies* became a major resource for European critiques of Spanish colonization, as the book came out in translations across Europe by the end of the sixteenth century, helping Protestants to paint Catholic imperialism as (in their eyes) exceptionally cruel.[20]

Even as Las Casas was mustering his rhetorical attack on Spanish abuses of natives, Spanish explorations into the North American interior proceeded. In the late 1530s, a Franciscan missionary named Marcos de Niza brought back reports to Mexico that he had seen one of the fabled Seven Cities of Gold. The viceroy of New Spain promptly commissioned Francisco Vásquez de Coronado to take a small army of Spanish and Mexican Indian soldiers, as well as six Franciscans, into northern Mexico to find this city. When the invaders came to a Zuni pueblo called Hawikku, Fray (or friar) Niza, who was guiding them, identified the place as the city of gold. The Spanish displayed a cross and assured residents that they came in peace. They gave the Indians rosary beads, and read a standard edict calling on them to "acknowledge the Church as the ruler and superior of the whole world, and the high priest called Pope, and in his name the king and queen." The Zunis responded with volleys of arrows. The Spanish attacked and killed hundreds of the residents of Hawikku, but found no gold. In his report to the viceroy, Coronado said that he would not "beat around the bush": Fray Niza had not "spoken the truth in anything he said." Coronado registered a number of observations about the Zunis, such as his opinion that they "eat the best tortillas I have seen anywhere." He thought that the Zunis "venerate water," for it generated corn and sustained life in the arid region.[21]

Pushing further east in search of the golden towns, Coronado's army provoked a rebellion among the Tiguex Pueblos, who lived north of present-day Albuquerque. Reports of Spaniards raping Indian women, and the Spaniards' relentless demands for supplies, instigated the hostilities. The Spaniards cut off the hands of some of the rebels, set war hounds on others, burned dozens of Pueblo men at the stake, and razed many of the Tiguex villages. Coronado eagerly received reports of another rumored golden city. These tales came via an Indian slave the Spanish called "El Turco" (the Turk) because he looked to them like a Moor. El Turco promised Coronado that there was a golden town called Quivira further east. (Some of the soldiers believed that El Turco was a witch doctor with gifts of supernatural knowledge.)[22]

Coronado, driven by the pursuit of fame and wealth, accepted the Turk's account and took his party into the Great Plains of what are now the panhandles of Texas and Oklahoma, and finally into Kansas. Near present-day Hutchinson, they arrived at Quivira, which amounted to villages of grass-thatched huts. The Indians there had no gold or silver. El Turco admitted under duress that he had lied about Quivira in order to get them out of New Mexico, hoping that Coronado's men and horses might die in the Great Plains' lonely stretches. Coronado's men strangled El Turco and quietly buried him in order not to raise suspicions among the other Indians. Before leaving, Coronado ordered the erection of one more cross, inscribed with the message that he, the Spanish general, had been there.[23]

Coronado's cross, placed deep in the North American interior, marked how far Spanish explorers, missionaries, and conquistadors had probed the continent by the 1540s. For all these strung-out expeditions and fevered quests for gold, Spanish imperial authorities were still focused on securing profitable trading routes and colonies, and countering the threat posed by European Protestant power. This explains the Spanish incursion into the Florida Atlantic coast in the 1560s. There, in 1565, Pedro Menéndez de Avilés founded St. Augustine, which would become the oldest continuously settled town founded by Europeans in the continental United States. (Menéndez had first sighted St. Augustine's harbor on the Catholic feast day of Augustine of Hippo.)[24]

The Spanish wished to secure an Atlantic coast harbor to protect shipping lanes between Spain and the Caribbean, where pirates often preyed on Spanish vessels. They had also learned that French Protestants, or Huguenots, had established Fort Caroline the year before at the site of present-day Jacksonville. (This was the first French colony in what would become the United States.) Less than two weeks after founding St. Augustine, Menéndez led an attack on Fort Caroline, which the Spanish forces overwhelmed. Menéndez told Spanish King Felipe II that he had killed over 130 devotees of the "evil Lutheran sect." (Technically, the Huguenots were followers of their fellow Frenchman John Calvin, not Martin Luther, but that distinction did not matter to Menéndez.) He executed another 150 Frenchmen he caught close to St. Augustine. Menéndez apparently feared that Protestants and local Native Americans might conspire together because of their similarly devilish religions. Executing them served "God Our Lord," he informed the king, "that we should thus be left more free from this wicked sect." The Spanish built a small fort, San Mateo, on the ruins of the Huguenots' settlement, but in 1568 a French privateer destroyed it and executed its Spanish garrison in retribution for Menéndez's killings.[25]

Over the next two years, Menéndez established outposts up and down the Florida coast. In 1570, he helped to build a Jesuit mission near the spot where the English would found Jamestown in 1607. The Jesuits hoped to evangelize local Indians, as well as to discover "an entrance into the mountains and on to China." (The dream of a westerly route to China would die a slow death in American history.) But in 1571, Indians attacked and killed the missionaries, who atypically had failed to bring soldiers with them.[26]

Conflicts with French and English privateers, as well as local Native Americans, wrecked nearly all of Menéndez's Florida settlements by the end of the sixteenth century. Like many Europeans, Menéndez theoretically hoped to see Native Americans convert to Christianity, but when they resisted imperial incursions, he concluded that they were recalcitrant and that the Spanish were wasting their missionary efforts. New Spain's Catholic bishops, mindful of the protests by Las Casas and others, disagreed, and recommended using vi-

olence and enslavement only as a last resort. In the years before his death in
1574, the conflicted Menéndez urged a "war of fire and blood" against Florida's
natives, but still spoke of spending his remaining days in Florida, working to
save the natives' souls.[27]

It was left to Franciscan missionaries, more quietly than Menéndez, to keep
evangelizing the native peoples of the southeast. The Catholic evangelistic
order of Franciscans, fired by the same kind of apocalyptic visions that undergirded Columbus's voyages, were responsible for much of the missionary
program that accompanied Spain's spread through the Americas. Columbus
brought Franciscans with him as early as his second New World visit, and in
1504, the pope made a Franciscan the first bishop in the New World. At Hernán
Cortés's request, King Charles V of Spain in 1524 appointed a group of twelve
apostle-like Franciscans to follow up Cortés's conquest in Mexico. One of the
pioneering Franciscans exulted that the evangelism of the Americas represented
a concluding point of Christian history: "Just as the name of God flourished at
the beginning of the Church in the East (which is the beginning of the earth) so
now, at the end of the centuries, it must flourish in the West (which is the end of
the earth)." The missionaries' intensity only grew with controversies related to
the Protestant Reformation, European contests with direct significance in the
New World.[28]

The Franciscans opened sustained missions in the American southeast in
the late sixteenth century. They established stations along the Atlantic coast,
along the Florida panhandle, and in the interior near present-day Gainesville.
The Franciscans discouraged mission Indians from retaining old practices that
smacked of pagan ritual. One Guale noted that they frowned upon "our dances,
banquets, feasts, celebrations, games and war." Some of the fathers' efforts met
staunch resistance, most notably in the 1597 uprising by the Guales of coastal
Georgia, who wrecked the missions and killed five Franciscans. Still, by their
peak in the late seventeenth century, the Florida missions consisted of forty
churches, staffed by fifty-two missionaries. The Spanish brought epidemic
disease to the Indians of the missions, making it difficult to maintain viable
populations. Up the South Carolina coast, the 1670 founding of Charles Town
(Charleston) by the English signaled a permanent imperial presence to rival
the Spanish in the southeast.[29]

As in Florida, exploited Pueblos also occasionally rose up against the Spanish
in New Mexico throughout the seventeenth century, with priests sometimes
falling victim to death by poisoning, bludgeoning, and other means. The pressures of disease, drought, attacks by native rivals, and the demanding Spanish
labor regime fostered conditions ripe for widespread revolt in 1680. Some Indi-

Frontal view of the Pyramid of the Sun, city of Teotihuacan, Mexico. Photograph copyright 2014 by Mariordo (Mario Roberto Durán Ortiz), Wikimedia Commons.

ans simply collapsed from hunger and perished where they lay in these years, as one priest reported seeing them "dead along the roads, in the ravines, and in their huts."[30]

Although some Pueblos undoubtedly accepted some or all of the friars' teachings about Jesus, it is hard to escape the conclusion that Christian "conversion" for many was partial, at best. Still, the Franciscans established a considerable presence in Pueblo towns, with a high point of forty-six missionaries in residence in 1656. This was roughly equivalent to the number of Pueblo villages in the area, although more than one friar often lived in central towns, close to other Spanish residents. (The entire Spanish population of New Mexico may not have been much more than a thousand just prior to 1680.) Some of the outlying towns went decades with no consistent pastoral oversight. The Franciscans, in contrast to Jesuit missionaries in New France, made little progress in learning Pueblo languages. Basic comprehension of native concerns was limited. Certain friars likely preyed sexually on Pueblo women. Bickering between secular and religious authorities in New Mexico afforded many opportunities for Pueblos to play Spanish officials against one another.

The effects of famine also exacerbated conflict between the Spanish, Pueblos, and nomadic Apaches, who saw the Spanish colonies as tempting targets for food and other supplies. (The Apaches had begun using horses, which the Spanish had tried to keep away from Native Americans. Horse riding made the Apaches effective raiders.) One priest wrote in 1669 that "the whole land is at war with the widespread heathen nation of the Apache Indians, who kill all the Christian Indians they can find and encounter. No road is safe; everyone travels at risk of his life, for the heathen traverse them all . . . they hurl themselves at danger like people who know no God nor that there is any hell." Towns like Hawikku, which had suffered from Coronado's attacks a century and a half earlier, fell victim to the Apaches, who in 1673 killed two hundred of the pueblo's residents, including its missionary.

Some Pueblos—a conglomeration composed of a great variety of language groups over hundreds of miles in northern New Mexico—turned back to native religious practices in the midst of their desperate circumstances. Yet the Franciscans suppressed hints of indigenous spirituality, sometimes brutally. In 1655, the Spanish accused a Hopi named Juan Cuna of worshipping pagan idols, and Fray Salvador de Guerra ("savior of war") whipped Cuna until he bled profusely. Cuna was whipped again later in the day, this time inside the mission church, and Guerra concluded the torture by smothering Cuna's flesh with burning turpentine, killing him. Although this kind of calculated viciousness was extreme, whipping or otherwise punishing Indians for idolatry was not unusual. In 1675, the Spanish hanged three Pueblos for sorcery and whipped forty-three others.[31]

The Spanish freed the forty-three accused sorcerers in response to Pueblo threats. One of the forty-three was a medicine man named Popé. Popé eventually fled to Taos, where he reportedly began to receive revelations from spirits he encountered in a kiva (a sacred underground chamber). The messages convinced him to formulate a plan for revolt, asserting that "the God of the Spaniards was worth nothing and theirs was very strong, the Spaniards' God being rotten wood."[32]

From his isolated location at Taos, Popé coordinated an elaborate secret plot to destroy the Spaniards in August 1680. The Spanish learned of the scheme with just a couple days' notice, and initial attacks shattered Spanish settlements. Pueblos laid siege to Santa Fé, where many of the survivors huddled for a month. In late September the Spanish abandoned Santa Fé and fled down the Rio Grande to El Paso/Juárez, where Franciscans had opened a mission in 1659.

The Pueblos left little doubt that this was a religious revolt, as they targeted missionaries and churches for retribution, born out of a "mortal hatred for our holy faith," as one Spanish officer put it. Popé himself reportedly emerged from Taos and traveled from village to village, demanding that the Pueblos "instantly break up and burn the images of the holy Christ, the Virgin Mary and the other saints, the crosses, and everything pertaining to Christianity, and that they burn the temples [and] break up the bells. . . . In order to take away their baptismal names, the water, and the holy oils, they were to plunge into the rivers and wash themselves." Twenty-one of New Mexico's thirty-three missionaries perished in the revolt, often after suffering torture from the rebels. Other Pueblos reportedly said that "now God and Santa Maria were dead, that they were the ones whom the Spanish worshiped, and that their own God whom they obeyed had never died."[33]

The Pueblo revolt was the most successful Native American rebellion ever against European colonizers. For thirteen years, the Spanish lingered in El Paso waiting for an opportunity to reconquer New Mexico. Spanish governor Diego Vargas finally brought an army into New Mexico in 1693, following a probing expedition into the territory a year earlier. The Spanish soldiers gave particular devotion to a statue of the Virgin Mary, called *Nuestra Señora de la Conquista*, reportedly first brought to New Mexico by Fray Alonso de Benavides.

This icon remains a powerful symbol in Santa Fé today, residing at the *La Conquistadora* chapel of Santa Fé's Cathedral Basilica of St. Francis of Assisi. Popé retains great cultural significance in New Mexico, too. The state sent a statue of him ("Po'pay") as the one hundredth addition to the U.S. Capitol's Statuary Hall Collection. Today Popé's likeness greets visitors at the Capitol Visitor Center.

By 1694 Vargas and the Spaniards had largely reconquered the kingdom, but not all was well. In 1696, the Pueblos again tried to evict the Spanish, killing five missionaries and burning a number of church properties. But Vargas was better prepared to face revolt, and he slowly broke down remaining Pueblo resistance (Popé himself had probably died around 1688). Never again did the dwindling Pueblo population attempt insurrection on such a massive scale.

After the reconquest, Franciscans found themselves somewhat marginalized in Spanish relations with New Mexico's Indians. Control of New Mexico seemed more pressing to Spanish authorities in light of the growing French presence in the Mississippi River Valley, symbolized by the explorations of the Sieur de La Salle down the river in 1682. Apaches brought reports of these new European colonizers to Santa Fé beginning in the 1690s. The Spanish also confronted a new Native American power, the Comanches, who in time would command the most formidable Indian "empire" within North America. Now Spanish political and military officials, not priests, tended to interface directly with Pueblo and other New Mexican Indians.[34]

Yet the Franciscans still came, with more modest results. Following earlier patterns, few friars made much progress in learning native languages, and there

were simply fewer Pueblos and other Indians available as candidates for evangelism after their demographic collapse. (From 1600 to 1750, the Pueblos' population may have declined by as much as 90 percent.) Although the Franciscans
may have nominally converted some 60,000 native New Mexicans by the 1630s,
their successors brought no more than 5,000 to the Catholic faith over the eighteenth century. The post-conquest missionaries engendered less hostility, with
only about seven martyred between the reconquest and the mid-eighteenth
century. From the beginning of the seventeenth century through the Pueblo
Revolt, almost fifty Franciscans had died at the hands of Native Americans.[35]

New Mexico governor Pedro Fermin de Mendinueta reflected on the prospects for successful evangelization of the region's Indians in a grim 1773 letter.
Although the kingdom had been much more peaceful since the reconquest, the
"reduction of the infidels" remained limited. Some converts participated, and
even assisted the Franciscans in Catholic rituals, but Mendinueta wondered
how much the Indians understood since so few priests spoke their languages,
and vice versa. Some villages were without a resident missionary, and might see
a priest only once a year when he arrived to perform baptisms and marriages.
Mendinueta assumed that this kind of "spiritual abandonment" would have
ill effects on the neophytes' faith. Missions among the Navajos, likewise, had
been attempted but abandoned when the proselytes "retired to the mountains
and left the missionaries alone." The governor doubted that the friars could
convince the Indians to return to the "tranquil magnificence of our Catholic
religion on account of their natural wild disposition which differs little from
the fierce beasts." Mendinueta drew similar conclusions about the Apaches,
Comanches, and other area Indians.[36]

Not all was well with the Spaniards' faith in New Mexico, either. In a 1778
account, Father Juan Agustin de Morfi wrote of the ethnic Spanish in much the
same terms as Mendinueta described the region's Indians. He suspected that
many Spanish residents rarely availed themselves of the church's sacraments,
and noted that priests struggled to oversee the dispersed settlements and farms.
"As a consequence," Morfi thought that many of the Spanish in New Mexico
"know less about religion than the Indians themselves." Crime and immorality
were rampant, according to Morfi, and "lewdness holds destructive sway here,
more so than among animals." In Morfi's view, the mission Pueblos' level of
piety was superior, as they faithfully attended mass and participated in the sacraments. Morfi was, of course, not an unbiased observer, and was frustrated with
corruption in the Spanish political and economic system. His reflections spoke
to the tenuous hold of faith even among some of the Spanish residents in the
kingdom, however.[37]

Image from Dutch translation of Bartolomé de las Casas's *The Destruction of the Indies* (1664). Peace Palace Library, The Hague. Photograph copyright 2014 by Hansmuller, Wikimedia Commons.

By the late eighteenth century, the kingdom of New Mexico was much more firmly under Spanish control than it had been a century earlier. In 1776, one priest described the capital of Santa Fé as a "rough stone set in fine metal." It compared quite unfavorably to Mexico City, the visitor wrote, "for in the final analysis it lacks everything." He estimated the population at just over two thousand. Santa Fé remained on the outer northern limits of Spain's American empire, along with more recently founded settlements in Texas and California. Missionaries had established the "holy faith" in New Mexico, but at quite a price for the evangelizers and the evangelized.[38]

HERNANDO DE SOTO'S EXPLORATIONS IN
THE AMERICAN SOUTHEAST (1541)

From Buckingham Smith, trans., *Narratives of the Career of Hernando de Soto* (New York, 1866), 108–10.

The Governor marched two days through the country of Casqui, before coming to the town where the Cacique was, the greater part of the way lying through fields thickly set with great towns, two or three of them to be seen from one. He sent word by an Indian to the Cacique, that he was coming to obtain his friendship and to consider him as a brother; to which he received for answer, that he would be welcomed; that he would be received with special good-will, and all that his lordship required of him should be done; and the chief sent him on the road a present of skins, shawls, and fish. After these gifts were made, all the towns into which the Governor came were found occupied; and the inhabitants awaited him in peace, offering him skins, shawls, and fish.

Accompanied by many persons, the Cacique came half a league on the road from the town where he dwelt to receive the Governor, and, drawing nigh to him, thus spoke:—

VERY HIGH, POWERFUL, AND RENOWNED MASTER:—

I greet your coming. So soon as I had notice of you, your power and perfections, although you entered my territory capturing and killing the dwellers upon it, who are my vassals, I determined to conform my wishes to your will, and hold as right all that you might do, believing that it should be so for a good reason, providing against some future event, to you perceptible but from me concealed; since an evil may well be permitted to avoid another greater, that good can arise, which I trust will be so; for from so excellent a prince, no bad motive is to be suspected. My ability is so small to serve you, according to your great merit, that though you should consider even my abundant will and humility in proffering you all manner of services, I must still deserve little in your sight. If this ability can with reason be valued, I pray you receive it, and with it my country and my vassals, of me and them disposing at your pleasure; for though you were lord of the earth, with no more good-will would you be received, served, and obeyed.

The Governor responded appropriately in a few words which satisfied the

Chief. Directly they fell to making each other great proffers, using much courtesy, the Cacique inviting the Governor to go and take lodging in his houses. He excused himself, the better to preserve peace, saying that he wished to lie in the field; and, because the heat was excessive, he pitched the camp among some trees, quarter of a league from the town. The Cacique went to his town, and returned with many Indians singing, who, when they had come to where the Governor was, all prostrated themselves. Among them were two blind men. The Cacique made an address, of which, as it was long, I will give the substance in a few words. He said, that inasmuch as the Governor was son of the Sun, he begged him to restore sight to those Indians: whereupon the blind men arose, and they very earnestly entreated him to do so. Soto answered them, that in the heavens above there was One who had the power to make them whole, and do whatever they could ask of Him, whose servant he was; that this great Lord made the sky and the earth, and man after His image; that He had suffered on the tree of the true cross to save the human race, and risen from the grave on the third day,—what of man there was of Him dying, what of divinity being immortal; and that, having ascended into heaven, He was there with open arms to receive all that would be converted to Him. He then directed a lofty cross of wood to be made and set up in the highest part of the town, declaring to the Cacique that the Christians worshipped that, in the form and memory of the one on which Christ suffered. He placed himself with his people before it, on their knees, which the Indians did likewise; and he told them that from that time thenceforth they should thus worship the Lord, of whom he had spoken to them, that was in the skies, asking Him for whatsoever they stood in need.

BARTOLOMÉ DE LAS CASAS DETAILS THE CRUELTIES OF THE SPANISH COLONIZATION OF THE AMERICAS (1542)

From Bartholomew de las Casas, *An Account of the First Voyages and Discoveries Made by the Spaniards in America* (London, 1699), 116–17.

The insatiable Covetousness of the Spaniards, who mind nothing but to amass together heaps of Treasure, makes 'em unwilling to suffer any Priest or Monk to come into those Cities where they are Masters, for fear their worldly Interest should receive considerable damage by that sort of Men; because (they say) it makes the Indians idle, to assemble 'em (as they do) to instruct 'em in the matters of Religion; for all the time they take up to preach to 'em, they detain 'em from the Work imposed on 'em. Sometimes when the poor Indians have been assembled for their instruction in Christianity, the Spaniards have insolently accosted 'em with Cudgels in their hands; taking such a number of 'em as they think fit, to carry their Baggage or any such like Service; and if they are unwilling to obey, they force 'em to it with Blows in the sight of all the rest, and in the presence of the Monks that instruct 'em; which is a great Scandal to our Religion, and a mighty Obstacle to their Conversion, who are strangely terrified and hinder'd in these pious Exercises as well as the Monks that preach to 'em, by this ill usage.

Another Inconvenience the Spaniards pretend they receive from these Instructions, is, that when the Indians are converted and plac'd in the number of Christians, they grow proud and insolent, thinking better of themselves than they are, and refuse to work so hard as they did before. For the Spaniards are very ambitious to command the Indians as their absolute Slaves, and to be obey'd, respected, and even ador'd by 'em; and therefore omit nothing that may hinder them from becoming Christians.

Sometimes 3 or 4 Towns or Villages are given up to the disposal of a certain number of Spaniards, and the Inhabitants distributed among 'em, to some more, to others fewer; and it often happens that a Woman falls to one Man's share, whose Husband falls to the Lot of another, and their Children to a third; so that they divide these miserable Families like Flocks of Sheep. They employ 'em in all sorts of service, as to manure the ground, to work in the Mines, and to carry Burdens in Journeys of 50 or 60 Leagues. And their Masters so constantly exact the hard Tasks of Work they set 'em, that the poor Wretches have not time to attend the Instructions of the Divine Word, and to learn the Rules of Christianity. These People, tho' free, have been made Slaves, and the greatest part of 'em destroy'd. Parents and Children have been slaughter'd together; Villages and Cities entirely ruin'd, and not a House left standing. And the Spaniards have no more regard to their Salvation, than if their Souls and Bodies died together, and were uncapable of eternal Rewards or Punishments.

The Spaniards undoubtedly have an Obligation of Duty upon 'em to instruct them in the Doctrine of Christ; but they are so ignorant themselves, that 'tis not much to be wonder'd at, if they take no care to inform others. . . .

A SPANISH REPORT ON THE REVOLT OF THE
PUEBLO INDIANS OF NEW MEXICO (1680)

From Charles Wilson Hackett, ed., *Revolt of the Pueblo Indians of New Mexico and Otermin's Attempted Reconquest* (Albuquerque, N.M., 1942), 177–78.

. . . the convocation and plot of the said Indians seems to have been so secret that they perpetrated their treason generally in all the jurisdictions of the kingdom, as was seen, beginning on the night of August 9, when the said Indians took up their arms and, carried away by their indignation, killed religious, priests, Spaniards, and women, not sparing even innocent babes in arms; and as blind fiends of the devil, they set fire to the holy temples and images, mocking them with their dances and making trophies of the priestly vestments and other things belonging to divine worship. Their hatred and barbarous ferocity went to such extremes that in the pueblo of Sandia images of saints were found among excrement, two chalices were found concealed in a basket of manure, and there was a carved crucifix with the paint and varnish taken off by lashes. There was also excrement at the place of the holy communion table at the main altar, and a sculptured image of Saint Francis with the arms hacked off; and all this was seen in one temple only, as we were marching out. The church of the villa was entirely consumed by fire before your lordship's eyes and those of this cabildo and of the people who were present in the siege to which the enemy subjected us. When they had us surrounded in the said casas reales, and fighting with them, because the said temple was not defended it caught fire and burned until it was consumed and entirely demolished, only the walls remaining. All this was in addition to the ravages and sacrileges that they committed in the other jurisdictions of thirty-four pueblos, and in the estancias and houses of the Spaniards of which the said New Mexico is composed, its settlements being so scattered and undefended that the people who are now in this army have escaped by a miracle. Here we have found that the prelate and the head of this church has lost eighteen clerical ministers and two lay religious, which make twenty-one. There have died besides more than three hundred and eighty Spaniards — men, women, and children — with some servants, among whom are seventy-three Spaniards of military age, all of whom have perished at the hands of the rebellious enemy, having been robbed of arms, haciendas, and everything they possessed. The same was done before your lordship's eyes, alike in the said villa, where they sacked our houses and set fire to them, and in the convents and estancias, for the truth of this is proved by what we saw for ourselves on the march which was made to leave the kingdom. We found the pueblos deserted, the convents and estancias sacked, and the horses, cattle, and other articles of our household goods on the mesas and in the roughest parts of the sierras, with the said enemy guarding all of it and verbally mocking and insulting us. There is no doubt that we should not have succeeded in making the said withdrawal if it had not been for divine assistance. . . .

3

The French Empire in America

In 1608, more than two thousand miles northeast of Santa Fé, the French established a settlement at a place local Indians called Kebec (Quebec), on the north bank of the St. Lawrence River. A lower town stood on the shores of the river, while an upper town perched on top of a rocky promontory, a stout location for a fortress. Aware of the new English colony of Jamestown, founded some eight hundred miles south in 1607, France had become worried that they might fall behind in the colonization of North America. Led by Samuel de Champlain, the French decided to plant a permanent colony away from the Atlantic coast, along the St. Lawrence, and among Native Americans who were key to the fur trade and who hopefully would receive evangelistic appeals from the Catholic Church. Champlain also figured that if the French kept following the St. Lawrence to the Great Lakes and into the west, they might find a water route to Asia.

Although no priests came with the first settlers, Champlain was a man of substantial Christian commitment, and he asked each soldier and sailor who came to Quebec "to examine his soul, to cleanse himself from his sins, to receive the sacraments and put himself in a state of grace so as to become afterward more free [*plus libre*] in his own conscience and in God's keeping, when he exposed himself to the mercy of the waves in a great and dangerous sea." In 1615, Champlain did bring missionaries with him to the St. Lawrence to pursue the conversion of native souls.[1]

The French had been venturing in Canada for some seven decades before Champlain founded Quebec. While the allure of gold and silver, and the pros-

43

pect of sugar plantations, seemed confined primarily to the lands of the Caribbean and Gulf of Mexico regions, the northern climes did yield abundant fisheries and furs. English and French explorers also probed for the elusive "Northwest Passage" that might offer a quicker trade route to Asia than the arduous eastward journeys from Europe.

Jacques Cartier made several journeys to Canada in the 1530s and 1540s, navigating parts of the Gulf of St. Lawrence and the river itself. He encountered Micmacs and Iroquoian Indians, among whom he planted a thirty-foot wooden cross that proclaimed long life to France's king. The region's Iroquoian king, Donnacona, understood the cross as a claim of sovereignty, and objected. Imitating the sign of the cross with his fingers and pointing at the wooden symbol, Donnacona gestured to the surrounding land, "as if he wished to say that all this region belonged to him," Cartier noted, "and that we ought not to have set up this cross without his permission."[2]

Cartier, a devout Catholic, reflected again the transcendent significance that many Europeans attached to these new American encounters. God intended for people across the world to accept the Christian gospel. As the gospel began in the Near East and spread west to Europe, so also was the faith, in the providence of God, spreading further west to the Americas, "just like the sun, carrying its light and its heat from east to west." Cartier connected this progression to the struggle against the "infants of Satan," including Protestants (Huguenots) and Muslims, and to Spain's missionary labors in the Caribbean and Mexico.[3]

Following a familiar grim pattern of contact, not long after Cartier's arrival among the Indians a major epidemic broke out with "marvelous and extraordinary symptoms," their bodies becoming swollen, bruised, and blackened. Although the French suffered from these maladies as well, cascading waves of disease, along with intertribal warfare, effectively eliminated native settlements along the St. Lawrence, opening the way for Champlain's permanent colony in the early seventeenth century.[4]

The Wendats, or Hurons, of the eastern Great Lakes became some of the French colonists' key allies. They were of Iroquoian background but broke with the Iroquois League in their friendship with the French (a choice that would bear bitter fruit for them in the end). As we saw in chapter 1, the Hurons shared many Native Americans' pervasively spiritual view of the natural world. Early European missionaries often overlooked the religious mentality of the Wendats and other natives because they assumed that religion entailed institutions, doctrines, and formal worship, along with practices. The Wendats certainly had beliefs; their religion was woven into the habits of daily life. One did not rush into any significant activity without acknowledging the spirits resident in the waters, the land, or the sky. The Wendats offered sacrifices to honor and appease spirits. They used tobacco as a ceremonial gift, for example, throwing handfuls into the fire when preparing to sleep or when requesting healing from an illness. To prepare for lengthy trips, Wendats sometimes placed bits of tobacco in the cracks of large rocks along the river, believing that this would protect them from accidents or attacks along the way.[5]

As with the Spanish, missionaries soon accompanied French settlement in Canada. In 1615, four French Recollet priests came to work among the Innus, a native group that lived along the north bank of the river. The Recollets, a reform branch of the Franciscans, decided to focus their evangelistic efforts on Innu youths. The missionaries found that Innu adults were reluctant to embrace conversion, and figured that they might more easily detach children and youths from aboriginal traditions. If they could train up children in French culture and Catholic piety, then perhaps those trainees would eventually take the gospel back to their own people.[6]

The Recollets opened a school for native children in Quebec in 1620. The same year, they sent one of their most promising students, the twelve- or thirteen-year-old Pierre-Anthoine Pastedechouan, to France for further education. Pastedechouan trained for five years at the La Baumette convent. He learned French and Latin, but also instructed prospective Recollet missionaries in the Innu language. In spring 1621, he received a public baptism and his Christian name, Pierre-Anthoine (after his royal French godparents), before a standing-room-only crowd. In spite of his tutoring sessions in Innu, by the end of his schooling he reportedly had begun to forget the language, and expressed reluctance to go back to Canada. Why, he supposedly asked the Recollets, would they want to send him "back to the beasts who do not know God"?[7]

Nevertheless, Pastedechouan did return to New France in 1626, to the Innu town at Tadoussac. An English attack in 1629 led to his temporary imprisonment, and subsequent French evacuation left Pastedechouan alone with the Innu relatives he had once denounced. The French returned in 1632, and the convert worked for a new Jesuit missionary, Paul Le Jeune. But the English intervention, and his time back among the Innu, had unsettled Pastedechouan, who now balked at taking communion. He admitted to Le Jeune that he found himself powerfully influenced by his surroundings, and unable to remain committed fully to Catholicism. "When I was with the English," he said, "I allowed myself to be influenced by their talk; when I am with the Savages, I do as they do; when I am with you, it seems to me your belief is the true one. Would to God I had died when I was sick in France, and I would now be saved." Struggling to reconcile with either the Jesuits or his Innu family, Pastedechouan apparently died alone in the woods, from exposure and starvation, in the mid-1630s. His case reminds us of the struggles of many Indian converts to find a permanent home amid clashing beliefs, competing loyalties, and colonial rivalries.[8]

Le Jeune represented the second, more enduring wave of French missionary activity in Canada, that of the Jesuits. The Jesuits, following the example of their order's missionary co-founder, Francis Xavier, engaged in a remarkable program of overseas missions in the sixteenth and seventeenth centuries, stretching from Japan to Mexico. They began arriving in New France in the mid-1620s. Some of the Jesuit "Black Robes," such as Paul Le Jeune, also worked among the Innu/Montagnais peoples. In the early 1630s, Le Jeune engaged Pastedechouan's older brother, the shaman Carigonan, and other Innus in remarkable exchanges that demonstrate how Native American leaders often modified, challenged, and rejected Christian missionaries' overtures on theological grounds. Le Jeune quizzed them as to where souls go after death. "Very far away," they said, "to a large village situated where the sun sets." Le Jeune insisted that North America was a large island, and that the yet-embodied souls they imagined could never cross the ocean's waters on foot. The Innu acknowledged that yes, sometimes the souls had to ford the water in places. Le Jeune replied that the water was too deep. "Thou art mistaken," they said, "either the lands are united in some places, or there is some passage which is fordable over which our souls pass."[9]

Le Jeune also quizzed the Innu leaders about what the departed souls did in the land of the dead. When they told him that most of their activity, including hunting, was nocturnal, Le Jeune protested that they could not see at night. "Thou art an ignoramus," they told him. "Thou hast no sense: souls are not like us, they do not see at all during the day, and see very clearly at night." They hunted for the souls of beavers, porcupines, moose, and other departed animals.[10]

Like the Recollets, early Jesuits envisioned working with native youths, instructing them in European languages and theology in order to raise up a cadre of indigenous missionaries (education and missions were primary foci of the Jesuits). Even though Native Americans had only oral languages, the Jesuits tended to view their dialects and intelligence as susceptible to Christian molding. Accordingly, the Jesuits worked harder than most European missionaries at learning native languages, but only with mixed results.

Following the great medieval Catholic philosopher Saint Thomas Aquinas, the Jesuits also emphasized common human reason and everyone's God-given ability to conceive divine truths. Possessing a formidable classical Christian education, they came hoping to build on some preexisting native concepts of God and morality, however corrupt those concepts may have become over time. In

Canada, the "Huron language will be your Saint Thomas and Aristotle," a veteran missionary warned. Some of the natives surpassed their highest expectations—or so the priests told supporters in reports to France. Le Jeune confessed that the Indians "evince a great deal of intelligence, but I would not have believed that they could reason so well, especially in the matter of our belief." Another Jesuit explained that though the Indians were barbarians, "there remained in their hearts a secret idea of the Divinity." Missionaries encouraged proselytes to consider the grand beauty of the created world: did its magnificence not suggest a divine creator? Over time, Jesuit estimations of native capabilities grew less optimistic. The devil had established a strong presence among these people, they reckoned.[11]

Although some early French Jesuits labored among the Innus, the order determined that the Wendats were the most promising native group for evangelization. They were key trading partners of the French, and relatively sedentary compared with other Canadian Indians. The Jesuits established a central mission at Sainte-Marie, about ninety miles north of present-day Toronto. By the late 1640s, some eighteen priests and as many as forty-six lay assistants worked in the Wendat missions.

The missionaries self-consciously used the technology and arts of European culture to convey an impression of superior power to the Wendats. Catholic piety was always more visually oriented than that of Protestants, but in Canada, that visual aspect seemed even more pressing due to language difficulties. They sought to make Sainte-Marie an "island of European culture," as one historian puts it, with beautiful displays in the mission chapel, as well as garden plots and stone-and-timber buildings that would not have looked out of place in provincial French towns in the seventeenth century. The Jesuits labored to endow their religious ceremonies "with a magnificence surpassing anything that the eyes of our Savages have ever beheld, all these things produce an impression on their minds, and give them an idea of the majesty of God." Printed images of saints, and of heaven and hell, dramatized the faith and captured the attention of proselytes. The Jesuits also assumed that the Indians, familiar only with oral language, would regard printed and handwritten text as a "secret worthy of astonishment."[12]

Travel into Huronia was daunting for the missionaries (starting with the transatlantic voyage), but immersion into the snowy woods seems to have been both harrowing and spiritually bracing. They spoke of the "sacred awe of these forests" and the "heavenly light one finds in the thick darkness of this barbarism." But the rigors of journeying through Canada, and life among their native proselytes, was full of daily difficulty and embarrassments, especially for a newly arrived minister. Canoe travel could be the most awful experience. Often physically incapable of the all-day paddling, the missionary could end up crouching "like a useless monkey among the baggage, his long robes tucked around his bare legs and feet, his head dipping to avoid the brain-rattling thump of a paddle as the sternman stood to negotiate obstacles and rapids." A ravaging diet of parched corn and unreliable water could create daily embarrassments. A Canadian mission was a job for the most zealous advocates of the Catholic Reformation, and a badge of spiritual honor. But "the joy that one feels when he has baptized a savage who dies soon afterwards, and flies directly to heaven to become an angel, certainly is a joy that surpasses anything that can be imagined," the Jesuits confessed. Then "one no longer remembers the sea, nor seasickness, nor the horror of past tempests." The missionaries took the reality of heaven and hell seriously; any sacrifice was worthwhile in light of the eternal stakes.[13]

The missionaries, who were usually in their mid-thirties, could not have known how central disease and death would become in their work. Epidemics of smallpox and the flu swept through Huronia repeatedly beginning in the 1630s. The Jesuits often waited to baptize converts until death seemed imminent, fearing the eternal consequences for Wendats who might receive baptism and later apostatize. Some Indians suspected that baptism hastened the converts' demise. One elderly Wendat told the Jesuits in 1637 that it was their fault he was dying: "I have seen you in a dream as persons who are bringing us misfortune," he asserted. The rampant sickness also positioned the missionaries as rivals to native shamans to demonstrate who wielded the more powerful medicine. Many of the Jesuits had acquired immunity to smallpox, so they survived at higher rates than the Wendats, including shamans. Although some native herbal remedies had palliative effects, the dances, games, and feasts they employed to counteract the epidemics did nothing. Neither did the Jesuits' bloodletting and purging, practices based on theories of balancing bodily humors.[14]

Missionaries figured that God's hand was behind the epidemics, and used them to encourage the Wendats to accept Christianity and repudiate their traditional practices. They exhorted converts to separate themselves from non-Christians, and sought to keep the bodies of deceased Wendat Christians from being buried in the ceremonial Feast of the Dead. (At the Lorette mission, priests did permit a disinterring and reburying ceremony on All Souls' Day.) In 1637, a Wendat council inquired of the Jesuits how they might secure the mercy of God in the midst of a besetting sickness. The missionaries told them to start obeying God's commands and to abandon their heathenish ways. The superior said that they should first "give up their belief in their dreams; 2nd, that their marriages should be binding and for life, and that they should observe conjugal chastity; 3rd he gave them to understand that God forbade vomiting feasts; 4th, those shameless assemblies men and women (I would blush to speak more clearly); 5th, eating human flesh; 6th, those feasts they call Aoutaerohi,—which they make, they say, to appease a certain little demon to whom they give this name." In spite of their desperate straits, the Wendats thought the Jesuits were asking too much—as if they were speaking of "overthrowing the country," the council averred.[15]

The evangelistic prospects in New France drew not only men, but also devout women to help establish a Catholic foothold. Indeed, Father Le Jeune appealed for women missionaries, asking, "is there not to be found some good virtuous woman who would wish to come to this country to gather up the blood of Jesus Christ by instructing these savage little girls?" Marie de l'Incarnation Guyart of the Ursuline monastery in Tours, France, had read some of the Jesuits' reports from New France, and in 1634 she had a vivid dream of the Virgin Mary and Jesus in a mountainous land shrouded in fog. She spoke with her Jesuit adviser, who told her that the place she had seen was New France. She believed that God wanted her to go there and make a "house for Jesus and Mary." Guyart envisioned demons oppressing the lost souls of America, "whom they snatched from the domain of Jesus Christ. . . . I yearned for these poor souls; I gathered them to my heart; I presented them to the Eternal Father."[16]

Guyart arrived in Canada in 1639 and helped to establish an Ursuline convent in Quebec. The sisters—a total of fourteen of them by 1650—worked at educating and catechizing Native American girls, with a growing number of French girls in residence as well. Sometimes native families sent students to the convent; sometimes Jesuits identified promising candidates for the school. Marie showed remarkable capacity for learning native languages to aid in instruction; by the 1660s she knew some of the Algonquin, Montagnais, Wendat, and Iroquois dialects. She found the work exhilarating, wondering if she found the schooling so "delectable" that she might love it too much. The Ursulines addressed the most basic cultural issues when the *filles sauvages* came to them, cleaning lice from their hair and teaching them to dress like French girls. The pupils learned to speak French and participated in the routines of Catholic liturgy and services.[17]

Guyart's letters, like the Jesuits' reports, reverberated across the Atlantic. In the early eighteenth century, they helped to inspire another Ursuline nun, Marie Tranchepain, to seek a similar North American mission. Receiving a vision almost identical to Guyart's, Tranchepain met with a Jesuit who wanted to sponsor a mission to Louisiana. In 1727 she and a company of Ursuline sisters arrived in New Orleans (a town founded by the French Mississippi Company in 1718), where they established a convent and school.[18]

In light of the formidable obstacles they faced, New France's missionaries needed stout conviction, especially as some began to fall victim to Iroquois' retributive attacks, enduring torture and martyrdom. Perseverance was one of the most impressive aspects of the Jesuits' mission to the native peoples, who respected those who suffered silently under torment. Isaac Jogues, whom the Hurons called Ondessonk ("bird of prey"), was captured by Mohawks in the early 1640s. The priest had his beard and fingernails torn out and his left thumb cut off, and his tormenters mangled another of his fingers with their teeth. But Jogues returned to Iroquoia in 1646, permanently scarred but willing to face martyrdom again—indeed, by the end of the year a group of Mohawks did kill him. Jesuits like Jogues could credibly testify that they did not fear death. "Why should we fear it?" they asked. "We believe in God; we honor, love, and obey him; and we are assured of eternal happiness in Heaven after our death."[19]

The 1630s and 1640s saw not only the advent of Jesuit missions, but also destructive wars between the Wendats and the confederated tribes of the Iroquois League. The Iroquois obtained superior weapons, including guns, from Dutch traders based in New Netherlands (New York), and used them against the Wendats, their competitors in the fur trade. The Wendats had also refused to ally with the powerful confederacy, and as the Iroquois lost growing numbers of their people to war and disease, they targeted the Wendats for annihilation or for adoption of captives into the alliance's tribes. (These "mourning wars" often featured the ritual adoption of prisoners of war to replace the deceased.)

These conflicts sometimes claimed missionaries' lives, fulfilling the Jesuits' expectation that martyrdom would precede the spread of the gospel in New France. The Jesuits were mindful of ancient church father Tertullian's precept that the blood of the martyrs is the seed of the church. Fathers Jean de Brébeuf and Gabriel Lalement perished in 1649 when Iroquois warriors overran the village of St. Ignace and tortured the priests at the stake. They reportedly mocked the rite of baptism by pouring boiling water over Brébeuf's head, then dismembered and cannibalized him. Deriding the Catholics' message of life after death, they told him, "we shall be the cause of thy Eternal happiness." Stories and pictures of the Jesuit martyrs' gruesome deaths were used in promotional literature in France to bring greater financial support for the missionaries' work.[20]

Conflict between the Wendats and Iroquois culminated with the near-total destruction of Huronia and its missions starting in 1648. The Jesuits baptized Wendats by the thousands as the region fell to the Iroquois, with reported scenes of mass killings of the Christian converts. In 1649, the Jesuits burned the Sainte-Marie mission to keep it from being taken by the Iroquois. Remaining Wendat refugees scattered east and west, from Quebec to Lake Michigan. Marie de l'Incarnation received the news from those who fled to Quebec. She called its effect on her an "inner crucifixion."[21]

Relations between the French and the Iroquois shifted significantly in the 1650s and 1660s, as military campaigns forced the confederacy to make alliances with the French, concluding with a French/Mohawk peace agreement in 1666–67. Jesuit missions among the Iroquois had already started in the 1650s, but in 1667 the Mohawks (the easternmost of the Iroquois tribes) agreed to allow missionaries into their villages, too. By 1668 the Jesuits had established missions among all five allied Iroquois tribes. The Iroquois became the Jesuits' new focus after the destruction of Huronia, although they still ministered to many Wendats who had known of the Catholics' gospel prior to their adoption into the Iroquois groups in the late 1640s.[22]

The most celebrated Mohawk convert of those years was Catherine Tekakwitha. Tekakwitha had lost her parents in a smallpox epidemic in the early 1660s, when she was about four years old. Most of what we know about Tekakwitha (as with so much of New France's Native American culture) comes from her Jesuit biographers. In 1675 she began studying for baptism with a missionary in her village of Gandaouagué in New York, about two hundred miles south of Montreal. On Easter Sunday, 1676, she received baptism in the mission chapel, and took the Christian name of Catherine ("Kateri"). As an exemplary convert, she began to participate in morning and evening prayers and Sunday mass, and "not to attend dream feasts, or dances or other Indian gatherings contrary to purity," wrote Claude Chauchetière.[23]

Not long after her conversion, Catherine relocated (with a number of other Mohawk Catholic converts) to the new Jesuit mission village of Kahnawake, just south of Montreal on the St. Lawrence. In these decades of war and shifting imperial fortunes, many Native Americans were on the move within North America, just as Europeans and Africans were moving across the Atlantic. Moving to Kahnawake meant aligning with the French, although Tekakwitha's new home maintained a distinctly Mohawk character. Some of the Catholic Mohawks undoubtedly kept a connection with traditional spiritual practices, but Catherine became involved with a women's confraternity that pushed into ever-greater heights of devotion and self-denial. They cared for the poor and sick, and strictly avoided the "pleasures of the body." They mortified the flesh by means such as bathing in an icy river, self-flagellation, and wearing hair shirts and iron girdles, devices meant to keep the skin constantly irritated. Without much direct evidence from the Mohawk Catholics themselves, it is difficult to characterize the significance of these rituals, but they likely would have seen them as a method of drawing ever closer to God, denying the flesh and cultivating the spirit.[24]

Self-mortification has a long Christian pedigree, but the ascetic practices of Catherine's confraternity were so intense—and seemingly independent—that they made some of the Jesuits anxious. (Marie de l'Incarnation, who died in 1672, had also practiced such disciplines as a young woman: she would put bitter herbs in her food, sleep as little as possible, and treat the "most foul-smelling wounds" of medical patients she oversaw, drawing close to them to smell the odor.) Chauchetière speculated that the devil was using the Mohawk penitents to "give this nascent Christianity a repugnant appearance." Another missionary noted that although he approved of certain self-denying habits, the women took them much further than he intended and that they often went by themselves to the woods to avoid clerical interference. There the women believed that "anything was permitted," the priests worried.[25]

Native converts, then, could adopt Christianity and put their own stamp on the faith, even in ways that gave the Jesuits pause. But the women's faith, including Catherine's, also concerned her fellow Mohawks. When Catherine made a vow of celibacy, some family and clan members were incredulous. Why would a twenty-three-year old take such a step? She reportedly told a missionary that marriage repulsed her now, and that she wished to have "none other than Jesus Christ as her spouse." She continued to pursue unauthorized penitent practices, depriving herself of sleep and food, and practicing self-flagellation, all of which degraded her health in 1679. In spite of warnings from priests and female friends, she continued the disciplines, and sometimes slept on a bed of thorns. One of the priests admitted that he admired her devotion but considered her imprudent. Her fame as an ascetic with extraordinary spiritual powers began to spread; the priests confirmed reports that divine light sometimes shone about her as she whipped herself. She died in April 1680, but the sickly Mohawk quickly acquired a reputation as a healing saint, with numerous reports of miraculous cures associated with prayers at her grave or touching her relics (such as her bones). As the Catholic Church grew more receptive to non-European saints in the late twentieth century, it beatified Catherine in 1980, then canonized her as a saint in 2012.[26]

Penitential practices like those of Tekakwitha apparently spread west with Catholic missions into the Great Lakes region, although the chief body of missionary reports, the *Jesuit Relations*, ended in 1672, after which the details of what we know about French mission stations taper off. An intriguing bit of material information was excavated from Fort St. Joseph, on the St. Joseph River near present-day Niles, Michigan, near the Indiana border. Fort St. Joseph was founded in 1691, partly to protect its affiliated Jesuit mission. In 2004 archaeologists discovered at the fort a cilice, a penitential device made of metal loops worn under the clothing to irritate the wearer's skin. The other items found with the cilice indicate it was probably left there in the second half of the eighteenth century. Its ends were blunted, suggesting that it may have been used moderately, more in accord with standard Jesuit practices. Because we cannot definitively trace the owner of the (quite rare, if not archaeologically unique) cilice, scholars cannot say for sure whether it was used, how often, or by whom. However, its discovery, along with the discovery of unearthed evidence such as crucifixes and other devotional items, tangibly suggests the spread of Jesuit and Catholic piety into the western reaches of France's American empire in the eighteenth century.[27]

French Jesuit missionaries continued to investigate the American interior after the French/Mohawk peace of the 1660s. The most celebrated journey in these years was Father Jacques Marquette's exploration of the Great Lakes and Mississippi River in 1673–74. Marquette and his companion, explorer Louis Joliet, sailed far south down the Mississippi to the mouth of the Arkansas River. He returned to the eastern shores of Lake Michigan, where he died (the exact location of his death is disputed) in spring 1675. As with Catherine Tekakwitha, Marquette's remains became objects of reverence, and not long after his passing, one of Marquette's friends reportedly pressed earth from the missionary's grave to his chest while praying for healing, and received immediate relief. Marquette's Indian converts made their own use of the missionary's body, however: two years later, Ottawas from the Jesuits' mission station at Michilimackinac disinterred his bones and dried them, in a manner reminiscent of Feast of the Dead rituals. Placing the bones in a bark box, they took his relics back to their mission. Indian and European Christians alike regularly made pilgrimage to Michilimackinac to petition God for aid at Marquette's tomb.[28]

Historians have not traditionally examined the issue of slavery in New France, but some have begun to unearth the realities of the Indian slave trade in the Great Lakes region. Jesuit missionaries routinely encountered Native American slaves (millions of whom were trafficked in the Americas during the colonial era, thousands of them in New France). Many priests owned Indian slaves, too. Most of these slaves were originally taken as captives by other Native Americans, and some ended up in the possession of the French, who often sold them into networks of the broader Atlantic slave trade.

At Father Marquette's Michilimackinac, a French fort on the far northern tip of Michigan's lower peninsula, a third of all entries in the church's baptismal records related to Indian slaves. Sometimes the lists indicated that a slave woman was presenting a child for baptism who had been fathered by the master. Other records remained silent about the father's identity. Slaves also appeared regularly in western French settlements, such as Fort St. Joseph and Fort Detroit (founded in 1701). Most of these slaves were women or children, who worked in the homes and fields of their owners.[29]

The Recollets and Jesuits registered few complaints about the practice of Indian slavery, knowing that the slaves were among the most common Catholic converts. A typical record of a slave baptism came from Jesuit Pierre Du Jaunay in 1744: "I solemnly administered holy baptism to a young Indian girl, aged about 10 or 12 years, a slave of Boiguilbert, sufficiently instructed and desiring holy baptism. She took the name of Anne." French settlers stood for the girl as godparents. Although it is impossible to know how much Catholic doctrine and piety "Anne" and most other converts embraced, baptism enveloped Indian slaves into the society of New France and the Catholic households of French and mixed-race settlers.[30]

By the late seventeenth century, New France remained small and isolated from Europe, with about 15,000 French settlers. Imperial developments elsewhere in North America and in Europe, still affected the French colonists. The upheavals of the "Glorious Revolution" in 1688–89 became especially significant. This episode not only led to the ouster of King James II of England, but also inaugurated two generations of periodic warfare between England and Europe's Catholic powers. In the English colonies, many of the royal governments faced civil unrest and rebellion in 1689, and New France authorities seized on the instability to launch raids on New York and New England, often led by equal numbers of Christianized Indians and French soldiers. Towns such as Schenectady, New York, and Salmon Falls, New Hampshire, suffered devastating attacks in 1690, with many of each village's residents killed or taken captive.[31]

New York and New England responded with several campaigns against Can-

"La pesche des Sauvages," from the *Codex Canadensis* (circa 1700),
Gilcrease Museum (Tulsa, Oklahoma). Photograph copyright 2014 by Pierre5018,
Wikimedia Commons.

ada and France's Indian allies, highlighted by Sir William Phips's expedition with 2,300 men against the fortress at Quebec in 1690, eight decades after Champlain founded the town. Although New Englanders kept the "wheel of prayer" going round and round for the troops, as Puritan minister Cotton Mather put it, the journey up the Atlantic coast and through the Gulf of St. Lawrence took an excruciatingly long time. An outbreak of smallpox decimated Phips's men. Once they finally reached the walled city in October 1690, his wearied army was unable to penetrate the citadel of the upper town. Priests reportedly placed a picture of the Holy Family on top of the cathedral, a tempting target that drew off useless cannon fire from the New England Protestants. Phips and his soldiers retreated in disgrace, with nearly half perishing before they returned to Massachusetts. Quebec's residents paraded with an image of the Virgin Mary in the lead, celebrating God's favor on them. This would represent only the beginning of focused religious and martial conflict between France and England's colonies in the coming decades.[32]

JESUIT MISSIONARY PAUL LE JEUNE ON
EARLY ENCOUNTERS WITH CANADIAN INDIANS (1637)

From Reuben Thwaites, ed., *The Jesuit Relations and Allied Documents* (Cleveland, 1898), 15: 29–35.

In our visits, we encountered a very sick old man. "My Nephews," (he said to us at first), "be welcome." He soon reversed the compliment when he learned what brought us there, for he said, the angry blood mounting to his face, "It is you people who are making me die; since you set foot in this house, six days ago, I have eaten nothing; and I have seen you in a dream as persons who are bringing us misfortune; it is you who are making me die." Observe that among these peoples nothing more need be said for a man to have his head split. In fact, notwithstanding the fine promises that I have just mentioned, we noticed afterwards so much coldness on all sides, and so great distrust of us, that we judged it wise to desist entirely from our visits. . . .

Our first Christian informed us of another report, similar to that of which we wrote last year, which certainly has had great vogue—namely, that we had brought a corpse from France, and that there was, without doubt, something in our tabernacle that made them die. These poor peoples lay the blame on a charm which they seek everywhere. Possibly this good man, or one of our Neophytes, may have spoken too freely of this precious deposit, since, for ourselves, we never speak to them about it until after a long proof of their faith.

This report was not yet smothered, when another one arose. Our crime was, they said, that we had established ourselves in the heart of the country that we might more easily procure its total ruin; to accomplish this, we had killed a little child in the woods by stabbing it with a bodkin, which had caused the death of a great many children. The devil was perhaps enraged because we had placed many of these little innocents in heaven. In short, we were rebuffed on all sides, so that, one day, when we strove to gain the good will of one of their sick people, who is among the most influential persons here, both he and his relatives began to abuse us. They took umbrage at our slightest act, some of them complaining that we kept our door closed in the morning. Possibly, they said, for some sorcery; others suspected us of some sinister design when in the early evening we sang our Litanies. In a word, they all agreed upon this point—that to put an end to their miseries they must make away with us as soon as possible, or else send us back to France. There was nothing, even to a weather vane that we had had placed on the top of a fir tree, which did not give them something to talk about. "For where are your wits," said one of the chief men, "you Nephews of mine? What does that piece of cloth mean, that I see placed so high up there?" But this complaint terminated pleasantly, when, after having learned that we placed it there to see from what quarter the wind blew, he reproached us for not having used a larger piece, that it might be seen from a greater distance.

Our clock was no longer visible, for they believed it to be the Demon of death, and our illuminated pictures represented to them nothing more than what was happening to their sick people. Merely seeing us walking about, they thought we were engaged in some witchcraft.

Here is the news that frightened us the most,—there was a report that Our Father Superior had been murdered. It was first brought to us by a terrified Savage, and two Captains of note related its details to others of our Fathers, even naming to them the murderer. Behold us, finally, miserable outcasts, as it were; for from that time on every one deserted us, and we were regarded only with dread. This reported assassination spread throughout the Country, when the Father, to console us, hastened to come and relieve us from our anxiety. He went, at the outset, to visit our Captain, who welcomed him as a man risen from the grave. The Old Men of the village came to welcome him, one after another. We could not impart the news of the Father's safety to the settlement of Saint Joseph until a week afterward, for lack of a messenger; the letters that they wrote us show plainly that the rumor passed for the truth among those of their village. In fact, both the little value that these peoples place upon the life of a man, and the reputation of being sorcerers, which infallibly drags death after it, render very palpable to us the evident obligations we are under to him who is the Master of our lives.

A JESUIT OBSERVES INDIANS' RITUALS IN CANADA (1642)

From Reuben Thwaites, ed., *The Jesuit Relations and Allied Documents* (Cleveland, 1898), 23: 53, 55–57.

There is hardly a day in the Year on which some Demon does not have special homage rendered unto him. But, as among Christians, after each Saint has had his own Day, there is a more solemn Festival on which all the Saints

Fathers Jean de Brébeuf and Gabriel Lalemant martyred
by Native Americans in New France. "P. Ioannes de
Brebeuf et P. Gabriel Lallemant Galli Soc. Iesu exco-
riato vertice," *Societas Jesu usque ad sanguinis et vitae
profusionem militans in Europea, Africa, Asia, et America*
(1675). Courtesy of the John Carter Brown Library at
Brown University.

are honored in Company, so likewise in this Country, after each Demon has
been honored in his turn, there is a public celebration in Winter, at which all
the Demons are honored on the same day. This celebration is called Onon-
houaroia, or "upsetting of brain," because all the youth, and even the women
and children, run about as if they were mad, insisting on obedience being paid
to their Demons by making them a present of something which they proffer
with an enigma, and which has been suggested to them in a dream.

Faith finds no difference between the sexes; it fortifies the courage of the
Women as well. Last Summer, the most famous Magician in the Country was
consulted to learn what success might be expected from the corn that had been

planted. He gave two answers,—in the first place, that it was necessary that each on should go every day to his field, throw some tobacco on the fire, and burn it in honor of the Demon whom he worshiped, calling aloud this form of prayer: "Listen, O Sky! Taste my tobacco; have pity on us."

Secondly, he ordered that no one should go to gather hemp (that was the time when they usually go to the untilled plains, in order to gather a certain wild plant, from which twine for their nets is made). And the wretch added that, if they failed to obey therein his Demon, all the grain would be lost. This command was at once proclaimed by the Captains; but the Christians would not offer sacrifices to the Devil, being resolved to die of hunger, rather than do so. Two sisters, who had agreed together to go out on the following day to gather hemp, thought that they could not without sin break this agreement; they went with bowed heads, and returned in the sight of all the Infidels. Complaints of this were made to the Captains, who proclaimed through the Village that a good harvest could not be expected, that the Christians would be the cause of famine, and that it was quite true that the Faith was the ruin of the Country. Every one accused these poor innocent women, but the hearts of the Faithful fear only God and sin. We do not know whether God willed to reward their Faith and to punish the impiety of the others; but we were witnesses that most of the corn did not ripen, especially that belonging to those who had sacrificed to the Devil, while our Christians gathered a fair crop.

MARIE DE L'INCARNATION ON THE URSULINES' SCHOOL FOR INDIAN GIRLS (1640)

From Joyce Marshall, trans. and ed., *Word from New France: The Selected Letters of Marie de l'Incarnation* (Toronto, 1967), 70–72.

We have every reason then, Madame, to praise the Father of mercies for those he has so abundantly poured upon our Savages since, not content with having themselves baptized, they are beginning to become settled and to clear the land in order to establish themselves. It seems that the fervour of the primitive Church has descended to New France and that it illuminates the hearts of our good converts, so that if France will give them a little help towards building themselves small lodges in the village that has been commenced at Sillery, in a short time a much further progress will be seen.

It is a wonderful thing to see the fervour and zeal of the Reverend Fathers of the Company of Jesus. To give heart to his poor Savages, the Reverend Father Vimont, the Superior of this mission, leads them to work himself and toils on the land with them. He then hears the children pray and teaches them to read, finding nothing lowly in whatever concerns the glory of God and the welfare of these poor people. The Reverend Father Le Jeune, the principal cultivator of this vineyard, continues to perform marvels there. He preaches to the people every day and has them do everything he wishes, for he is known to all these nations and is held among them as a man of miracles. And indeed he is indefatigable beyond anything that might be said in the practice of his ministry, in which he is seconded by the other Reverend Fathers, all of whom spare neither life nor health to seek those poor souls that the blood of Jesus Christ has redeemed.

There has been a great persecution among the Hurons in which one of the Fathers was almost martyred by the blow of a hatchet. A club was broken upon him in detestation of the faith he preached. There has been a like conspiracy against the others, who were overjoyed to suffer. Despite all this, at least a thousand persons have been baptized. The devil has worked in vain. Jesus Christ will always be the Master—may he be praised forevermore.

There is talk of giving us two girls of this nation and two Algonkins, these in addition to the eighteen that have filled our seminary, not to speak of the day-girls that come here continually. I assure you, Madame, that in France it will be hard to believe the benedictions God continually pours upon our little seminary. I shall give you a few particulars so as to acquaint you with our consolation.

The first Savage seminarian that was given to us, Marie Negabamat by name, was so used to running in the woods that we lost all hope of keeping her in the seminary. The Reverend Father Le Jeune, who had persuaded her father [Noël Negabamat] to give her to us, sent two older Christian girls with her. These remained with her for some time in order to settle her, but to no avail, for she fled into the woods four days later, after tearing a dress we had given her to pieces. Her father, who is an excellent Christian and lives like a saint, ordered her to return to the seminary, which she did. She had not been here two days when there was a wonderful change. She seemed no longer to be herself, so disposed was she to prayer and the practices of Christian piety, so that today she is an example to the girls of Quebec, although they are all very well brought-up. As soon as she has committed a fault, she comes to ask pardon on her knees and she does the penance she is given with incredible submissiveness and amiability. In a word, it is impossible to look at her without being touched by devotion, so marked is her face by innocence and inner grace.

At the same time we were given a big girl of seventeen years whose name is Marie Amiskouevan. One could not see anything more tractable, more innocent, or more candid even than this girl, for we have never surprised her in a lie, which is a great virtue among the Savages. If her companions accuse her, she never excuses herself. She is so ardent in praying to God that it is never necessary to advise her to do so; she even leads the others, and it seems as if she were their mother, so much charity has she toward them. She has great intelligence for retaining what is taught her, especially the mysteries of our holy Faith, which makes us hope she will do great good when she returns to the Savages. She is sought in marriage by a Frenchman, but it is intended to give her to a man of her own nation because of the example it is hoped she will give the other Savages. If God would give someone in France the devoutness to help her build a little house, this would undoubtedly be a work of very great merit. This girl has helped us greatly in the study of her tongue because she speaks French well. In a word, she wins everyone's heart by her sweetness and her fine qualities.

4

VIRGINIA AND THE CHESAPEAKE

Colonies were on Europeans' minds in 1607–08, as Spaniards founded Santa Fé, English settlers founded Jamestown, and the French established Quebec. These were tiny outposts in a burgeoning system of transatlantic trading networks that spanned the ocean from Europe to the Americas and Africa. Jamestown was not England's first effort at American colonizing, but it was the first permanent effort. In 1607, 104 Englishmen (there were only males among them) established the new colony in Virginia. One of the first things they did was build a chapel on the banks of the James River. Captain John Smith recalled that they hung an old sail from trees to serve as an awning. "Our walls were rails of wood, our seats unhewed trees, till we cut planks, our pulpit a bar of wood nailed to two neighboring trees," Smith said. That structure served as the church until they upgraded and "built a homely thing like a barn." There they had prayer services every morning and evening, two sermons every Sunday, and a communion service every three months.[1]

In 1608 the barn-like church burned, and Jamestown colonists replaced it with a much more imposing structure, sixty-four by twenty-four feet: by far the largest building in the settlement. For many years, archaeologists assumed that the foundations of this church, along with the whole original Jamestown fort, had been lost to erosion in the river. But in the 1990s, excavations revealed the buried remains of the fort on land. In the decades since, the site has yielded millions of artifacts and the remains of buildings, including the 1608 church. It was discovered underneath Civil War–era earthworks in 2011, revealing perhaps the oldest Protestant church remains in North America. The church was the scene of the most celebrated (and controversial) wedding of the American colonial era, that between John Rolfe and Pocahontas.[2]

Early Virginia colonists did not come with clear religious purposes, as did settlers of Massachusetts, nor did Virginians mobilize the kind of missionary effort as Catholic New Spain or New France. Yet from the beginning, religion was everywhere in colonial Virginia, dominating the Virginians' physical landscape, its laws, and its mores.

✦ ✦ ✦

When you consider the context of imperial struggle between Europe's Catholic and Protestant powers, this religious emphasis in Virginia should not be a surprise. The key organizers and promoters of the Virginia venture had extensive experience in the English conquest of Catholic Ireland, and viewed English territorial expansion through the lens of confessional and military conflict. One of the most important advocates of English colonization was Oxford-educated minister Richard Hakluyt, who reflected much of the prevailing English mindset in his "Discourse on Western Planting," the first effort by an Englishman to make an imperial, economic, and religious case for westward expansion. In 1584 Hakluyt presented this document to Elizabeth I, the "virgin queen" to whom it was dedicated.[3]

Hakluyt led with religion when justifying the colonization program. It was not enough to employ financial and imperial arguments, although he used those, too. Western settlements, he argued, would serve "the gospel of Christ, whereunto the princes of the Reformed Religion are chiefly bound, amongst whom her Majesty is principal." The minister averred that the native people living between Florida and Canada were idolaters, worshipping the sun, moon, and stars. Who would reach these benighted people with the gospel? Would Catholics get to them first? Hakluyt cited the apostle Paul in Romans 10, noting that whoever called on the name of the Lord would be saved. But how would they believe without faithful Christians to proclaim the good news to them? "It is necessary," Hakluyt concluded, "for the salvation of those poor people which have [been] sitting so long in darkness and in the shadow of death, that preachers should be sent unto them."[4]

Hakluyt proposed that the best way to evangelize native Virginians was to plant functioning English colonies among them and learn their languages. (Hakluyt glumly noted that this would take time, what with the apostolic "gift of tongues being now taken away.") If they proceeded wisely and discreetly, the English could "distill into their purged minds the sweet and lively liquor of the gospel." Recklessness marked the missionary strategy of the Spanish. This was not the English way. Hakluyt compared the English enterprise to that of Paul in the Book of Acts, chapter 16, when he had a vision of a man from Macedonia saying, "Come over into Macedonia, and help us." Even so, "the people of AMERICA cry out unto us . . . to come and help them, and bring unto them the glad tidings of the gospel." If not a direct fulfillment of prophecy, western expansion would replay key sequences from the biblical record.[5]

In promoting colonization, Hakluyt also emphasized countering the Spanish and Catholic threat in the Americas. He noted their corrupting religious effects, and also their barbarous treatment of native people, quoting Bartolomé de las Casas at length to demonstrate the "tyrannies and devilish doings of the Spaniards." Although Las Casas helped to bring the worst abuses of the Spanish conquests to light among European Catholics, his writings may have gained even more attention from critics of Spanish rule like Hakluyt, giving powerful ammunition to the case for countering Catholic colonies with Protestant ones. These English advocates typically failed to mention the brutalities of the Irish conquest in the mid-1500s, which saw rampant executions of men, women, and children, as well as the posting of severed heads on pikes as warnings to prospective Irish resisters.[6]

Challenging Catholic hegemony in the Americas was part of a fabric of justifications for English colonization, but there was no question that as of the late 1500s, the English felt they were behind in western expansion. Many believed that colonies could function as a pressure release for the teeming masses of England's landless poor, especially in London. Even if they did not produce America's long-rumored gold and silver or a water route to the East Indies, colonies would supply raw materials for English production, as well as new markets for refined goods. Richard Hakluyt's lawyer cousin (inconveniently, also named Richard Hakluyt) summarized the goals of colonization as these:

1. To plant Christian religion.
2. To trafficke.
3. To conquer.

"Or," Hakluyt said, "to do all three."[7]

Walter Ralegh, a veteran of the Irish conquests, received knighthood and a commission from the queen to explore lands across the Atlantic in the mid-1580s. Elizabeth charged him to "discover, search, find out, and view such remote, heathen, and barbarous lands, countries, and territories not actually possessed of any Christian Prince." Hakluyt and others predicted that "in all the world the like abundance is not to be found" as in the mid-Atlantic region. In 1585 Ralegh brought about a hundred colonists to Roanoke Island, on the outer banks of the North Carolina coast (then considered part of greater Virginia).[8]

Roanoke did not prove quite as fertile as the colonists imagined, so they inaugurated what became a typical English survival strategy: taking food from Indians. By 1586, this policy led to resentment, culminating in bloodshed between the colonists and their Algonquin neighbors. The first Roanoke colonists left soon thereafter. Ralegh was not ready to give up on Virginia, however, and sent a new detachment of colonists led by John White in 1587, hoping to found a new settlement on the shores of the Chesapeake Bay. An impatient ship's captain dumped the colonists at Roanoke Island again, and hurried off for the pirating grounds of the Caribbean. The same problems as before plagued the new colonists, so John White returned to England for guidance and to replenish supplies. He expected to go back to Roanoke soon, but English and Spanish conflict intervened, highlighted by the Spanish Armada's failed attack on England in 1588. In that episode, repeated delays, defeats, and phenomenal storms resulted in the loss of more than fifty Spanish ships, much to the delight of English Protestants. A commemorative medal declared that "Jehovah blew with His wind and they were scattered."

The ruin of the Spanish Armada indirectly perpetuated the suffering and uncertainty of the Roanoke colonists, and when after three years White returned, he happened upon one of the greatest mysteries of the American colonial era. The Roanoke settlement was deserted. No evidence suggested an attack by Indian or Spanish forces. Only one clue remained—the word "CROATOAN" carved into a tree. Croatoan was the name of a neighboring island, but it is not clear whether this meant that the colonists escaped there and stayed, or continued further north to the Chesapeake region. Later reports of white settlers among Native Americans in Virginia suggested the latter, but the fate of America's original English colonists remains uncertain.

Twenty years passed before the English could summon the initiative to launch another colony, but the Roanoke colony was an important first step. It generated lingering interest in the untapped possibilities in the Chesapeake, as described in Thomas Hariot's 1588 *Brief and True Report of the New Found Land of Virginia.* Hariot, a close friend of Ralegh's, went on one of the exploratory visits to Roanoke. His *Brief and True Report* focused on the natural abundance of the place, making a case that a real settlement could work in Virginia and become more than a pirate's cove. In spite of the Roanoke colonists' strife with Indians, Hariot asserted that the "natural inhabitants" of Virginia were "not to be feared, but that they shall have cause both to fear and love us." The fear would result from the Roanoke Indians' inferior war-making technology, as they lacked iron weapons and guns. Hariot reckoned that "some religion they have already, which although it be far from the truth, yet being as it is, there is hope that it may be the easier and sooner reformed." Although they believed in many gods, he thought they also acknowledged one chief, eternal god.[9]

To the north of the Roanoke Indians lived the people of the Powhatan chiefdom. They resided along the rivers of eastern Virginia, or Tsenacommacah, as they called their lands. Roughly 20,000 natives lived in the region when English settlers arrived. These Indians reportedly honored a "great good God" named Ahone who was the perfect creator but who remained detached from the Powhatans' daily affairs. The god Okeus, by contrast, was active, vengeful, and malicious, and the Powhatans believed that they needed to pacify Okeus, lest they provoke his wrath.[10]

Indians in Virginia all worked at providing material sustenance, but in different roles according to gender. Men hunted and fished, and women grew vegetables and gathered nuts and berries. The only Powhatans who took a nonagricultural role in society were the priests or shamans, who maintained temples and advised chiefs. John Smith observed some of these priests during an audience with Wahunsonacock (the tribal name of the chief Powhatan). As he waited to meet the chief, there "came skipping in a great grim fellow, all painted over with coal, mingled with oil; and many snakes' and weasels' skins stuffed with moss, and all their tails tied together, so as they met on the crown of his head in a tassel." With "hellish voice and a rattle," the priest and other shamans danced about a fire encircled with corn and corn meal. Smith concluded that they intended the ceremony's symbols to represent Virginia, the ocean, and Smith's far-off home.[11]

Wahunsonacock presided over a formidable Algonquin-speaking confederacy in the early 1600s. Through a combination of diplomatic and martial skills, he brought together an alliance of thirty tribes between the (soon-to-be-named) James and Potomac rivers. One of the early settlers described the chief as a "strong and able savage, sinewy, active, and of a daring spirit, vigilant, ambitious, [and] subtle to enlarge his dominions." He reportedly had more than a hundred wives and commanded a tributary network through which he received gifts, including animal skins and tobacco. He represented an established political and religious entity that the English colonists struggled to understand, much less conquer.[12]

The expedition to settle Jamestown entered the Chesapeake Bay on April 26, 1607, and before sailing up the James River to find a suitable place to plant the colony, they "set up a cross" on the shore to announce their presence and their faith to the native peoples. One of the early leaders explained that the English hoped "by degrees to change [the Indians'] barbarous natures, make them ashamed the sooner of their savage nakedness, inform them of the true God, and of the way to their salvation, and finally teach them obedience to the King's majesty and to his governors in those parts." The English did not bring any missionaries specifically tasked with evangelizing the Indians, although they did bring ministers with them. The first, Robert Hunt, was a disciple of Richard Hakluyt. He spoke to the colonists upon the planting of the cross, and administered what was likely the first Protestant communion service in North America in 1607. Hunt died under unknown circumstances about a year after his arrival.[13]

Unlike the Catholic colonists and their missionary orders, Protestants tended to see the missionary enterprise as a matter of setting up Christian villages, and bringing Indians into the life of those communities when appropriate. Commending the Virginia colony in 1609, the Reverend Robert Gray argued that it was every Christian's duty to "venture either with his person or with his purse, to bring the barbarous and savage people to a civil and Christian kind of government." Gray knew that some might object, asking what right the English had to take the Indians' land from them. He replied that the Indians were not properly using the land in an agricultural sense. The English meant only to take a small portion of it, in any case. If war became necessary "to reclaim and reduce those savages from their barbarous kind of life," it would be justified. "Those people are vanquished to their unspeakable profit and gain, which by conquest are abridged of the liberty of sin and impiety," the minister wrote. The focus was not on the fate of individual Indians, some of whom might well die in the conquest, but on Powhatan society as a whole, which Gray and the Virginia promoters insisted would benefit in this life, and the next, by coming under the dominion of Protestant Christendom and English government.[14]

The English struggled to establish a viable society in the Chesapeake, however. Some sixty miles up the river they named for their king, they founded Jamestown on the north shore. Building a triangular fort and the ramshackle chapel, the colonists began to contemplate how to sustain themselves in the New World. They had formidable factors working against them. Aside from the strength of the Powhatans, they built their fort next to a marshy swamp, a perfect breeding ground for disease-bearing mosquitoes, which would wreak havoc on the Jamestown settlers. The colonists, imagining that few of them would stay very long, and that the material abundance of the land would support them, failed to bring many people who knew about growing food.

Disease, violence, and starvation ensued. Already by late 1608, perhaps 144 of 244 colonists who had come to Jamestown had died. In the winter of 1609–10, the colony experienced a "starving time" during which about half of the colony's 220 residents died, some in Indian attacks, but the majority from disease and starvation. They ate whatever they could find: horses, dogs, rats, snakes. There were even reports of cannibalism.[15]

Leaders routinely complained of the colonists' lazy habits. One Virginia governor said that instead of planting lifesaving crops in the spring, the settlers entertained themselves with "their daily and usual works, bowling in the streets." This strange juxtaposition of desperation and idleness resulted from a number of factors: disease and malnutrition, growing despair over the mounting death rates, poisoning from salty, unclean water supplies, disappointment over not discovering precious metals, and unfamiliarity with the type of work required to sustain themselves.[16]

In 1611, Virginia leaders instituted a program of martial law, and some of the regulations revealed fears that Jamestown's problems came partly from spiritual irreverence. The laws threatened dire punishments for disrespectful or irreligious behavior. They threatened with death anyone who derided the doctrine of the Trinity, or any "known articles of the Christian faith." Those who took God's name in vain could have a stiletto thrust through the tongue. Even if authorities rarely enforced such statutes (the legal code was published in England), their presence conveyed the impression that the colony really was devoted to the "glorie of God."[17]

Desperation about the colony also fueled endemic conflict with the Powhatans, from whom the English constantly demanded food. Both sides took captives and committed atrocities against the other, ranging from torture to the cold-blooded murder of women and children. The capture and conversion of Wahunsonacock's daughter Pocahontas, and her marriage to John Rolfe, seemed to validate the colony's aspirations to evangelize the Indians. Pocahontas had earlier played a key role in "saving" Captain John Smith from execution by Wahunsonacock. Smith—whose writings are our only record of the episode—recorded that Pocahontas took Smith's head in her arms and pleaded with her father to release him. What was likely happening was that Smith was being ritually adopted into the Powhatan tribe, and Pocahontas was performing an assigned role in the ceremony.[18]

Later the English captured Pocahontas and set out to teach her the English language and Christian doctrine. It is difficult to know what Pocahontas's view of her marriage to John Rolfe was, but Rolfe explained that he married her "for the good of this plantation, for the honor of our country, for the glory of God, for my own salvation, and for the converting to the true knowledge of God and Jesus Christ, an unbelieving creature, namely Pocahontas." He also conceded his personal motivations, however, saying that his "heart and best thoughts" were entangled with the teenage girl. She and Rolfe, at the behest of the colony's promoters, soon made their way to England, where she died in 1617.[19]

Early on, Roanoke colonists had noticed local Indians cultivating a plant that the Spanish called tobacco. Thomas Hariot said that tobacco smokers were "notably preserved in health, and know not many grievous diseases wherewithall we in England are oftentimes afflicted." The Indians, Hariot believed, used tobacco as a sacrifice to appease their gods. After nine years at Jamestown, the English seized upon tobacco as their economic salvation. Although some, including King James I, tried to discourage the habit, tobacco was already popular across Europe, and Virginia had ideal soils and climate for growing the crop. The trade expanded phenomenally over the seventeenth century, from 200,000 pounds produced in 1624, to 10 million in 1660, to 30 million by the end of the century. The tobacco business inextricably connected Virginia settlers and workers, English planters, indentured servants, and (soon) African slaves to the broader Atlantic economy. It also meant that the English forced Virginia's Indians off more and more of their traditional lands, disrupting the Powhatans' food supplies even as the English continued to expect Indians to provide "tributes" in corn. (More tobacco also meant less land for cultivating food.) The tobacco boom created ever-deeper resentments among the Powhatans, who were determined not to allow themselves to be treated as a subjected people.[20]

The prospects for the tobacco trade made it imperative that the Virginia colony get its house in order, which required a major transformation. The bitter catalyst for that transformation came in a cataclysmic attack by the Powhatans in 1622, who, in an effort to rescue themselves from the debilitating control of the English, killed more than 350 settlers, or nearly a third of the Virginia colonists. The synchronized assault by hundreds of Powhatans did not spare "either age or sex, man, woman, or child," Virginia investor Edward Waterhouse grimly reported. Settlements by 1622 had spread into the interior on both sides of the James River, and nineteen villages fell under the onslaught.[21]

The year 1622 dramatically changed the character of the Virginia experiment. First, the Powhatans' attack convinced the crown to seize control of the colony from the Virginia Company and turn it into England's first royal colony. Second, the rebellion by the "Native Infidels" dashed the Virginia proprietors' dreams of bringing Native Americans into English Christian society, and justified, according to Waterhouse, a posture of war against the Indians, in order to "destroy them who sought to destroy us." For the next two years, the

English engaged in a host of retaliatory actions. In one episode they feigned peace negotiations with a group of Indians, plying them with poisoned alcohol and killing many in their sickened stupor. The Powhatans, led by their aging chief Opechancanough, attempted another uprising to protect their lands in 1644, but it too failed. Opechancanough, who was reportedly almost a hundred years old, died in English captivity when a guard shot him in the back. Some of the English began to suggest that the Indians would never convert to Christianity because of a kind of "hereditary heathenism," in historian Rebecca Goetz's term, which predisposed them against the gospel.[22]

The end of the Virginia Company and the advent of royal control signaled a new era of stability and prosperity for the colony, accompanied by growing numbers of indentured servants and slaves to work the tobacco fields. The maturation of the English slave trade took some time, but starting with a shipment of "20 and odd Negroes" in 1619, the wealthiest planters in Virginia were eager to bolster their plantations and fortunes by the use of slave labor. Less wealthy farmers tended to depend more on white indentured servants until the early eighteenth century.[23]

We will consider the development of the English Atlantic slave trade at greater length in chapter 8, but both slaves and indentured servants faced grim conditions in early Virginia, conditions much more desperate than those faced by free settlers. White indentured workers normally exchanged four or seven years of labor for passage to the New World. That approximately three-quarters of the English colonists in the seventeenth century came initially as indentured servants speaks to the harsh realities of life in England at the time, especially among the urban poor. Some did not come voluntarily, however; English authorities deported some convicts and orphans to the Chesapeake. One of the colony's secretaries reckoned that Virginia had become "a sink to drain England of her filth and scum." Servants who survived the terms of their indenture might be able to acquire land for themselves—something that would have been unthinkable had these destitute people stayed in England.[24]

Many of the early servants did not survive their terms of service, however, falling victim to violence and disease, exacerbated by the physical stresses of the tobacco fields. In the peculiar logic of bound servitude, the lives of indentured servants, though they were English and not African, may have seemed less valuable to planters because of their temporary contracts. If an owner worked a servant to death, not much was lost. With slaves, the master owned the worker's labor for life, and that of his or her children, too. Female indentured servants came in small numbers, but those who did emigrate sometimes found themselves particularly vulnerable in the male-dominated Chesapeake.

One abusive planter gave his servant Elizabeth Abbott as many as five hundred lashes as a punishment, leaving her "body full of sores and holes" and putrefying, untreated wounds. Because of women's scarcity in the Chesapeake, however, many female servants could expect better prospects for marriage than in England—but this was contingent upon them living through their contracted period of service.[25]

Starting in 1634 the Virginia colonists had unwelcome neighbors in the Chesapeake, the settlers of the Maryland colony. In 1632 King Charles I gave a charter for the colony to Cecil Calvert, the second Lord Baltimore, who with his father George had converted to Roman Catholicism in the 1620s. The Calverts envisioned Maryland as a refuge for long-persecuted English Catholics. That prospect did not charm Protestant authorities in America. The savvy Calverts knew that anti-Catholic animus could scuttle plans for the colony, so they circulated a paper titled "Objections Answered Touching Maryland." Perhaps the most pressing question they addressed was whether Maryland's Catholics would threaten Virginia or the New England colonies with a subversive religious presence. In the worst case, Protestants feared, the Maryland colonists might ally with the Spanish and seek to dominate the Atlantic coast for the Catholic cause. In time, they might even "shake off any dependence on the Crown of England." But the Calverts denied any such intentions, noting that "any people as long as they may live peaceably under their own government, without oppression either in spirituals or temporals," would want to live in harmony with their neighbors. Nevertheless, rumors about Maryland Catholic conspiracies persisted. Whispers that Maryland Catholics had contracted with Seneca Indians for the "total destroying of all the Protestants" continued to foment mistrust among Chesapeake Protestants in 1688, on the eve of the Glorious Revolution. That event would not only displace the Catholic king James II, but also the Catholic leaders of Maryland, in favor of a Protestant royal governor.[26]

As it turned out, not that many English Catholics emigrated to Maryland, but a number of Protestant dissenters did, including Quakers and Puritans. This unplanned religious diversity forced Maryland's assembly to adopt the landmark 1649 "Act Concerning Religion." Although the act threatened blasphemers with punishments including death, it prohibited Marylanders from calling each other epithets, including "heretic, schismatic, idolater, puritan, independent, Presbyterian, popish priest, Jesuit, Jesuited papist, Lutheran, Calvinist, Anabaptist, Brownist, Antinomian, Barrowist, Roundhead, Separatist, or any other name or term in a reproachful manner relating to matters of religion." More substantially, the act guaranteed that no one who professed faith in Jesus Christ would suffer persecution for his or her religion, nor be denied "the free exercise thereof," nor be compelled to contribute to or attend another denomination's church. Although the majority of Maryland Protestants abandoned these principles after the Glorious Revolution, this was the first instance in English law when all Christians were promised free exercise of religion, with no harassment from civil authorities.[27]

By the 1670s, the Virginia colony had become much more successful than its grim early years might have predicted. Indeed, the colony became a victim of its own success. It was still a place of grave risk but considerable opportunity for the destitute people of England, and some poor English men went from being indentured servants to independent tobacco farmers. But by the 1670s, opportunities had begun to dissipate. Much of the best land for cultivation and transport of tobacco to market was taken up, and the farther west one settled, the more likely conflict with neighboring Indians became. Violence broke out between the westernmost English settlers and the Susquehannocks in 1675 over English attempts to push the Susquehannocks off their lands in Virginia and Maryland. White frustration over the difficulties of acquiring the Indians' territory, as well as jealousy over the frontier Occanneechees' role as middlemen in trade networks with other major Indian tribes, fueled conditions ripe for anti-Indian violence, and ultimately for rebellion against Virginia authorities.[28]

Long-serving governor William Berkeley noted the misery of trying to rule over "a people where six parts of seven at least are poor, indebted, discontented, and armed." Berkeley had first served as Virginia's governor from 1642 to 1652, but lost his office during the English Civil War. He was reappointed by the restored king Charles II in 1660, and dreamed of turning Virginia into a stable, economically diverse colony. At his own plantation, Berkeley saw some success in cultivating silk, hemp, wine, and other products. (He and other Virginia elites strangely overlooked their greatest opportunity for diversification, which would have been selling grain to the burgeoning sugar islands of the Caribbean.) But troubles with poor whites and Indians eventually wrecked Berkeley's hopes for Virginia.[29]

In 1675 violence between the Susquehannocks and frontier settlers spread into incessant rounds of recriminations and murders. The English clamored for a campaign to destroy as many Indians as possible, regardless of whether they were friend or foe. Berkeley was reluctant to authorize what today we might call an ethnic cleansing campaign. He proposed instead that the colony bolster its frontier with new forts. Freed former servants found this tepid response unacceptable, and seized upon a leader in the governor's cousin, Nathaniel Bacon. Bacon was an elite Englishman, but in a quest for political power he adopted the role of the people's champion. When Bacon initiated unauthorized military campaigns against frontier Indians, Berkeley declared him a traitor, and Bacon turned his forces against Jamestown.

Bacon looked to God and the people of Virginia to vindicate his cause. If there was "a just God to appeal to, if religion and justice be a sanctuary here, if to plead the cause of the oppressed . . . be treason, God Almighty judge and let the guilty die," he thundered. Bacon excoriated the way that Berkeley used heavy taxes to enrich his friends and relatives. Let us "see what sponges have sucked up the public treasure and whether it has not been privately contrived away by unworthy favorites and juggling parasites," he demanded. Bacon offered freedom to servants who would run away from their masters to fight against Berkeley, and a number of African slaves also participated in the revolt. Bacon signed his proclamation "General by the consent of the people." Coming four years before the Pueblo Revolt, Bacon's Rebellion was the largest violent English uprising in the colonies before the American Revolution.[30]

Bacon's militia entered Jamestown and burned it to the ground in September 1676, as Berkeley and his allies fled across the Chesapeake to Virginia's Eastern Shore. A hostile account noted how they "in the most barbarous manner convert[ed] the whole town into flames, cinders, and ashes, not so much as sparing the church, and the first that ever was in Virginia." This was a brick church from the mid-1600s that had eventually replaced the original church building (the one recently discovered at the Jamestown site). The "sacrilegious action" destroyed the building except for the church tower, the only seventeenth-century structure that remains standing at Jamestown today. It appeared as if Bacon might well take control of mainland Virginia, but a month after razing Jamestown, Bacon died of the "bloody flux," or dysentery. English reinforcements soon arrived, Berkeley was replaced with a new governor, and royal officials reduced the most onerous taxes on the people.[31]

Improved stability, declining English immigration, and increased availability of slaves from Africa meant that Virginia soon transitioned into an era of great tobacco planters, who owned vast properties and legions of slaves, and who would dominate Virginia politics and economic life through the Revolution. The tensions between rich and poor whites remained, but after Bacon's Rebellion, Virginia became a much more racially stratified and slavery-based society than it was in the seventeenth century. The world that Jamestown represented was passing away. Williamsburg, roughly eight miles inland from Jamestown, situated on less swampy property, would become the colony's new capital in 1699. It would be a capital for the slave-owning tobacco lords, and of Virginia's emerging resistance movement against Britain in the 1760s.

THOMAS HARIOT DESCRIBES THE NATIVE
INHABITANTS OF THE COLONIAL SOUTH (1588)

From Thomas Hariot, *A Brief and True Report of the New Found Land of Virginia* (1588; repr., New York, 1903), E–E4.

OF THE NATURE AND MANNERS OF THE PEOPLE.

I speak a word or two of the natural inhabitants, their natures and manners, leaving large discourse thereof until time more convenient hereafter: now only so far forth, as that you may know, how that they in respect of troubling our inhabiting and planting, are not to be feared; but that they shall have cause both to fear and love us, that shall inhabit with them.

They are a people clothed with loose mantles made of deerskins, and aprons of the same round about their middles; all else naked; of such a difference of statures only as we in England; having no edge tools or weapons of iron or steel to offend us withal, neither know they how to make any: those weapons that they have are only bows made of witch hazle, and arrows of reeds; flat edged truncheons also of wood about a yard long, neither have they anything to defend themselves but targets made of barks; and some armors made of sticks wickered together with thread.

Their towns are but small and near the sea coast but few, some containing but 10 or 12 houses, some 20, the greatest that we have seen have been but of 30 houses: if they be walled it is only done with barks of trees made fast to stakes, or else with poles only fixed upright and close one by another.

Their houses are made of small pokes made fast at the tops in round form after the manner as is used in many arbories in our gardens of England, in most towns covered with barks, and in some with artificial mats made of long rushes; from the tops of the houses down to the ground. . . .

Their manner of wars amongst themselves is either by sudden surprising one another most commonly about the dawning of the day, or moonlight; or else by ambushes, or some subtle devises: Set battles are very rare, except it fall out where there are many trees, where either part may have some hope of defense, after the deliverie of every arrow, in leaping behind some or other.

If there fall out any wars between us and them, what their fight is likely to be, we having advantages against them so many manner of waies, as by our discipline, our strange weapons and devises else; especially by ordinance: great and small, it may be easily imagined; by the experience we have had in some places, the turning up of their heels against us in running away was their best defense.

In respect of us they are a people poor and for want of skill and judgment in the knowledge and use of our things, do esteem our trifles before things of greater value: Notwithstanding in their proper manner considering the want of such means as we have, they seem very ingenious. For although they have no such tools nor any such crafts, sciences and arts as we; yet in those things they do, they show excellence of wit. And by how much they upon due consideration shall find our manner of knowledge and crafts to exceed theirs in perfection, and speed for doing or execution, by so much the more is it probable that they should desire our friendship and love, and have the greater respect for pleasing and obeying us. Whereby may be hoped if means of good government be used, that they may in short time be brought to civility, and the embracing of true religion.

Some religion they have already, which although it be far from the truth, yet being as it is, there is hope it may be the easier and sooner reformed.

They believe that there are many Gods which they call *Montóac*, but of different sorts and degrees; one only chief and great God, which hath been from all eternity. Who as they affirm when he purposed to make the world, made first other gods of a principal order to be as means and instruments to be used in the creation and government to follow; and after sun, moon, and stars, as petty gods and instruments of the other order more principal. First they say were made waters, out of which by the gods was made all diversity of creatures that are visible or invisible.

For mankind they say a woman was made first, which by the working of one of the gods, conceived and brought forth children: And in such sort they say they had their beginning.

But how many years or ages have passed since, they say can make no relation, having no letters nor other such means as we to keep records of the particularities of times past, but only tradition from father to son.

They think that all the gods are of human shape, and therefore they represent them by images in the forms of men, which they call *Kewasówok*. . . .

They believe also the immortality of the soul, that after this life as soon as the soul is departed from the body according to the works it hath done, it is either carried to heaven the habitacle of gods, there to enjoy perpetual bliss and happiness, or else to a great pit or hole, which they think to be in the furthest parts of their part of the world toward the sunset, there to burn continually: the place they call *Popogusso*. . . .

What subtlety so ever be in the *Wiroances* and priests, this opinion worketh so much in many of the common and simple sort of people that it maketh them have great respect to their governors, and also great care what they do to avoid torment after death, and to enjoy bliss; although notwithstanding there is punishment ordained for malefactors, as stealers, whoremongers, and other sorts of wicked doers; some punished with death, some with forfeitures, some with beating, according to greatness of the facts.

And this is the sum of their religion, which I learned by having special familiarity with some of their priests. . . .

Most things they saw with us, as mathematical instruments, sea compasses, the virtue of the loadstone in drawing iron, a perspective glass whereby was showed many strange sights, burning glasses, wildfire works, guns, books, writing and reading, spring clocks that seem to go of themselves, and many other things that we had, were so sprang unto them, and so far exceeded their capacities to comprehend the reason and means how they should be made and done, that they thought they were rather the works of gods than of men, or at the leastwise they had been given and taught us of the gods. Which made of them to have such opinion of us, as that if they knew not the truth of god and religion already it was rather to be had from us, whom God so specially loved them from a people that were so simple, as they found themselves to be in comparison of us. Whereupon greater credit was given unto that we spake of concerning such matters.

Many times and in every town where I came, according as I was able, I made declaration of the contents of the Bible; that therein was set forth the true and only GOD and his mighty works, that therein was contained the true doctrine of salvation through Christ, with many particularities of miracles and chief points of religion, as I was able then to utter, and thought fit for the time. And although I told them the book materially and of itself was not of any such virtue, as I thought they did conceive, but only the doctrine therein contained yet would many be glad to touch it, to embrace it, to kiss it, to hold it, to their breasts and heads, and over all their body with it; to show their hungry desire of that knowledge which was spoken of.

NATHANIEL BACON JUSTIFIES HIS REBELLION AGAINST VIRGINIA'S GOVERNMENT (1676)

From Nathaniel Bacon, "Proclamations of Nathaniel Bacon," *Virginia Magazine of History and Biography* 1, no. 1 (July 1893): 55–61.

If virtue be a sin, if piety be guilt, all the principles of morality, goodness, and justice be perverted. We must confess that those who are now called rebels

The Massacre of the Settlers. Engraved by Matthaus Merian after a work by Theodore de Bry, Frankfurt, Germany (1634). The Colonial Williamsburg Foundation.

may be in danger of those high imputations, those loud and several bulls would affright innocents and render the defense of our brethren and the inquiry into our sad and heavy oppressions, treason. But if there be as sure there is a just God to appeal to, if religion and justice be a sanctuary here, if to plead your cause of the oppressed, if sincerely to aim at his Majesty's honor and the public good without any reservation or by interest, if to stand in the gap after so much blood of our dear brethren bought and sold, if after the loss of a great part of his Majesty's colony deserted and dispeopled freely with our lives and estates to endeavor to save the remainders be treason, God Almighty judge and let guilty die. But since we cannot in our hearts find one single spot of rebellion or treason or that we have in any manner aimed at the subverting your settled government or attempting of the person of any either magistrate or private man notwithstanding the several reproaches and threats of some who for sinister ends were disaffected to us and censured our inno[cent] and honest designs, and since all people in all places where we have yet been can attest our civil, quiet, peaceable behavior far different from that of rebellion and tumultuous person let truth be bold and all the world know the real foundations of pretended guilt. We appeal to the country itself what and of what nature their oppressions have been or by what cabal and mystery the designers of many of those whom we call great men have been transacted and carried on, but let us trace these men in authority and favor to whose hands the dispensation of the country's wealth has been committed; let us observe the sudden rise of their estates composed with the quality in which they first entered this country or the reputation they have held here amongst wise and discerning men, and let us see whether their extractions and education have not been vile, and by what pretense of learning and virtue they could so soon into employments of so great trust and consequence, let us consider their sudden advancement and let us also consider whether any public work for our safety and defense or for the advancement and propagation of trade, liberal arts or sciences in here extant in any [way] adequate to our vast charge, now let us compare these things toget[her] and see what sponges have sucked up the public treasure whether it hath not been privately contrived away by unworthy favorites and juggling parasites whose tottering fortunes have been repaired and supported at the public charge, now if it be so judge what greater guilt can be then to offer to pry into these and to unriddle the mysterious wiles of a powerful cabal let all people judge what can be of more dangerous import then to suspect the so long safe proceedings of some of our grandees and whether people may with safety open their eyes in so nice a concern. . . .

Another main article of our guilt is our design not only to ruin and extirpate all Indians in general but all manner of trade and commerce with them. Judge who can be innocent that strike at this tender eye of interest; since the right honorable the governor hath been pleased by his commission to warrant this trade who dare oppose it, or opposing it can be innocent, although plantations be deserted, the blood of our dear brethren split, on all sides our complaints, continually murder upon murder renewed upon us. . . .

If it should be said that the very foundation of all these disasters the grant of the beaver trade to the right honorable governor was illegal and not grantable by any power here present as being a monopoly, were not this to deserve the name of rebel and traitor.

Judge therefore all wise and unprejudiced men who may or can faithfully or truly with an honest heart attempt your country's good, their vindication and liberty without the aspersion of traitor and rebel, since as so doing they must of necessity gall such tender and dear concerns, but to manifest sincerity and loyalty to the world, and how much we abhor these bitter names, may all the world know that we do unanimously desire to present our sad and heavy grievances to his most sacred Majesty as our refuge and sanctuary, where we do well know that all our causes will be impartially heard and equal justice administered to all men.

THE DECLARATION OF THE PEOPLE

For having upon specious pretenses of public works raised unjust taxes upon the commonality for the advancement of private favorites and other sinister ends but no visible effects in any measure adequate.

For not having during the long time of his government in any measure advanced this hopeful colony either by fortification, towns or trade.

For having abused and rendered contemptible the majesty of justice, of advancing to places of judicature scandalous and ignorant favorites.

For having wronged his Majesty's prerogative and interest by assuming the monopoly of the beaver trade.

By having in that unjust gain bartered and sold his Majesty's country and the lives of his loyal subjects to the barbarous heathen.

For having protected, favored, and emboldened the Indians against his Majesty's most loyal subjects never contriving requiring or appointing any due or proper means of satisfaction for their many invasions, murders and robberies committed upon us.

For having when the army of the English was just upon the track of the Indians, which now in all places burn, spoil and murder, and when we might with ease have destroyed them who then were in open hostility for having expressly countermanded and sent back our army by passing his word for the peaceable demeanor of the said Indians, who immediately prosecuted their evil intentions committing horrid murders and robberies in all places being protected by the said engagement and word passed of him the said Sir William Berkeley having ruined and made desolate a great part of his Majesty's country, have now drawn themselves into such obscure and remote places and are by their successes so emboldened and confirmed and by their confederacy so strengthened that the cries of blood are in all places and the terror and consternation of the people so great, that they are now become not only a difficult, but a very formidable enemy who might with ease have been destroyed, etc. When upon the loud outcries of blood the assembly had with all care raised and framed an army for the prevention of future mischiefs and safeguard of his Majesty's colony.

For having with only the privacy of some few favorites without acquainting the people, only by the alteration of a figure forged a commission by we know not what hand, not only without but against the consent of the people, for raising and effecting of civil wars and distractions, which being happily and without bloodshed prevented.

Remains of the 1639 Jamestown Church tower (with 20th-century reconstruction on the original foundations). Photograph copyright 2014 by Tony Fischer, Wikimedia Commons.

For having the second time attempted the same thereby, calling down our forces from the defense of the frontiers, and most weak exposed places, for the prevention of civil mischief and ruin amongst ourselves, whilst the barbarous enemy in all places did invade, murder, and spoil us his Majesty's most faithful subjects.

Of these aforesaid articles we accuse Sir William Berkeley, as guilt of each and every one of the same, and as one, who hath traitorously attempted, violated, and injured his Majesty's interest here, by the loss of a great part of his colony, and many of his faithful and loyal subjects by him betrayed, and in a barbarous and shameful manner exposed to the incursions and murders of the heathen.

. . .

And we do further demand that the said Sir William Berkeley, with all the persons in this list, be forthwith delivered up, or surrender themselves, within four days, after the notice hereof, or otherwise we declare, as followeth. That in whatsoever house, place, or ship, any of the said persons shall reside, be hidden, or protected, we do declare, that the owners, masters, or inhabitants of the said places, to be confederates, and traitors to the people, and the estates of them, as also of all the aforesaid persons to be confiscated, this we the commons of Virginia do declare desiring a prime union among ourselves, that we may jointly, and with one accord defend ourselves against the common enemy. And let not the faults of the guilty, be the reproach of the innocent, or the faults or crimes of ye oppressors divide and separate us, who have suffered by their oppressions.

These are therefore in his Majesty's name, to command you forthwith to seize the persons above mentioned, as traitors to ye king and country, and them to bring to middle plantation, and there to secure them, till further order, and in case of opposition, if you want any other assistance, you are forthwith to demand it in the name of the people of all the counties of Virginia.

Nath Bacon, Gen'l
By the Consent of ye People

AN ASSAULT ON A SERVANT, CHARITY DALLEN (1649)

From Warren M. Billings, ed., *The Old Dominion in the Seventeenth Century: A Documentary History of Virginia, 1606–1689* (Chapel Hill, N.C., 1975), 136–37. Lower Norfolk County Order Book, 1646–51, fol. 120.

The deposition of Joseph Mulders aged 23 years or thereabouts sworn and examined sayeth:

That Deborah Fernehaugh, the mistress of this deponent, did beat her maidservant in the quartering house before the dresser more like a dog then a Christian, and that at a certain time, I felt her head, which was beaten as soft as a sponge, in one place, and that as there she was a weeding, she complained and said, her backbone as she thought was broken with beating, and that I did see the maid's arm naked which was full of black and blue bruises and pinches, and her neck likewise and that afterwards, I told my mistress of it and said that two or three blows could not make her in such a case, and after this my speeches she chided the said maid for showing her body to the men, and very often afterwards she the said maid would have shown me how she had been beaten, but I refused to have seen it, saying it concerns me not, I will do my work and if my mistress abuse you, you may complain, and about eight days since, being about the time she last went to complain, I knew of her going, but would not tell my mistress of it, although she asked me, and said I could not choose but know of it, and further he sayeth not.

sworn the 31st July 1649

Thomas Bridge Clerk of Court
The Marke of Joseph X Mulders

Michael Mikaye aged 22 years of [*sic*] thereabouts, sworn and examined, sayeth verbatim as the above mentioned deponent sayeth and deposeth and further sayeth not sworn the 31st July 1649

Thomas Bridge Clerk of Court
The Marke of Michael X Mikay

Upon the depositions of Joseph Mulders and Michael Mikaye of the misusage of Charetie Dallen, by her mistress Deborah Fernehaugh, and by many other often complaints, by other sufficient testimonies, and although the said Deborah hath had advertisement thereof from the Court yet persisteth in the very ill usage of her said servant, as appeareth to the board, it is therefore ordered that the said Charetie Dallen shall no longer remain in the house or service with her said mistress, but is to be and continue at the house of Mr. Thomas Lambard [Lambert], until such time as the said Deborah Fernehaugh shall sell or otherwise dispose of her said servant, for her best advantage of her the said Deborah.

5

NEW ENGLAND

In the fall of 1620, 102 colonists sailed for the New World aboard the *Mayflower*. They originally set out to find a home near the mouth of the Hudson River, where four years later the Dutch would establish New Amsterdam on Manhattan Island. But they ended up settling at Cape Cod Bay, more than two hundred miles to the north, at a place they called Plymouth. Plymouth had once been the site of a significant Native American village, but the Patuxet tribe had suffered an epidemic that left only scattered bones and abandoned buildings behind.[1]

The leaders of the Plymouth colony were Separatist Christians, who had become convinced that the Church of England was irredeemably corrupt. Groups began meeting in "separate" churches in England, which elicited persecution from English authorities. Many of the English Separatists eventually left to go to the free environs of Holland. But Dutch society had its own traps. Would the Separatists' children fall under Dutch influences and renounce the purity of properly Reformed, biblical principles? A group of the English Separatists ultimately decided to seek a new home in America. They were among the first of a number of English, French, and German and other Protestant dissenters who pursued spiritual liberty on the Atlantic's western shores.

Aboard the *Mayflower*, forty-one of the arriving men gathered in November 1620 and signed a short document that committed to a self-governing system of government honoring God and protecting the common good. They agreed to form a "civil body politic" that would preserve the primary aims of the venture: "the glory of God, and advancement of the Christian faith, and honor of our king and country." The 153-word "Mayflower Compact" struck themes that transcended the tiny outpost: self-government, the creation of a political union by common consent, and a settlement devoted to God's glory. The Separatists were ultimately absorbed by the larger Puritan colony of Massachusetts, but the New England colonies together exercised an outsized influence in their vision of religious purpose. That spiritual mission also cast the New England colonies' failings, and violence against Native Americans, in a harsher light.

The series of events leading to the Puritans' migration in 1630 began a hundred years earlier, with the English Reformation. England's split with the Church of Rome originated in Henry VIII's feud with the pope over his desire to have his marriage to Catherine of Aragon annulled, resulting in the creation of an independent Church of England. For the next three decades, England saw convulsions over its vacillating devotion to Protestantism and Catholicism. During the short tenure of Edward VI (1547–53), the archbishop of Canterbury, Thomas Cranmer, led the English church toward stronger alliances with continental Reformers, including Geneva's John Calvin. The reign of Mary Tudor wrenched England back toward Catholicism, with the martyrdom of key Protestant leaders, including Cranmer. In 1556, Cranmer was supposed to issue a complete recantation of Protestantism in his final address prior to his execution in Oxford, but instead he denounced the pope as "Christ's enemy, and antichrist, with all his false doctrine." Cranmer was burned at the stake.[2]

Queen Elizabeth I's ascension to the throne in 1559 would secure England for Protestantism, if for no other reason than her long tenure. But Elizabeth's church preserved many of the ceremonies and practices that Reformed leaders wanted to expunge, such as elaborate clerical vestments and the observation of saints' days. This set the stage for tension between English Protestants over the extent of the Reformation within the church. The "Puritans," as they became known to their enemies, sought a simpler church, purified of its remaining "popish" corruptions and closer to what they saw as the New Testament blueprint. Elizabeth, her successor King James I, and their leading church officials engaged in occasional battles with Puritan and Separatist leaders. Some Separatists of Scrooby, England, were imprisoned and put under surveillance prior to their departure for Holland in 1608. For the Puritans, the point of greatest crisis began in the 1620s, when James I's son Charles I assumed the throne.

Charles I seemed determined to take England further away from Reformed principles and into a cozier relationship with Catholic piety and Catholic European powers. Puritans were especially concerned about his marriage to Henrietta Maria of France, a Catholic herself, who arranged for Catholic masses at royal residences. Soon-to-be Puritan immigrant Thomas Hooker, referencing Malachi 2:11–12, lamented that "an abomination is committed, Judah hath married the daughter of a strange God." Charles I's church authorities, led by archbishop William Laud, removed growing numbers of Puritan preachers from their parishes, including future New Englanders John Cotton and John Davenport.[3]

Like the Plymouth Separatists nine years earlier, some English Puritans began to contemplate a refuge in the New World. Through savvy political maneuvering, some well-connected Puritans, including lawyer John Winthrop, secured a charter for the Massachusetts Bay Company in 1629, and guaranteed that the quasi-independent charter could not be changed by the Puritans' enemies. They transferred the physical copy of the charter to Massachusetts.

Many Puritans believed—in ways paralleling the beliefs of their Catholic rivals—that they were living in the last days before Christ's return to earth, or at least the inauguration of God's thousand-year reign of peace on earth, the millennium. Popular Puritan writer Thomas Brightman even averred that the Book of Revelation's "seventh trumpet" had blown in 1558, with the death of Queen Mary and the ascension of Elizabeth. "Now is the last act begun," Brightman wrote, "of a most long and doleful tragedy, which shall wholly overflow with scourges, slaughters, [and] destructions, but after this theater is once removed, there shall come in room of it a most delightful spectacle of perpetual peace." English Protestants watched domestic and foreign affairs with keen interest sparked by these apocalyptic assumptions. In 1618, an incident on the Continent, in Prague, in which a crowd of Protestants tossed several Catholic officials out of a tower window (they survived the seventy-foot fall by landing in a pile of horse manure), precipitated the Thirty Years' War. This complex conflict engulfed most of Europe, and often pitted Catholic powers against Protestants. The "wars and rumors of wars" that Jesus himself had forecast seemed to be at hand.[4]

With these thoughts in their minds, certain English Puritans prepared to depart for the New World. Perhaps, as violence and corruption descended over Europe, the migrants thought they could establish a godly refuge and beacon in the New World. Historians debate whether the Puritans' mentality was primarily defensive (escaping and restoring a biblical society for themselves) or offensive (establishing Massachusetts as an example to England, with hope that Massachusetts's leaders would go back to England to rule when God brought down Charles I). In either case, John Winthrop made the classic statement of the Puritans' mission in his "Model of Christian Charity" address, which he probably gave aboard the *Arbella*, the ship that brought him to Massachusetts (the sermon itself was not published until more than two centuries later). Paraphrasing the

Gospel of Matthew, Winthrop told the Puritan emigrants that "we shall be as a city upon a hill. The eyes of all people are upon us. So that if we shall deal falsely with our God in this work we have undertaken, and so cause him to withdraw his present help from us, we shall be made a story and a by-word through the world."[5]

During the "Great Migration" of the 1630s, about 21,000 English settlers came to New England. The average immigrants were farmers or people of middling professions—lawyers or merchants—who came as whole families: a mother, father, and children. This stood in stark contrast to many other European colonies (especially Virginia) that initially drew mostly male immigrants. Although she subsequently ran afoul of Puritan authorities, Anne Hutchinson's family was typical among the early immigrants. She was forty-three at the time of her departure with her merchant husband William and their children. They went to Boston to follow their beloved pastor, John Cotton. The Hutchinsons came to America for religious reasons—but it was religion in the context of relationships. As admired pastors and other leaders such as Winthrop went to the New World, it prepared the way for thousands of like-minded English families to follow.[6]

As the Puritans soon found out in Hutchinson's case, they did not all believe the same things about theology and the Christian life. But there were certainly characteristic Puritan tenets that grew out of their Calvinist origins. John Calvin was one of the Puritans' favorite authors, and between the mid-sixteenth and mid-seventeenth centuries, his translated works made him the most-published writer in England. Other Reformers, such as Martin Luther, influenced the Puritans, as did older writers such as Saint Augustine. But the Bible was the preeminent guide for Puritans. The Bible gave the Puritans a framework for church order. As biblical "primitivists," they sought to understand the Bible line by line, to believe its truths, to implement its requirements, and to jettison everything rooted in nonbiblical traditions.

The Puritans understood from Scripture and Reformed writers that God was inexpressibly powerful, and that he ruled as a sovereign over mankind. God even controlled the eternal destinies of men and women, choosing to rescue some from the just penalty for their sins: eternal wrath in hell. These saints were the "elect," who were selected for salvation, for reasons only fully understood by God. As Puritan theologian William Perkins wrote, God is not required to deal with all people equally, or to justify his eternal decrees to mankind. "God is not thus bound," Perkins concluded, "because he is a sovereign, and absolute Lord over all his creatures, and may do with his own what he will."[7]

God was also loving and gracious, having provided his only son, Jesus Christ, as a substitute on the cross to endure the punishment that sinners deserved. God was perfectly good and just, attributes that met together in Jesus's perfect life, purposeful death, and victorious resurrection. People were fatally broken by sin, their will and judgment standing against God's ways, unless God came in by his Holy Spirit to rescue them. In what they termed the Covenant of Grace, God initiated salvation for the elect by regenerating them by the Holy Spirit and giving them the gift of faith. The terminology of "covenants"—derived from the Book of Genesis—distinctively marked Puritan theology and practice: nations, colonies, churches, and individuals all could stand in covenant relationships with God.

Some have depicted the Puritans as obsessive killjoys, and the English Reformers certainly did not hesitate to make the Bible's moral codes known to congregants or political leaders. The Puritans believed that the state should regulate behavior in accord with the Bible's Ten Commandments. Early New Englanders required settlers to honor Sunday as the Sabbath. Sabbath-breakers and those who failed to attend church faced legal punishments. Allowing people to disobey God's revealed moral law threatened to provoke God's judgment against the whole society. But many Puritans also seemed to relish earthly delights such as marital sex and good drink (though not drunkenness). Puritans did not oppose alcohol consumption per se. To the contrary, one group of English Reformers in Dorchester in 1622 built a brewhouse, and used the proceeds from beer sales to fund programs for the assistance of impoverished youths.[8]

The Separatists at Plymouth shared many of the theological views of the Puritans, even if they differed about the Church of England's redeemability. The *Mayflower* arrived too close to winter to do much construction, so many of the first Plymouth settlers huddled together on the boat. Losing their storehouse to a fire, the colonists suffered terribly, and half died during that first winter. Spring brought new hope in the form of warmer weather and the arrival of two Indians who could speak English, Samoset and Squanto. These men helped the Plymouth settlers establish diplomatic relations with the Wampanoag tribe and its leader, Massasoit.

Early relations between Plymouth and its Indian neighbors were relatively peaceful, a fact commemorated today in Americans' annual observation of the November Thanksgiving holiday. We do not actually know much about what happened in that initial celebration in fall 1621. Edward Winslow, an assistant to Plymouth governor William Bradford, wrote that the governor commissioned a special occasion with feasting on "fowl" (perhaps turkey?). "Many of the Indians [came] amongst us, and among the rest their greatest king Massasoit, with some ninety men, whom for three days we entertained and feasted." The Indians also brought deer to add to the bounty. "We have found the Indians very faithful in their covenant of peace with us," Winslow happily reported. He noted that the Wampanoags were a people "without any religion or knowledge of God." Occasional gruesome violence still marked the Plymouth colony's relationship with local Native Americans. In 1623, mindful of the Indian uprising in Virginia the year before, the English settlers launched a preemptive assault on some Massachusetts Indians. They killed a number of Massachusetts people, including their tribal leader, whose decapitated head ended up on top of the Plymouth fort "for a terror unto others," as Governor Bradford put it.[9]

In the summer of 1630, John Winthrop's group of settlers came to Boston and began establishing the framework for the new Massachusetts government. Winthrop would serve as governor, and a General Court met quarterly to deal with legislative and judicial affairs. The court restricted voting privileges to male church members, befitting the religious vision of the colony. The 1641 *Body of Liberties* laid out a kind of bill of rights, which enjoined the colonists to use their liberty to honor God, not to indulge sin. "The free fruition of such liberties, immunities, and privileges as humanity, civility, and Christianity call for as due to every man in his place and proportion without impeachment and infringement has ever been and ever will be the tranquility and stability of churches and commonwealths," the authors noted.

The *Body of Liberties* assured colonists that they would not suffer from government coercion or unfair judicial proceedings. It singled out women for protection from domestic violence and from being left destitute at their husband's death. It also offered servants some protection from abuse, and mandated that slavery be restricted to those who voluntarily sold themselves into bondage or those taken in just wars. Cruelty to "brute creatures," or domestic animals, was forbidden. The code threatened capital punishment for a host of crimes, including blasphemy, witchcraft, homosexual acts, and bestiality.[10]

Winthrop, whose leadership as governor was often challenged by Puritan rivals, explained his concept of the people's duties and freedoms in his 1645 "Little Speech on Liberty" before the General Court. Once the people elect their magistrates, Winthrop warned, they had a covenant responsibility to respect and obey them, as the governor's authority came from God. "The covenant between you and us is the oath you have taken of us, which is to this purpose, that we shall govern you and judge your causes by the rules of God's laws and our own, according to our best skill." The carnal liberty that humans exercised led only to evil and rebellion, but what Winthrop termed "civil," "federal," or "moral" liberty was "exercised in a way of subjection to authority; it is the same kind of liberty wherewith Christ has made us free." This kind of liberty under authority also marked the godly submission of a wife to her husband, he said, or the church to Jesus Christ. Freedom of self-determination or individual conscience had little place in the Puritan vision of liberty.[11]

Yet the Puritans did believe that people related to God on an individual basis, which accounts for persistent outbreaks of dissent in early New England. For example, the brilliant but mercurial Roger Williams arrived in Boston in 1631. Leaders offered him the pastorate of First Church Boston, but Williams declined because he had become convinced that the Puritans needed to repudiate the Church of England as "Antichristian." Shuttling between Plymouth and the Puritan towns, Williams began criticizing Massachusetts authorities for their unfair treatment of Indians. He also objected to Massachusetts's persecution of those who violated the first four of the Ten Commandments, those which forbade idolatry and required Sabbath-keeping. These were matters of conscience, he argued, and not fit for state oversight. After several contentious appearances before the General Court, Massachusetts authorities ordered him to leave the colony in 1635. In 1636, Williams established Providence, in what would become the Rhode Island colony. Rhode Island, under Williams's leadership, offered residents freedom of conscience, as the government declined to enforce any particular brand of Christian orthodoxy. This made Rhode Island a refuge for a number of other New England dissenters, including the family of Anne Hutchinson.

As Williams's controversy with Massachusetts festered, so also was Hutchinson generating concern because of home-group meetings she held to discuss Puritan sermons. These assemblies first attracted only women, but Hutchinson soon also drew in some men. Hutchinson began criticizing Boston ministers for teaching works righteousness, or the idea that a person's good deeds could make him or her acceptable to God. Only her favorite pastors, John Cotton and John Wheelwright, properly emphasized that a person could do nothing to make themselves fit for salvation. A wrenching, mystical experience of regeneration by the Holy Spirit of God was the only path to salvation, Hutchinson argued.

The gap between Hutchinson and the pastors she criticized was not really that large, but it revealed a constant tension in Puritan and Reformed theology. If God saved people by grace alone, then what place did good works have in the Christian life? Hutchinson's critics labeled her an "antinomian," someone who rejects the moral law of God. The clash between these positions dated to sixteenth-century England, but Hutchinson's case tested whether there was room for such differences of opinion—especially when one side's leading advocate was female—in early Massachusetts. Hutchinson's boldness made it more likely that the colony would act against her. When one of her pastoral rivals, John Wilson, would take the pulpit at First Church Boston, she and her devoted followers would get up and leave.

Although John Cotton decided to make peace with his clerical colleagues, John Wheelwright defended Hutchinson and received a sentence of banishment for it. In late 1637 the General Court summoned Hutchinson herself for trial, in which (as was typical of such proceedings in the era) her guilt was presumed. When the judges pressed Hutchinson to justify her theological criticisms, she insisted that God had given her a gift of prophecy (or insight into scriptural truth) that she was compelled to exercise. Moreover, she claimed to have received her understanding of Scripture by the "immediate revelation" of the Holy Spirit, or "by the voice of [God's] own spirit" to her soul. To the judges, this smacked of the sectarian radicalism of groups like the Quakers. They assumed that God would not communicate with any layperson in a manner that contradicted the teaching of ministers. The court banished her, and she and her family left for Rhode Island in 1638.[12]

In spite of these controversies, seventeenth-century Puritans managed to preserve relatively uniform faith and practice in their "Bible commonwealth." At mid-century, Massachusetts maintained one pastor for every 415 people, as compared with Virginia, which had one for every 3,239. The law required people in Massachusetts to attend church, where they would hear lengthy, learned sermons focused on the biblical text. Every church had its "horse-shed" Christians, as historian David Hall has called them, those who preferred to hang around the horse shed and chat rather than sit through the sermon. But the average Puritan was not bored in church: church meetings broke up the monotony of the week's incessant chores, and many Puritans were keen to listen and learn more about the Bible. They had their chances—the typical New Englander heard about seven thousand sermons during his or her lifetime.[13]

In spite of this religious intensity, church membership rates remained somewhat low during the first two decades of settlement in New England, and even showed signs of decline by the 1650s. Scholars have debated how to interpret these patterns, with some suggesting it reflected apathy, while others have argued that it actually reflected great seriousness among laypeople about membership. Puritans believed in a church membership composed of "visible saints," or those who had gone through a convincing experience of conversion through

Christ. Prospective members often had to relate their experience, including their struggles with sin, to the church members, who would decide whether to accept the candidate. The mid-century testimony of Elizabeth Dunster (the sister of Harvard's first president) was typical: she spoke of desiring Christ as savior, but for some time she was not sure if she would break through to conversion. Even though a powerful sermon on Christ's words "Come to me, all ye weary and heavy laden" broke her heart and seemed to make her "willing," she somehow still felt an "inability to come." Other Scripture passages, and her sense of love for other church members, boosted her confidence and made her ready to apply for membership. Still, she worried about ongoing struggles with sin, and confessed that she still sometimes found her heart "dead and sluggy."[14]

Those admitted to membership could take communion, or the Lord's Supper, as well as have their children baptized. Because the apostle Paul issued severe warnings against those who took the Supper in an "unworthy" manner, even some pious people hung back. By the 1650s, fewer and fewer people were joining the churches, which also meant that there were growing numbers of unbaptized children. In 1662, Massachusetts pastors crafted a compromise policy, known as the Halfway Covenant, which allowed baptized nonmembers to have their own children baptized. It was an uneasy settlement that reminded some of the parish system of the Church of England, where baptism of infants represented more of a cultural rite of passage than a sacred privilege available only to elect parents. The tension led some to split off as Baptists, who rejected infant baptism altogether.

Like most other European colonies, the Massachusetts Bay Company justified its existence in part by reference to the conversion of Native Americans. This ambition was most strikingly displayed on the seal of the company, which featured an Indian saying "Come over and help us," a reference to the apostle Paul's vision of a man from Macedonia pleading for help in the Book of Acts, chapter 16. In one of the company's early meetings in London, organizers asserted that the "main end of the plantation" was "the conversion of the savages." There were a number of problems with this stated objective. First, the original settlers did not commission missionaries, unlike the Spanish or French colonies. Second, among all the early American Christian movements, Puritanism was one of the most dependent upon literacy in a written, European language. Puritanism was a book-centered faith, with the heaviest focus on the English Bible. Work at translating the Scriptures into native languages would be slow and imperfect.[15]

   The most obvious problem with the Puritans evangelizing Native Americans was that before any sustained missionary program could begin, the Puritans had already engaged in a vicious war with the Pequot Indians of Connecticut. (The Connecticut and New Haven colonies, originally separate, were founded by Puritans in 1636 and 1638, respectively.) Tensions between the English and Pequots grew during the 1630s. As in Virginia, colonists required the Pequots to pay "tribute" to them in the form of wampum, the beads and shells that functioned as currency among northeastern Indians. The New Englanders often exchanged the wampum for beaver furs supplied by the Abenaki Indians to their north. Outrage over episodic killings of English people escalated anger between the groups, and the English allied with Narragansett and Mohegan tribes to eliminate the Pequots.[16]

   The violence in the Pequot War was regionally limited, but its brutality was dizzying. Both the English and Indians dismembered and distributed body parts of the vanquished with regularity. The celebrated Mohegan chief Uncas, who broke with the Pequots and cooperated with the English in the war, delivered "five Pequots' heads" to Connecticut's Fort Saybrook as a sign of his allegiance. Captain John Underhill, one of the leaders of the anti-Pequot forces, said that the severed heads "mightily encouraged the hearts of all, and we took this as a pledge of [the Mohegans'] further fidelity." (The Bible gave a bit of precedent for such practices, as in Judges 7, when Gideon's warriors brought back the heads of two leaders of the Israelites' enemies.) As Plymouth colonists had done with the severed Massachusett man's head, Saybrook's defenders topped their fort with the Pequot heads. The traffic in body parts continued through the war, and even Roger Williams received three pairs of Pequot hands in late summer 1637. Unlike a number of Puritan leaders, Williams balked at the gift, saying that he had "always shown dislike to such dismembering of the dead." Nevertheless, Williams recognized their ritual significance and sent them on to John Winthrop.[17]

   The most notorious incident of the war came in May 1637 at a Pequot village on the Mystic River in Connecticut. New Englanders and their Indian allies surrounded the settlement—filled with hundreds of women, children, and elderly men—and set it ablaze, burning most of the Pequots there to death. Many who tried to escape were struck down with swords and "hewed to pieces," reported William Bradford. Pequots were "frying in the fire, and the streams of blood quenching the same; and horrible was the stink and scent thereof; but the victory seemed a sweet sacrifice, and they gave the praise thereof to God," Bradford said. Citing Psalm 110:6, Captain John Mason wrote that "God was above them, who laughed his enemies and the enemies of his people to scorn, making them as a fiery oven. . . . Thus did the Lord judge among the heathen, filling the place with dead bodies!" John Underhill explicitly cited Old Testament precedents for this kind of tactic. "Sometimes the Scripture declares women and children must perish with their parents. . . . We had sufficient light from the word of God for our proceedings." The Pequots were decimated by the war, yet a 1638 agreement between the Puritans and their Indian allies stipulated that any remaining Pequots should be enslaved to work in settlers' homes, deported to work the plantations of the Puritan colony at Providence Island (off the coast of Nicaragua), or executed and decapitated.[18]

This outcome reminds us that the Puritans did traffic in Indian and African slaves (as well as white indentured servants). Still, no one would have confused the nature of the labor systems of the northern and southern colonies. While Virginia and other southern colonies depended on cash crops for trade, the New England colonies were less profitable, with more diverse, modest economies and subsistence farming. Wealthy New England families, especially in port cities, did own slaves and servants, and many pastors' families also possessed a household slave or two. One visitor to Boston in 1687 made the exaggerated claim that virtually every house had at least one slave, but this observation demonstrates that in the cities of New England, slavery was pervasive, if not dominant. By 1700, perhaps about one thousand blacks lived in New England, many of them slaves.[19]

In spite of the Pequot War's ravages, the Puritans did attempt some missionary work among Indian people beginning in the 1640s. The key English minister in this effort was John Eliot, who had come to Massachusetts in 1631. In the early 1640s Eliot began to learn Algonquian with the help of a bilingual Indian tutor, a young captive from the Pequot War and Eliot's servant. In 1651 Eliot established his first "praying town" for Indian converts in Natick, Massachusetts. During four decades of ministry to Native Americans, Eliot helped bring around 1,100 Indians to profess Christianity, supervised the production of a number of Algonquian-language religious translations, including one of the Bible, and founded fourteen praying towns.[20]

Like many Puritans, Eliot was fascinated with eschatology, or the theology of the last days, and he understood his missionary work in apocalyptic terms. He believed that the New World and native evangelization offered unique opportunities to reestablish the true practice of biblical Christianity without having to fight against European corruption. Eliot remained cognizant of the English Civil War and wars on the Continent, in which Eliot figured that Christ meant

to "overthrow Antichrist by the wars of the Lamb." He told English correspond-
ents that he hoped it would also "be some comfort to your heart to see the
Kingdom of Christ rising up in these western parts of the world; and some
confirmation it will be, that the Lord's time is come to advance and spread His
Blessed Kingdom, which shall (in his season) fill all the earth."[21]

Eliot knew that conversion would disrupt social and family structures for Native Americans, and to a large extent, he encouraged those disruptions. One of
his first converts was an older woman who died subsequent to accepting the
Puritans' gospel. On her deathbed she told her daughters not to go back among
her non-Christian relatives, "for they pray not to God, keep not the Sabbath,
commit all manner of sins and are not punished for it." Eliot erected praying
towns so that the Indians, like the mission Indians of the Spanish southwest,
would become sedentary farmers. But he found that many, even those interested in Christianity, were unwilling to move near the English, "because they
have neither the tools, nor skill, nor heart to fence their grounds." If they did not
build fences, the "English cattle" would spoil their corn.[22]

Eliot planned praying towns in places "somewhat remote from the English,
where they must have the word constantly taught, and government constantly
exercised." The proselytes would learn trades and farming techniques. They
would wear English-style clothing, and the men would cut their hair short. The
praying towns attracted Indians from tribes especially decimated by the arrival
of the English. Although many converts struggled to give conversion testimonies that convinced Eliot and other Puritan observers, Natick did establish a
small native congregation in 1660.[23]

The extent to which native converts in New England (and elsewhere) actually internalized Christian belief is disputed. Some likely experimented with
Christian adherence to test its efficacy, or in hope of improving their material
conditions. When family members or tribal leaders accepted Christianity, it
made it easier for others to follow. Some undoubtedly found Christianity satisfy-
ing at an intellectual or spiritual level, too. One intriguing case of native appro-
priation of Christian faith came at the Puritan missions on Martha's Vineyard.
There, the father and son missionaries Thomas Mayhew, Sr. and Jr., as well
as John Cotton, Jr., saw perhaps the greatest successes among New England's
Indians prior to King Philip's War in the 1670s.

Martha's Vineyard Wampanoags not only understood core Christian concepts,
but also filtered them through preexisting native categories, a process that historian David Silverman calls "religious translation." Wampanoag converts assisted
missionaries in the work of translating Christian terminology into Wampanoag

words. They cultivated the concept that Wampanoag converts were not rejecting their previous beliefs in favor of a foreign alternative, but that Christianity represented a recovery of spiritual truths that lay hidden in the shadowy
Wampanoag past. Most of Martha's Vineyard's native population embraced this
contextualized kind of Christianity by the end of the seventeenth century.[24]

The Mayhews and Cotton depended on native translators and converts to
defend and propagate the faith. As documented in Cotton's journal, Christian
Wampanoags quizzed the missionary about ethical and doctrinal topics; he recorded some 470 questions in all. Some of their questions must have stumped
the Englishman. "How many sorts of sinners are there in the world? . . . how
many sorts of faith are there? . . . what are the keys of the kingdom of heaven?"
Women occasionally participated in these exchanges, as Mary Amanhut asked
Cotton why children were baptized as infants, and if that sacrament washed
away their sin, why do they keep on sinning when they grow up? The questions ran from the mundane to the transcendent. One convert at Chappaquid-
dick named Jonathan asked Cotton both "what was a constable's office?" and
"whether Christ and his saints should live again upon earth?" In 1659, Puritans
approved the organization of a Wampanoag church, and in 1670, Cotton and
John Eliot participated in the ordination of Hiacoomes, one of the most influential converts. He was the first ordained Native American pastor in North
America.[25]

Whatever successes Puritan missionaries enjoyed were disrupted again by King
Philip's War in 1675–76, a conflict that that nearly shattered New England,
similar to the way that the Pueblo Revolt would ravage Spanish New Mexico
five years later. Simmering frustration between the English and many native
groups exploded when the body of a Harvard-trained Christian Indian, John
Sassamon, was discovered in an icy pond. The English accused "King Philip,"
the Wampanoag sachem Metacom, and his henchman of murder. They apprehended three Wampanoag suspects and hanged them for the crime, opening
a spiraling conflict that devastated the native and English populations of New
England. When English arbitrators approached Metacom, ostensibly to avoid
war, the sachem cited as his "grand complaints" against the colonists a series of
bogus land deals in which the English had cheated the Wampanoags and other
Indians, the colonists' eagerness to sell Indians alcohol, and the Wampanoags'
fear "that any of their Indians should be called or forced to be Christian Indians." Metacom rallied other tribes to his cause, but so did the English: without

the aid of Indian allies, including (ironically) the Pequots, the English would likely have lost Massachusetts altogether.[26]

Horrors reminiscent of the Pequot War marked King Philip's War. The English assault on the Narragansett fort in Rhode Island's Great Swamp featured tactics similar to Mystic River atrocities in 1637. Thousands of Indians, mostly women and children, huddled in wigwams within the fort, and the English settlers began burning the fort and waited for survivors to emerge, where they struck them down, including "squaws and papooses," or shot them with flintlock muskets. Even one of the English reports regarded the episode as "a carnage rather than a fight, for everyone had their fill of blood." The report estimated that five hundred Indian men died there, as well as many "women and children, the number of which we took no account of."[27]

Native fighters committed their share of violence, often (like the Pueblo rebels) mocking and repudiating Christianity as they went. During an attack on Sudbury, Massachusetts, an Indian chased an elderly Englishman into a swamp, and the Indian reportedly exclaimed, "Come Lord Jesus, save this poor Englishman if thou canst, whom I am now about to kill," before striking him down and leaving him for dead. One Goodman Wright apparently believed that he would hold out the Bible to protect himself during an Indian attack, but when the talisman failed him, the attackers slew Wright, "ripped him open and put his Bible in his belly." Countless English reports painted King Philip's forces as evil, bloodthirsty, "barbarous creatures," as Mary Rowlandson's celebrated captivity narrative put it.[28]

The war wrecked the praying towns and scattered their residents. Some of the newer, western towns allied with King Philip. Others sought refuge with French Catholics to the north. In fall 1675, Massachusetts authorities mandated that the remaining friendly Christian Indians be evacuated and detained at Deer Island, in Boston Harbor. This was ostensibly for the natives' protection, but many English did not trust any Indians, Christian or otherwise, and felt more comfortable with them safely ensconced at Deer Island. Some were sold into Caribbean slavery, while those who remained suffered under squalid winter conditions on the island. John Eliot and his missionary colleague Daniel Gookin visited them and found the environs "bleak and cold, their wigwams poor and mean, their clothes few and thin." Gookin and Eliot asked for adequate supplies, which angered some of the English, who resented any provisions going to the praying Indians. Some proposed that they be rounded up again, deported, or even executed. When Gookin continued to push for better treatment, one man reportedly called him an "Irish dog" and "the son of a whore, a bitch, a rogue." Gookin received death threats. When spring came, authorities released the detainees on Deer Island, which had become a death trap. Half of the praying Indians had died during the winter.[29]

The war began to peter out in mid-1676 as Philip's forces, riddled with epidemic disease, started running out of food and ammunition. Then in August, an Indian ally of the English shot Philip to death. The English, with the help of an Indian "executioner," dismembered Philip's body, and gave Philip's killer one of the sachem's hands. The English victors kept Philip's head, and on August 17, 1676, Plymouth celebrated a day of thanksgiving, capped by the public display of Philip's head on a tall pole in Plymouth. It was fifty-five years since Philip's father Massasoit attended the "first thanksgiving" there in Plymouth. (It was also fifty-three years since the English had posted the head of the Massachusett sachem at the Plymouth fort.) Metacom's head stayed there for some years, to remind Indians of the terrible consequences of the uprising. Cotton Mather, Boston's most prolific author of the early 1700s, reportedly even yanked off the jaw from the skull on a visit to the town some years later. Transcendent aspirations and ugly realities clashed in the early years of Puritan settlement in New England.[30]

ANNE HUTCHINSON'S HERESY TRIAL TESTIMONY (1637)

From [Thomas] Hutchinson, *The History of the Province of Massachusets-Bay, from the Charter of King William and Queen Mary, in 1691, until the Year 1750* (Boston, 1767), 507–13.

MRS. H: If you please to give me leave I shall give you the ground of what I know to be true. Being much troubled to see the fallenness of the continuation of the church of England, I had like to have turned separatist; whereupon I kept a day of solemn humiliation and pondering of the thing; this scripture was brought unto me—he that denies Jesus Christ to be come in the flesh is antichrist—this I considered of and in considering found that the papists did not deny him to be come in the flesh, nor we did not deny him—who then was antichrist? Was the Turk antichrist only? The Lord knows that I could not open scripture; he must by his prophetical office open it unto me. So after that being unsatisfied in the thing, the Lord was pleased to bring the scripture out of the Hebrews. He that denies the testament denies the testator, and in this did open unto me and give me to so that those which did not teach the new covenant had the spirit of antichrist, and upon this he did discover the ministry unto me and ever since I bless the Lord, he hath let me see which was the clear ministry and which the wrong. Since that time I confess I have been more choice and he hath let me to distinguish between the voice of my beloved and the voice of Moses, the voice of John Baptist and the voice of antichrist, for all those voices are spoken of in scripture. Now if you do condemn me for speaking what in my conscience I know to be truth I must commit myself unto the Lord.

MR. NOWELL: How do you know that that was the spirit?

MR. H.: How did Abraham know that it was God that bid him offer his son, being a breach of the sixth commandment?

DEP. GOV.: By an immediate voice.

MRS. H.: So to me by an immediate revelation.

DEP. GOV.: How! an immediate revelation.

MRS. H.: By the voice of his own spirit to my soul, I will give you another scripture, Jer. 46: 27,28—out of which the Lord showed me what he would do for and rest of his servants. But after he was pleased to reveal himself to me I did presently like Abraham run to Hagar. And after that he did let me see the atheism of my own heart, for which I begged of the Lord that it might not remain in my heart, and

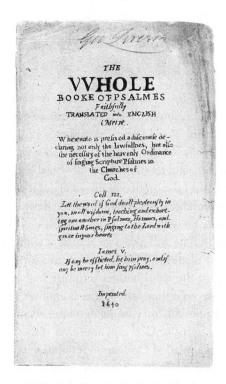

Title Page, Bay Psalm Book (1640),
Library of Congress Special Collections.
This was the first book printed in British
North America. Library of Congress.

being thus, he did show me this (a twelvemonth after) which I told you of before. Ever since that time I have been confident of what he hath revealed onto me.

. . . You have power over my body but the Lord Jesus hath power over my body and soul, and assure yourselves thus much, you do as much as in you lies to put the Lord Jesus Christ from you, and if you go on in this course you begin you will bring a curse upon you and your posterity, and the mouth of the Lord hath spoken it.

DEP. GOV.: What is the scripture she brings?

MR. STOUGHTON: Behold I turn away from you.

MRS. H.: But now having seen him which is invisible I fear not what man can do unto me.

GOV.: Daniel was delivered by miracle; do you think to be delivered so too?

MRS. H.: I do here speak it before the court. I look that the Lord should deliver me by his providence.

MR. HARLAKENDEN: I may read scripture and the most glorious hypocrite may read them and yet go down to hell.

MRS. H.: It may be so . . .

MR. ENDICOT: I would have a word or two with leave of that which hath thus far been revealed to the court. I have heard of many revelations of Mr. Hutchinson's, but they were reports, but Mrs. Hutchinson I see doth maintain some by this discourse, and I think it is a special providence of God to hear what she hath said. Now there is a revelation you see which she doth expect as a miracle. She saith she now suffers and let us do what we will she shall be delivered by a miracle. I hope the court takes notice of the vanity of it and heart of her spirit. Now because her reverend teacher is here I should desire that he would please to speak freely whether he doth condescend to such speeches or revelations as have been spoken of, and he will give a great deal of content.

MR. COTTON: May it please you Sir. There are two sorts of revelations, there are [defaced] or against the word besides scripture both which [defaced] and tending to danger more ways than one—there is another sort which the apostle prays the believing Ephesians may be made partakers of, and those are such as are breathed by the spirit of God and are never dispensed but in a word of God and according to a word of God, and though the word revelation be rare in common speech and we make it uncouth in our ordinary expressions, yet notwithstanding, being undefined in the scripture sense I think they are not only lawful but such as Christians may receive and God bear witness to it in his word, and usually he doth express it in the ministry of the word and doth accompany it by his spirit, or else it is in the reading of the word in some chapter or verse and whenever it comes flying upon the wings of the spirit.

MR. ENDICOT: You give me satisfaction in the thing and therefore I desire you to give your judgment of Mrs. Hutchinson; what she hath said you hear and all the circumstances thereof.

MR. COTTON: I would demand whether by a miracle she doth mean a work above nature or by some wonderful providence for that is called a miracle often in the psalms.

MRS. H.: I desire to speak to our teacher. You know Sir what he doth declare though he doth not know himself [something wanting] now either of these ways or at this present time it shall be done, yet I would not have the court so to understand me that he will deliver me now even at his present time.

DEP. GOV.: I desire Mr. Cotton to tell us whether you do approve of Mrs. Hutchinson's revelations as she hath laid them down.

MR. COTTON: I know not whether I do understand her, but this I say, if she doth expect a deliverance in a way of providence—then I deny it.

"The figure of the Indians' fort or palizado in New England and the manner of the destroying it by Captayne Underhill and Captayne Mason," in John Underhill, *News from America* (1638), Library of Congress Rare Book and Special Collections Division.

DEP. GOV.: No Sir, we did not speak of that.

MR. COTTON: If it be by way of miracle then I would suspect it.

DEP. GOV.: Do you believe that her revelations are true?

MR. COTTON: That she may have some special providence of God to help her is a thing that I cannot bear witness against.

DEP. GOV.: Good Sir, I do ask whether this revelation be of God or no?

MR. COTTON: I should desire to know whether the sentence of the court will bring her to any calamity, and then I would know of her whether she expects to be delivered from that calamity by a miracle or a providence of God.

MRS. H.: By a providence of God I say I expect to be delivered from some calamity that shall come to me.

GOVER.: The case is altered and will not stand with us now, but I see a marvelous providence of God to bring things to this pass that they are. We have been hearkening about the trial of this thing and now the mercy of God by a providence hath answered our desires and made her to lay open herself and the ground of all these disturbances to be by revelations . . . there is no use of the ministry of the word nor of any clear call of God by his word, but the ground work of her revelations is the immediate revelation of the spirit and not by the ministry of the word, and that is the means by which she hath very much abused the country that they shall look for revelations and are not bound to the ministry of the word, but God will teach them by immediate revelations and this hath been the ground of all these tumults and troubles, and I would that those were all cut off from us that trouble us, for this is the thing that hath been the root of all the mischief.

COURT: We all consent with you.

GOV.: Aye it is the most desperate enthusiasm in the world, for nothing but a word comes to her mind and then an application is made which is nothing to the purpose, and this is her revelations when as it is impossible but that the word and spirit should speak the same thing.

NATIVE AMERICAN CHRISTIAN CONVERTS
IN NEW ENGLAND (1653)

From [John] Eliot and [Thomas] Mayhew, *Tears of Repentance: Or, A Further Narrative of the Progress of the Gospel amongst the Indians in New-England* (London, 1653), B–B1, 7–10.

In these times the prophecies of Antichrist his downfall are accomplishing. And do we not see that the Spirit of the Lord, by the word of prophecies, hath raised up men, instruments in the Lord's hand, to accomplish what is written herein. And the spirit of prayer, and expectation of faith is raised generally in all saints, by the same word of prophecy. In like manner the Lord having said, "That the gospel shall spread over all the earth, even to all the ends of the earth; and from the rising to the setting sun; all nations shall become the nations and kingdoms of the Lord and of his Christ." Such words of prophesy hath the Spirit used to stir up the servants of the Lord to make out after the accomplishment thereof; and hath stirred up a mighty spirit of prayer, and expectation of faith for the conversion of the Jews, (yea all Israel) and of the Gentiles also over all the world. For this cause I know every believing heart, awakened by such Scriptures, longeth to hear of the conversion of our poor Indians, whereby such prophecies are in part begun to be accomplished. Yea, the design of Christ being to erect his own kingdom, in the room of all those dominions, which he doth, and is about to overturn: You shall see a spirit by such words of prophecy poured forth upon the saints (into whose hands Christ will commit the managing of his kingdom on earth) that shall carry them forth to advance Christ to rule over men in all affairs, by the word of his mouth, and make him their only Law-giver and supreme Judge, and King. . . .

THEN WABAN WAS CALLED FORTH, WHOSE
CONFESSION WAS AS FOLLOWETH; NO FORMER CONFESSION
OF HIS BEING READ UNTO THE ELDERS.

Before I heard of God, and before the English came into this country, many evil things my heart did work, many thoughts I had in my heart; I wished for riches, I wished to be a witch, I wished to be a Sachem; and many such other evils were in my heart: Then when the English came, still my heart did the same things; when the English taught me of God (I coming to their houses) I would go out of their doors, and many years I knew nothing; when the English taught me I was angry with them: But a little while ago after the great sickness, I considered what the English do, and I had some desire to do so as they do; and after that I began to work as they work; and then I wondered how the English come to be so strong to labor; then I thought I shall quickly die, and I feared lest I should die before I prayed to God; then I thought, if I prayed to God in our language, whether could God understand my prayers in our language; therefore I did ask Mr. Jackson, and Mr. Mayhew, if God understood prayers in our language? They answered me, God doth understand all languages in the world. But I do not know how to confess, and little do I know of Christ; I fear I shall not believe a great while, and very slowly; I do not know what grace is in my heart, there is but little good in me; but this I know, that Christ hath kept all God's commandments for us, and that Christ doth know all our hearts, and now I desire to repent of all my sins: I neither have done, nor can do the commandments of the Lord, but I am ashamed of all I do, and I do repent of all sins, even of all that I do know of: I desire that I may be converted from all my sins, and that I might believe in Christ, and I desire him; I dislike my sins, yet I do not truly pray to God in my heart: no matter for good words, all is the true heart; and this day I do not so much desire good words, as thoroughly to open my heart: I confess I can do nothing, but deserve damnation; only Christ can help me and do for me. But I have nothing to say for myself that is good; I judge that I am a sinner, and cannot repent, but Christ hath deserved pardon for us.

This confession being not so satisfactory as was desired, Mr. Wilson testified, that he spoke these latter expressions with tears, which I observed not, because I attended to writing; but I gave this testimony of him, that his conversation was without offence to the English, so far as I knew, and among the Indians, it was exemplary: his gift is not so much in expressing himself this way, but in other respects useful and eminent; it being demanded in what respect, I answered to this purpose, that his gift lay in ruling, judging of cases, wherein he is patient, constant, and prudent, insomuch that he is much respected among them, for they have chosen him a ruler of fifty, and he ruleth well according to his measure. It was further said, they thought he had been a great drawer on to religion; I replied, so he was in his way, and did prevail with many; and so it rested.

THE NEXT THAT WAS CALLED, WAS WILLIAM OF SUDBURY,
HIS INDIAN NAME IS NATAÔUS;
HIS FORMER CONFESSION READ BEFORE THE ELDERS,
WAS AS FOLLOWETH:

I confess that before I prayed, I committed all manner of sins, and served many gods: when the English came first, I going to their houses, they spoke to me of your God, but when I heard of God, my heart hated it; but when they said the devil was my god, I was angry, because I was proud: when I came to their houses I hated to hear of God, I loved lust in my own house and not God, I loved to pray to many gods. Five years ago, I going to English houses and they speaking of God, I did a little like of it, yet when I went again to my own house, I did all manner of sins, and in my heart I did act all sins, though I would not be seen by man. Then going to your house, I more desired to hear of God; and my heart laid, I will pray to God so long as I live. . . . I believe that Christ hath redeemed us, and I am glad to hear those words of God; and I desire that I might do all the good ways of God, and that I might truly pray unto God: I do now want graces, and these Christ only teacheth us, and only Christ hath wrought our redemption, and he procureth our pardon for all our sins; and I believe that when believers die, God's angels carry them to heaven: but I want faith to believe the Word of God, and to open my eyes, and to help me to cast away all sins; and Christ hath deserved for me eternal life: I have deserved nothing myself; Christ hath deserved all, and giveth me faith to believe it.

MARY ROWLANDSON'S ACCOUNT OF BEING TAKEN
CAPTIVE BY NATIVE AMERICANS (1675)

From Mary Rowlandson, *The Sovraignty & Goodness of God*, 2d ed. (Cambridge, Mass., 1682), 1–12.

On the tenth of February 1675 came the Indians with great numbers upon Lancaster: Their first coming was about sun-rising; hearing the noise of some guns, we looked out; several houses were burning, and the smoke ascending to heaven. There were five persons taken in one house, the father, and the mother and a sucking child they knocked on the head: the other two they took and carried away alive. There were two others who being out of their garrison upon some occasion were set upon, one was knocked on the head, the other escaped: Another there was who running along was shot and wounded, and fell down. He begged of them his life, promising them money (as they told me) but they would not hearken to him and knocked him in head, and stripped him naked and split open his bowels. Another seeing many of the Indians about his barn, ventured and went out, but was quickly shot down. There were three others belonging to the same garrison who were killed; the Indians getting up upon the roof of the barn, had advantage to shoot down upon them over their fortification. Thus these murderous wretches went on, burning, and destroying before them.

At length they came and beset our own house, and quickly it was the dolefulest day that ever mine eyes saw. . . . Some in our house were fighting for their lives, others wallowing in their blood, the house on fire over our heads, and the bloody heathen ready to knock us on the head, if we stirred out: Now might we hear mothers and children crying out for themselves, and one another, *Lord, what shall we do?* Then I took my children (and one of my sisters, hers) to go forth. . . . No sooner were we out of the house, but my brother-in-law (being before wounded, in defending the house, in or near the throat) fell down dead, whereat the Indians scornfully shouted, and hallowed, and were presently upon him, stripping off his clothes, the bullets flying thick, one went through my side, and the same (as would seem) through the bowels and hand of my dear child in my arms. One of my elder sister's children, named William, had then his leg broken, which the Indians perceiving, they knocked him on head. Thus were we butchered by those merciless heathen, standing amazed, with the blood running down to our heels. . . . The Indians laid hold of me, pulling

me one way, and the children another, and said, *Come go along with us*; I told
them they would kill me; they answered, if I were willing to go along with them,
they would not hurt me.

Oh, the doleful sight that now was to behold at this house: *Come behold the
works of the Lord, what desolations he has made in the earth*. Of thirty-seven
persons who were in this one house, none escaped either present death, or a
bitter captivity, save only one, who might say as he, Job, 1.15, *And I only am
escaped alone to tell the news*. . . . It is a solemn sight to see so many Christians
lying in their blood, some here, and some there, like a company of sheep torn
by wolves. All of them stripped naked by a company of hell-hounds, roaring,
singing, ranting, and insulting, as if they would have torn our very hearts out;
yet the Lord by his Almighty power preserved a number of us from death, for
there were twenty-four of us taken alive and carried captive.

I had often before this said, that if the Indians should come, I should choose
rather to be killed by them than taken alive, but when it came to the trial my
mind changed; their glittering weapons so daunted my spirit, that I chose rather
to go along with those (as I may say) ravenous bears, then that moment to end
my days; and that I may the better declare what happened to me during that
grievous captivity. I shall particularly speak of the several removes we had up
and down the wilderness.

THE FIRST REMOVE

Now away we must go with those barbarous creatures, with our bodies
wounded and bleeding, and our hearts no less than our bodies. About a mile
we went that night up upon a hill with sight of the town where they intended
to lodge. There was hard by a vacant house (deserted by the English before, for
fear of the Indians) I asked them whither I might not lodge in the house that
night? To which they answered, what will you love English men still? This was
the dolefulest night that ever my eyes saw. Oh the roaring, and singing and
dancing, and yelling of those black creatures in the night, which made the
place a lively resemblance of hell. And as miserable was the waft that was there
made, of horses, cattle, sheep, swine, calves, lambs, roasting pigs, and fowls
(which they had plundered in the town) some roasting, some lying and burning, and some boiling to feed our merciless enemies; who were joyful enough
though we were disconsolate. To add to the dolefulness of the former day, and
the dismalness of the present night: my thoughts ran upon my losses and sad be-
reaved condition. All was gone, my husband gone (at least separated from me,
he being in the bay; and to add to my grief, the Indians told me they would kill
him as he came homeward), my children gone, my relations and friends gone,

our house and home and all our comforts within door and without, all was gone (except my life). . . .

THE SECOND REMOVE

But now, the next morning I must turn my back upon the town, and travel with them into the vast and desolate wilderness, I knew not whither. It is not my tongue or pen can express the sorrows of my heart, and bitterness of my spirit, that I had at this departure: but God was with me, in a wonderful manner, carrying me along, and bearing up my spirit, that it did not quite fade. . . .

After this it quickly began to snow, and when night came on, they stopped; and now down I must sit in the snow, by a little fire, and a few boughs behind me, with my sick child in my lap; and calling much for water, being now (through the wound) fallen into a violent fever. . . .

THE THIRD REMOVE

The morning being come, they prepared to go on their way: one of the Indians got up upon a horse and they set me up behind him, with my poor sick babe in my lap. A very wearisome and tedious day I had of it; what with my own wound, and my child's being so exceeding sick, and in a lamentable condition with her wound. It may be easily judged what a poor feeble condition we were in, there being not the least crumb of refreshing that came with either of our mouths, from Wednesday night to Saturday night, except only a little cold water. This day in the afternoon, about an hour by sun, we came to the place where they intended, viz., an Indian town, called Wenimessat, northward of Quahaug. When we were come, Oh the number of pagan (now merciless enemies) that there came about me, that may say as David, Psalm 17.13, *I had fainted, unless I had believed, &c.* The next day was the Sabbath: I then remembered how careless I had been of God's holy time: how many Sabbaths I had lost and misspent, and how evilly I had walked in God's sight: which lay so close unto my spirit, that it was easy for me to see how righteous it was with God to cut off the thread of my life, and cast me out of his presence forever. Yet the Lord still showed mercy to me, and upheld me. . . .

Thus nine days I sat upon my knees, with my babe in my lap, till my flesh was raw again; my child being even ready to depart this sorrowful world, they bode me carry it out to another wigwam (I suppose because they would not be troubled with such spectacles). Whither I went with a very heavy heart, and down I sat with the picture of death in my lap. About two hours in the night, my sweet babe, like a lamb departed this life, on Feb. 13, 1675. It being about six years and five months old. It was nine days from the first wounding, in this miserable condition, without any refreshing of one nature or other, except a little cold water. I cannot but take notice, how at another time I could not bear to be in the room where any dead person was, but now the case is changed; I must and could lie down by my dead babe, side by side all the night after. I have thought since of the wonderful goodness of God to me, in preserving me in the use of my reason and senses, in that distressed time, that I did not use wicked and violent means to end my own miserable life.

6

THE MIDDLE COLONIES

In the mid-1620s a Dutch West India Company bureaucrat wrote a report from the New World to officials at The Hague. The note explained that a ship had just returned from the Dutch settlement of New Netherlands. "Our people are in good heart and live in peace there; the women also have borne some children there." Then came what to Dutch recipients would have seemed another mundane detail, but to modern readers it leaps off the page: "They have purchased the Island Manhattes from the Indians for the value of 60 guilders." Thus began European settlement on Manhattan Island, at New Amsterdam, a tiny outpost of the Dutch empire.[1]

The notion that the Dutch "purchased" Manhattan from resident Lenni Lenapes may mislead us: the Indians did not transfer ownership of the land to the Dutch, nor did they pack up and leave. They probably received goods valued at roughly sixty guilders with the understanding that they gave the Dutch permission to build a settlement on the southern tip of the island (which they did). But the Indians stayed around, and the Dutch relied on them for sustenance and guidance. There was not much limitation on space—well into the eighteenth century one could walk from lower Manhattan and quickly get to uncultivated woods.

Like Virginia, the colony of New Netherlands was business-minded. Dutch-Indian relations focused on furs more than faith, and Dutch ministers made few attempts to evangelize the region's native peoples. New Amsterdam's first pastor, Jonas Michaelius, took a dim view of Indians (he did not think much of the Dutch population either). "As to the natives of this country, I find them entirely savage and wild, strangers to all decency, yea, uncivil and stupid as garden poles, proficient in all wickedness and godlessness; devilish men, who serve nobody but the devil, that is, the spirit, which, in their language, they call Menetto. . . . They have so much witchcraft, divination, sorcery, and wicked tricks, that they cannot be held in by any bands or locks. . . . How these people can best be led to the true knowledge of God and of the Mediator Christ, is hard to say." Some Indians did indicate occasional interest in learning the Dutch language and Christian doctrine. Reformed ministers tutored one of them in the 1650s so that he could "repeat the commandments" in Dutch, and they gave him a Bible. They hoped he might become a missionary to his people, but soon the Indian began drinking heavily, pawned his Bible, and "turned into a regular beast." Resentments and misunderstandings often spiraled into violence.[2]

Within a year of the Dutch "acquisition" of Manhattan, settlers had built about thirty wooden houses, a stone trading hut and storage house operated by the West India Company, and a fort, should relations with Indians turn sour. The New Amsterdam fort stood roughly where today's National Museum of the American Indian is located, across from Manhattan's Battery Park.

The "Island Manhattes" was a marginal settlement in the burgeoning Dutch empire of the early seventeenth century. The Dutch established Europe's most formidable carrying and fishing fleet, and founded trading posts across the world, from India to west Africa to Brazil. The United Provinces of the Netherlands became perhaps the most diverse place in Europe by the beginning of the seventeenth century, its relatively tolerant atmosphere attracting refugees from across Europe (including, as we have seen, radical Separatists from England).

The Synod of Dort in 1618 formally committed the Dutch Reformed Church to Calvinist orthodoxy, banishing a number of Arminian pastors (those who rejected the doctrine of predestination and other Calvinist distinctives) or stripping them of their clerical position. But in the era of New Netherlands' founding, the Dutch remained relatively tolerant in practice. It is easy to overstate the Dutch commitment to religious freedom, though: authorities across the empire generally employed a policy of "connivance," or selectively overlooking the meetings of those outside the Dutch Reformed fold. As long as dissenting Christians or Jews did not insist upon open worship, authorities in the Netherlands ignored and tolerated their presence. Such practices also characterized diverse New Netherlands, which mandated that residents could practice no "other divine worship than that of the Reformed religion . . . without however persecuting anyone on account of his religion, but leaving to everyone the freedom of his conscience."[3]

The Netherlands, which had only begun to win its independence from Spain in the late sixteenth century, sought to challenge Catholic imperial power on the world stage. That desire set the context for Englishman Henry Hudson's explorations, commissioned by the Dutch East India Company, which aimed to find a northern or western route to the East Indies. In the early nineteenth century, Delaware and Mahican elders related an oral tradition of the European and native encounter, which has some resonances of Hudson's arrival in New York. The Indians, the story went, regarded the European ship as a "large canoe or house, in which the great Mannitto" lived. The Indians set about preparing gifts, sacrifices, and dances, to appease this great new power. Europeans often interpreted such reactions as indicating that the Indians regarded them as gods, but this is probably too colored with monotheistic assumptions. When confronted with new people and powerful technology, such as Hudson's ship, Indians regarded them in the traditional native sense of "Manitou": beings or things with extraordinary power. A Manitou required careful treatment.[4]

Prior to the settlement at Manhattan, the Dutch set up a trading post at the future site of Albany, which they first named Fort Nassau, and later Fort Orange. This was the first Dutch settlement in North America. The Dutch population there remained small, as Fort Orange served the fur trade, and was as much an Iroquois (especially Mohawk) town as a Dutch one.

Serious Dutch efforts at colonization in the western hemisphere began with the establishment of the powerful Dutch West India Company in 1621. The West India Company was ambitious and martial, designed to "proceed in a warlike manner against the common enemy," the kingdom of Spain. The proprietors assured Dutch officials that the native people of the Americas were "so barbarous, and have so few wants (inasmuch as they feel no desire for clothing . . .)," that it would be inexpensive to create a major Dutch colonial presence there. The company sought to disrupt the Portuguese and Spanish colonial presence in the Atlantic world by establishing strongholds for trade, shipping, and piracy. That plan was "so graciously blessed by God . . . that great wealth has thereby been brought to [the Netherlands], and the enemy's finances thrown into such arrears and confusion, that no improvement is to be expected therein, except from the cessation of our arms," Dutch proprietors explained.[5]

The boldest Dutch seventeenth-century colonial effort in the Americas was not at Manhattan, but in northeastern Brazil, where in 1630 they took over Portuguese holdings in order to create New Holland. Although the Dutch invested far more resources in Brazil than in New Netherlands, the colony never achieved stability because of dangers posed by Indians and the remaining Portuguese. After twenty years the Portuguese reconquered the area. But the Dutch retained control of much of the slave trafficking trade in the Americas. Establishing large American farming settlements was not a primary concern of the West India Company, which preferred to administer small trading posts and entrepôts.

Nevertheless, establishing a trading presence meant that the Dutch needed more than a West India Company office in a colony, and in the 1620s they began to welcome various refugees, often ones with intense religious commitments, into New Netherlands. The earliest families to come to New Netherlands were Protestant French and Walloons, many of whom had earlier settled in Leiden and had associated with English Separatists there. They signaled the bustling diversity and religious fervor that came to mark the Middle Colonies.

Pastor Jonas Michaelius was a veteran of the Dutch Atlantic empire before his arrival in New Netherlands, having already served for several years at a West African Dutch outpost. Michaelius struggled with language and translation difficulties, both among his communicants, who mostly spoke French, and among the Indians, with whom he could barely speak at all. The only favorable thing he discovered about the Indians was that they did not mock "the godlike and glorious majesty of their Creator as the Africans dare to do." Otherwise, he determined that they had virtually no knowledge of the true God. He found their language "peculiar" with "many guttural letters, which are formed more in the throat than by the mouth, teeth and lips, to which our people are not accustomed." The Dutch could learn enough to make trade deals with them, but not to explain Christian doctrine. Michaelius even suspected that the natives hid much of their language from the colonists. He regarded their speech as a "made-up, childish language; so that even those who can best of all speak with the savages, and get along well in trade, are nevertheless wholly in the dark and bewildered when they hear the savages talking among themselves."

Like other European Christian observers, Michaelius figured that it would be best to separate young proselytes from their parents, to protect them from the Indians' "heathenish tricks and deviltries." The young Indians should not forget their native language, however, as it would be the means by which converts would go on to evangelize their own people. He reminded himself that God had power to give life to the dead, which was all the more necessary, "as the wrath and curse of God, resting upon this miserable people, is found to be the heavier."[6]

Michaelius found New Netherlands an inhospitable place. His wife perished shortly after their arrival, leaving him with three small children. Good help was hard to find, and he complained that the "Angola [female] slaves [*d'Angoolsche slavinnen]*" were "thievish, lazy, and useless trash." The company provided acreage for him, but he could not find reliable indentured servants, and horses, cows, and slaves were in short supply. Fresh food was likewise scarce, so he mostly ate the meager fare one would expect on board ships: beans, gray peas, barley, and salted fish. Michaelius did not last long in New Netherlands. After he feuded with the colony's director, Peter Minuit, whom the minister regarded as "a compound of all iniquity and wickedness," the company replaced both Michaelius and Minuit in 1631.[7]

As Dutch settlement expanded, familiar violence with Native Americans arose, too. Murders and recriminations between Dutch settlers and the Raritan Indians prompted the Dutch to announce bounties for Raritan Indian heads delivered to New Amsterdam. Willem Kieft, the colony's director, began a series of raids against neighboring Indians in the early 1640s, including an attack on Pavonia, on the New Jersey bank of the Hudson. The killing of Indians there elicited a critical description reminiscent of Las Casas's accounts of the conquest of the Americas. "Infants were torn from their mother's breasts, and hacked to pieces in the presence of their parents, and pieces thrown into the fire and in the water, and other sucklings, being bound to small boards, were cut, struck, and pierced, and miserably massacred." Captain John Underhill, the veteran of the Pequot War in New England who had subsequently come to Long Island and aligned with the Dutch, led an attack on the Algonquin village at Pound Ridge, which the Dutch forces burned in a manner similar to the English attack at Mystic River in 1637. Several hundred men, women, and children died in the conflagration. By the mid-1640s, New Netherlands had descended into incessant rounds of attacks and torture. Among the colonists who died were Puritan dissenter Anne Hutchinson and her family, who had come to New Netherlands after spending several years in Rhode Island.[8]

Pieter Stuyvesant, the son of a Calvinist pastor from Friesland (northern coastal Holland), brought some order to New Netherlands when he became the colony's director in 1647. Stuyvesant had served the Dutch empire in South America and the Caribbean, and he lost a leg during an attack on Spanish St. Maarten. Stuyvesant discovered that New Amsterdam was a run-down, ramshackle village where residents pitched all manner of trash—"rubbish, filth, ashes, oyster-shells, [and] dead animals"—into the streets. Outhouses drained directly into the town's lanes, where hogs wallowed in excrement.[9]

Stuyvesant's New Amsterdam remained small and diverse. French Jesuit missionary Isaac Jogues visited the colony in the 1640s and observed "four or five hundred men of different sects and nations," including as many as eighteen different languages. Jogues found the religious environment especially varied, in spite of the official role of the Dutch Reformed Church. "No religion is publicly exercised but the Calvinist, and orders are to admit none but Calvinists, but this is not observed; for there are in the colony besides the Calvinists, Catholics, English Puritans, Lutherans, Anabaptists, here called [Mennonites]." Jogues was mistaken about New Netherlands banning the non-Reformed, but he captured the peculiar situation of functional religious diversity operating below the official canopy of Dutch Calvinism.[10]

The Dutch policy of "conniving" at religious difference did not extend to dissenters who wished to publicly practice their faith, or who sought to proselytize in the colony. In the 1640s and 1650s, growing numbers of dissenters (like the ill-fated Hutchinson family) moved to the colony, precipitating anxiety among Dutch officials. Some Lutherans "saucily" agitated for full freedom of worship. (One of the Dutch pastors complained that a new Lutheran minister was a "wild, drunken, unmannerly clown, more inclined to look into the wine can than into the Bible. He would prefer drinking brandy two hours to preaching one.")[11]

Small numbers of Jews also arrived in New Amsterdam in the 1650s. Some two dozen of them came in 1654, fleeing Brazil after the Dutch surrendered to the Portuguese there. One of the Dutch ministers bemoaned the presence of the Jews ("godless rascals") in addition to the "Papists, Mennonites, and Lutherans among the Dutch; also many Puritans and Independents and many atheists and various other servants of Baal among the English. . . . It would create a still greater confusion if the obstinate and immovable Jews came to settle here." Prompted by concerns of illicit meetings and ignorant preachers, Stuyvesant and the governing council of the colony promulgated new regulations in 1656, banning non–Dutch Reformed religious meetings, on threat of fines. They emphasized that they meant to suppress public displays of non-Reformed religion, not private reading of the Bible or family worship.[12]

No one engaged in more flamboyant displays than Quakers, who began to appear in New Netherlands in 1657. The Quakers, or "Friends," were among the most radical of the new Protestant sects generated during the English Civil War. They believed that all people retained within them God's presence, which they called the "Inward Light." Although traditional Protestants taught that the Holy Spirit resided within believers, the Quakers believed that Christ's Light lay within everyone, regardless of whether they were converted, and regardless of one's social standing, gender, or ethnicity. God's Light was waiting to be discovered, a process that would begin with one's conversion as a Quaker.

Although they did not reject the Bible, Quakers placed great emphasis on the revelation of God in their meetings, which followed no preplanned agenda and featured no learned clergy. Friends sat in silence until the Spirit moved one of them to speak. Rejecting cherished conventions, the Quakers mobilized itinerant preachers (women and men) to evangelize across Europe and America.

Some Quaker itinerant women demonstrated provocatively in colonial towns. In New Netherlands, two such women shook and screamed in the street, insisting that all should repent, for the day of judgment was at hand. (The Quakers got their name because of such shaking in spiritual ecstasy, or because they called on people to tremble before God's power.) After imprisoning the women briefly, the Dutch expelled them. Another Quaker preacher, Robert Hodgson, was detained for illegal preaching but continued exhorting devotees from a window. Authorities clapped him into a filthy dungeon in New Amsterdam and sentenced him to two years of hard labor "with a Negro at the wheel-barrow." He would not comply with the sentence, so officials incessantly whipped him with a tar-covered rope, keeping him conscious on a bare diet of bread and water. Hodgson eventually agreed to begin serving his sentence, but Stuyvesant released him, contingent upon his leaving the colony.[13]

Quaker agitation prompted another ordinance in 1657, warning residents to inform authorities about the activities of Quaker missionaries, and not to house them. The policy elicited a protest from residents of Vlissingen (Flushing), which has become known as the Flushing Remonstrance (1657). Although its immediate impact was minimal, the Remonstrance set an important precedent for freedom of religion in America. The petitioners argued that as Christians, they could not treat Quakers treacherously, but would welcome them "as God shall persuade our consciences." Stuyvesant was unconvinced, and he sentenced the lead petitioner to a fine or banishment for supporting the "abominable sect of Quakers, who vilify both the political authorities and the Ministers of the Gospel and undermine the State and God's service." New Netherlands was hardly alone in its official hostility toward Quakers. Massachusetts executed several Quaker missionaries for returning to the colony after banishment in the years 1659–61.[14]

The Quakers represented just one sign of the Middle Colonies' religious and ethnic diversity at the time of the English conquest of New Netherlands in 1664. Officially, the English took over a Dutch colony, but in fact they absorbed people of many ethnicities, including Africans, Finns, French Huguenots, Germans, Norwegians, Swedes, and Native Americans. Some of the European settlers had come seeking fortunes, some escaping religious persecution, and some were looking for a place to set up a godly refuge.

Just before the English takeover, a small group of utopian Mennonites led by Pieter Plockhoy came to New Netherlands. They founded a settlement on the lower Delaware, at a place evocatively named Whorekill. In the Netherlands and England, Plockhoy had dabbled in a range of religious and philosophical utopian thought. In the 1650s, he moved among the political leaders of England's Interregnum, telling the Lord Protector, Oliver Cromwell, that England needed to establish a unified Christian state, one that offered full toleration of all sects. Plockhoy published *The Way to the Peace and Settlement of These Nations*, which, in its subtitle, averred that "the liberty of speaking (which every one desires for himself) is opposed against Antichrist, for the procuring of his downfall, who will not grant the same to others." Plockhoy affirmed the great Protestant war against the Roman Antichrist, but he warned of "little Antichrists" who used political coercion in spiritual matters. "It belongs only to God and Christ to have dominion over consciences, and to magistrates to prevent any from exercising lordship over the consciences of others; in so doing they would be true maintainers and defenders of Liberty," Plockhoy declared.[15]

The Restoration of Charles II was a major disappointment to Plockhoy, and he returned to the Continent with thoughts of seeking shelter in the New World. His brother had already gone to New Netherlands, so Plockhoy applied for a land grant to start a settlement at Whorekill. Plockhoy proposed a charter for the settlement that would grant full religious liberty to all. There would be a strong communal bent, with much property held in common and assurances of provision for the indigent. Despite his paeans to religious liberty, Plockhoy warned that "all eccentric persons such as obstinate papists which are strongly attached to the Roman chair, parasitic Jews, Anglican headstrong Quakers and Puritans, and rash and stupid believers in the millennium, besides all present-day pretenders to revelation, etc., will have to be carefully averted from this Christian civilian society."[16]

In 1663, his group of forty-one settlers arrived at Whorekill, where Plockhoy's utopian vision turned into a disaster. The Dutch in the area (unlike in New Amsterdam) decided to resist the occupying English forces in 1664, resulting in violence and thoroughgoing conquest of the lower Delaware region. This included Whorekill, where the English commander reported that they took what "belonged to the Quaking Society of Plockhoy to a very naile." Plockhoy himself seems to have died within a year of his arrival. Many colonists' dreams—both religious and financial—perished in the difficult circumstances they found in the New World.[17]

✦ ✦ ✦

Time ran out for Dutch New Netherlands in the 1660s. Conflict between England and Holland made New Amsterdam's presence between Connecticut and Maryland more conspicuous to English authorities. In 1664, the recently restored king of England, Charles II, sent an expedition against New Amsterdam. Although Stuyvesant wished to fight, English negotiators (including John Winthrop, Jr.) convinced the Dutch to give up New Amsterdam. The king renamed the town and colony for his brother, James Stuart, the Duke of York. Because this was an instance of English Protestants conquering Dutch Protestants, the English extended toleration to the Dutch Reformed Church, promising that the "Dutch here shall enjoy the liberty of their consciences in Divine Worship." The English assumed control of the lucrative fur trade, and in the 1670s they cemented an alliance with the Iroquois League that became known as the Covenant Chain.

The English continued to consolidate their hold over the Middle Colonies as, in the same year they conquered New Netherlands, they formed the New Jersey colony between the Hudson and Delaware rivers. For two decades, New Jersey was split into East and West Jersey, the former dominated by Scots immigrants, the latter by English Quakers. One of West Jersey's sponsors was William Penn, who in 1682 established Pennsylvania, the second major English settlement of the Middle Colonies, as a refuge for persecuted English and European Quakers. In spite of Quakerism's radical tendencies, Penn himself was an aristocrat whose family was owed a substantial debt by the crown. To pay off this debt, Charles II granted Penn title to the Pennsylvania colony.

Penn envisioned Pennsylvania as a "free colony for all mankind that should go thither, more especially those of my own profession, not that I would lessen the civil liberties of others because of their persuasion." The Restoration era, beginning in the 1660s, had seen harsh persecution of Quakers in England. Penn himself had spent time in jail for illegal preaching and subversive publishing. A decade before the founding of the colony, Penn became an activist for religious freedom, defining liberty of conscience as more than the "liberty of the mind," but instead the "exercise of ourselves in a visible way of worship." While Dutch authorities had seen religious liberty as freedom of thought and freedom from coercion, Penn's colony would allow all denominations to meet in public.[18]

The colony would not tolerate polytheism or atheism, however, nor would it countenance gross immorality. Its guarantee of freedom of "religious persuasion, or practice, in matters of faith and worship" extended only to those who believed in "the one Almighty and eternal God." Pennsylvania's early laws also recommended that all residents observe the Sabbath, and warned that the "wildness and looseness of the people provoke the indignation of God against a country." Accordingly, the proprietors banned a long list of practices, including

the "drinking of healths, obscene words, incest, sodomy, rapes, whoredom, fornication, and other uncleanness."[19]

Penn mustered hundreds of investors and thousands of colonists, getting
Pennsylvania off to a solid start. Within four years of its initial settlement, the
colony had more than eight thousand settlers, more than New Netherlands had
at the time of the English conquest of 1664. Many of these Pennsylvanians were
Quakers from the British Isles, but there were also significant numbers of Anglicans, as well as nonconformists, including Presbyterians, Baptists, and Catholics. The colony drew Dutch Calvinists, and German Lutherans and Pietists,
many of whom settled in Germantown, northwest of Philadelphia.

Penn's capital, the "City of Brotherly Love," was laid out in a rectangle between the Delaware and Schuylkill rivers. The systematic grid pattern of streets
gave Philadelphia a much more orderly appearance than older colonial towns
such as Boston. The city, and the colony generally, thrived due to a favorable
combination of conditions. Quakers tended to move as families, and employed
fewer indentured servants. Due to a shorter growing season, Pennsylvania saw
less cultivation of tobacco, and more of wheat, a crop that demanded less intensive labor and thus encouraged family-based farms.

The colony enjoyed a relatively placid relationship with the region's Native
Americans, due to good timing on the Quakers' part, and also to their convictions regarding fair treatment of Indians. Penn said that he wished to break
from earlier English and Spanish patterns by dealing honestly with the Lenni
Lenapes and other native peoples. He regretted the "unkindness and injustice
that has been too much exercised towards [Indians] by the people of these parts
of the world." The early Quakers took only land secured through negotiated
contracts and treaties. They made a number of major purchases along the Delaware and Schuylkill from 1682 to 1684, buying land from Lenape and Susquehannock leaders in order to secure the colony's core tracts.[20]

These early precedents helped Pennsylvania avoid the violence, resentment,
and rebellion that had beset Virginia, New Mexico, New Netherlands, and
New England. The Quakers' late arrival on the colonial scene also meant that
they were dealing with Indian populations already weakened by epidemics and
war. The area's major tribal group, the Lenni Lenapes, had dwindled to perhaps
five thousand people by the time of Pennsylvania's founding, and they were content to enter agreements with the English as a buffer against the hostile Iroquois
League. In spite of their evangelistic work among the English, the Quakers made
almost no effort to proselytize Native Americans. They regarded Indians as cul-
turally inferior, and expected that once natives came under English colonial
rule, they should accept the laws and customs of the newcomers. And even

though Penn dealt in relative fairness in land acquisitions, there was never any question in his mind that those deals would happen.[21]

In a letter Penn wrote to the "Kings of the Indians" in 1681, a year before he arrived in Pennsylvania, Penn noted that there was "one great God and Power" who had created all humans alike, and to whom all people would give account of their lives. That God had commanded him (and all people) to love others and not make "mischief." "This great God hath been pleased to make me concerned in your parts of the world," he told them, and his king had granted him a province there. He only wished to build up the province with their "love and consent." After saying that he would come to meet them soon, in the manuscript of the letter Penn added an interlinear note: "in the mean time I have sent my commissioners to treat with you about land and a firm league of peace." Penn's letter spoke to his religious conviction that the Quaker colony must set a new precedent, but it reflected the general English understanding that relations with Indians had sunk to an unprecedented low in King Philip's War (1675–76) in New England. Murderous hatred of Indians had also fueled the beginnings of Bacon's Rebellion, which almost brought down the Virginia colony in 1676. It seems unlikely that Penn knew about the Pueblo Revolt in New Mexico in 1680 at the time of his 1681 overture to Indian sachems. What he already knew about the English colonies' troubles, however, made him determined to break patterns of unrestrained land seizures, unresolved grievances, gruesome violence, and unremitting war.[22]

Penn's good intentions for the colony did not spare it from internal divisions and theological wrangling. The most serious religious dispute, the Keithian schism, came in the early 1690s, and illustrated the weakness of Quaker authority in the New World. (The schism played out in Penn's absence—the founder spent relatively little time in his colony, having left in 1684, and returning only in 1699.) George Keith was a Quaker missionary who arrived in 1685 to help organize East and West Jersey; he went on to teach at Philadelphia's Latin School, and to do battle with the Quakers' Puritan adversaries in New England, especially the father-son tandem of Increase and Cotton Mather. In a 1689 book, Keith proclaimed the Puritans' form of church to be "No True Church of Christ," called on New Englanders to repent, and sought to refute the "gross Abuses, Lies, and Slanders of Increase Mather."[23]

Keith soon became concerned about theological drift among Quakers in America, too. He worried that their beliefs were drifting too far from the counsel of Scripture. Yes, the "Spirit of Christ" was the key to apprehending the vital

truths of God, Keith conceded, but the Spirit had inspired the writers of Scripture, making the Bible a required guide for all Christians. Keith grew alarmed
by the opinions of Public Friends (de facto ministers, although Quakers did not
practice ordination) in Philadelphia, who seemed to disparage the Scripture
and Christ himself. Some reportedly said that faith in a historical or bodily
Christ was not necessary. One leader asked "what good or profit can the name
of Christ do us?"[24]

Reminiscent of Anne Hutchinson's meetings in Boston a half-century earlier,
Keith began holding separate assemblies in Philadelphia to teach against doctrinal fallacies. Some Public Friends asked Keith to terminate his sessions, a request Keith interpreted as a strategy to "cloak error and heresies." The ministers
named a formal committee to confront Keith, but he mocked their authority
as "rank popery" and said that none of them preached "Christ rightly." The
Philadelphia Meeting of Ministers removed Keith as a pastor, deploring his
divisive behavior. They said that Keith had abused Quaker leaders, calling them
"fools, ignorant heathens, infidels, silly souls, liars, heretics, [and] rotten ranters
. . . , foaming out his own shame." The unrepentant Keith continued to see
the controversy as a matter of illicit power in the church. The ministers were
encroaching "upon our Christian Liberty" in a way that "savors too much of
the Church of Rome."[25]

The Philadelphia meeting's judgment against Keith was circulated to Quaker
meetings throughout the colonies, reflecting how a disagreement over theological particulars had become a broad contest over Quaker power in the colonial
setting. Keith's supporters set up a separate yearly meeting in Pennsylvania. Civil
authorities even indicted Keith for libel, as the dissenter had reportedly said that
the top colonial magistrate "was not fit to be a governor, and that his name would
stink." Keith mercilessly criticized Quaker ministers who also served as politicians, saying that the blurring of church and state had corrupted them. (Most of
the leading political officials in Philadelphia were also Public Friends.)[26]

Keith became nearly deranged by the mainstream Quakers' attacks on him.
His indignation culminated in a bizarre scene at the Philadelphia meetinghouse,
where he and his followers barged in and erected a separate speakers' gallery
for Keithian ministers. A brawl ensued, and both galleries were demolished. Although Keith kept trying to establish separate meetings for his followers, now
called the "Christian Quakers," his movement was sputtering, and by early 1694
Keith had left the colony for England. Disowned by London's Yearly Meeting
as well, Keith converted to Anglicanism and became an Anglican minister and
missionary in 1702.[27]

During the course of the dispute with Quaker authorities, Keith and his supporters produced a remarkable antislavery tract, *An Exhortation and Caution to Friends Concerning Buying or Keeping of Negroes*. This was another front that Keith opened in his attack on his wealthy antagonists, some of whom trafficked in slaves. It was one of the earliest antislavery documents in American history, suggesting the religious roots of American criticism of slave owning. (Slave holding also had its biblical defenders.) "Blacks and Tawnies [Native Americans] are a real part of mankind," Keith wrote, "for whom Christ hath shed his precious blood, and are capable of salvation, as well as White Men." They possessed the Inward Light just as much as any people. True Christians should seek the "inward and outward" liberty of all people, Keith warned, so participating in the slave trade was unjust. That trade violated the Golden Rule, and it hindered evangelism. Because slaves were taken and transported against their will, the traffic implicated slave merchants and owners in "man-stealing," which was explicitly prohibited in I Timothy 1. This was a pioneering stance. Unfortunately, Keith seems to have abandoned the subject of slavery from this point forward. His published argument did not keep him from enlisting later with the Anglican Society for the Propagation of the Gospel, an organization that acquired a Barbados plantation with hundreds of slaves.[28]

With its ethnic and religious diversity, the Middle Colonies were taking on distinctive New World qualities. Yet political and economic developments across the Atlantic kept shaping life in Pennsylvania and New York. In the late 1680s, the former New Amsterdam was shaken by the Glorious Revolution (an event we will discuss at length in chapter 9). Indeed, the removal of the Catholic King James II in England precipitated a "rebellion" in New York City under the leadership of Jacob Leisler who, like Pieter Stuyvesant before him, was the son of a Calvinist minister from the Continent (in Leisler's case, Germany). When news arrived of the ascension of King William and Queen Mary to the English throne, Leisler and a colonial militia attacked the city's fort, sending New York's royal deputy governor, Francis Nicholson, back to England. In the 1680s crown officials had consolidated the New England colonies, as well as the Jerseys and New York, into a tax-hungry political unit called the Dominion of New England, much to the consternation of colonists like Leisler.

Leisler briefly became governor of New York by popular acclamation. The new monarchs hesitated to proclaim Leisler as the legitimate administrator of the colony, especially when the mercurial Leisler's leadership began to spawn bitter opposition from New Yorkers, especially among English residents and the Anglicized Dutch. The crown finally appointed a new governor, the appropri-

1694 Society of Friends Meetinghouse, Flushing, New York.
Library of Congress Prints and Photographs Division.

ately named Henry Sloughter, who arrived in New York in 1691 and demanded
that Leisler surrender the city's fort, now dubbed Fort William for England's
Dutch king. Leisler did give up after some months of struggle, and Sloughter had him tried and executed for treason. On May 16, 1691, the executioner
hanged Leisler, then took him down from the gallows and beheaded him.

Leisler's angry supporters, many of them traditional Dutch Calvinists, sang
Psalm 79 in protest before dispersing. The choice of text was quite purposeful:

> O god, the heathen are come into thine inheritance; thy holy temple have
> they defiled; they have laid Jerusalem on heaps.
> The dead bodies of thy servants have they given to be meat unto the fowls
> of the heaven, the flesh of thy saints unto the beasts of the earth. . . .
> Pour out thy wrath upon the heathen that have not known thee, and upon
> the kingdoms that have not called upon thy name.
> For they have devoured Jacob, and laid waste his dwelling place.[29]

Bitterness about the outcome of Leisler's Rebellion would taint New York politics for decades. But the would-be Dutch Jerusalem at "Manhattes" was irrevo-
cably subdued. The outcome of the ill-fated Calvinist's rebellion signaled that
for New York (like all of England's American colonies), the second half of the
colonial era would be marked by a British imperial power that overshadowed
American diversity and assertions of autonomy. Indeed, for the American col-

onies, the period from the Glorious Revolution to the American Revolution would be marked by increasing stability. England's colonies saw a trend toward greater integration with the culture and politics of the empire's center at London. Yet imperial conflict between Europe's Catholic and Protestant powers would also keep festering, and colonists would continue to interpret those conflicts through the lens of religion.

EUROPEANS FIRST ARRIVE AT MANHATTAN ISLAND
(ACCOUNT FROM 1801)

From "Indian Tradition of the First Arrival of the Dutch at Manhattan Island, Now New York," in New-York Historical Society, ed., *Collections of the New-York Historical Society, Second Series*, vol. 1 (New York, 1841), 71–74.

The following account of the first arrival of European at York Island, is verbatim as it was related to me by aged and respected Delawares, Momeys and Mahicanni (otherwise called Mohigans, Mahicanders) near forty years ago. It is copied from notes and manuscripts taken on the spot. They say:

A long time ago, when there was no such thing know to the Indians as people with a *white skin* (their expression), some Indians who had been out a-fishing, and where the sea widens, espied at a great distance something remarkably large swimming, or floating on the water, and such as they had never seen before. They immediately returning to the shore apprised their countrymen of what they had seen, and pressed them to go out with them and discover what it might be. These together hurried out, and saw to their great surprise the phenomenon, but could not agree what it might be; some concluding it either to be an uncommon large fish, or other animal, while others were of opinion it must be some very large house. It was at length agreed among those who were spectators, that as this phenomenon moved towards the land, whether or not it was an animal, or anything that had life in it, it would be well to inform all the Indians on the inhabited islands of what they had seen, and put them on their guard. Accordingly, they sent runners and watermen off to carry the news to their scattered chiefs, that these might send off in every direction for the warriors to come in. These arriving in numbers, and themselves viewing the strange appearance, and that it was actually moving towards them (the entrance of the river or bay), concluded it to be a large canoe or house, in which the great Mannitto (great or Supreme Being) *himself* was, and that he probably was coming to visit them. By this time the chiefs of the different tribes were assembled on York Island, and were counselling (or deliberating) on the manner they should receive their Mannitto on his arrival. Every step had been take to be well provided with a plenty of meat for a sacrifice; the women were required to prepare the best of victuals; idols or images were examined and put in order; and a grand dance

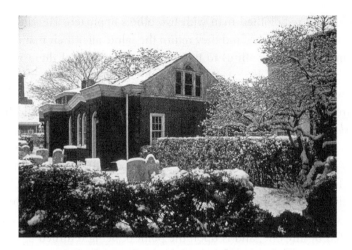

Gloria Dei (Old Swedes') Church National Historic Site,
Philadelphia. Courtesy of the National Park Service. In use
since 1700, this is the oldest church building in Pennsylvania.

was supposed not only to be an agreeable entertainment for the Mannitto, but might, with the addition of a sacrifice, contribute towards appeasing him, in case he was angry with them. The conjurors were also set to work, to determine what the meaning of this phenomenon was, and what the result would be. Both to these, and to the chiefs and wise men of the nation, men, women, and children were looking up for advice and protection. Between hope and fear, and in confusion, a dance commenced. While in this situation fresh runners arrive declaring it a house of various colours and crowded with living creatures. It now appears to be certain that it is the great Mannitto bringing them some kind of game, such as they had not before; but other runners soon after arriving, declare it a large house of various colours, full of people, yet of quite a different colour than they (the Indians) are of; that they were also dressed in a different manner from them, and that one in particular appeared altogether red, which must be the *Mannitto* himself. They are soon hailed from the vessel, though in a language they do not understand; yet they shout (or yell) in their way. Many are for running off to the woods, but are pressed by others to stay, in order not to give offence to their visitors, who could find them out, and might destroy them. The house (or large canoe, as some will have it), stops, and a smaller canoe comes ashore with the red man and some others in it; some stay by this canoe to guard it. The chiefs and wise men (or councilors) had composed a large circle, unto which the red-clothed man with two others approach. He salutes them with friendly countenance, and they return the salute after their manner. They are lost in admiration, both as to the colour of the skin (of these whites) as also to their manner of dress, yet most as to the habit of him who wore the red clothes, which shone[1] with something they could not account for. He must be the great Mannitto (Supreme Being), they think, but why should he have a *white skin?*[2] A large hockhack[3] is brought forward by one of the (supposed) Mannitto's servants, and from this a substance is poured out into a small cup (or glass) and handed to the Mannitto. The (expected) Mannitto drinks; has the glass filled again, and hands it to the chief next to him to drink. The chief receives the glass, but only smelleth at it, and passes it on to the next chief, who does the same. The glass thus passes through the circle without the contents being tasted by any one; and is upon the point of being returned again to the red-clothed man, when one of their number, a spirited man and great warrior jumps up—harangues the assembly on the impropriety of returning the glass with the contents in it; that the same was handed them by the Mannitto in order that they should drink it, as he himself had done before them; that this would please him; but to return what he had given to them might provoke him, and be the cause of their being destroyed by him. And that, since he believed it for the good of the nation that the contents offered them *should* be drank, and as no one was willing to drink it *he would*, let the consequence be what it would; and that it was better for one man to die, than a whole nation be destroyed. He then took the glass and bidding the assembly a farewell, *drank it off.* Every eye was fixed on their resolute companion to see what an effect this would have upon him, and he soon beginning to stagger about, and at last dropping to the ground, they bemoan him. He falls into a sleep, and they view him as expiring. He awakes again, jumps up, and declares that he never felt himself before so happy as after he had drank the cup. Wishes for more. His wish is granted; and the whole assembly soon join him and become intoxicated.[4]

1. [Editor's note] Lace.

2. Their own expression.

3. Their word for gourd, bottle, decanter, &c.

4. The Delawares call this place (New York Island) *Mannahattanink* or *Mannahachtanink* to this day. They have frequently told me that it derived its name from this general *intoxication*, and that the word comprehended the same as to say, *the island or place of general intoxication.*

This Mahicanni, (otherwise called Mohiggans by the English, and Mahicanders by the Low Dutch), call this place by the same name as the Delawares do; yet think it is owing or given in consequence of a kind of wood which grew there, and of which the Indians used to make their bows and arrows. This wood the latter (Mohicanni) call "*gawaak.*"

After this general intoxication had ceased (during which time the whites had confined themselves to their vessel), the man with the red clothes returned again to them, and distributed presents among them, to wit, beads, axes, hoes, stockings, &c. They say that they had become familiar to each other, and were made to understand by signs; that they now would return home, but would visit them next year again, when they would bring them more presents, and stay with them awhile; but that, as they could not live without eating, they should then want a little land of them to sow some seeds in order to raise herbs to put in their broth. That the vessel arrived the season following, and they were much rejoiced at seeing each other; but that the whites laughed at them (the Indians), seeing they knew not the use of the axes, hoes, &c., they had given them, they having had these hanging to their breasts as ornaments; and the stockings they had made use of as tobacco pouches. The whites now put handles (or helves) in the former, and cut trees down before their eyes, and dug the ground, and showed them the use of the stockings. Here (say they) a general laughter ensued among them (the Indians), that they had remained for so long a time ignorant of the use of so valuable implements; and had borne with the weight of such heavy metal hanging to their necks for such a length of time. They took every white man they saw for a Mannitto, yet inferior and attendant to the *supreme Mannitto*, to wit, to the one which wore the red and laced clothes. Familiarity daily increasing between them and the whites, the latter now proposed to stay with them, asking them only for so much land as the hide of a bullock would cover (or encompass), which hide was brought forward and spread on the ground before them. That they readily granted this request; whereupon the whites took a knife and beginning at one place on this hide, cut it up into a rope not thicker than the finger of a little child, so that by the time this hide was cut up there was a great heap. That this rope was drawn out to a great distance, and then brought round again, so that both ends might meet. That they carefully avoided its breaking, and that upon the whole it encompassed a large piece of ground. That they (the Indians) were surprised at the superior wit of the whites, but did not wish to contend with them about a little land, as they had enough. That they and the whites lived for a long time contentedly together, although these asked from time to time more land of them; and proceeding higher up

---

The universal name the Monseys have for New York, is *Laaphawachking*, which is interpreted, the place of *stringing beads* (*wampum*). They say this name was given in consequence of beads being here distributed among them by the Europeans; and that after the European vessel had returned, wherever one looked, one would see the Indians employed in stringing the beads or wampum the whites had given them.

the Mahicanittuk (Hudson river), they believed they would soon want all their country, and which at this time was already the case.

[Here ends this relation.[5]]

A DUTCH PASTOR DESCRIBES THE WORK OF THE QUAKERS (1657)

From Hugh Hastings, ed., *Ecclesiastical Records State of New York*, vol. 1 (Albany, N.Y., 1901), 399–400.

Reverend, Pious, Very Learned Fathers and Brethren in Christ:—

Just after closing our recent letter of August 5th, it happened that on August 6th (or 12th) a ship came from the sea to this place, and approached the Fort, having no flag flying from the topmast, nor from any other place on the ship; only from the foremast a small burgee floated to indicate the wind. We could not decide whether she was Dutch, French, or English. They fired no salute before the fort, as is usual with ships on their arrival. When the Fiscal went on board, they tendered him no honor or respect. When the master of the ship came on shore and appeared before the Director-General, he rendered him no respect, but stood still with his hat firm on his head, as if a goat. The Director-General could with difficulty get a word from any of them. He only learned that they had come from London in about eight weeks. When asked as to the condition of Holland, France, etc., hardly a word could be drawn from them. At last information was gained that it was a ship with Quakers on board. The following morning early they hoisted anchor and sailed eastward, towards Hellgate, as we call it, in the direction of New England. We suppose they went to Rhode Island; for that is the receptacle of all sorts of riff-raff people, and is nothing else than the sewer (latrina) of New England. All the cranks of New England retire thither. We suppose they will settle there, as they are not tolerated by the Independents in any other place. Last year there also arrived at Boston, in New England, several of these Quakers, but they were immediately put in prison and then sent back in the same ship. Probably fearing the same

---

5. At the head of this article there is a typographical error in the name of a tribe of Indians, —*Momeys* should be MONSEYS, often written *Minsis*. For an exact account of this and other Delaware nations, see GALLATIN's "Synopsis of the Indian Tribes," a work of extraordinary ability, contained in *Transactions of American Antiquarian Society*, vol ii, p. 44, &c.

thing, these Quakers came this way, and then passed on. But they did not pass from us so hastily, as not to leave some evidences of their having been here, for they left behind two strong young women. As soon as the ship had fairly departed, these began to quake and go into a frenzy, and cry out loudly in the middle of the street, that men should repent, for the day of judgment was at hand. Our people not knowing what was the matter, ran to and fro, while one cried "Fire," and another something else. The Fiscal, with an accompanying officer, seized them both by the head, and led them to prison. On their way to jail, they continued to cry out and pray according to their manner, and continued to do the same when in prison. We perceive from this circumstance that the devil is the same everywhere. The same instruments which he uses to disturb the churches in Europe, he employs here in America. We trust that our God will baffle the designs of the devil, and preserve us in the truth, and bring to nothing these machinations of Satan. Finally, we commend your Reverences to the protection of the Most High, while we beseech him to bless us all in the ministry, to the edification of his church.

> *Your dutiful servants,*
> *Joannes Megapolensis*
> *Samuel Drisius*

Amsterdam, in New Netherland,
August 14th, 1657

WILLIAM PENN ON THE INDIANS OF PENNSYLVANIA (1683)

From William Penn, *A Letter from William Penn, Proprietary and Governour of Pennsylvania in America, to the Committee of the Free Society of Traders* (London, 1683), 5–7.

XI. The NATIVES I shall consider in their persons, language, manners, religion and government, with my sense of their original. For their persons, they are generally tall, straight, well-built, and of singular proportion; they tread strong and clever, and mostly walk with a lofty chin. Of complexion black, but by design, as the Gypsies in England. They grease themselves with bear's fat clarified, and using no defense against sun or weather, their skins must needs be swarthy. Their eye is little and black, not unlike a straight-looked Jew. The thick lip and flat nose, so frequent with the East-Indians and Blacks, are not common to them: for I have seen as comely European-like faces among them of both, as on your side the sea; and truly an Italian complexion hath not much more of the white, and the noses of several of them have as much of the Roman.

XII. Their language is lofty, yet narrow, but like the Hebrew; in signification full, like short-hand in writing; one word serveth in the place of three, and the rest are supplied by the understanding of the hearer. Imperfect in their tenses, wanting in their moods, participles, adverbs, conjunctions, interjections: I have made it my business to understand it, that I might not want an interpreter on any occasion. And I must say, that I know not a language spoken in Europe, that hath words of more sweetness or greatness, in accent and emphasis, than theirs . . . .

XIII. Of their customs and manners, there is much to be said, I will begin with children. So soon as they are born, they wash them in water, and while very young, and in cold weather to choose, they plunge them in the rivers to harden and embolden them. Having wrapped them in a clout, they lay them on a straight thin board, a little more than the length and breadth of the child, and swaddle it fast upon the board to make it straight: wherefore all Indians have flat heads; and then they carry them at their backs. The children will go very young, at nine months commonly, they wear only a small clout round their waist, till they are big; if boys they go a-fishing till ripe for the woods, which is about fifteen; then they hunt, and after having given some proofs of their manhood, by a good return of skins, they may marry, else it is a shame to think of a wife. The girls stay with their mothers, and help to hoe the ground, plant corn, and carry burdens and they do well to use them to that young, they must do when they are old, for the wives are the true servants of their husbands: otherwise the men are very affectionate to them.

XIV. When the young women are fit for marriage, they wear something upon their heads for an advertisement, but so as their faces are hardly to be seen, lest when they please: the age they marry at, if women, is about thirteen and fourteen, if men, seventeen and eighteen, they are rarely older.

XV. Their houses are mats, or barks of trees set on poles, in the fashion of an English barn, but out of the power of the winds, for they are hardly higher than a man; they lie on reeds of grass. In travel they lodge in the woods about a great fire, which the mantle of duffels they wear by day, wrapped about them, and a few boughs stuck round them.

XVI. Their diet is maize, or Indian corn, diverse ways prepared; sometimes roasted in the ashes, sometimes beaten and boiled with water, which they call hominy; they also make cakes, not unpleasant to eat: They have likewise several sorts of beans and peas that are good nourishment; and the woods and rivers are their larder.

XVII. If an European comes to see them, or calls for lodging at their house or wigwams they give him the best place and first cut. If they come to visit us, they salute us with an *Itah*, which is as much as to say, *Good be to you*, and set them down, which is mostly on the ground close to their heels, their legs upright; may be they speak not a word more, but observe all passages. If you give them anything to eat or drink, well, for they will not ask: and be it little or much, if it be with kindness, they are well-pleased, else they go away sullen, but say nothing.

XVIII. They are great concealers of their own resentments, brought to it, I believe, by the revenge that hath been practiced among them, in either of these, they are not exceeded by the Italians. . . . Some of the young women are said to take undue liberty before marriage for a portion; but when married, chaste; when with child, they know their husbands no more, till delivered, and during their month, they touch no meat, they eat, but with a stick, lest they should defile it; nor do their husbands frequent them, till that time be expired.

XIX. But in liberality they excel, nothing is too good for their friend; give them a fine gun, coat, or other thing, it may pass twenty hands before it sticks; light of heart, strong affections, but soon spent: the most merry creatures that live, feast and dance perpetually, they never have much, nor want much. . . . Since the Europeans came into these parts, they are grown great lovers of strong liquors, rum especially, and for it exchange the richest of their skins and furs. If they are heated with liquors, they are restless till they have enough to sleep; that is their cry, *some more, and I will go to sleep*, but when drunk, one of the most wretchedest spectacles in the world.

XX. In sickness impatient to be cured, and for it give anything, especially for their children, to whom they are extremely natural; they drink at those times a *teran* or decoction of some roots in spring water; and if they eat any flesh, it must be of the female of any creature. If they die, they bury them with their apparel, be they men or women, and the nearest of kin fling in something precious with them, as a token of their love. Their mourning is blacking of their faces, which they continue for a year. They are choice of the graves of their dead; for lest they should be lost by time and fall to common use, they pick off the grass that grows upon them, and heap up the fallen earth with great care and exactness.

XXI. These poor people are under a dark night in things relating to religion, to be sure, the tradition of it; yet they believe a god and immortality, without the help of metaphysics; for they say, there a great king that made them, who dwells in a glorious country to the southward of them, and that the souls of the good shall go thither, where they shall live again. Their worship consists of two parts, sacrifice and cantico. Their sacrifice is their first fruits; the first and fattest buck they kill, goeth to the fire, where he is all burnt with a mournful ditty of him that performeth the ceremony, but with such marvelous fervency and labor of body that he will even sweat to a foam. The other part is their cantico, performed by round-dances, sometimes words, sometimes songs, then shouts, two being in the middle that begin, and by singing and drumming on a board direct the chorus. Their postures in the dance are very antic and differing, but all keep measure. This is done with equal earnestness and labor, but great appearance of joy. In the fall, when the corn cometh in, they begin to feel one another. There have been two great festivals already, to which all come that will. I was at one myself; their entertainment was a great seat by a spring, under some shady trees, and twenty bucks, with hot cakes of new corn, both wheat and beans, which they make up in square form in the leaves of the stem, and bake them in ashes; and after that they fell to dance. But they that go must carry a small present in their money (it may be six pence) which is made of the bone of a fish; the black is with them as gold, the white, silver; they call it wampum.

XXII. Their government is by kings, which they call *sachema*, and those by succession, but always of the mother's side. For instance, the children of him that is now king will not succeed, but his brother by the mother, or the children of his sister, whose sons (and after them the children of her daughters) will reign, for no woman inherits; the reason they render for this way of descent is that their issue may not be spurious.

XXIII. Every king hath his council, and that consists of all the old and wise men of his nation, which perhaps is two hundred people: nothing of moment is undertaken, be it war, peace, selling of land or traffic, without advising with them; and which is more, with the young men too. 'Tis admirable to consider, how powerful the kings are, and yet how they move by the breath of their people. . . .

XXIV. The justice they have is pecuniary. In case of any wrong or evil fact, be it murder itself, they atone by feasts and presents of their wampum, which is proportioned to the quality of the offense or person injured, or the sex they are of: for in case they kill a woman, they pay double, and the reason they render is that she breedeth children, which men cannot do. 'Tis rare that they fall out, if sober, and if drunk, they forgive it, saying, it was the drink, and not the man, that abused them.

XXV. We have agreed, that in all differences between us, six of each side shall end the matter. Don't abuse them, but let them have justice, and you win them. The worst is, that they are the worse for the Christians, who have propagated their vices and yielded them tradition for ill, and not for good things. But as low an ebb as they are at, and as glorious as their own condition looks, the Christians have not outlived their sight with all their pretensions to a higher manifestation. What good then might not a good people, where there is so distinct a knowledge left between good and evil? I beseech God to incline the hearts of all that come into these parts to outlive the knowledge of the natives, by a fixed obedience to their greater knowledge of the will of God, for it were miserable indeed for us to fall under the just censure of the poor Indian conscience, while we make profession of things so far transcending.

XXVI. For their original, I am ready to believe them of the Jewish race, I mean of the stock of the ten tribes, and that for the following reasons: first, they were to go to a land not planted or known, which to be sure Asia and Africa were, if not Europe, and he that intended that extraordinary judgment upon them might make the passage not uneasy to them, as it is not impossible in itself from the easternmost parts of Asia, to westernmost of America. In the next place, I find them of like countenance, and their children of so lively resemblance, that a man would think himself in Duke's Place or Berry-Street in London, when he seeth them. But this is not all, they agree in rites, they reckon by moons, they offer their first fruits, they have a kind of Feast of Tabernacles; they are said to lay their altar upon twelve stones; their mourning a year, customs of women, with many things that do not now occur.

7

THE COLONIAL SOUTH AND CARIBBEAN

In 1670, colonists from Barbados, seeking more room to spread the fortune of the Caribbean colonies, founded Charles Town. It was named for King Charles II, and placed a new colony in between English Virginia and Spanish Florida. For all the attention Americans give to the thirteen mainland colonies, which would revolt against England in 1776, the Caribbean colonies were the great cash producers of England's western empire. They generated wealth and a number of younger sons of planters, who also dreamed of exploiting the abundant land and warm climate of the lower South.

The lead proprietor of Carolina was Lord Anthony Ashley Cooper, the first earl of Shaftesbury. With the help of his secretary, the thirty-seven-year-old John Locke, Cooper drew up Carolina's Fundamental Constitutions, a plan of government offering generous land holdings and religious toleration. In order to receive protection as a legitimate church, communicants had to affirm monotheism, the public worship of God, and provide for a way of bearing inviolate witness to the truth, whether by laying one's hand on the Bible, kissing the Bible, or raising one's right hand.

The Constitutions acknowledged the presence of Carolina's non-Christian native people, who were "utterly strangers to Christianity, whose idolatry, ignorance, or mistake gives us no right to expel or use them ill." The sponsors aspired to set a good example for all, including "Jews, heathens, and other dissenters from the purity of Christian religion." The proprietors hoped that non-Christians might not be frightened away from the faith because of oppressive religious policies. Perhaps a free Carolina would be a place where they would be "won over to embrace and unfeignedly receive the truth."

Befitting its Caribbean origins, the proprietors knew that African slaves would be an integral part of their experiment. The colony would be built upon slavery, but the proprietors wished that enslavement would not drive Africans from the Christian fold. Could they have it both ways? Charity, they recognized, obliged them to desire the welfare of all souls, but faith would not alter anyone's civil status. Before God, even slaves were fully capable of faith, the same as any free white person. Yet the proprietors made the law of slavery clear: "every freeman of Carolina shall have absolute power and authority over his negro slaves, of what opinion or religion soever."[1]

Carolina's combination of Christianity and slavery proved unstable (and, by the 1850s, unsustainable). It would produce daily consternation among slaves, and occasional mass revolts. Slavery in Carolina was not restricted to Africans, as many of the region's Indians also fell into bound labor. Native American enslavement produced deep grievances and devastating war by the end of the first generation of Carolina settlement.

In the meantime, in 1670 about two hundred English people, formerly of the West Indies, established Charles Town. In 1680 they relocated the fledgling town to a peninsula at the confluence of two rivers, looking out at a fine harbor that opened into the Atlantic. The English named the rivers the Ashley and the Cooper.

In hopes of countering Spanish power, the English established colonies in the Caribbean, beginning in 1624 with St. Christopher. The key seventeenth-century English Caribbean colony was Barbados, founded in 1627. Because of sugar cultivation, Barbados would become the most profitable colony among England's American possessions. As in the Middle Colonies, the Dutch played an important role in Barbados's economic foundations. Dutch financiers helped the English colonists open the colony's first sugar mills in the 1630s, and Dutch slave traffickers enabled the quick growth of the colony's slave system. By 1650, Barbados had become a full-blown slave society. Its population density was higher than any other place in the English empire except for London. From a mid-century peak of some 30,000 white inhabitants, the Anglo population slowly declined over the second half of the seventeenth century, while the black population burgeoned. By 1660, blacks outnumbered whites; by 1680, more than 46,000 slaves labored in Barbados's sugarcane fields. Fewer than two hundred great planters came to dominate Barbados's economy, with each owning more than one hundred acres and sixty slaves. Even though Barbados was larger than most of the Lesser Antilles islands, its land area remained quite limited. The island is only twenty-one miles long and fourteen wide. By 1680, the era of white opportunity had ended, helping to explain the desire of many Barbadians to seek new lands in the lower South.[2]

The strong population majority of enslaved blacks on Caribbean islands made white masters nervous, and in 1675 Barbadian whites believed that they narrowly averted an island-wide slave revolt. White authorities made gruesome examples of suspected conspirators: a rapidly assembled court convicted seventeen leaders and executed them, some by burning, and some by beheading. The headless bodies of some slaves were paraded through Speightstown, on the northwestern end of the island, before being burned. The Barbadian assembly cracked down on slaves' movements between plantations, attempting to prevent the kinds of conversations that supposedly fueled the conspiracy. Slaves were prohibited from carrying clubs and similar weapons, and from playing drums and other instruments that they might use to communicate signals. The assembly applied these strictures to Native American as well as African slaves, and banned the further importation of "Indian slaves from New England." Native Americans had long represented a minority of the Caribbean (and American) slave population, but given that some of the Indian slaves were coming on the market following King Philip's War, Barbadian masters were unenthusiastic about importing those who might be rebels. If they continued bringing in New England Indians, the assembly worried, "greater mischief may happen to this island than from any Negroes." Barbados's governor reckoned that the Indians had "imbibed something of the spirit of rebellion, a devil that I doubt will not be laid with prayers and fasting."[3]

The suspected 1675 rebellion marked a turning point in Christian missions to the island's African laborers. Anglicans and Quakers had both made modest inroads among black Barbadians, but many planters came to believe that the missionaries—especially Quakers—were abetting the rebels. Now some Barbadian gentlemen openly opposed the evangelization of slaves, saying that "the conversion of slaves to Christianity would not only destroy their property but endanger the island, inasmuch as converted negroes grow more perverse and intractable than others." During earlier stages of English colonization, there was widespread uncertainty among both planters and Anglican authorities about whether slave conversions would legally require manumission, since Christians were typically not seen as deserving slavery. But after 1660, the Church of England clarified that the colonies should seek to Christianize their slaves.[4]

Quakers began arriving in Barbados in the 1650s, but initially directed most of their evangelistic efforts toward whites. By 1680 they had six assemblies on the island, with several hundred members. Many Quaker converts on Barbados owned slaves, and prominent Quaker minister George Fox encouraged them in the early 1670s to mitigate slavery's effects by treating slaves fairly and giving them Christian education. In the aftermath of the ostensible rebel plot, many white Barbadians reacted against Quaker overtures to blacks. The island council passed a measure "to prevent the people called Quakers, from bringing Negroes to their meeting." It threatened those who broke this law with seizure of their slaves. Some Quakers did run afoul of the measure, such as Ralph Fretwell, who was "prosecuted for eighty Negroes being present at a meeting in his house." In the 1680s Barbados's governor ordered that the Quaker meeting-house of Bridgetown be gutted and boarded up. Formal Christian evangelistic work would languish on Barbados until the arrival of evangelical missionaries in the 1760s.[5]

Far to the north of Barbados, the isolated Atlantic island of Bermuda was formally colonized by the English in 1612. Settlers immediately built St. Peter's Church in St. George's, Bermuda, which is the oldest continuously operating Anglican church in the Americas. The colony had a strong Puritan influence from the outset. A Spanish visitor reported in 1639 that the island had "5 or 6 churches, which the people of every parish attend from their farms on Sunday morning and evening to hear the sermons preached by the ministers, the service lasting more than 3 hours." In the era of the English Civil War, the colony was wracked by conflict between Anglican and Puritan "Independent" factions. A Bermudan Puritan petition to Parliament elicited an order from the House of Commons that Independents in all English colonies should have "liberty of their consciences in matter of God's worship."[6]

Tranquility in religion or politics was difficult to achieve during the Civil War, especially following the beheading of King Charles I in 1649. Bermuda went through successive governments, and Presbyterian authorities worked to suppress Independents (who, unlike Presbyterians, believed in full autonomy of the local congregation). The 1640s had seen a major outbreak of English witchcraft accusations, and in the early 1650s, those charges spilled over into Bermuda. As with the more famous Salem, Massachusetts, crisis four decades later, witchcraft was notoriously difficult to interpret. On one hand, English people (as well as Indians, Africans, and other Europeans) believed in the possibility of magic arts and demonic covenants. On the other, witchcraft accusations seem to have run along social fault lines, though we can rarely say that accusers were intentionally making false charges of witchcraft.

In any case, in 1651 Bermuda saw its first recorded charges of witchcraft, against Anne Bowen and Jeane Gardiner. Authorities tasked some women to search Bowen and Gardiner's bodies for suspicious protrusions that might mark them as witches, but the women could find none. Further investigation revealed a damning "blewe spott" in Gardiner's mouth, however, and authorities put her through the water test. (Witchcraft lore held that witches could not sink.) Gardiner failed the test, and a jury convicted Gardiner of witchcraft. She had reportedly afflicted a mulatto woman with dumbness and blindness for two hours, as well as performing other unnamed malevolent acts. Authorities executed Gardiner by hanging on a small island in St. George's harbor in May 1651. Four more people were hanged for witchcraft over the next several years, mimicking similar witch hunts in England and New England during those same decades. An analysis of the accused suggests (as was often the case elsewhere) that they came from poorer sections of Bermudan society, and each had prior history of conflict or other notoriety. The accusations did not track precisely with religious tensions, so we should be hesitant about interpreting them as a front for settling scores between denominational rivals. Nevertheless, the outbreak of accusations and executions spoke to the pervasively religious mindset of Bermudans. Conflicts in the English church and state, and even the methods of pursuing suspected witches, affected similar controversies in the Americas in the seventeenth century.[7]

The Puritan "diaspora" radiated through the lower South and Caribbean. Perhaps the most intriguing Puritan colonial project outside of New England came at Providence Island, off the coast of Nicaragua. While Massachusetts functioned as something of a Puritan refuge, Providence Island had more militant plans to challenge Spanish hegemony in the Caribbean. In 1630, the same year that the Puritan migration to Massachusetts began, Puritan gentlemen also founded the Providence Island Company. The organizers envisioned the colony as a profitable, godly society, and a thorn in Spain's side. But the colony's mercantile, military, and spiritual purposes never seemed to mesh. One proprietor confessed that "we well hoped (according to our intention) that we had planted a religious colony in the isle of Providence, instead whereof we find the root of bitterness plentifully planted amongst you, an industrious supplanting one of another, and not a man there of place (a strange thing to consider) but he doth both accuse and is accused; these are uncomfortable fruits of religion." While early Massachusetts was wracked by controversies over dissenters such as Roger Williams and Anne Hutchinson, feuding over politics and religion defined Providence Island's brief history.[8]

Providence Island was, during its short life, a slave colony. By the mid-1630s slaves probably represented about half the population, but the colony never seized upon the turn to sugar that proved so lucrative for Barbados and other Caribbean locales. Following a failed Spanish attack on the island in 1635, proprietors stepped up privateering (legalized piracy) with expeditions against Spanish shipping to the nearby coastal ports of Portobelo and Cartagena. "Annoying the Spaniard" was always one of Providence's primary goals.[9]

One of the lead Providence proprietors, Lord Saye and Sele, engaged in a heated exchange of letters with Massachusetts's John Winthrop in 1640–41, debating which colony was a better choice for Puritan settlers. Although Puritan principles drove both, Providence was the more hierarchical and imperial-minded. Lord Saye and Sele insisted that Providence was in the superior geographic location for "the advancement of the gospel and putting down the great adversary thereof, that man of sin, whereunto as you are now you neither are able nor are likely to be to put your hands to the least wheel that is to be turned about in that work, otherways than by well wishing thereunto." In Lord Saye and Sele's mind, Massachusetts was not the main event of Puritan colonization in the New World.[10] Not long after his exchange with Winthrop, the Puritan experiment at Providence ended, with the arrival in May 1641 of a formidable Spanish fleet from Cartagena. English and African defenders briefly attempted to stop the Spanish invaders, but they realized that resistance was pointless. The Spanish conducted a formal conquest ceremony, and celebrated Catholic mass in the Puritans' church.[11]

Barbados and Jamaica would more than make up for the English loss of Providence Island. As historian Richard Dunn put it, Jamaica was "founded in blood." The English seized it from the Spanish in 1655 and the island became the key English hub of buccaneering. As the relatively small Barbados ran out of available acreage, Jamaica and Carolina became two of the most desirable alternatives for aspiring English landowners. After the first four decades of English control, Jamaica's wild era of the privateers passed, and in its place rose the "sugar and slave system in its starkest and most exploitative form."[12]

The English took Jamaica as a meager afterthought during the Western Design campaign, sponsored by England's Lord Protector Oliver Cromwell in 1654–55 to crush the Spanish Caribbean. An attack on Hispaniola failed, so the English forces, led by Admiral William Penn (father of the Quaker founder), assaulted lightly guarded Jamaica instead. Although disease often ravaged new arrivals to the island, the population rose from about 3,500 in 1661 to more than 17,000 in 1673, by which time slaves had become a majority. This was also the heyday of the buccaneers, especially the most celebrated English pirate of the century, Henry Morgan. Morgan and his henchmen sacked a series of Spanish cities from Cuba to Venezuela. Spanish diplomatic protests briefly shut down Morgan's operations, but after Morgan visited London in the early 1670s, bringing with him bounteous gifts (bribes), he secured both a knighthood and permission to continue his piratical exploits.[13]

Jamaica's capital Port Royal (originally Fort Cromwell) was a wild outpost on the watery Caribbean frontier during the years of Morgan's dominance. It was both literally and figuratively an unstable place, built precariously on the end of a ten-mile-long sand spit. Brothels and bars sprang up in the closely packed streets. But faith also played a conspicuous role in early Port Royal, with Quaker and Presbyterian meetinghouses, an Anglican church, a Catholic chapel, and a Jewish synagogue. Sugar merchants dominated the town, as one visitor observed that they lived "in the height of splendor, in full ease and plenty, being sumptuously arrayed, and attended on, and served by their Negro slaves."[14]

Many Jamaican lives, from sugar barons to slaves, came to an abrupt end when a catastrophic earthquake dumped more than half of Port Royal into the sea in 1692. Thousands on the island drowned, and the earthquake's effects killed thousands more in the squalid aftermath. Two of the town's forts, the wharves, many shops and houses, and St. Paul's Anglican church all spilled into the churning waters. Even the town's graveyard was upended in the disaster, adding to the number of corpses bobbing in the water when the shaking subsided. One Quaker wrote that many "great men who were so swallowed up with pride, that a man could not be admitted to speak with them, and women whose top-knots seemed to reach the clouds, now lie stinking upon the water, and are made meat for fish and fowls of the air." The new town of Kingston, Jamaica, just across the harbor, supplanted Port Royal as the colony's key city. By the mid-eighteenth century Kingston had become the third largest town in Britain's American colonies, and Jamaica had become Britain's most valuable colony.[15]

In the 1670s, many whites began leaving Barbados for destinations in the English Atlantic, including Jamaica, Antigua (established as an English colony in the 1630s, following a visit by Christopher Columbus in the 1490s), Boston, and London. The English metropolis was perhaps the most common destination: many colonists came to America with the intention of returning to England. But Barbadians and others from the West Indies also played a critical role in shaping the fledgling settlement at Carolina. These settlers ran the gamut from planters with slaves and servants to merchants, sailors, and small farmers. Barbadian immigrants known as the "Goose Creek men" congregated around a settlement a few miles north of Charles Town, and dominated the politics of early Carolina. Barbadian slavery helped turn Carolina into a slave society almost immediately. Virginia had been founded six decades earlier, but slavery was only just becoming the core of its labor regime at the time of Charles Town's birth.[16]

Although it took some experimentation for Carolinians to discern which staple cash crops (rice, and later indigo) would sustain the colony, there was little doubt that the inspiration for its founding was economic. Yet familiar religious and imperial concepts — evangelizing the Indians, and countering the Spanish — appeared in the promotional literature regarding Carolina. Early Carolina governor John Archdale, a Quaker, saw all European colonization in a providential framework. He marveled at how "the hand of God was eminently seen in thinning the Indians, to make room for the English." He reckoned that God had arranged civil wars between the Indians, as well as "unusual sicknesses," to reduce their numbers and make way for English settlers. God had left them an "American Canaan, a Land that flows with Milk and Honey." Archdale warned Carolinians to honor their commitment to religious liberty, as by intra-Christian quarrelling they would "lose the essential badge of Christianity, and so can never be instruments to propagate the gospel amongst the heathens."[17]

Indian evangelization never became a major priority in Carolina, however. Instead, colonists worked to integrate Indians — many of them decimated by disease — into the Carolina economy of guns, deerskins, and slaves. As one observer put it, the Carolinians were "absolute masters over the Indians . . . within the circle of their trade." Such mastery was never as absolute as some Europeans might have imagined, but the English were resourceful in creating networks of Indian dependence, and preventing much-feared Native American alliances with Africans. Indians who stayed on good terms with the Carolinians received consistent supplies of guns and ammunition. Native Americans provided the English with deerskins, as well as slaves they took captive from enemy tribes. Some Indians also served as trackers to hunt down runaway African slaves.[18]

The deerskin trade altered many tribes' relationships with both deer and the English, as Indians shifted from consuming deer for subsistence to hunting deer for an international market. Between 1698 and 1715, Charles Town merchants exported about 53,000 deerskins annually. The number dropped precipitously during the Yamasee War of the mid-1710s, but took off again after it. The deerskin trade (like the fur trades in New France) penetrated deep into the continent's interior. Most skins went through Charles Town until the emergence of Savannah as a major port in the mid-eighteenth century. Hundreds of thousands of pounds of deerskins shipped out each year by the eve of the American Revolution, and one estimate suggested that by 1764, the southeastern deer trade produced 800,000 pounds of deerskin annually. Native American men hunted and killed the deer, while Indian women processed the carcasses. Often they left the animals' meat and bones in the forest to rot.[19]

English alliances with southeastern Indians influenced Spanish networks in Florida. The Spanish depended on their mission stations in north Florida to maintain friendly relations with tribes, including the Guale, Timucua, and Apalachee Indians. These missions became targets for the Carolina English and their Native American allies. Beginning in 1680, Carolina forces attacked missions at Santa Catalina and Jekyll Island (coastal Georgia). Then, as part of the imperial War of Spanish Succession (Queen Anne's War), South Carolina governor James Moore attacked but did not quite conquer St. Augustine, Florida, in 1702. Two years later, Moore assembled an army of white and Indian slave raiders and invaded north Florida, razing thirty-two Apalachee missions and villages. The Spanish abandoned north Florida's missions network, leaving them only with St. Augustine in Florida.[20]

Florida was marginal to the larger Spanish American empire, with its valuable mines and farms in Central and South America. Relatively few of the hundreds of thousands of Spaniards who came to the Americas in the sixteenth and seventeenth centuries went to either Florida or New Mexico. St. Augustine remained the key Spanish settlement in Florida during the colonial era, although it was difficult "to get anyone to go to St. Augustine because of the horror with which Florida is painted," wrote a governor of Cuba in 1673. "Only hoodlums and the mischievous go there from Cuba," he said. Spanish political officials in Florida often governed in absentia. Authorities also sent criminals and exiles from Spain, or other places in the empire, to Florida. Nevertheless, there were signs of growing stability in St. Augustine as of 1700, when about 1,500 people lived there, including African slaves and Spanish-speaking Indians. St. Augustine's landowners often held farms outside of the town, but maintained an official residence in the coastal village.[21]

Although Indian evangelization did not feature prominently in early Carolina, religion did make a major imprint on the colony. The Fundamental Constitutions set a (contested) pattern of religious toleration, but early leaders — many of them having relocated from Bermuda or Barbados — squabbled over the relative influence of Puritanism and high-church, anti-Puritan Anglicanism. Moreover, the need to recruit more English and European settlers resulted in religious diversity, just as it did in Pennsylvania in these same decades. Hundreds of Puritans left Restoration England for Carolina. Captain Benjamin Blake, for example, had served in Oliver Cromwell's navy but decided to come to Carolina when it became evident that the Catholic James, Duke of York, would succeed Charles II as king. Blake, like other Puritan migrants in the 1680s, figured that the "miseries they endured [under Charles II] were nothing to what he foresaw would attend the reign of a Popish Successor; wherefore he resolved to remove to Carolina." Blake's son would serve as governor of Carolina at the end of the century.[22]

A number of Quakers from Barbados and England arrived in Carolina in the 1670s. Immigration from Barbados picked up following its slave rebellion scare in 1675, after which Barbadian officials became less friendly toward Quakers and their scruples. Anthony Ashley Cooper actively recruited a number of London Quakers to Carolina. One of the best known of these was Mary (Fisher) Crosse, who had already traveled widely as a Quaker missionary in England, the Ottoman empire, Massachusetts, and the West Indies. She and her family came to Charles Town in 1680 and assisted in the formation of a Quaker meeting there.[23]

Dissenters from Scotland added to the ethnic and religious diversity of early Carolina. Scottish Presbyterian Covenanters were devoted to a National Covenant of religion signed in 1638, which had committed Scotland to defend Presbyterianism as the true religion. The Covenanters fell under dire persecution in Scotland during the 1680s, in what they came to call the "Killing Time." Covenanters sponsored the short-lived Stuarts Town colony in 1684, near Port Royal and the future site of Beaufort, South Carolina. This tiny village faced tensions over the Indian trade with English authorities in Charles Town, and was vulnerable to Spanish incursions. The Scots participated in an attack on Spanish missions, which elicited a furious response by the Spanish. Stuarts Town was destroyed and burned in 1686, but Covenanters retained important religious and cultural influence in Carolina.[24]

Perhaps the most distinctive refugee group populating Carolina were French Protestants, or Huguenots, many of whom left France over the course of the seventeenth century. Many departed after the revocation of the Edict of Nantes in 1685, which took away the tolerated status they had once enjoyed in Catholic France. A minority of Huguenots ventured to America, and in the years following 1685, a majority of Huguenot immigrants elected to go to Carolina. Huguenots began arriving in Carolina in 1680, even before the revocation. They established Huguenot congregations in Charles Town and several outlying communities. In 1706, Carolina formalized an Anglican Church establishment, and outlying Huguenot churches merged into Church of England parishes rather than suffer the disadvantages of nonconformity. The Charles Town French congregation, however, remained distinctively Huguenot and Calvinist. In 1699, the Charles Town French church had 195 adherents, which represented about half of the Carolina Huguenot population at the time. (The Charleston French Protestant Church remains in operation today, and is apparently the only independent French Calvinist congregation in the United States.)[25]

Protestant migrants also flowed into Carolina from other English colonies. For example, Baptist pastor William Screven brought much of his Maine Baptist congregation to South Carolina by the mid-1690s. Screven had emigrated from England to Maine in the 1660s. By the early 1680s, Screven had become convinced that infant baptism was not biblical, and began promoting the Baptists' distinctive practice of baptizing adult believers alone, instead of infants. He and his followers affiliated with Boston's Baptist congregation, but Screven ran afoul of authorities in Maine (which was part of Massachusetts), who fined him for illegal preaching. The pressure these Baptists encountered in New England helped push them to Carolina, where dissenters in the 1690s could expect friendlier treatment. Screven ministered in and around Charles Town for two decades. The Baptists drew criticism from Anglican and Congregationalist leaders, including John Cotton, Jr., who briefly served as pastor of Charles Town's Independent (Congregationalist) Church in the late 1690s.[26]

In spite of its reputation for a relatively secular quality, early Carolina featured a striking range of Anglican, Congregationalist, Quaker, Baptist, and Huguenot churches. This amounted to a per capita ratio of one church per five hundred residents, which made Carolina one of the most churched of the English colonies. The colony would take a decisive step away from religious pluralism in the first decade of the 1700s, as the South Carolina assembly passed laws giving the Anglican Church established status, over reservations expressed by the court of Queen Anne. Dissenters enlisted the celebrated nonconformist writer Daniel Defoe to defend their interests in London polemics. In his *Case of the Dissenters in Carolina*, Defoe argued for religious liberty in the face of state power. "If any government breaks in upon the liberty of conscience, it breaks in upon an indefeasible right of the people, and commits a violation, which must necessarily turn to the prejudice of the community," Defoe asserted. "Though some religious bodies of men may have better securities than others, yet there can be no security to any, but that can outlive the change of opinion in the government, but that of an universal and absolute toleration."[27]

Anglicanism was ascendant in Carolina, further demonstrated by the arrival of missionaries sponsored by the Society for the Propagation of the Gospel

St. Peter's Church (1620), St. George's, Bermuda. Photograph
copyright 2011 by JoeyBagODonuts, Wikimedia Commons.

(SPG) in 1702, and the appointment of the colony's first Anglican commissary,
Gideon Johnston, in 1708. As seen in the absorption of Huguenot congregations,
the Anglicans made their denomination dominant, yet laypeople continually
placed dissenting and Puritan types of demands on Anglican ministers. Some
would not kneel at the Lord's Table to receive communion, and a few even insisted upon baptism by immersion, in the preferred mode of the Baptists. SPG
missionary Francis Le Jau admitted that he would baptize by dipping when
requested to do so. At first sight, the argumentative Carolinians dismayed Commissary Johnston, who ranted that these people were "the vilest race of men
upon the earth. They have neither honor, nor honesty, nor religion enough to
entitle them to any tolerable character, being a perfect medley or hotch-potch,
made up of bankrupt pirates, decayed libertines, sectaries, and enthusiasts of all
sorts who have transported themselves hither [from other English colonies] and
are the most factious and seditious people in the whole world." Far from being
a secular people, Carolinians were dizzyingly religious.[28]

The initiatives of the Anglicans' Society for the Propagation of the Gospel were designed to consolidate Anglican adherence among whites, but the
growth of the southern slave population did not escape church authorities' notice. As the number of Carolina African slaves grew from about 2,400 in 1700 to
at least 20,000 in 1730, ministers realized that they needed to try to bring slaves
into Christian community. As in early Virginia and the Caribbean, a number
of slave masters resisted such overtures, fearing that conversion would lead to
expectations of freedom, or even foster rebellion. In a widely distributed ser-

mon preached before SPG officials, Bishop William Fleetwood contended that the English had an obligation to evangelize slaves, who would enjoy eternal bliss should they embrace the Christian faith. He assured his audience that the liberty of the gospel was spiritual, not physical: "freedom from their sins, freedom from the fears of death, and everlasting misery, and not from any state of life," Fleetwood advised. Conversion would make slaves more obedient, and evangelism offered the prospect of creating a more benevolent, Christianized slave system. Many southern white colonists were not so sure about African or Indian evangelization. The Virginia House of Burgesses in 1715 even debated a bill that would have suppressed Christian instruction of Native Americans by the SPG.[29]

SPG missionary Francis Le Jau had a markedly transatlantic personal history: born in France, and educated in Dublin, Ireland, he served in the West Indies before taking a parish in Goose Creek, South Carolina. Le Jau was one of many who distributed copies of Fleetwood's sermon, and who tried to follow through on the mandate of slave evangelization. A number of Africans and Indians showed interest in baptism, and Le Jau followed up with doctrinal teaching. He invited "children, servants and slaves to come to be instructed in the church," but he left it up to the discretion of masters who should attend, and when. Le Jau was disappointed with the results, as few came to his classes (or were allowed to attend). Le Jau reckoned that although a number of masters publicly commended his evangelistic efforts, "it seems by their whispers and conduct, they would not have me urge of contributing to the salvation, instruction, and human usage of slaves and free Indians." He struggled to convince some parishioners "to make a difference between slaves and free Indians, and beasts." Some slave couples wished to have a Christian marriage, but Le Jau could not secure their masters' permission to marry them. He recoiled at the brutality toward slaves that he witnessed: one slave woman, accused of burning her master's home, was "barbarously burnt alive near my door," Le Jau wrote, "without any positive proof of the crime." He counseled her before the execution, and she professed her innocence to the last. Le Jau also condemned lurid punishments of enslaved people, such as the amputation of male slaves' testicles, or of female slaves' ears, for running away. Even though Le Jau and other early SPG missionaries found aspects of the slave system troubling, it was difficult to resist its power over southern society. Le Jau himself went on to own at least three slaves.[30]

Following a typical pattern in the Americas, the SPG's aspirations for evangelism were wrecked by violence. In 1715, resentments surrounding the trade in

Indian slaves and deerskins erupted into war with the Yamasees, who along with Creek and Catawba allies killed hundreds of traders and settlers, sending many white Carolinians into Charles Town for refuge. The English in Carolina and Virginia cut off weapons supplies to the Yamasee rebels. Then South Carolina (North Carolina had been established as a colony with a separate governor in 1712) enlisted Cherokee and Tuscarora allies to fight against the Yamasees, who were decimated and sought sanctuary among the Spanish near St. Augustine. The war saw the eradication of most of Carolina's experienced traders with Indians, and it largely signaled the end of Native Americans' participation in the colony's slave trade, even though Indian slavery remained legal, and a useful diplomatic tool. Historian Alan Gallay estimates that somewhere between 30,000 and 50,000 southern Native Americans were sold in the British slave trade between 1670 and the Yamasee War. From that point forward, the growth of Carolina slave trafficking would depend mostly on the importation of Africans. Already by 1710, blacks outnumbered whites in Carolina, and by 1730, there were two enslaved people for every free person in the colony.[31]

The enslavement of Africans came with its own dangers. The sheer numerical advantages held by the enslaved Carolinians frightened whites, and the 1720s and 1730s were rife with rumored slave insurrections. Whites' worst fears came true at the Stono River outside of Charles Town in September 1739, where a group of slaves began killing whites and taking guns and ammunition. They made their way south toward Spanish Florida, hoping to find asylum there. In the end, they rallied about eighty or a hundred slaves to the rebellion, but whites mustered a militia, who attacked and killed most of the Stono rebels. The militia decapitated many of them, posting their heads on stakes along the road to Charles Town.

In the absence of direct sources explaining their motives, it is hard to discern what precipitated the Stono Rebellion, aside from the grinding abuses and deprivations of enslavement. However, religion—in particular, the rebels' Catholic convictions—may have also influenced the goals and timing of the revolt. Many of the African insurrectionists came from the Kongo, where Catholic missionaries from Portugal had inculcated their faith for centuries. Francis Le Jau observed this Catholic Portuguese influence among some of his own parish's slaves, who spoke good English and wished to receive communion from him. He "proposed to them to declare openly their abjuring the errors of the Romish Church" before he would receive them at communion. This Catholic heritage suggests that the rebels may have felt a religious commonality with the Spanish, who offered to free slaves held by the English should they escape to St. Augustine. Rumors suggested that in the same month as the insurrection, Georgia officials (Georgia was founded in 1732) had seized a Spaniard who they suspected was a Catholic priest plotting to foment slave rebellion. Evidence suggests that the Stono rebels may have even timed the revolt for the weekend of September 8–9 because they connected it to that Saturday's commemoration of the Virgin Mary's nativity. They carried banners of white cloth, a color closely associated with the mother of Jesus in Kongolese religious imagery.[32]

Even though "by the blessing of God the Negroes were defeated," as the South Carolina assembly put it, slavery had become entrenched as Carolina's chief source of labor and wealth, and as its greatest quandary. "With regret we bewailed our peculiar case," the assemblymen said, "that we could not enjoy the benefits of peace like the rest of mankind, and that our industry should be the means of taking from us all the sweets of life and of rendering us liable to the loss of our lives and fortunes." Following on the great potential demonstrated in Barbados and the West Indies, Carolina had become much like its parent colonies, dependent on slavery yet fearing the consequences of that dependence, and the black majorities that it created. Carolina slave masters were already discovering what Thomas Jefferson would lament eighty years later: slave masters had, as it were, "the wolf by the ear, and we can neither hold him, nor safely let him go."[33]

ANGLICAN MINISTER FRANCIS LE JAU DESCRIBES
SLAVES' RELIGIOUS DEVOTION (1709)

From Frank J. Klingberg, ed., *The Carolina Chronicle of Dr. Francis Le Jau, 1706–1717* (Berkeley, Calif., 1956), 60–61.

Our Congregation is generally of about 100 Persons, sometimes more, several that were inclinable to some of the dissenting partys shew themselves pritty constant among us, and I do what possible to edify them and give them satisfaction in their doubts. On Sunday next I design God willing to baptise two very sensible and honest Negro Men whom I have kept upon tryal these two Years. Several others have spoken to me also; I do nothing too hastily in that respect. I instruct them and must have the consent of their Masters with a good Testimony and proof of their honest life and sober Conversation: Some Masters in my parish are very well satisfyed with my Proceedings in that respect: others do not seem to be so; yet they have given over opposing my design openly; it is to be hoped the good Example of the one will have an influence over the others. I must do the Justice to my Parishioners that tho' many Young Gentlemen are Masters of Great Estates, they and almost all the heads of all our Neighbouring families are an Example of Sobriety, honest & Zeal for the Service of the Church to all the province.

To remove all pretence from the Adult Slaves I shall baptise of their being free upon that Account, I have thought fit to require first their consent to this following declaration *You declare in the Presence of God and before this Congregation that you do not ask for the holy baptism out of any design to free yourself from the Duty and Obedience you owe to your Master while you live, but meerly for the good of Your Soul and to partake of the Graces and Blessings promised to the Members of the Church of Jesus Christ.* One of the most Scandalous and common Crimes of our Slaves is their perpetual Changing of Wives and husbands, which occasions great disorders: I also tell them whom I baptise, *The Christian Religion dos not allow plurality of Wives, nor any changing of them: You promise truly to keep to the Wife you now have till Death dos part you.* I[t] has been Customary among them to have their feasts, dances, and merry Meetings upon the Lord's day, that practice is pretty well over in this Parish, but not absolutely: I tell them that present themselves to be admitted to Baptism, they must promise they'l spend no more the Lord's day in idleness, and if they do I'l cut them off from the Comunion.

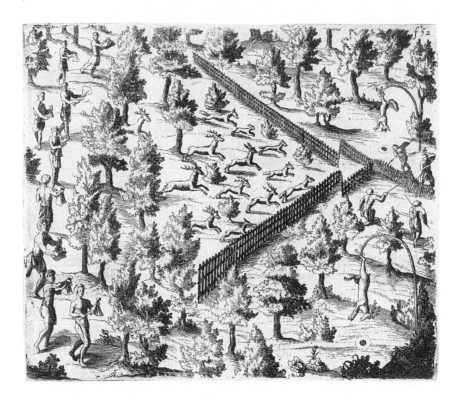

Native Americans hunting deer. From Samuel de Champlain, *Voyages et descovertures faites en la Nouvelle France* (1619). Courtesy of the John Carter Brown Library at Brown University.

These I most humbly Submit to the judgment of my Superiors whose Commands and instructions I will follow while I live: I see with an incredible joy the fervor of several of those poor Slaves. Our free Indians our Neighbours come to see me, I admire the sense they have of Justice, and their patience; they have no Ambition; as for their sense of God, their Notions are obscure indeed, but when we take pains to Converse with them, in a jargon they are able to understand: We perceive their Souls are fit Materials which may be easily polish't, they agree with me about the duty of praying, & doing the good & eschewing the evil. The late Colonel Moore and our present Governor have in a great measure put a Stop to their perpetual murdering one another which some of them cannot to this day conceive to be evil. Some of them to whom the Devil has formerly appeared, as they coldly declared to myself, say that evil Spirit never incites them to any thing more than hatred, revenge, and Murder of those that offend them.

I am told still that if anything opposes the publishing of the Gospel among the Indians it shall be the manner how our Indian Trade is carryed on, chiefly the fomenting of War among them for our people to get Slaves.

THE SOUTH CAROLINA ASSEMBLY DESCRIBES THE YAMASEE WAR AND STONO REBELLION (1740)

From *Report of the Committee Appointed by the General Assembly of South Carolina in 1740* (Charleston, S.C., 1887), 14–15, 17–19.

In 1715 Peace being sometime concluded between the Crowns, the Yemassee Indians, who before the settlement of this Province, had lived in amity with the Government at St. Augustine, but afterwards Removed and Settled on a Body of land opposite Port Royal Island living Contiguous to and in the most Intimate manner with the settlers in those parts, having been Ill used By some of the Traders amongst them, were so far Disgusted that they Broke out in war with this Province, by massacreing, on the 15th April, above eighty of the Inhabitants of Granville County. But it was manifest that they were prompted to this severe Resentment of their usage, whatever it as, by the Spaniards at St. Augustine. For though those Yemassees had, During Queen Anne's war, been the greatest Instruments of Constantly Disturbing and harrassing them in so much that not a man dared for a long time to go out of the sight of the Castle, and Destroying even their Castle, yet on the very day this war Broke out the Yemassees shewed so much Confidence in the Spaniards that they sent away their women and children in their own boats by water to Augustine, and having Ravaged the Country, Killed many more and doing all the mischief they could, so that all the Southern parts were broken up to about the Distance of 20 miles from Charlestown, they themselves soon after Retreated to St. Augustine also, where they were Received, Protected, and Encouraged to make frequent Incursions from thence into the Settlements of this Province; and being oftentimes headed by Spaniards, they cut off several of the settlers and Carried off their slaves. The slaves themselves at length, taking advantage from those things, deserted their own accord to St. Augustine, and upon being Demanded back by this Government, they were not Returned. . . .

In 1738, although Peace subsisted, and Governour Johnston, after his arrival here, renewed the before mentioned Stipulation, another method was taken up by the Spaniards to answer their Ends. Hitherto the Government of St. Augustine had not dared to acknowledge, much less to Justify, the Little Villanies and violences offered to our Properties, but now an Edict of his Catholic Majesty himself was Published by beat of Drum Round the town of St. Augustine, where many Negroes, belonging to English Vessels, which carried thither Supplies of Provisions, &c., had the opportunity of hearing it, promising Liberty and protection to all slaves that should desert thither from any of the English Colonies, but more especially from this, and Least that should not prove sufficient of itself, Secret measures were taken to make it Known to our Slaves in General, in Consequence of which numbers of Slaves did, from time to time, by Land and water, Desert to St. Augustine, and the better to facilitate their escape, carried off their masters' Horses, Boats, &c. — Some of them first Committing murder, and were accordingly received and declared free. Our Present Lieut. Govern'r, by Deputies sent from hence on that occasion to Signior Don Manuel de Montiano, the Present Govern'r of St. Augustine, Set forth the manner which those slaves had Escaped, and Redemanded them pursuant to the stipulation between the two Governments, and to the peace subsisting between the Crowns. Notwithstanding which, though that Government acknowledged those Slaves to be there, yet producing the King of Spain's said Edict, he Declared that he could not Deliver them up without a positive order for that Purpose from the King, and that he should continue to Receive all others that should Resort thither, it having been an article of Complaint against his Predecessour that he had not put the said Edict in force Sooner. The Success of those Deputies being too well known at their Return, Conspiracies were formed and attempts made by more Slaves to Desert to Augustine, but as every one was by this time alarmed with apprehensions of that nature, by great vigilance they were prevented from succeeding.

In Sept'r. 1739, our Slaves made an Insurrection at Stono, in the Heart of our settlements not 20 miles from Charlestown, in which they massacred 23 whites after the most Cruel and Barbarous manner to be conceived, and having got arms and ammunition out of the store, they bent their Course to the Southward, burning all the Houses on the Road, but they marched so slow in full confidence of their own Strength, from their first success, that they gave time to a party of our Militia to Come up with them. The number was in a manner Equal on both sides, and an Engagement wherein one fought for Liberty and Life, the other for their Country and everything that was dear to them, ensued such as may be supposed in such a case, but by the Blessing of God the Negroes were Defeated, the greatest part being Killed on the spot or taken, and those that then escaped were so closely pursued and hunted, day after day, that in the End all but 2 or 3 men were Killed or Taken and Executed. That the Negroes would not have made this Insurrection had they not Depended on St. Augustine for a place of Reception afterwards was very certain, and that the Spaniards had a hand in prompting them to this particular Action, there was but little Room to Doubt. For in July preceding, Don Pedro, Capt. of the Horse at St. Augustine, came to Charlestown in a Launch with 20 or 30 men (one of which was a Negro that spoke English very well), under a Pretence of Delivering a letter to General Oglethorpe, altho' he could not possibly be Ignorant that the General resided at Frederica, not half the Distance from St Augustine; and in Return he was seen at Times to put into every one of our Inlets on the Coast. And in the very month in which the above Insurrection was made, the General acquainted our Lieut. Gov'r by the Letter that the Magistrates at Savannah in Georgia had seized a Spaniard, whom he took to be a priest and that they thought, from what they had Discovered, that he was Employed by the Spaniards to procure a general Insurrection of the Negroes. On this occasion Every Breast was filled with concern, Evil Brought home to us within our very Doors awakened the attention of the most unthinking. Every one that had any relation, any Tie of nature, every one that had a life to lose, were in the most Possible manner Shocked at such Danger daily hanging over their Heads. With Regret we bewailed our peculiar case that we could not Enjoy the Benefits of peace like the Rest of mankind, and that our Industry Should be the means of taking from us all the Sweets of life and of Rendering us Liable to the Loss of our Lives and Fortunes. With Indignation we looked at St Augustine like another Sallee, (Alsatia?) that Den of thieves and Ruffians, Receptacle of Debtors, Servants, and Slaves, Bane of Industry and Society, and Revolved in our minds all the Injuries this Province had Received from thence ever since the first Settlement; that they had from first to Last in times of Profoundest Peace, both Publickly and privately, by themselves, Indians and Negroes, in every shape, molested us, not without some Instances of uncommon Cruelty. . . .

RICHARD LIGON RECORDS A SLAVE REBELLION, AND SLAVE RELIGION, ON BARBADOS (1657)

From Richard Ligon, *A True and Exact History of the Island of Barbadoes*, second edition (London, 1673), 45–48.

. . . some cruel Masters will provoke their Servants so, by extream ill usage, and often and cruel beating them, as they grow desperate, and so joyn together to revenge themselves upon them.

A little before I came from thence, there was such a combination amongst them, as the like was never seen there before. Their sufferings being grown to a great height, and their daily complainings to one another (of the intolerable burdens they labour'd under) being spread throughout the Island; at the last, some amongst them, whose spirits were not able to endure such slavery, resolved to break through it, or dye in the act; and so conspired with some others of their acquaintance, whose sufferings were equal, if not above theirs; and their spirits no way inferiour, resolved to draw as many of the discontented party into this plot, as possibly they could; and those of this perswasion, were the greatest numbers of Servants in the Island. So that a day was appointed to fall upon their Masters, and cut all their throats, and by that means, to make themselves only freemen, but Masters of the Island. And so closely was this plot carried, as no discovery was made, till the day before they were to put it in act: And then one of them, either by the failing of his courage, or some new obligation from the love of his Master, revealed this long plotted conspiracy; and so by this timely advertisement, the Masters were saved: Justice Hethersall (whose servant this was) sending Letters to all his friends, and they to theirs, and so one to another, till they were all secured; and, by examination, found out the greatest part of them, whereof eighteen of the principal men in the conspiracy, and they the first leaders and contrivers of the plot, were put to death, for example to the rest. And the reason why they made examples of so many, was, they found these so haughty in their resolutions, and so incorrigible, as they were like enough to become Actors in a second plot, and so they thought good to secure them; and for the rest, to have a special eye over them.

It has been accounted a strange thing, that the Negroes, being more than double the numbers of the Christians that are there, and they accounted a bloody people, where they think they have power or advantages; and the more bloody, by how much they are more fearful than others: that these should not commit some horrid massacre upon the Christians, thereby to enfranchise themselves, and become Masters of the Island. But there are three reasons that take away this wonder; the one is, They are not suffered to touch or handle any weapons: The other, That they are held in such awe and slavery, as they are fearful to appear in any daring act; and seeing the mustering of our men, and hearing their Gun-shot, (than which nothing more is terrible to them) their spirits are subjugated to so low a condition, as they dare not look up to any bold attempt. Besides these, there is a third reason, which stops all designs of that kind, and that is, They are fetch'd from several parts of Africa, who speak several languages, and by that means, one of them understands not another: For, some of them are fetch'd from Guinny and Binny, and some from Cutchew, some from Angola, and some from the River of Gambia. And in some of these places where petty Kingdomes are, they sell their Subjects, and such as they take in Battle, whom they make slaves; and some mean men sell their Servants, their Children, and sometimes their Wives; and think all good traffick, for such commodities as our Merchants send them.

When they are brought to us, the Planters buy them out of the Ship, where they find them stark naked, and therefore cannot be deceived in any outward infirmity. They choose them as they do Horses in a Market; the strongest, youthfullest, and most beautiful, yield the greatest prices. Thirty pound sterling is a price for the best man Negroe; and twenty five, twenty six, or twenty seven pound for a Woman; the Children are at easier rates. And we buy them so, as the sexes may be equal; for, if they have more Men than Women, the men who are unmarried will come to their Masters, and complain, that they cannot live without Wives, and desire him, they may have Wives. And he tells them, that the next ship that comes, he will buy them Wives, which satifies them for the present; and so they expect the good time: which the Master performing with them, the bravest fellow is to choose first, and so in order, as they are in place, and every one of them knows his better, and gives him the precedence, as Cows do one another, in passing through a narrow gate; for, the most of them are as near beasts as may be, setting their souls aside. Religion they know none; yet most of them acknowledge a God, as appears by their motions and gestures: For, if one of them do another wrong, and he cannot revenge himself, he looks up to Heaven for vengeance, and holds up both his hands, as if the power must come from thence, that must do him right. Chaste they are as any people under the Sun; for, when the men and women are together naked, the never cast their eyes towards the parts that ought to be covered; and those amongst us, that have Breeches and Petticoats, I never saw so much as a kiss, or embrace, or a wanton glance with their eyes between them. Jealous they are of their Wives, and hold it for a great injury and scorn, if another man make the least courtship to his Wife. And if any of their Wives have two Children at a birth, they conclude her false to his Bed, and so no more adoe but hang her. We had an excellent Negro in the Plantation, whose name was Macow, and was our chief Musician; a very valiant man, and was keeper of our Plantine-Grove. This Negroe's Wife was brought to bed of two Children, and her Husband, as their manner is, had provided a cord to hang her. But the Overseer finding what he was about to do, enformed the Master of it, who sent for Macow, to disswade him from this cruel act, of murdering his Wife, and used all perswasions that possibly he could, to let him see, that such double births are in Nature, and that divers presidents were to be found amongst us of the like; so that we rather praised our Wives, for

their fertility, than blamed them for their falseness. But this prevailed little with
him, upon who custom had taken so deep an impression; but resolved, the next
thing he did, should be to hang her. Which when the Master perceived, and
that the ignorance of the man, should take away the life of the woman, who was
innocent of the crime her Husband condemned her for, told him plainly, that if
he hang'd her, he himself should be hang'd by her, upon the same bough; and
therefore wish'd him to consider what he did. This threatning wrought more
with him then all the reasons of Philosophy that could be given him; and so let
her alone; but he never car'd much for her afterward, but chose another which
he lik'd better. For the Planters there deny not a slave, that is a brave fellow, and
one that has extraordinary qualities, two or three Wives, and above that number
they seldom go: But no woman is allowed above one Husband.

At the time the wife is to be brought a bed, her Husband removes his board;
(which is his bed) to another room (for many several divisions they have, in
their little houses,) and none above six foot square. And leaves his wife to God,
and her good fortune, in the room, and upon the board alone, and calls a neighbour to come to her, who gives little help to her delivery, but when the child is
born, (which she calls her Pickaninny) she helps to make a little fire near her
feet, and that serves instead of Possets, Broaths, and Caudles. In a fortnight,
this woman is at work with her Pickaninny at her back, as merry a soul as any
is there: If the Overseer be discreet, she is suffer'd to rest her self a little more
than ordinary; but if not, she is compelled to do as others do. Times they have
of suckling their Children in the fields, and refreshing themselves; and good
reason, for they carry burthens on their backs; and yet work too. Some women,
whose Pickaninnies are three years old, will, as they work at weeding, which a
stopping work, suffer the wee Pickaninny, to sit a stride upon their backs, like
St. George a Horse-back; and there Spur his mother with his heels, and sings
and crows on her back, clapping his hands, as if he is mean to flye; which the
mother is so pleas'd with, as she continues her painful stooping posture, longer
than she would do, rather than discompose her Jovial Pickaninny of his pleasure, so glad she is to see him merry. The work which the women do, is most of
it weeding, a stooping and painful work; at noon and night they are call'd home
by the ring of a Bell where they have two hours time for their repast at noon;
and at night, they rest from six, till six a Clock next morning.

On Sunday they rest and have the whole day at their pleasure; and the most
of them use it as a day of rest and pleasure; but some of them who will make
benefit of that dayes liberty, go where the Mangrave trees grow, and gather the
bark, of which they make ropes, which they truck away for other Commodities,
as Shirts and Drawers.

In the afternoons on Sundayes, they have their Musick, which is of kettle drums, and those of several sizes; upon the smallest the best Musician playes, and the other come in as Chorasses: the drum all men know, has but one tone; and therefore variety of tunes have little to do in this musick; and yet so strangely they varie their time, as 'tis a pleasure to the most curious ears, and it was to me one of the strangest noises that ever I heard made of one tone; and if they had the variety of tune, which gives the greater scope in Musick, as they have of time, they would do wonders in that Art.

8

AFRICANS AND ATLANTIC WORLD SLAVERY

In 1626, not long after the Dutch purchased the "Island Manhattes" from the Lenni Lenape Indians, the first enslaved people arrived on that island. The Dutch West India Company owned these eleven slaves, and used them to build the colony's fort, to construct roads, and to clear trees and brush. When the Dutch established farms, slaves began working on those as well. New Amsterdam slowly saw its slave population grow. In the 1650s, the Netherlands lost control of Brazil to Portugal, and when that happened, slavery became even more entrenched in the social and economic fabric of Manhattan, a trading center that was more needed than ever in Dutch commerce. An especially large delivery of African people arrived on board the *Witte Paert* in 1655: three hundred men, women, and youths had been stowed in the ship's hold, under such wretched conditions that the stench of urine, feces, and other human waste stunk across the city's wharfs. Although Charles Town would later surpass it, by the 1660s New Amsterdam had become mainland North America's key port in the slave trade.[1]

Because of their lack of large-scale plantations, we often do not associate the northern colonies with slavery. The actual slave population lagged in the colonies north of the Chesapeake, and the number of slaves, both African and Indian, grew larger the further south you went, from Virginia to Carolina to the Caribbean. Yet the northern colonies all had slaves, and more importantly, port cities like New York, Newport, and Philadelphia were integral to the broader Atlantic slave trading system. Traders in the north bought and sold slaves, arranged for their transportation, and consumed the goods their labor produced. In early America, no region was without slaves, and all colonies played roles in

Atlantic slavery, which composed both the most vital and vitiating link joining the societies of Europe, Africa, and North and South America.

The opening of the traffic in enslaved African people began in the late medieval period when Portugal colonized the west coast of Africa. The Portuguese called the coastal region of present-day Ghana the Gold Coast, which spoke to their initial colonizing intentions: the discovery of precious metals. In 1482 the Portuguese founded the port of Elmina on the Gold Coast, physically moving a pre-built medieval fortress there that became the Castle São Jorge da Mina. Trade and mining along the Gold Coast did bring significant wealth into Portuguese coffers, first in gold, then in slaves. The Dutch would conquer Elmina in 1637, but by 1682, the fort and surrounding town had about 20,000 residents, making it the largest European settlement in West Africa.[2]

The Portuguese also evangelized the kingdom of Kongo, south of the Gold Coast region, where Christianity made its deepest early impact in West Africa. The Portuguese did not entirely colonize Kongo, yet Kongolese elites and royalty accepted Christian teachings from almost the beginning of interactions with Europeans. Some of these elites traveled back and forth from Portugal, learning Portuguese and Latin, and Catholic theology, and introducing the king of Kongo, Nzinga a Nkuwu, to Christianity. The king received Christian baptism after receiving revelatory dreams and miracles, including the finding of a peculiar cross-shaped black stone near the kingdom's capital. In the early sixteenth century, Kongolese king Afonso I called upon Saint James the Greater (the patron saint of Spain and Portugal) under duress in a battle, and subsequently routed his enemies. His foes "saw a white cross in the sky and a great number of armored horsemen which so frightened them that they could think of nothing else but to flee." Saint James's Day, July 25, became a Kongolese national holiday, and Christian figures became central to Kongolese cultural identity. Afonso arranged for the education of the Kongolese elites in Catholicism, including his own son Henrique, who eventually became a priest and bishop.[3]

Understanding African religious beliefs prior to European contact presents challenges similar to that of pre-contact Native Americans. A paucity of written records, and the biases of European accounts, obscures our view. Nevertheless, some common themes emerge about African religions as Christians observed them: there was a spiritual realm, which humans could not see, but which could impinge on human affairs. Divine or spirit beings could send revelations to communicate with humans. Humans could appease spiritual powers through the use of charms, prayers, and sacrifices, and some gained access to malevolent spiritual power through witchcraft and sorcery. Those who died passed into the spiritual otherworld. Although Europeans often reacted with puzzlement or disdain toward West African religious practices, the theologies behind these practices offered certain points of commonality with late medieval Christianity. Those commonalities set the stage for the emergence of African Christianity in both eastern and western regions of the Atlantic basin. As with some Native American people, many Africans' lack of concern for precise doctrine facilitated their adherence to Christianity, even if that adoption was not as wholesale as European missionaries might have liked.[4]

A French merchant and writer named Jean Barbot wrote about his visits to the African coast in the late 1600s, concluding that the native peoples were "gross ignorant pagans." He observed that many West Africans wore charms to preserve them from danger, and that they had a supreme god, Canou, whom they saw as an omniscient being who would judge all people according to their works. Observing one fertility ceremony, Barbot watched as participants dabbed their cheeks with blood and then powdered their faces with rice meal. They broke off an orange tree and sacrificed a chicken, allowing the bird's blood to drip into the stump. This was to ensure "success in their business of the next day, which was to begin sowing of the rice," Barbot concluded. The region's priests or shamans were also considered healers and herbalists. Barbot explicitly compared the shamans' social and religious roles to the priests found among the natives of Florida, and of New France, connecting sites of cultural interaction across the far-flung Catholic Atlantic.[5]

Many of the earliest Africans whom Europeans shipped to and throughout the Americas were what historian Ira Berlin has termed "Atlantic creoles," those familiar already with Atlantic trade networks. They spoke languages of those networks, in addition to local African languages in which they were raised. ("Creoles" may include people of mixed-race background, with multiple cultural influences and competence in more than one language.) Many of them had knowledge of Christian or Muslim practices, and although they may not have repudiated the animistic religions of their upbringing, many were comfortable with supplementing those practices with devotion to Jesus or to Allah.

These pioneering creoles came to European colonies in the Americas that initially featured a mixed labor system with white, Indian, and African servants and slaves. Only later would the societies from the Chesapeake southward make the shift to plantations worked by non-creole Africans, who came directly from Africa's interior. The non-creoles would be relatively unfamiliar with European language, culture, or religion. The early growth of slavery in New Netherland, then, was not all that different from that in the Chesapeake—there was no strict racialized hierarchy between different kinds of workers. New Netherland's slaves mingled with Dutch settlers as well as Germans, French Protestants, and Jews. Many of these early slaves worked on their own, on a contract basis, learning the Dutch language and often joining the Dutch Reformed Church. During the first decades of slavery in New Amsterdam, around twenty-six black couples married in the town's Dutch church, and baptized their children there as well.[6]

These creole slaves marked the early scenes of African slavery in the New World, but in most locations south of the Middle Colonies, the creole migrants were supplanted upon the coming of plantation agriculture. The large-scale production of a cash crop—sugar, rice, or tobacco—required the involuntary importation of legions of workers from Africa. Many of them could expect either to die en route across the Atlantic, or soon after arriving, due to disease or the harsh conditions of working in the fields. Plantation agriculture dated back to the medieval period in the Old World, and by the late sixteenth century, sugar cultivation on plantations became a fixture in South American colonies. The plantation regime then transformed the Caribbean colonies, and finally the southern mainland colonies of North America. All these became "slave societies," meaning not just ones that had slaves, but places where economy and society were inextricably shaped by slavery. Slaves represented a conspicuous presence, and were often the majority of the population.

Race was not originally the defining feature of the labor systems of the western Atlantic world. Indentured whites, Native Americans, and creole Africans might well serve in the same areas or on the same farms. But as the system focused increasingly on the work of Africans, it also became more racially defined, both in practice and in law. In Barbados, early laws tended to distinguish between the free and unfree, instead of white and black. In the 1650s, however, as the massive turn to sugar began, evidence appeared of special legal disadvantages for black slaves. In 1661 the Barbadian assembly passed separate legal codes for the "good governing of servants," and for the "better ordering and governing of Negroes." African, Negro, and slave were assumed to be the same things in the latter code. It characterized African workers as a "heathenish, brutish, and an uncertain dangerous pride of people." "Heathen" implied non-Christian, while "brutish" implied animal-like qualities, and "uncertain" meant unstable and untrustworthy. White indentured servants were granted some basic civil rights under their code; slaves were not. Slaves (any "Negro") who physically assaulted a "Christian" could be whipped for the first offense, have his or her "nose slit" for the second, and face execution for a third incident. The separation of free and slave in Barbados was now enshrined in laws with both religious and racial overtones.[7]

Jamaica adopted this kind of slave code sooner in its evolution as a sugar colony than Barbados did. Jamaica briefly tried cocoa as its principal crop in the 1660s, but switched to sugar in the 1670s. By the early 1670s, blacks accounted for half the island's population, and whites struggled to suppress runaways and violence against the masters. By the 1680s Jamaica's African population had grown to about 24,000, while the number of whites declined to about 7,500. In 1681, the Jamaican assembly passed a servant and a slave code, following precedents established in Barbados. The Jamaican politicians not only made a clear distinction between indentured servants and slaves, but also introduced the actual word "white" into the legislation, adding to the English repertoire of terms for racial differences. In earlier Caribbean laws, "Christian" had usually stood for white, but the term "white" had appeared occasionally in earlier European and colonial literary sources and legal codes. In a 1676 letter to South Carolina's governor, for instance, the English Lords of Trade inquired "what number of Whites, Blacks, or Mulattos" had been born in the colony in recent years. The implicit problem with contrasting "Christians" and "slaves" was that doing so raised the question of whether Africans who converted to Christianity would necessarily gain their freedom. A 1684 Jamaican act made clear that conversion did not alter one's enslaved status. Carolina lawmakers adopted much of the 1684 Jamaica slave law in their own 1691 statute, just as the mainland lower South was settling on rice as its slave-grown cash crop.[8]

As noted by Anglican missionary Francis Le Jau, South Carolina pioneered a system of severe punishments against slaves, who after the Yamasee War of 1715 were generally presumed to be African. In Carolina's 1696 Slave Act, the colony stipulated that male or female runaways would be branded with the letter R. For a second offense, owners could cut off an ear of a female slave, or the testicles of a male slave. The law threatened to seize the slaves of owners who refused to follow through on these measures. A 1701 law added that a gelded slave who ran away again could have one of his Achilles' tendons severed, and also placed major restrictions on slaves' ability to congregate and carry guns.[9]

The practice of castration caused a furor in a Baptist congregation in Carolina in 1710, prompting them to write a fellow Baptist congregation in England to inquire whether they should discipline a master who made "a eunuch of his slave." The Carolina church explained that the law endorsing gelding was necessary, as it would prevent "vagrancy, theft, robbery, insurrections, and out-rages" by the slaves. The church further suggested that masters should follow the Old Testament and enact more severe punishments for a "heathenish servant," since blacks were "rude, unpolished people, whose nature requires a stricter hand." Carolina slaves were familiar with cattle herding, including the gelding of young bulls, and the threat and practice of castration implicitly served as a "method of bestializing black men," and furthered the distance between white and African workers.[10]

Virginia's turn to slavery transpired over a longer period of time, as its supply of African slaves in the early and mid-1600s was limited by imperial and economic factors in the broader Atlantic world. Virginia planters struggled to establish the colony as an important player in the transatlantic slave trade. But those Virginia elites who had the resources and connections turned to slave labor in the tobacco fields as soon as they could. On the eve of Bacon's Rebellion in the 1670s, large-scale planters who owned mostly black instead of white laborers had begun to emerge in the Tidewater region of Virginia. Bacon's Rebellion—fueled by resentments of white servants who had lived through their terms of indenture—may have implicitly cautioned some planters of the risks of overdependence on white indentured servants. But many of those planters had already begun building their workforce upon African slaves, anyway. By the 1710s, a number of the large planters had hundreds of slaves working for them, with relatively few white servants, and even modest landowners were getting access to affordable enslaved people.[11]

As seen in the Caribbean and lower South, the growth of African slavery in Virginia came with increased codification of racial categories that set "black" or "negro" apart from "white" or "Christian." This created anxiety about the sexual mixing of races, which precipitated a 1662 Virginia law stipulating that "children got by any Englishman upon a negro woman" would follow the sta-tus of the woman, meaning that mixed-ethnicity children born to a black slave woman would be slaves, too. It also threatened punishments against any "Chris-tian [who] shall commit fornication with a negro," implying that Africans were by definition non-Christian (ignoring the slaves who had Christian influences in their African background, or who affiliated with Anglican churches in the colony). Yet in 1667 the legislature passed another statute regarding slave chil-dren, clarifying that when masters allowed the children of slaves to be baptized, that did not make the children free. The legislature hoped to relieve masters from fear of Christianizing their slaves, although the statute does not seem to have had that effect. Many remained reluctant about evangelistic overtures toward blacks and Native Americans. One woman told Anglican minister Morgan Godwyn that baptism was "to one of those [slaves] no more beneficial, than to her black bitch." When Godwyn left Virginia to minister in Barbados, he found similar resistance, as some planters believed that "baptizing of their negroes is the ready way to have all their throats cut," or to foment slave rebellion.[12]

The laws of early Virginia mixed religious and racial categories to define the nature of slavery. A 1682 statute specified that slaves, whether Africans, Indians, or "Moors," were people brought into the colony who did not have a Christian background. A 1705 law specified the rights of "white Christian" servants, admonishing masters to show "Christian care and usage of all Christian servants." It remained silent about the rights of (African, or perhaps Indian) slaves, and prohibited "negros, mulattos, or Indians" from owning Christians as servants. It warned again of punishments for interracial sex or marriage, deploring the "abominable mixture and spurious issue" that resulted from such unions. It also sought to prevent ministers from conducting mixed-race marriages, with the threat of fines of ten thousand pounds of tobacco for doing so.[13]

West African society was transformed by the expansion of plantation slavery in the Americas. Early African slaves tended to be those who were already in some sort of legal or religious trouble prior to their journey to the western hemisphere. But after 1700, African slave hunters penetrated deep into the interior of the continent, stealing millions of Africans away, and slaying millions more. In this sense, a cruel "new world" came to the African continent in the wake of European colonization of West Africa and the Americas, just as a new world came to the Native Americans of the North and South American interiors. Young, healthy African men were special targets of the slave merchants, who knew that the American plantations were hungry for workers with the greatest endurance.[14]

The "Middle Passage" across the Atlantic was viewed with horror by many captives, who were already distressed by their capture and journey to the coast, and who assumed that a terrible fate awaited them at the other end of the ocean journey. Hundreds of slave ships experienced attacks from the shore or, more commonly, insurrections on board the ships. Reflecting the increased rate of trafficking, most of the documented onboard insurrections happened in the eighteenth century. Slave ship rebels were generally unsuccessful, failing to take control of the boat or to kill the crew. The slaves themselves generally bore the brunt of deaths and injuries in attempted insurrections, although many more died of exposure and disease than in shipboard battles. Perhaps the greatest effect that such incidents had on the traffic in slaves was that the ever-present specter of revolt raised shippers' costs in crewmen and weaponry. The cumulative financial burden of this added inefficiency in the trade may have prevented hundreds of thousands of extra slaves from being shipped across the ocean in the eighteenth century.[15]

Just as Africans participated in the enslavement of Africans, they also played a role in policing slaves during the Middle Passage. According to one captain's explanation, African "guardians" were bought by English Royal African Company, with thirty or forty assigned to a ship, to keep slaves from fighting among themselves, to report any rebel schemes, and to make sure the slaves cleaned up the "filth and nastiness" that accumulated in the ship's hold. Male guardians were probably in the majority, but ships also employed female guardians. The captain deputized some guardians with a cat of nine tails as a sign of authority. Although the guardians remained subordinate in the hierarchy of the trafficking system, police duties offered a more interdependent relationship with the ship's captain, and more power over fellow slaves. Yet when the ships arrived in the Americas, the separate status of the guardians vanished, at least from the European perspective. Presumably most of them were sold in the same procedures as all the other slaves on board.[16]

The latest statistics on the transatlantic slave trade suggest that nearly eleven million Africans disembarked in the Americas from the sixteenth to the nineteenth centuries. The Portuguese dominated the early and late stages of the trade, and accounted for a little under half of the whole traffic in African slave transports over its 350-year history. Accordingly, Portuguese Brazil was the most common point of disembarkation for enslaved African workers, roughly 4.8 million of them. The British Caribbean was the next most common destination, followed by Spanish America and the French Caribbean. American historians have devoted a disproportionate share of attention to chattel slavery in the area that would become the United States, because of an interest in national history, the growth of American slavery, and the coming of the Civil War. Although slavery in the United States continued to grow numerically and geographically after the United States banned slave imports in 1808, it is instructive to note that mainland North America only came in fifth in the rank of areas receiving the most slaves from Africa. (Some 10 percent of mainland American slaves arrived there in ships that had originally delivered slave cargos to the Caribbean.) All told, mainland North America received roughly 388,000 slaves over the course of the trade. Over time the United States' traffic in slaves became dependent on natural increase of the enslaved population, and slave trading in and among the southern states. Almost four million slaves lived in the United States as of the 1860 census.[17]

In the British Caribbean, Jamaica and Barbados led the way in the slave trade by taking in about a million and a half million people, respectively. Saint-Domingue (Haiti) received about three-quarters of a million enslaved laborers from Africa, while Carolina and Georgia received about 210,000 Africans over the course of the trade. The Chesapeake brought in 128,000 enslaved people during its two centuries of international slave trafficking.

The numbers in the slave trade are dizzying, yet each one of these millions of people had his or her own personal story of injustice and deprivation. Most of those individual stories are now lost to history. In terms of arrivals, Africans far outpaced European immigrants to the Americas from Columbus's journeys to the 1820s; about four of every five immigrants was from Africa during this period. It was the largest long-distance coerced transport of people in history, and it dramatically reworked the demographics of both sub-Saharan Africa and the Americas. The changes were all the more marked when you consider the collapse of Native American populations that was transpiring at the same time. Although death rates could also be high for African slaves, the flood of forced immigration, especially in the eighteenth century (and in Brazil in the first half of the nineteenth) had a kind of replacement effect in the Americas. Africans provided a dispensable, and yet indispensable, labor force for the sugar, rice, and tobacco plantations of the New World.

In British America, Jamaica became the most profitable colony by the mid-eighteenth century, the base of a sugar empire built upon the lives and deaths of hundreds of thousands of Africans. By 1788, 90 percent of the Jamaican population was enslaved. It was a deadly place for all who came there. Few Jamaicans, whether white, black, or Native American, were born on the island. Death could come in many ways: from disease, exhaustion, malnutrition, violence, or accidents. The merchant ships that traversed the Atlantic frequently carried disease with them. Smallpox was the most feared, as it ruthlessly cut down those who had not already endured a childhood bout with it. Inoculation remained an experimental (and risky) preventive, and did not become widely practiced in the Caribbean until the early nineteenth century. Masters put a premium on slaves who displayed scars from earlier cases of smallpox and thus had gained immunity from it.[18]

Sugar was Britain's most profitable colonial crop, and it was also the most taxing and dangerous. The "great gang," composed largely of (relatively) able-bodied men, did the most backbreaking, perilous labor in Jamaica, cultivating and harvesting the sugarcane fields, working the sugar mills, and tending their processing fires. These slaves could expect to be sick or injured perhaps half of their prime working years, and the male slaves (those who had not perished at some earlier stage of the trade, of course) died at an average age of forty-two years. Women were often shielded from the most demanding field work, and though they hardly lived under safe conditions, they could expect to live several years longer on average than male slaves. Infants born to slaves lived under tenuous conditions, and perhaps half of all children born did not survive to their first birthday. Because so many children died, Jamaica's slave population was not growing by natural means; more imported workers were always required.[19]

Although masters wanted to keep their slaves alive for economic reasons, overseers often drove slaves beyond limits of endurance in a short-sighted quest for productivity. One planter complained about an aggressive overseer who was "driving everything to the Devil to make a great crop to get himself a name," but who did not realize that it would ruin the labor force for future seasons. The slaves would say of such whites that "Buckra make whip do every ting, but make life, and that it no able to do, but make plenty dead."[20]

It is hard to know the precise extent or frequency of the brutality meted out against the slaves of the Caribbean, because masters and overseers would not have typically recorded the most violent treatment of African workers. Among the most grotesque punishments recorded came from the diary of Thomas Thistlewood, a Jamaican planter who was known to deal out whippings of up to 350 lashes. He also practiced what he called "Derby's dose," in which he had a slave defecate into the mouth of an offender, and then had that slave's mouth wired shut.[21]

In terms of imported workers and death rates, the Caribbean islands were the chief scene of action in British America. But the lower South and Chesapeake had, by the beginning of the eighteenth century, entered an era of deep dependence on African laborers, as well. Carolina saw its population go from roughly 1,200 people (one thousand whites and two hundred blacks) at the time of Charles Town's founding to a black majority population of about 18,400 in the year 1720 (9,900 blacks, 6,500 whites, and 2,000 Native American slaves). By that year, rice dominated South Carolina's economic fortunes, accounting for more than half of the value of all of the colony's exports. The same changes would come later to the coastal plains of the Georgia colony (founded in 1732) and East Florida (which came under British control in 1763).[22]

By 1720 three-quarters of South Carolina slaves worked on plantations with ten or more slaves, and the dominance of large-scale planters grew as the

Slaves processing sugar. From *Naaukeurige versameling der gedenk-waardigste zee en land-reysen na Oost en West-Indiën* (1707). Courtesy of the John Carter Brown Library at Brown University.

American Revolution approached. As in the Caribbean, most of the plantation slaves worked in gangs. Planting began in the spring and ran nearly into summer. Slaves alternately flooded and drained the fields to manage moisture and weeds, but some mid-summer weeding happened by hand. Harvest came in September, and the picked rice was threshed and processed, often by female workers. The winter months saw field preparations, plus elaborate construction projects, as the laborers built canals, gullies, dams, and floodgates to manage the low country tidal flows.[23]

The conditions on the rice plantations led to high rates of mortality, which, if perhaps not as high as in Jamaica or Barbados, still meant that slaves were not naturally replacing themselves with children. Distressed and exhausted slave women suffered high rates of miscarriage and low rates of conception, and many of their children died in infancy. Some Carolina rice slaves had a certain degree of autonomy, in spite of the difficult work conditions. Planters delegated direct oversight to slave drivers, who were often slaves themselves. Workers also operated by the task system, under which planters mandated that a day's worth of work entailed a certain amount of planting, threshing, and cleaning. Once that standard task was completed, slaves might be able to reclaim some of their days for their own purposes. Masters and owners were often not resident at the farms themselves, but lived a day or more of travel away in Charles Town or another coastal location.[24]

Slaves represented about half the population of Charles Town through the eighteenth century, but slave life there, and in Savannah, was quite different from that on the plantations. Slaves lived in proximity to white families, often serving them as cooks and maids. Most of them learned English, and many adopted Christianity. Slave men worked at the docks, in the transport of goods, and as craftsmen. Indeed, certain slave artisans became so sought after that some whites complained that they pushed Anglos out of the skilled labor market.[25]

Enslaved women in the rice ports also occupied an entrepreneurial niche as street vendors. These women so dominated the cities' markets for meat and produce that whites grumbled about their extortionist practices. A 1778 visitor estimated seeing some sixty "Negro wenches" in Charles Town's markets and lanes, selling baked items, vegetables, and fruits. Some women would meet blacks coming from the countryside and buy up their farm products before they got to Charles Town's streets, leading some residents to protest that "poor honest white people" were cut out of the business. Anxieties about black economic independence could mix with other kinds of fears. One runaway slave advertisement warned about a woman named Amey, who was a "pretty black [and] very sensible" slave, and was apparently somewhere "in Charles-Town selling things about the streets, pretending to be a free woman."[26]

Dependence on African slavery also swept over the Chesapeake in the late 1600s. White indentured servants and Indian slaves had worked alongside Africans there for years, just as in the lower South, but the 1690s saw exponential growth in the number of slaves imported, especially along the York River, north of Williamsburg. Between 1695 and 1700, Virginians imported more enslaved Africans than they had in the previous two decades combined. Yet that pattern of importation never translated into a numeric majority of slaves, in contrast to South Carolina and the Caribbean. By 1740, Africans and African Americans represented about 40 percent of Virginia's population, up from about 10 percent in the 1680s. Increasing numbers of these slaves came straight from Africa's interior, with little knowledge of English language or culture. Many wore the distinctive marks of their African tribal society, including filed teeth and ritual scars.[27]

The case of St. Mary's, Maryland's southernmost county on its western shore, illustrated how the turn to heavy use of African slaves slowly proceeded in one

Chesapeake location. As of the 1720s, slave owning there was still dominated by small numbers of elite families, and probate records indicate that two-thirds of white households still did not possess enslaved workers. But the slave population was poised for dramatic growth, from about 12 percent of St. Mary's people to about 40 percent on the eve of the Revolution. By the 1730s, the Chesapeake slave population was contributing to its own growth through natural increase. Over the middle decades of the eighteenth century, many more farmers acquired slaves. By the 1760s, records suggested that a majority of white households in St. Mary's owned slaves. The use of slave labor became common among non-owners, too, as large planters rented the labor of their surplus slaves to farmers of more modest means. Thus, between 1720 and 1760, St. Mary's, and much of the Chesapeake region, transformed from an elite slave-owning society to a popular slave society, where the institution of slavery touched the lives of a majority of white families.[28]

We can only piece together fragmentary records, at best, of most of the slaves coming into the Chesapeake in the decades before the American Revolution. We know more about a young enslaved woman named Kate than we do about most others. In 1772, she came to Bermuda Hundred, in the fast-growing Virginia Piedmont area, which received a much higher percentage of imported slaves in the years after 1750 than it had in the earlier colonial decades, when the eastern Tidewater area dominated the slave trade. By the end of the Revolution, more of Virginia's roughly 230,000 slaves lived in the Piedmont than the Tidewater. Newspapers advertised that the *Polly*, the ship that brought Kate to Virginia, had a cargo of four hundred and fifty "fine healthy slaves" total. A local legislator, Paul Carrington, bought fifty of those slaves, planning to resell almost all of them, save for the girl he estimated was eighteen years old, whom he gave the English name Kate. Soon Carrington sent Kate a short distance away to his Robins plantation, which was worked exclusively by slaves—Carrington did not even keep a white overseer there. Just under two years after her arrival in the Piedmont, Kate gave birth to a son. She went on to have three other recorded children, all of whom likely became the property of Paul Carrington, Jr., when he married in 1785. We do not know who fathered her children. Her arrival in the Piedmont instead of the Tidewater, and residence at a middling plantation with some separation from whites, reflected broader trends in the later decades of slavery in the Chesapeake.[29]

The new enslaved arrivals were concentrated on tobacco farms, living under harsh conditions and the threat of (legally backed) punishments for insubordination. In one ugly 1708 instance, Robert "King" Carter asked permission from the Lancaster County court to dismember "two incorrigible negroes of his named Bambarra Harry and Dinah." The court approved his request, hoping that the punishment would promote the "better reclaiming [of] the said negroes and deterring others from ill practices." The Lancaster authorities specifically authorized Carter to "dismember the said negroes . . . by cutting off their toes." Behind closed doors some masters engaged in other punishments, too: Virginia planter William Byrd made a young slave who repeatedly wet his bed to drink a "pint of piss" to teach him a lesson. He and other masters used horse's bits on runaways and other disorderly Africans.[30]

In the northern colonies, slavery never became as integral to the domestic farming economy as it did in regions to the south. But northern seaport merchants invested in the Atlantic slave trade, and slaves continued arriving in those seaports—usually coming from the Caribbean, rather than direct from Africa—in small numbers through the beginning of the Revolution. Slavery was more urban-centered in the north: Philadelphia's population was about one-sixth enslaved in the early eighteenth century. Still, most slaves living in the northern colonies worked on farms in rural areas. One of their most common employments was raising food for export to the land-starved sugar islands. These enslaved people typically worked in small groups alongside whites, including their owners. Compared with the field slaves further south, they tended to have many tasks to do in any season, such as conventional farm work, transport and courier services, and household duties.

In New York City, the North's key slave port, the Anglican Society for the Propagation of the Gospel made a concerted effort to evangelize blacks beginning in the early 1700s. Elias Neau, a French Huguenot and merchant, was the SPG's most important worker there, running a mission school for slaves (both Native American and African), white servants, and free blacks. Neau was flexible in his instruction methods, attempting to use some basic Indian and African dialects to translate the Lord's Prayer, and leaning on hymn-singing for English instruction. As in the southern colonies, Neau's efforts tested the tolerance of New York slave owners, who worried about the subversive effects of literacy, conversion, and baptism. He wrote of encountering "vulgar prejudice in those parts, that if the Negroes were baptized, they would cease to be slaves; though neither the law nor the gospel does authorize any such opinion." As in other English colonies, some New York statutes suggested that slaves were not Christians, implying that conversion might entail emancipation. Neau advocated a new law that would allay slave masters' fears. New York should stipulate that the slaves' "religion should make no alteration in their condition," Neau believed.[31]

Neau got his wish with a 1706 New York law that countered the "ground-less opinion that hath spread itself in this colony, that by the baptizing of such Negro, Indian or Mulatto slave they would become free and ought to be set at liberty." The law made clear that baptizing a slave did not mean that he or she would attain liberty. It also stipulated that children born to slaves, re-gardless of ethnicity, would follow the legal status of the mother and remain slaves themselves. This statute heralded the transition seen earlier in the South and Caribbean toward identifying non-white skin color, including "Negro, In-dian, Mulatto, and Mestee," with hereditary slavery. Neau's school suffered a dreadful setback in the early 1710s when about twenty-five enslaved New York-ers rose up against whites, burning a number of residences and killing nine people. Twenty-one alleged conspirators were tortured and killed by a variety of means, including hanging and burning at the stake. Some white New Yorkers blamed Neau and his school for stoking the revolt. Two of Neau's pupils were among the executed. One of the students, Robin, was accused of killing his master, who had refused to allow Robin to be baptized. For his crimes, Robin was hung up in chains and allowed slowly to die. The city passed new rules limiting slaves' ability to congregate or move about town, especially after dark. Neau kept operating his school until his death ten years later, in 1722, but he complained that white New Yorkers were "strangely prejudiced with a horrid notion, thinking that the Christian knowledge will be a means to make their slaves more cunning and apt to wickedness."[32]

The 1712 city code made manumission of slaves more difficult in New York, and also barred freed blacks from owning property. These restrictions prevented the advent of distinct black residential areas of the city. Instead, the largest num-bers of slaves actually lived in the most affluent areas of town, on the property of New York's wealthiest families. The most distinct separate space granted to African Americans in New York was their burial ground, used for most of the eighteenth century, and only rediscovered in 1991 as a result of construction of an office building in the city. Excavations discovered the skeletons of more than four hundred men, women, and children, but tens of thousands of Africans may have been interred in the burial ground during the eighteenth century.[33]

Tinkering with the city's slave codes did not alleviate the dread of slave revolt, an anxiety that afflicted any colony with significant concentrations of enslaved people. This fear exploded in New York in 1741 when a multiethnic group of African, Afro-Spanish, Irish, and Anglo laborers began burning city buildings, beginning with Fort George, the center of British imperial power in the colony. An epidemic of arson followed over several weeks, with a number of dwellings, outbuildings, and businesses succumbing to flames. Affluent whites suspected that workers were setting the fires. Then whites caught a slave, Cuffee, running away from the scene of a storehouse fire. Cuffee's arrest led to the detention of more than a hundred blacks.[34]

An investigation traced the conspiracy to the tavern of a white family, the Hughsons, who had cooperated with certain slaves to sell stolen materials. Two slaves named Caesar and Prince, along with Caesar's girlfriend, Irishwoman "Peggy" Sorubiero, worked at the center of the ring of thieves and arsonists. About thirty Irish men and women were ostensibly involved. They cooperated with a number of Gold Coast slaves, who took courage from the ministrations of "Doctor" Harry, who may have served as an Akan shaman. In the end, New York authorities executed thirty slave men as co-conspirators, and expelled more than seventy enslaved men and women.[35]

The arson conspiracy hardly led to the demise of New York City slavery, but it did help change its characteristics. In the 1740s, male slaves went from a slight majority to a strong minority of the town's slave population. Whites, convinced that black creoles with a Spanish background were central to the uprising, imported more slaves directly from Africa. But the black population in New York City remained fairly stable, at about 20 percent.[36]

From northern seaports to southern and Caribbean plantations, many early Americans came to the New World as enslaved or indentured laborers. The institution of slavery was an inescapable economic and social reality in most places. Even in the rural North, owning a slave or two became one of the common prerogatives of the genteel. But whatever its prominence in places like New York City, the influence of slavery grew heavier the further south you went in the Americas. As of 1720, there were about 14,000 slaves in the northern colonies, with the highest number in New York. More than 42,000 lived in the Chesapeake, more than half of those in Virginia. Almost 12,000 lived in South Carolina. Far more slaves—more than all the mainland British colonies combined—lived in the British Caribbean, especially Jamaica and Barbados. By 1730, some 219,000 enslaved people labored in those islands.[37]

The degrading conditions and ravenous demands of slavery prompted a great deal of legal and theological boundary-setting, in hopes of stabilizing and justifying the system. Yet from New York to Jamaica, white colonists could never escape the fear that the enslaved, indentured workers, and their free collaborators would pursue liberty by whatever means necessary. The experiences of New York City in 1712 and 1741, South Carolina in 1739, and countless other small-scale episodes of resistance confirmed that elites had reason to be concerned.

A RUNAWAY SLAVE AD (1766)

From Maryland *Gazette* (Annapolis), Oct. 2, 1766.

Ran away from the subscriber living in Baltimore-Town, on the 7th of September last, a Negro Girl, named Hagar, about 14 years of age, of a brownish complexion, remarkable long fingers and toes, has a scar under one of her breasts, supposed to be got by a whipping: Had on when she went away, an Osnabrig[38] shift and petticoat very much patched, and may now be very ragged, an iron collar about her neck, which it is probable she has got off, as it was very poorly riveted. She is supposed to be harboured in some negro quarter, as her father and mother encourages her in elopements, under a pretence that she is ill used at home.

Whoever takes up the said girl, and brings her to me, shall have, if taken 10 miles from home twenty shillings reward, if 20 miles forty shillings, and if further three pounds, paid by

WILLIAM PAYNE

N.B. All persons are forbid to harbour the said negro, as they shall answer the contrary at their peril.

JAMAICAN SLAVES' BURIAL RITUALS (1739)

From Charles Leslie, *A New and Exact Account of Jamaica*, 3d ed. (Edinburgh, 1740), 322–26.

The most of the Slaves are brought from the Coast of Guiney; when they first arrive, 'tis observed they are simple and very innocent Creatures, but they soon turn to be roguish enough: And when they come to be whipt, urge the Example of Whites for an Excuse. Their Notions of Religion are very inconsistent, and vary according to the different Countries they come from: But they have a Kind of occasional Conformity, and join without Distinction in their solemn Sacrifices and Gamboles. They generally believe there are Two Gods, a good and a bad One; the First they call *Naskew* in *Papaw* Language, and the other *Timnew*: The good God, they tell you, lives in the Clouds, is very kind and favours Men; 'twas he that taught their Fathers to till the Ground, and to hunt for their Subsistence. The evil God sends Storms, Earthquakes, and all Kind of Mischief. They love the one dearly and fear the other as much. Their Notions are extremely dark; they have no Idea of Heaven, further than the Pleasures of returning to their native Country, where they believe every Negroe goes after Death: This Thought is so agreeable that it cheers the poor Creatures, and makes the Burden of Life easy, which otherways would be quite intolerable. They look on Death as a Blessing: 'Tis indeed surprising to see that what Courage and Intrepidity some of the will meet their Fate, and be merry in their last Moments; they are quite transported to think their Slavery is near an End, and that they shall revisit their happy Native Shores, and see their old Friends and Acquaintance. When a Negroe is near about to expire, his Fellow-Slaves kiss him, with a good Journey, and send their hearty Recommendations to their Relations in *Guiney*. They make no Lamentations, but with a great deal of Joy inter his Body, firmly believing he is gone home and happy.

When any Thing about a Plantations is missing, they have a solemn Kind of Oath which the oldest Negroe always administers, and which by them is accounted so sacred, that except they have the express Command of their Master or Overseer, they never set about it, and then they go very solemnly to Work. They range themselves in that Spot of Ground which is appropriate for the Negroe's Burying place, and one of them opens a Grave. He who acts the Priest takes a little of the Earth, and puts into every one of their Mouths; they tell, that if any has been guilty, their Belly swells and occasions their Death. I never saw an Instance of this but one; and it was certainly Fact that a Boy did swell, and acknowledged the Theft when he was dying: But I am far from thinking there was any Connection betwixt the Cause and the Effect; for a Thousand Accidents might have occasioned it, without having Recourse to that foolish Ceremony.

I have discoursed them about the Immortality of the Soul, and some other important Points, but I observed their Notions of these Matters were extremely obscure, yet from the Customs they use at their Burials, I can gather some faint Remains of their Knowledge in that Article. When one is carried out to his Grave, he is attended with a vast Multitude, who conduct his Corps in something of a ludicrous Manner: They sing all the Way, and they who bear it on their Shoulders, make a Feint of stopping at every Door they pass, and pretend, that if the deceast Person had received any Injury, the Corps moves to-

Runaway slave advertisement, North Carolina
Gazette (1752). Courtesy of the University of North
Carolina at Greensboro, University Libraries.

wards that House, and that they can't avoid letting it fall to the Ground when
before the Door. When they come to the Grave, which is generally made in
some Savannah or Plain, they lay down the Coffin, or whatever the Body happens to be wrapt up in; and if he be one whole Circumstances could allow it
(or if he be generally liked, the Negroes contribute among themselves) they
sacrifice a Hog. The Way they do it is this; the nearest Relation kills it, the
Intrails are buried, the four Quarters are divided, and a kind of Soup made,
which is brought in a Calabash or Gourd, and, after waving it three Times, it is
set down, then the Body is put in the Ground; all the while they are covering
it with Earth, the Attendants scream out in a terrible Manner, which is not the
Effect of Grief but of Joy; they beat on their wooden Drums, and the Women
with their Rattles make a hideous Noise: After the Grave is filled up, they place
the Soup which they had prepared at the Head, and a Bottle of Rum at the
Feet. In the mean Time cool Drink (which is made of the *Lignum: Vitæ* Bark)
or whatever else they can afford, is distributed amongst these who are present;
the one Half of the Hog is burnt while they are drinking, and the other is left to
any Person who pleases to take it; they return to Town or the Plantation singing
after their Manner, and so the Ceremony ends.

COURT RECORDS OF THE ARSON PLOT IN NEW YORK CITY (1741)

From Daniel Horsmanden, *The New York Conspiracy, Or A History of the Negro Plot* (New York, 1810), 35–40.

"Gentlemen of the grand jury,

It is not without some concern that I am obliged at this time to be more particular in your charge, than for many preceding terms there hath been occasion. The many frights and terror which the good people of this city have of late been put into, by repeated and unusual fires, and burning of houses, give us too much room to suspect, that some of them at least did not proceed from mere chance, or common accidents; but on the contrary, from the premeditated malice and wicked purposes of evil and designing persons; and therefore it greatly behoves us to use our utmost diligence, by all lawful ways and means, to discover the contrivers and perpetrators of such daring and flagitious undertakings: that, upon conviction, they may receive condign punishment. . . .

"I am told there are several prisoners now in jail, who have been committed by the city magistrates, upon suspicion of having been concerned in some of the late fires; and others, who under pretence of assisting the unhappy sufferers, by saving their goods from the flames, for stealing, or receiving them. This indeed, is adding affliction to the afflicted, and is a very great aggravation of such crime, and therefore deserves a narrow inquiry: that so the exemplary punishment of the guilty (if any such should be so found) may deter others from committing the like villainies; for this kind of stealing, I think, has not been often practised among us.

"Gentlemen,

"Arson, or the malicious and voluntary burning, not only a mansion house, but also any other house, and the out buildings, or barns, and stables adjoining thereto, by night or by day, is felony at common law; and if any part of the house be burned, the offender is guilty of felony, notwithstanding the fire afterwards be put out, or go out of itself.

"This crime is of so shocking a nature, that if we have any in this city, who, having been guilty thereof, should escape, who can say he is safe, or tell where it will end?

"Gentlemen,

"Another Thing which I cannot omit recommending to your serious and diligent inquiry, is to find out and present all such persons who sell rum, and other strong liquor to negroes. It must be obvious to every one, that there are too many of them in this city; who, under pretence of selling what they call a penny dram to a negro, will sell to him as many quarts or gallons of rum, as he can steal money or goods to pay for.

"How this notion of its being lawful to sell a penny dram, or a pennyworth of rum to a slave, without the consent or direction of his master, has prevailed, I know not; but this I am sure of, that there is not only no such law, but that the doing of it is directly contrary to an act of the assembly now in force, *for the better regulating of slaves*. The many fatal consequences flowing from this prevailing and wicked practice, are so notorious, and so nearly concern us all, that one would be almost surprised, to think there should be a necessity for a court to recommend a suppression of such pernicious houses: thus much in particular; now in general.

"My charge, gentlemen, further is, to present all conspiracies, combinations, and other offences, from treasons down to trespasses; and in your inquiries, the oath you, and each of you have just now taken will, I am persuaded, be your guide, and I pray God to direct and assist you in the discharge of your duty.

Court adjourned until to-morrow morning ten o'clock.

SUPREME COURT.

WEDNESDAY, APRIL 22.

Present, the second justice. The court opened, and adjourned until ten o'clock to-morrow morning.

The grand jury having been informed, that Mary Burton could give them some account concerning the good stolen from Mr. Hogg's, sent for her this morning, and ordered she should be sworn; the constable returned and acquainted them, that *she said she would not be sworn, nor give evidence*; whereupon they ordered the constable to get a warrant from a magistrate, to bring her before them. The constable was some time gone, but at length returned, and brought her with him; and being asked why she would not be sworn, and give her evidence? She told the grand jury she would not be sworn; and seemed to be under some great uneasiness, or terrible apprehensions; which gave suspicion that she knew something concerning the fires that had lately happened: and being asked a question to that purpose, she gave no answer; which increased the jealousy that she was privy to them; and as it was thought a matter of the utmost concern, the grand jury was very importunate, and used many arguments with her, in public and private, to persuade her to speak the truth, and tell all she knew about it. . . .

Accordingly, she being sworn, came before the grand jury; but as they were proceeding to her examination, and before they asked her any questions, she told them she would acquaint them with what she knew relating to the goods stolen from Mr. Hogg's, but would say nothing about the fires.

This expression thus, as it were providentially, slipping from the evidence, much alarmed the grand jury; for, as they naturally concluded, it did by construction amount to an affirmative, that she could give an account of the occasion of the several fires; and therefore, as it highly became those gentlemen in the discharge of their trust, they determined to use their utmost diligence to sift out the discovery, but still she remained inflexible, till at length, having recourse to religious topics, representing to her the heinousness of the crime which she would be guilty of, if she was privy to, and could discover so wicked a design, as the firing houses about our ears; whereby not only people's estates would be destroyed, but many person might lose their lives in the flames: this she would have to answer for at the day of judgment . . . and she gave the following evidence, which however, notwithstanding what had been said, came from her, as if still under some terrible apprehensions or restraints.

Deposition, No. 1—Mary Burton, being sworn, deposeth,

1. "That Prince (*a*) and Caesar (*b*) brought the things of which they had robbed Mr. Hogg, to her master, John Hughson's house, and that they were handed in through the window, Hughson, his wife, and Peggy receiving them, about two or three o'clock on a Sunday morning. (*c*)

2. "That Caesar, prince, and Mr. Philipse's negro man (Cuffee) used to meet frequently at her master's house, and that she had heard them (the negroes) talk frequently of burning the fort; and that they would go down to the Fly (*d*) and burn the whole town; and that her master and mistress said, they would aid and assist them as much as they could.

(*a*) Mr. Auboyneau's negro.	(*b*) Vaarck's negro.
(*c*) 1st March, 1740, 1.	(*d*) The east end of the city.

3. "That in their common conversation they used to say, that when all this was done, Caesar should be governor, and Hughson, her master, should be king.

4. "That Cuffee used to say, that a great many people had too much, and others too little; that his old master had a great deal of money, but that, in a short time, he should have less, and that he (Cuffee) should have more.

5. "That at the same time when the things of which Mr. Hogg was robbed, were brought to her master's house, they brought some indigo and bees wax, which was likewise received by her master and mistress.

6. "That at the meetings of the three aforesaid negroes, Caesar, Prince, and Cuffee, at her master's house, they used to say, in their conversations, that when they set fire to the town, they would do it in the night, and as the white people came to extinguish it, they would kill and destroy them.

7. "That she has known at times, seven or eight guns in her master's house, and some swords, and that she has seen twenty or thirty negroes at one time in her master's house; and that at such large meetings, the three aforesaid negroes, Cuffee, Prince, and Caesar, were generally present, and most active, and that they used to say, that the other negroes durst not refuse to do what they commanded them, and they were sure that they had a number sufficient to stand by them.

8. "That Hughson (her master) and her mistress used to threaten, that if she, the deponent, ever made mention of the goods stolen from Mr. Hogg, they would poison her; and the negroes swore, if ever she published, or discovered the design of burning the town, they would burn her whenever they met her.

9. "That she never saw any white person in company when they talked of burning the town, but her master, her mistress, and Peggy."

This evidence of a conspiracy, not only to burn the city, but also destroy and murder the people, was most astonishing to the grand jury, and that any white people should become so abandoned as to confederate with slaves in such an execrable and detestable purpose, could not but be very amazing to every one that heard it; what could scarce be credited; but that the several fires had been occasioned by some combination of villains, was, at the time of them, naturally to be collected from the manner and circumstances attending them.

THE GLORIOUS REVOLUTION AND THE LINKS
OF EMPIRE IN ENGLISH AMERICA

When word arrived in Boston in April 1689 that King James II had been deposed, the people of Massachusetts expelled their own royal authorities. Thousands of armed men went into the streets, demanding and securing the surrender of Dominion of New England governor Edmund Andros. Massachusetts immediately pursued a positive relationship with the new English monarchs, William and Mary, and a restoration of the revered Massachusetts charter, which John Winthrop had won for the colony six decades earlier.

A rebellion normally warrants an official explanation, and Boston leaders issued one on April 18, 1689. But the way it began seemed peculiar—the inhabitants began the story of their own Glorious Revolution with a reference to the (bogus) "horrid Popish Plot" to assassinate Charles II and forcibly convert Protestants, the ostensible conspiracy that had sensationalized London in 1678. In that plot, the Bostonians said, the "bloody devotees of Rome had in their design and prospect no less than the extinction of the Protestant religion." New England had become a target of that global scheme too, led by those who "were intoxicated with a bigotry inspired into them by the great Scarlet Whore." That malicious Catholic spirit, the Boston Declaration trumpeted, led to the revocation of the Massachusetts charter and the creation of the larger Dominion of New England in 1686. Even troubles with Native Americans on the New England frontier appeared to be a "branch of the plot." Thus, Bostonians seized upon their opportunity to expel the Andros regime and save New England from the power of "popery and slavery."[1]

The Glorious Revolution shook English America from New England to the Caribbean. Although it played out differently according to local circumstances, religious and political fears blended together to make 1688–89 a watershed in the English monarchy, empire, and colonies. It marked the key political turning point in the history of English colonization of America prior to the American Revolution. Although the Glorious Revolution revealed the depth of American colonial unrest in 1689, it also set the stage for decades of relative peace between crown and colonists. English Americans believed that James II's removal had committed England (after 1707, Britain) to defending Protestant Christianity around the world.

American colonists' reactions to the Glorious Revolution centered on two common themes: the venting of political resentments, and the rhetoric of anti-Catholicism. The most straightforward ouster of a royal governor came in the Leeward Islands and Antigua, where Sir Nathaniel Johnson was an unapologetic supporter of James II. Even after it became clear that William and Mary had supplanted King James II, Johnson would not declare his support for the new monarchs. Rumors began to swirl that Johnson was contemplating an alliance with the French on nearby Martinique. Under pressure, Johnson resigned and left the islands in July 1689.[2]

In Barbados, which saw nothing of the massive unrest in Massachusetts, anti-Catholicism still became a useful tool for Lieutenant Governor Edwyn Stede to consolidate his faction's control of the island. In the 1680s, new fear about the Catholic menace mixed with ever-present white Barbadian anxieties about slave revolt. Fear of revolt focused not only on Africans, but also on Irish Catholic indentured servants, who remained a significant presence in the sugar islands. Long-standing fears of Spanish power also meshed in the 1680s with growing concern about French assertiveness in the Caribbean.[3]

This backdrop of imperial and religious uncertainty explained how Stede and his Barbadian supporters responded to Catholic or crypto-Catholic leaders on the island, especially Irish attorney general Thomas Montgomery, who was reputed to be Catholic, and Catholic planter Willoughby Chamberlain. When these two welcomed the ministrations of a shadowy French Jesuit priest called "Father Michel," Barbadian Protestant fears began to surge. Father Michel reportedly held mass at the homes of both Montgomery and Chamberlain, with perhaps hundreds of Irish workers in attendance. Montgomery and Willoughby, some whispered, recruited fellow Catholics to these services, even promising "treats" for the island's Catholics who attended.[4]

All the colonies went through unsettling months from November 1688 to April 1689, as they received contradictory reports about what was happening in England. By February, Lieutenant Governor Stede and his followers had decided to cast their lot with William and Mary, but issued an equivocal statement of support. All it made clear was that Catholicism was bad, lamenting the "subtile, wicked, horrid and abominable contrivances of Popish Recusants, and more particularly those called Jesuits, who going about with their head and father the devil . . . have for many years been undermining and endeavoring to destroy, overturn, and utterly abolish the truly ancient, Catholick and apostolic Protestant faith." But Stede hesitated to endorse the expulsion of James II, still not knowing which way events would proceed. Stede cleverly played on Barbadian fears about French and Irish Catholicism, however, to target his enemy Thomas Montgomery. Charging Montgomery and Willoughby with sheltering the Jesuit missionary and planning a Catholic coup, Stede had both of them imprisoned. The elusive Father Michel left the island. Stede even wrote to New York's ill-fated populist governor Jacob Leisler in 1690 and commended him for his "Zeale in Their Majties Service" and in "the true Reformed Religion." Anti-Catholicism could only do so much for Stede, however, as he remained unpopular with many Barbadian planters. By 1692 he had returned to England, where Stede received knighthood from King William.[5]

In Maryland, Catholic and anti-Catholic sentiment synced more closely with reality than anywhere else in America. Its proprietary government remained in Catholic hands, in spite of an overwhelming Protestant popular majority. Resentment against colony's Catholic proprietors had been building for years, and in the late 1680s anti-Catholic rumors began to fuel rebellious sentiments among Maryland's Protestants. According to one "unbiased account," Maryland Protestants resented the "growth of Popery and arbitrary power in England" and in their colony, where five Catholic officials monopolized political power. They imposed unreasonable taxes on the people, and offered only a "bare, politic pretence of liberty of conscience" for Protestants. Catholic priests and Jesuits reportedly lived in luxury, while Protestant pastors struggled with poverty.[6]

Maryland Protestants asserted that when rumors began to circulate about James II being deposed, Catholic officials and Jesuits spread lies among the people, telling them that James II was defeating the "rebels as they termed the Protestants." They warned of the formidable power of New France and its Native American allies, and predicted that soon the French and Indians would overrun the English Protestant colonies. With these falsehoods and other "black mouth scandals and impious curses" the Catholics railed against the new monarchs, and against English Protestantism.[7]

Maryland officials took steps to ward off rebellion in early 1689, including an order that all colonists deliver their firearms to county sheriffs (ostensibly for repair and readiness in the event of a Dutch invasion). Then rumors spread that a massive Indian and French army had assembled, possibly at proprietor Lord Baltimore's behest, with a commission to invade the colony and destroy Protestants. Proprietary officials went out of their way to deny and defuse tales of a Catholic-Indian scheme, and the council president even mandated that sheriffs return the people's guns to them.[8]

Virginia formally hailed William and Mary as the new monarchs in late April 1689. Maryland's refusal to follow its southern neighbor's example became more conspicuous as weeks passed. It is not clear whether this delay was intentional or not. Lord Baltimore, residing in England, claimed that he had repeatedly sent instructions to the colony to affirm the new king and queen. The postponed announcement opened the door for outright Protestant rebellion, a movement that found its leader in the Maryland proprietors' longtime rival, John Coode. Ten years earlier Coode had been tried for sedition in the colony for supposedly threatening to overthrow the proprietary government, which Coode claimed was in league with Indians.[9]

Coode had been ordained as an Anglican minister, in addition to his service as a leader in Maryland's militia. His anti-Catholic zeal was unsurpassed. Coode led an armed force against the colonial capital of St. Mary's. While proprietary officials tried to raise support to defend the colony, they found many Marylanders unwilling to assist them. Many believed "that Coode rose only to preserve the country from the Indians and papists and to proclaim the king and queen." Lord Baltimore's supporters gave up the capital and retreated to Baltimore's nearby estate. But Coode's men surrounded the property and summoned reinforcements. Meanwhile, the proprietary faction alleged that Coode's supporters continued spreading rumors about a Catholic-Indian conspiracy, and that they had even forged a letter regarding news of an Indian attack on English settlers. Baltimore's allies had no option but to surrender, which they did on August 1, 1689, removing the last Catholic center of power in English North America. Benedict Calvert, the fourth Lord Baltimore, would regain control of the colony only by renouncing Catholicism and adopting Anglicanism. George I granted the Maryland title to the fifth Lord Baltimore (who also accepted Anglicanism) after the fourth's death in 1715.[10]

Massachusetts governor Edmund Andros was not a Catholic, but his opponents accused him of Catholic sympathies, and of conspiring with Native Americans and the French. This was ironic, as Andros had attempted in the mid-1680s to bring the region of Maine more fully under Massachusetts's control. (In between Massachusetts and Maine, New Hampshire had received a separate royal charter in 1679, but became part of the Dominion of New England in 1686.) Maine was especially volatile territory, as it stood in between poorly defined French and English imperial claims, and it was the traditional home of Abenaki Indians, who tended to side with the French (who were less land-hungry than the English). Andros had commissioned several attacks on the French post and Jesuit mission of Castine, on the coast at the mouth of the Penobscot River. English families at Casco, Maine, soon faced strikes in 1688 from Native American allies of the French. A series of raids followed, and Andros decided to lead an expedition far into northeastern Maine, establishing garrison posts along the way.[11]

These actions made sense to Andros, but edgy colonists interpreted them in a malevolent light. Why drain New England towns of fighting-age men just when their families needed them most? Rumors swirled that Andros meant to leave Massachusetts vulnerable, and that he might encourage Mohawk Indians to attack the colony while his expedition was detained in the northeast. Andros was further rumored to have visited "praying" Indians at Natick, giving them Catholic devotional books, and promising them that a combined French, Irish, and Indian army would overrun Boston. (People in New York heard similar reports about Andros's dark designs for Manhattan.)[12]

When news arrived in August 1688 that James II's wife had given birth to a son, James Francis Edward (who would become known as the "Old Pretender"), everyone knew that unless James II was removed, the monarchy would remain Catholic. Some in England argued that the child was an impostor, snuck in just to secure the royal line for Catholics. Andros and Dominion officials dutifully mandated days of thanksgiving to be celebrated in New York and Boston, in spite of the agitation over the news of the successor's birth. The Dominion government specifically wrote to Cotton Mather, one of Boston's leading pastors, insisting that he have the thanksgiving proclamation read aloud at his church, and that he "do then and there publicly stir up your hearers to the solemn work of the day, as is required by the same, and hereof you are not to fail." Congregationalist ministers were less than enthused about the thanksgiving mandate for the royal heir. After the ousting of James II and Andros, Mather exuded about "what has been done by God for the English Nation, in its deliverance, from the spiritual mischiefs of Popery," praising God that England was no longer "priest ridden by the Janizaries of Antichrist!"[13]

As in Maryland, Andros's officials hesitated to respond to the uncertain reports about James II's removal. In some cases, they repressed the news accounts.

This only fed the anxiety of militant Protestant colonists, and by April 1689, Andros's supporters said that Boston was boiling with "foolish and nonsensical stories, and pretended wonderful discoveries of horrid plots." This was not just a matter of a few anti-Andros officials crafting a pretense for revolution, as Andros's friends noted that the stories captured the imaginations of the "ignorant multitude" and made the majority of the people ready to revolt. Exotic stories flew fast and furious: Andros had taken "all the youth of the country to the eastward, on purpose to destroy them," and he poisoned their rum to do the job. Moreover, rumors insisted that the "Indian war was but a sham," Andros was fraternizing with "Squaws," and he had given orders that no solider was allowed to kill an Indian. Fears of Native Americans and Catholics, and resentments against the Dominion, blended into a toxic anti-Andros mix.[14]

The tension finally exploded on April 18, 1689. For days there was a "general buzzing among the people," Andros wrote, "great with expectation of their old charter." Thousands of people gathered in the streets demanding that Andros surrender and turn over control of the town's two (lightly defended) forts. The governor was detained and reluctantly gave in to the rebels. The royal government was overthrown without any killings. Word of Andros's ouster spread to Long Island, which identified religiously more with New England than New York. Long Island colonists also began removing Dominion of New England officials. Then attention turned to New York City, which was rumored to be the target of a French attack. Others said that royal officials intended to set upon Protestant worshipers the first Sunday of June, killing them in their churches. The besieged lieutenant governor Francis Nicholson faced charges that he was a secret Catholic, and that he was harboring French or Irish Catholic soldiers at the city's fort. Finally the Jacob Leisler–led militia confronted Nicholson and his officials, and secured control of the fort. By June 1689, the Dominion of New England was no more, falling in the wake of James II's removal. Anti-Catholic sentiment focused resentment against the Dominion and other representatives of James II's power in America. Barbados's governor Edwyn Stede had survived by channeling that resentment against actual Catholic officials, but the leaders of Maryland, Massachusetts, and New York failed to direct colonists' fury against anyone but themselves.[15]

The Glorious Revolution did not satiate anti-Catholic sentiment in America; to the contrary, it inaugurated seven decades in which Anglo-Americans would participate in interminable conflicts that they interpreted as episodes in the global Protestant-Catholic clash. In a sense, these conflicts did not resolve until the end of the Seven Years' War in the 1760s. In the meantime, colonial officials embraced the energized Protestant commitment of the English monarchy and empire by attacking French and Spanish American holdings on multiple fronts. In King William's War, which immediately followed the Glorious Revolution, colonial officials sought to dislodge the French from Quebec and the Leeward Islands.

On St. Christopher, Irish servants in the summer of 1689 rose up in the name of James II and sought to "kill, burn, and destroy all that belongs to the Protestant interest in that island." It was at this time that the pro-Stuart (James's family line) governor of the Leeward Islands, Nathaniel Johnson, resigned his charge. Soon the English gave up St. Christopher altogether, but Edwyn Stede assembled a militia to retake the island and stabilize other English possessions. The Barbadians took over the French-controlled St. Bartholomew Island, where the English, in a comical report, claimed to have gotten a Franciscan priest drunk, and he "spoke Latin so fluently on transubstantiation, that he confounded himself on his own argument." The English then recruited a three-thousand-man force that included soon-to-be-pirate William Kidd, and assaulted St. Christopher, routing the island's French, Irish, and Carib Indian defenders. Across the empire, English observers celebrated the victory and hoped that it would "root the French interests out of that part of the world."[16]

Leaders in the Middle Colonies and New England had similar ambitions for "rooting out" the French from Quebec. New France had long been an irritant to English colonists, and in early 1690 a joint French and Indian attack on Schenectady, New York, confirmed many northern colonists' desire to launch an invasion of Canada. Albany merchant Robert Livingston led a delegation to New England to argue for intercolonial cooperation in the fight against the French. The delegates reminded the New Englanders that the French had "gained much upon the Indians by sending their clergymen amongst them not so much to convert their souls as their beaver and other trade to Canada." Livingston called for a combined English campaign against Quebec, believing that if the French were removed, the region's Native Americans would have no choice but to ally with the English. Moreover, Livingston and his men contended that the expedition had transcendent significance, as there were "diverse good omens that God Almighty has determined the downfall of Anti-Christ in our days, [and] this is the only means in all probability to effect it in America."[17]

New Englanders, led by Sir William Phips, initiated the multipronged invasion of Canada by attacking the small, lightly fortified capital of Acadia at Port

Royal. The fort fell easily to Phips's eight hundred men, and the English soldiers captured two Jesuit priests there. Then Phips's troops desecrated Port Royal's Catholic chapel, breaking icons, cutting down the cross, and pulling down the high altar. But Port Royal was the easiest part of Phips's work. French-allied Indians soon resumed their attacks in Maine, but New York's and Massachusetts's leaders struggled to recruit enough soldiers—Anglo or Native American—for the planned overland attack on Montreal, and naval crusade against Quebec. Officials decided to abandon the idea of assaulting Montreal. The erratic New York governor Jacob Leisler was enraged, implying that this setback was yet another episode in the dark popish conspiracy. Leisler went so far as to put Connecticut military leader (and future governor) Fitz-John Winthrop in jail because of the debacle, implying that he was a Catholic sympathizer. Leisler's failed crusade helped to ensure his removal as governor and, ultimately, his execution. He and his supporters never let go of the anti-Catholic narrative they assigned to his troubles, however. Resentful friends of the departed Leisler said his enemies were minions of "the dragon, the whore, and the croaking frogs of the pit."[18]

In spite of the collapse of the venture against Montreal, New Englanders vowed to push forward with the Quebec campaign. They hoped it would ensure the "extirpation or subjugation of the French and Indians, who by the bloody instigation of fiery Jesuits, were designing no less against us and consequently all the English America." While Phips's armada of thirty-four ships and more than two thousand men lumbered up the coast and along the St. Lawrence River, an Indian messenger notified the French of their imminent arrival. By the time they arrived, the city was well prepared, and the English assault turned into a disaster. Phips's ships limped back to New England, buffeted by bad weather and shipboard disease. The confidence that inspired the campaign wilted in the face of failure. Edmund Andros's replacement, Simon Bradstreet, mused that for inscrutable reasons, through a series of unfavorable providences, God had "spit in our face."[19]

The failure of the expedition, as well as continuing threats from France and Spain in the Americas, helped to push most colonists into a deeper, warmer relationship with the English empire than ever before. From the Glorious Revolution through the end of the Seven Years' War in the 1760s, colonists largely understood that, whatever frustrations came along with British imperial authority, they were worth it because Britain was the great world defender of Protestantism. This sentiment took on different nuances across the English colonies: in South Carolina, for example, it helped planters welcome imperial power to combat the Spanish in Florida. The southern elites worried about the attraction that the Spanish might hold for runaway slaves, especially slaves with a Catholic background.

The British Protestant mentality also helped Massachusetts stomach the disappointment of the new charter they received in 1692. Gone was the Dominion of New England, but the new charter did not offer the same kind of independence as had the original Puritan one. The governor of Massachusetts was now a royal appointee, and Congregationalists (no longer in any useful sense "Puritans" after 1692) had to tolerate the presence of other Protestants, including Church of England ministers and missionaries.

New Englanders dealt with the Catholic threat in a direct way because of the still-entrenched presence of French Catholics in Quebec. Even when war was not officially declared in Britain, New Englanders often faced vicious local skirmishes with the French and allied Native Americans. Politicians and pastors made much out of the role of Jesuit missionaries in stirring up Indian conspiracies against the English. Massachusetts's royal governor in 1700 warned the legislature about "French Jesuits debauching those Indians," and lawmakers responded by banning all Catholic priests, including Jesuits, from the province. New England's fear of Jesuit intrigues crested in the 1720s (a time of diplomatic peace between Britain, France, and Spain) during "Father Rale's War," which focused on the ministry of Father Sebastien Rale among Abenakis at Norridgewock, Maine. Concern over Rale's subversive work prompted a 1724 Massachusetts expedition against Norridgewock, in which Massachusetts forces executed Rale on the spot. Boston minister Cotton Mather wrote that "the barbarous and perfidious Indians in our Eastern Country, being moved by the instigation of the Devil and Father Rallee; have begun hostilities upon us. They did it, when the French hopes of a fatal revolution on the British Empire, deceived them." Anger toward the Abenakis, Rale, and the Jesuits telescoped into an episode of transcendent and transatlantic significance.[20]

The colonists' commitment to the British empire became even more fixed after the crisis of succession that followed Queen Anne's death in 1714. She died without surviving children, raising the prospect that a Catholic relative of hers might take the throne. But according to the terms of the 1701 Act of Succession, the crown passed over dozens of closer kin, going to (the non-English-speaking) George I of Hanover in Germany. This seemed to settle the question of the Protestant succession for the foreseeable future. George I's accession spawned a failed 1715 Jacobite uprising in Britain, in which supporters of the Stuart line tried to install Anne's half-brother James Stuart as king. The events of the mid-1710s convinced many in Anglo-America that the Hanoverian line needed prayerful, militant support. Benjamin Colman, the leading pastor in early eighteenth-century Boston, spoke for many when he preached that Americans' "adherence to the Protestant Succession in the House of Hanover, is our fidelity to CHRIST and his holy religion."[21]

For the "average" white colonist, it is difficult to know how much these sorts of imperial sentiments captured their thinking. Undoubtedly it did so more on patriotic holidays such as November 5, or Guy Fawkes' Day, when Anglo-Americans often engaged in anti-Catholic festivities, including burning the pope in effigy. (November 5 originally marked the foiling of Fawkes's plot to blow up Parliament in 1605, but it took on a more providential cast when it also became the day that King William landed in England during the Glorious Revolution.) Regular colonists also clung to the British empire when imperial war came close to their homes, welcoming the supplies and military presence that association with Britain conveyed.

On a day-to-day basis, however, typical farmers and merchants in English America connected with the empire not through politics or war, but through commerce. Although the English colonies never became as profitable as London thought they should be, the colonies remained inextricably connected to England's Atlantic world through buying and selling goods. They exported crops to regional, continental, and European markets, and imported an ever-growing array of products (as well as bound and enslaved workers). As soon as southern planters seized on their cash crop, from Chesapeake tobacco in the 1610s, to Caribbean sugar in the mid-1600s, and to Carolina rice in the early 1700s, their farms and plantations engaged with the transatlantic marketplace. New England and Middle Colonies farmers tended not to have as much of a presence in British and European markets, but starting in the second half of the seventeenth century, they supplied markets in their own seaport towns, and in the land-starved Caribbean. Initial settlements in the backcountry were often more subsistence-oriented, but soon even many backcountry farmers found production outlets at least for regional markets.[22]

Among foodstuffs, West Indies sugar was the key to the British imperial trades. British imports of sugar rose from 8,000 tons in 1663, to over 25,000 in 1710, to 97,000 tons in 1775. Increasingly, that sugar was being consumed in Britain and Ireland—sugar consumption there skyrocketed from four pounds per capita in the early 1700s to eleven pounds at the time of the American Revolution. (This growth correlated to the massive increase in Britain's tea imports from east Asia, which rose a hundredfold in value over that same time period.) Similarly, by 1770 more than 90 percent of the products shipped from the Caribbean to mainland North America was sugar or its derivatives, molasses and rum. Chesapeake tobacco exports slowed in the early eighteenth century, but with the turn to widespread use of African slave labor, British imports of tobacco rose rapidly in the middle decades of the century, tripling between the 1720s and 1770s. Most of that tobacco was re-exported elsewhere in Europe by the 1770s. Likewise, the vast majority of rice and West Indian coffee imported to England and Scotland at mid-century was transported out of the country for sale on the Continent.[23]

Large plantation masters produced primarily for market (and in many cases imported the food needed for daily sustenance), while many small farmers worked primarily for subsistence and engaged local markets only through modest sales and bartering. Perhaps the most typical model was "composite farming," in which a farm family produced for both market and subsistence, the balance between the two depending heavily on prices and the bounty of a particular season. Women and men saw more differentiation in their farm roles over the course of the eighteenth century: while women tended to work in gardens, in chicken coops, and at spinning wheels and looms for subsistence, men were more likely to produce the crops, wood, or meat that went to market. Women also took over the primary responsibility for weaving from men, at least in eighteenth-century New England. Two-thirds or more of rural New England households owned a spinning wheel by mid-century. There was more uniformity to the subsistence aspect of a farm family's work than the market component. The northern colonies might sell surplus apples, fish, beef, pork, or dairy, or they might produce goods like maple sugar, tanned hides, or furniture for sale. The southern colonial farmers and their slaves produced crops like tobacco and indigo that had no role in subsistence, and both sugar and rice growers produced far more of those crops than households needed.[24]

Even in early eighteenth-century America, white colonists had access to a surprising array of consumer goods imported from Britain. In places without stores, peddlers brought items for sale into rural communities. An (unlicensed) peddler named William Moore, for example, came to Berwick, Maine, in 1721. Both men and women purchased his wares: Sarah Gooding bought muslin, silk, and thread, as well as "a yard and quarter of lace for a cap." Patience Hubbard got a pair of garters, while Sarah Stone came away with an unnamed parcel of "small trifles." In much of America, such interactions were the most immediate connections that people like Hubbard and Stone made with what historian T. H. Breen has called the "empire of goods." The number of exports from England to America grew nearly eightfold over the first three-quarters of the eighteenth century. Over roughly the same time period, the mainland American population also grew about eight times over, while exports to Britain expanded by about 500 percent. All this activity suffused the colonies with British goods on the eve of the Revolution.[25]

Anglo-Americans may have been relative latecomers to the revolution in consumption, as historian James Axtell has noted that eastern Native Americans went through a similar process starting in the seventeenth century. The fur trade, from beaver skins in the north to deerskins in the south, offered new sources of cash to many Indians, who used the proceeds to buy European products. Most famously (and damagingly) they bought alcohol and firearms, but the most common products they bought were fabric and clothes. Some have suggested that the fur trade could just as easily be called the cloth trade, so pervasive was British and European fabric in markets and diplomacy with native people. Woolen blanketing was especially valued because it was lighter and dried more quickly than fur-based clothes. James Logan was one of the key merchants in the trade networks with Native Americans in Pennsylvania in the early eighteenth century. His account books from the 1710s show that clothes, fabric, and accessories represented almost 60 percent of the items he imported from Britain and Holland to sell to Native Americans. Firearms and tools composed about 30 percent.[26]

The Anglo-Americans' "consumer revolution" picked up speed in the three decades before the Revolution. Wealthier families could afford more goods than those of modest means, but even poor white families found that by 1750 they could purchase basic furniture, flatware, ceramic dishes, cups, and linens. Coffee, hot chocolate, and tea became common in cities and towns, as well as accompanying items like pewter or silver bowls for table sugar, and sturdier cups suited for holding hot liquids. (One saw similar linking patterns in English consumption—an increasing volume of tea imports from Asia also meant growing sugar imports from the West Indies.) A traveling German pastor, impressed by the wide range of cloths, household goods, and luxury drinks and food he saw, wrote in the early 1750s that "it is really possible to obtain all the things one can get in Europe in Pennsylvania." Although it is challenging to know why particular consumers bought these discretionary products, some have argued that fashionable goods, and the way consumers used them (serving tea, for example), became badges of "membership in class-conscious social groups" in British America. Especially in a colonial setting that could be quite unsettled, buying and using the new products could signify that you and your family belonged to the ranks of the genteel, or at least aspired to belong to that class.[27]

Growing population and social equilibrium in the early eighteenth century, after the ravages of the seventeenth century, facilitated more successful marketing of a diverse range of products among the colonists. In Virginia, to-bacco firms operating out of Glasgow set up many new retail shops in the mid-eighteenth century, enabling small farmers to deal directly with the Scottish importers for goods and credit. A Hanover County merchant noted that twenty-five such stores were within eighteen miles of him, with more set to open soon. A 1728 probate of a rural Virginia store suggests the typical state of the early inventories: numerous containers, from boxes to barrels, held a dizzying array of items, including books, hats, spectacles, stoneware, combs, sugar, tools, ce-ramics, and bread. War and broadly shared Protestant sensibilities undoubtedly bolstered British nationalism in the colonies, but the experience of consuming these kinds of imported goods integrated average white (and sometimes African American and Native American) colonists into the everyday workings of the British empire. It also prepared them to be touchy about imperial policies that might hinder the affordability of those products.[28]

The consumer revolution was seen in luxury items like sugar, tea, wine, or colorful clothes. But the British empire and its colonies also generated an enor-mous range of products to supply the needs of the plantation economy and its workers. Slaves had little discretionary income, or freedom to spend it, but the consumer revolution still touched their working lives. The slaves themselves were made into human commodities. But they also required food, clothing, and farm implements such as the plantation hoe. The Crowley metalworking business of northeastern England was the preeminent supplier of the modest, iron-headed hoe, producing hundreds of thousands of them over the eighteenth century. They tailored different kinds of hoes for different American plantation regions: the Chesapeake, Carolina, and the Caribbean. Each was tailored to the type of work that slaves needed to do in the tobacco, rice, and sugarcane fields. Manufacturers also issued different sizes of hoes for women, men, and children.[29]

The plantation economy and the desire for luxury goods combined in less obvious ways than just sugarcane production. For example, West Indian farmers realized that as they needed to clear land for cultivation, they could also use felled trees as commodities. Not only could they use the timber for building materials, but some special woods, especially mahogany, emerged as material of choice for luxury furniture. These impulses led to dramatic reworking of the Caribbean landscape: already by the 1660s, Barbados was largely deforested. Not long after sugar cultivation took hold, planters found that they needed to import timber from the American mainland. Planters tended to move forward with deforestation, even though some realized that razing the woods meant de-priving themselves of a valuable commodity to export besides sugar. To English settlers in the Caribbean, woods seemed like unused territory, with a murky reputation as havens for runaway slaves. Once the rain forests were decimated, there was little point in replanting trees that could take hundreds of years to mature again into harvestable products. Mahogany's scarcity helped give it an elite aura for consumers in America and Britain. Portrait artists often depicted their subjects seated on, or next to, polished mahogany furniture, which accentuated their other signs of gentility, especially clothes and hairstyles.[30]

The Glorious Revolution represented a hinge moment in colonial American history, as it signaled the colonies' fuller economic, religious, and imperial integration with the English empire. London was now indisputably the colonies' metropolitan core. Especially after the Hanoverian settlement of 1714 left little doubt about the Protestant succession in the British monarchy, colonists expressed religious devotion to the empire and monarch, even as they wished to remain free from imperial meddling and taxes. The Glorious Revolution also signaled the moment at which the mainland and Caribbean colonies began to take on fundamentally different roles in the empire. The large sugar planters came to depend a great deal on imperial support, especially against French and Spanish threats and competition in the sugar trade. By contrast, for the first half of the eighteenth century, the mainland colonies were the beneficiaries of what historians have traditionally called "benign neglect." If the Glorious Revolution did not return quasi-independent status to Massachusetts, both that colony and most of the others on the mainland entered an era of formal sympathy for the empire, along with strong functional autonomy and self-government. The key institutions in this autonomy were the colonies' lower houses of their legislatures. Out from under the more controlling and seemingly ominous policies of the Stuart kings, the mainland colonies thrived and stabilized in the first decades of the 1700s. Growing populations were supplemented by more British and European immigration, much of which expanded into the trans-Appalachian interior. Land ownership for whites remained a more viable prospect on the American mainland than in the Caribbean or in Britain. Although the Caribbean colonies remained attached to the empire in both principle and practice, the mainland colonies stayed under the Protestant canopy of the empire but began to grow independent in ways that neither colonists nor crown fully understood.[31]

It was not coincidental that the commercial and consumer revolutions in Anglo-America came after the Glorious Revolution. By the mid-1700s, Britain had successfully forged an American empire that was producing and receiving more goods in the transatlantic trades, and the colonies were importing thousands of enslaved workers to produce (and consume) many of those goods. Although commerce was the most immediate connection to the empire for many English colonists, the empire's role as the great defender of Protestantism—and opponent of what Boston's leaders called the "Scarlet Whore"—gave it a symbolic capital that helped command the colonists' allegiance, especially as long as Catholic power remained an imminent threat in North America.

THE DECLARATION OF THE REASON AND MOTIVE FOR THE PRESENT APPEARING IN ARMS OF HIS MAJESTY'S PROTESTANT SUBJECTS IN THE PROVINCE OF MARYLAND (1689)

From William Hand Browne, ed., *Archives of Maryland: Proceedings of the Council of Maryland, 1687/8–1693* (Baltimore, 1890), 101–7.

Although the nature and state of Affairs relating to the government of this Province is so well and notoriously known to all persons any way concerned in the same, as to the people Inhabitants here, who are more immediately interested, as might excuse any declaracōn or apologie for this pres^{nt} inevitable appearance; Yet forasmuch as (by the plotte contrivances insinuacōns remonstrances and subscriptions carryed on, suggested, extorted and obtained, by the Lord Baltemore, his Deputys Representatives and officers here) the injustice and tyranny under which we groan, is palliated and most if not all the particulars of our grievances shrowded from the eyes of observacōn and the hand of redress, Wee thought fitt for general satisfaccōn, and particularly to undeceive those that may have a sinister account of our proceedings to publish this Declaracōn of the reasons and motives inducing us thereunto. His Lordships right and title to the Government is by virtue of a Charter to his father Cecilius from King Charles the first of blessed memory how his present Lordship has managed the power and authority given and granted in the same wee could mourn and lament onely in silence, would our duty to God, our allegiance to his Vicegerent, and the care & welfare of ourselves and posterity permit us.

In the first place in the said Charter is a reservation of the fayth and allegiance due to the Crown of England (the Province and Inhabitants being imediately subject thereunto) but how little that is manifested is too obvious, to all unbyasted persons that ever had anything to do here the very name and owning of that Sovereign power is some times crime enough to incurr the frownes of our superiors and to render our persons obnoxious and suspected to be ill-affected to the government. The ill usage of and affronts to the Kings Officers belonging to the customes here, were a sufficient argument of this. Wee need but instance the busines of Mr Badcock and Mr Rousby, of whom the former was terribly detained by his Lordshipp from going home to make his just complaints in England upon which he was soon taken sick, and t'was more then probably conjectur'd that the conceit of his confinement was the chief cause of his death which soon after happened.

The latter was barbarously murthered upon the execucōn of his office by one that was an Irish papist and our Cheif Governor. . . .

In the next place Churches and Chappels, which by the said Charter should be built and consecrated according to the Ecclesiastical lawes of the Kingdom of England, to our greate regrett and discouragement of our religion, are erected and converted to the use of popish Idolatary and superstition, Jesuits and seminarie preists are the only incumbents; (for which there is a supply provided by sending our popish youth to be educated at St Omers) as also the Chief Advisers and Councellors in affaires of Government, and the richest and most fertile land sett apart for their use and maintenance, while other lands that are piously intended, and given for the maintenance of the Protestant Ministry, become escheats, and are taken as forfeit, the ministers themselves discouraged, and noe care taken for their subsistance.

The power to enact Laws is another branch of his Lordshipp's authority, but how well that has been executed and circumstances is too notorious. . . .

Nor is this nullyfyeing and suspending power the only grievance that doth perplex and burthen us in relacōn to Laws, but these laws that are of a certain and unquestioned acceptacōn are executed and countenanced, as they are more or less agreable to the good liking of our Govr in particular, one very good lawe provides that orphan children should be disposed of to persons of the same religion with that of their dead parents. In direct opposition to which several children of protestants have been committed to the tutlage of papists, and brought up in the Romish Superstition. Wee could instance in a young woman that has been lately forced by order of Council from her husband committed to the custody of a papist, and brought up in his religion.

T'is endless to enumerate the particulars of this nature, while on the contrary those laws that enhance the grandeur and income of his said Lordshipp are severely imposed and executed especially one that is against all sense, equity, reason and law punishes all speeches, practices and attempts relating to his Lordship and Government that shall be thought mutinous and seditious by the Judge of the provincial Court, with either whipping, branding, boreing through the Tongue, fines, imprisonments, banishment or death, all or either of the said punishments at the discretion of the said Judges, who have given a very recent and remarkable proof of their authority in each particular punishment aforesaid, upon several the good people of this Province, while the rest are in the same danger to have their words and acōns lyable to the construction & punishment of the said Judges, and their lives and fortunes to the mercy of their arbitrary fancies, opinions and sentences.

TO THESE GRIEVANCES ARE ADDED

Excessive Officers Fees, and that too under Execucōn directly against the Law made & provided to redress the same, wherein there is no probability of a legall remedy, the Officers themselves that are partys and culpable being Judges. The like Fee being imposed upon and extorted from Masters and Owners of Vessels trading into this Province, without any Law to Justifie the same, and directly against the plaine words of the said Charter that say there shall be no imposition or assessment without the consent of the Freemen in the Assembly to the great obstruccōn of trade and prejudice of the Inhabitants.

The like excessive Fees imposed upon and extorted from the owners of Vessels that are built here or do really belong to the Inhabitants contrary to an Act of Assembly made and provided for the same, wherein moderate and reasonable Fees are ascertained for the promoting and incouragement of Shipping and navigation amongst ourselves.

The frequent pressing of men, horses, boats, provisions and other necessarys in time of peace and often to gratifie private designs and occations, to the great burthen and regrett of the Inhabitants contrary to Law and several Acts of Assembly in that case made and provided.

The seirvice and apprehending of Protestants in their houses with armed force consisting of Pap^sts and that in time of peace, thence hurrying them away to Prisons without Warrant or cause of comittment these kept and confined with popish guards a long time without tryall.

Not only private but publick outrages, & murthers committed and done by papists upon Protestants without redress, but rather conived at and tolerated by the cheif in authority, and indeed it were in vain to desire or expect any help or other measures from them being papists and guided by the Councills and instigacōn of the Jesuits, either in these or any other grievances or oppresions, and yet these are the men that are our Cheif Judges at the Comon Law in Chancery of the Probat of Wills and the Affairs of Administration in the Upper House of Assembly, and Cheif military Officers and Commanders of our forces, being still the same individuall persons, in all these particular qualifications & places.

These and many more even infinit pressures and Calamitys, wee have hitherto layne with patience under and submitted to, hoping that the same hand of providence that hath sustained us under them would at length in due time release us. And now at length for as much as it hath pleased Almighty God, by meanes of the great prudence and conduct of the best of Princes our most gracious King William to putt a check to that great inudation of Slavery and Pop-

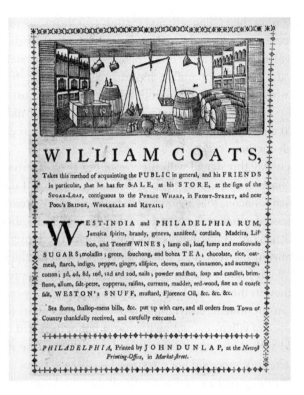

A colonial shopkeeper's wares. From William Coats,
"Takes this Method of Acquainting the Public" (Philadelphia, 1772). The Library Company of Philadelphia.

ery, that had like to overwhelm their Majestys Protestant Subjects in all their
Territorys and Dominions (of which none have suffered more or are in greater
danger than ourselves) Wee hoped and expected in our particular Stations and
qualifications, a proportionable shew in soe great a blessing.

But our greatest grief and consternation, upon the first news of the great
overture and happy change in England, wee found ourselves surrounded with
strong and violent endeavours from our Governors here (being the Lord Balte-
mores Deputys and Representatives) to defeat us of the same.

Wee still find all the meanes used by these very persons and their Agents,
Jesuits, Priests, and lay papists that are of malice can suggest to devise the obedience and loyalty of the inhabitants from their most sacred Majestys to that
height of impudence that solemn masses and prayers are used (as we have very

good informacōn) in their Chappells and Oratorys for the prosperous success of the popish forces in Ireland, and the French designs against England, whereby they would involve us, in the same crime of disloyalty with themselves and render us obnoxious to the insupportable displeasure of their Majesties.

Wee every where have not only publick protestations against their Majesties rights and possessions of the Crown of England, but their most illustrious persons vilefied and aspected with the worst and most trayterous expressions of obloquie and detraction.

Wee are every day threatened with the loss of our lives, libertys and Estates of which wee have great reason to think ourselves in eminent danger by the practises and machinacons that are on foot to betray us to the French, Northern and other Indians of which some have been dealt withall, and others invited to assist in our distruccōn, well remembering the incursion and invade of the said Northern Indians in the year 1681, who were conducted into the heart of this Province by French Jesuits, and lay sore upon us while the Representatives of the Country, then in the Assembly were severely prest upon by our superiours to yield them an unlimited and tyrannicall power in the Affairs of the Militia As so great a piece of villany cannot be the result but of the worst of principles, soe wee should with the greatest difficulty believe it to be true if undeniable evidence and circumstances did not convince Us.

Together with the promises we have with all due thinking and deliberacōn considered the endeavours that are making to disunite us among ourselves, to make and inflame differences in our neighbour Collony of Virginia, from whose friendshipp, vicinity great loyalty and samenes of Religion wee may expect assistance in our greatest necessity. Wee have considered that all the other branches of their Majesty's Dominions in this part of the world (as well as wee could be informed) have done their duty in proclaiming and asserting their undoubted right in these & all other their Majesties Territoryes & Countys.

But above all with due and mature deliberacōn wee have reflected upon that vast gratitude and duty incumbent likewise upon us, to our Sovereign Lord and Lady the King and Queene's most Excellent Majesty's in which as it would not be safe for us, soe it will not suffer us to be silent in soe great and general a Jubilee, withall considering and looking upon ourselves, discharged, dissolved and free from all manner of duty, obligacōn or fidelity to the Deputy Gov' or Chief Magistrate here as such they having departed from their Allegiance (upon which alone our said duty and fidelity to them depends) and by their Complices and Agents aforesaid endeavoured the destruccōn of our religion, lives, libertys, and propertys all which they are bound to protect.

These are the reasons, motives and considerraccōns which wee doe declare have induced us to take up Arms to preserve, vindicate and assert the sovereign Dominion and right of King William and Queen Mary to this Province; to defend the Protestᵗ Religion among us, and to protect and chelter the Inhabitants from all manner of violence, oppression and destruccōn, that is plotted and designed against them, the which wee doe solemnly declare and protest wee have noe designes or intentions whatsoever.

For the more effectual Accomplishment of which, wee will take due care that a full and free Assembly be called and conven'd with all possible expedicōn by whom we may likewise have our condicōn circumstances, and our most duty-full addresses represented and tendered to their Majesties, from whose great wisdom, justice and special care of the protestant religion wee may reasonably and comfortably hope to be delivered from our present calamity and for the future be secured under a just and legall Administracōn from being ever more subjected to the yoke of arbitrary government of tyranny and popery.

In the _ of _ wee will take care, and doe promise that no person now in armes with us, or that shall come to assist us shall committ any outrage or doe any violence to any person whatsoever that shall be found peaceable and quiet and not oppose us in our said just and necessary designes, and that there shall be a just and due satisfaccōn made for provisions and other necessarys had and received from the Inhabitants and the souldiers punctually and duely payed in such wayes and methodes as have been formerly accustomed or by Law ought to bee. And wee doe lastly invite and require all manner of persons whatsoever residing or Inhabiting in this Province, as they tender their Allegiance, the Protestant Religion, their Lives, fortunes and Families, to ayd and assist us in this our undertaking.

Given under our hands, Maryland the 25th day of July in the first year of their Majesties Reign Anno Dom: 1689.

> *John Coode*
> *Hen. Jowles*
> *Jno Cambell*
> *Hum: Warren*
> *Kenelm Cheseldyn*
> *Wm Purling*
> *Wla Blackiston*
> *Ricd Clouds.*

"Jamaica Negroes cutting canes in their working dresses." From Henry T. De La Beche, *Notes on the present condition of the Negroes in Jamaica* (1825). Courtesy of the John Carter Brown Library at Brown University.

AN ADVERTISEMENT FOR CONSUMER GOODS AND A SLAVE (1728)

From *The American Weekly Mercury* (Philadelphia), June 27, 1728.

"To be sold by Evan Morgan in Market-street, in Philadelphia, at the Corner Shop over against the Pillory, very good Barbadoes Rum, Madeira Wine, Sugar, Mellassoes, Salt, Spunges, and Neeple Shels so to draw Womens Brests with; and likewise a very likely young Negroe Man of about 21 Years of Age, a Cooper by Trade to be sold, or hired out by the Year . . . "

RUMORS ABOUT CATHOLIC/INDIAN CONSPIRACY
IN NEW ENGLAND (1689)

From James Phinney Baxter, ed., *Documentary History of the State of Maine*, vol. 4 (Portland, Me., 1889), 446–47.

Sudbury [Mass.] 3 January 1688/89
The testomonies of Joseph Graues seni^r aiged 46 yers or thear abouts
And of mary Graues aiged thirty yers or thear abouts and of John Rutter aiged 40 years Wittnesseth that Solomon thomas Indian Being att the house of Joseph Graues: wee heard said Soloman thomas Say That when ye fight att the East ward, should bee: if the Indians had the better of itt as: the English did retreate ye friend Indians wear near to shoot them downe but if the [English] gett the day wee say nothing. that in the spring french and Irish would Com to Boston as many and all one as Indians for that was the first plase that was to bee destroyed and after that the Countery tounes would bee all one nothing.

That the Governour had Given said Solomon a booke that was better then the bible and all that would not turn to the govornor reledgon and owne that booke should bee destroyed/ in which booke hee the said thomas said was the pictur of our Savior and of the virgen Mary and the twelve apostls and the governour says when we pray wee pray to the virgen Mary, and when the fight shoold bee att East ward the governor woold sit in his Wigwam and say o braue Indians this and much mor may bee said.

Joseph Graues Mary Graues John V Rutter
           her marke W . *his marke* X .

The Great Awakening

When Samuel Niles, a Narragansett Indian from Rhode Island, was about forty years old, he heard about a new religious excitement among neighboring Anglo-Americans. Soon he was drawn into meetings at a Westerly, Rhode Island, church, and made a profession of faith in Jesus Christ. He received baptism, and gained admission to membership and communion, or the Lord's Supper, probably around 1743. Some sixty Native Americans joined the Westerly church in 1742 and 1743, but white missionary and pastor Joseph Park noted with concern that the Narragansetts met by themselves "for prayer and praise" a couple nights a week. They were starting to function as a separate church. The gifted Niles wanted to begin "exhorting," or informally preaching, in the Westerly church meetings, but Park and other leaders did not like this idea. Park upbraided Niles and his supporters "for becoming noisy, by speaking and praying, in his meeting."

Tensions rose until Niles led a secession of native believers from the church in 1750. They met in Narragansett wigwams for their assemblies, which sometimes ran late into the night. Then they built a tiny meetinghouse, twenty-five feet square. Squabbles with white and Indian brethren alike whittled the church's numbers, but the Narragansett church appointed three of their own members to ordain Niles to the ministry. During the ordination service, there was a great outpouring of the Holy Spirit, such that the Indian Christians wept, prayed, and cried out, all at the same time, for almost an hour. Another white minister worried that while the (apparently) illiterate Niles was well intentioned, he relied too much on the leading of the Holy Spirit instead of the Bible. He leaned too heavily, whites feared, on "feelings, impressions, visions, appearances and directions of angels and of Christ himself in a visionary way."[1]

This was the Great Awakening in the Narragansett Christians' world. The revivals of the mid-eighteenth century were transatlantic in scope and significance, and participants had a strong sense that they were part of a movement of God that was much larger than themselves. Widespread printed materials—including revival newspapers and cheap books—spread the word about revivals happening in America, in Britain, and on the Continent. They publicized the work of celebrity evangelists, headed primarily by the English Anglican itinerant George Whitefield, the wonder of the age. But the revivals also had specific local contours that revealed much about tensions over race, gender, and church practice.

Some traditional church leaders opposed the Great Awakening, seeing it all as frothy spiritual nonsense. Some welcomed the conversion of many to new faith in Christ, but worried about the destabilizing features of the revivals—they worried that if the awakenings went too far, they could disrupt traditional social lines built around ethnicity, gender, education, and age. But for many like Samuel Niles, the revivals inaugurated a life-transforming encounter of spiritual focus and authority. Sometimes they experienced transcendent dreams or visions, and received the immediate guidance of the Holy Spirit. For Samuel Niles and countless others who typically had no "voice" in Anglo-American culture, these were bracing, even revolutionary experiences.

The Great Awakening, the greatest upheaval in English America prior to the American Revolution, represented a remarkable confluence of a number of factors, some religious, others cultural. Participants saw the revivals as the work of God, by the Holy Spirit, the third person of the divine Trinity. Protestants in Britain and Europe had deep traditions of awakening going back to the early 1600s. Some regarded the Protestant Reformation itself as an outbreak of revival. In awakenings, large numbers of people experienced "conversion" by the power of the Holy Spirit, who convicted people of their sin and convinced them that the only way of salvation lay through faith in Jesus Christ, who had died on the cross to bring forgiveness of sins to those who would receive it. (Some also found their faith in Christ renewed during the revivals, even if they did not experience salvation for the first time.) Those who did not accept Christ's forgiveness were left to their own sin and guilt, which would rightly earn them eternal condemnation in hell, the awakening pastors taught. Salvation and conversion were works of the Spirit, given by the grace of God. Morality and religiosity remained important as signs of true faith, but in a certain sense, they did not matter. What mattered was being "born again" and made fit for heaven, as Jesus had taught in the Gospel of John, chapter 3. These were the distinctive beliefs of these Protestant Christians whom historians typically call "evangelicals."[2]

Hannah Heaton, a farm woman from Connecticut, had also heard much about the revivals. Devout family members quizzed her about her spiritual state until she too entered her conversion ordeal. She had thoughts of suicide, fearing that she could never break through to salvation. She worried that if she went to pray alone, she might encounter her dark enemy, the devil. Indeed, one time she thought she felt the devil "twitch" her clothes. At night she would look out the window, thinking she might see the first glimmers of Jesus returning to earth in judgment. Finally, she went to a revival meeting and "the power of God came down." Many were crying out to be saved. In the midst of the noisy throng, she began to pray for mercy, and then she had a vision: "I thought I saw Jesus with the eyes of my soul," she wrote, "standing up in heaven. A lovely god-man with his arms open, ready to receive me, his face was full of smiles, he looked white and ruddy and was just such a savior as my soul wanted." Soon she experienced a peace and happiness unlike anything she had known before. "It seemed as if I had a new soul and body both," she testified.[3]

+ + +

What accounts for the timing of the Great Awakening? Participants would have pointed to God's role in precipitating the revivals, but there were clear earthly factors as well. In many of the colonies, there was a growing sense of cultural crisis leading up to the awakenings. This was especially true in New England, which had seemingly lost its way after the first two generations of English settlement. New Englanders were generally pleased with the outcome of the Glorious Revolution and the ouster of King James II and Dominion of New England governor Edmund Andros, but that success was followed by the botched Quebec invasion in 1690.

Then came the Salem witchcraft controversy and executions of 1692. Most of the accusations of witchcraft came from young women and girls against older women, many of whom were widows and may have had a reputation for irritability or unorthodox ideas. The judges in the trials admitted as valid evidence stories about the "specters" of the older women appearing to the tormented, demanding that they sign the devil's "book." Eventually nineteen accused witches were executed by hanging. (Another man was pressed to death with stones, and two dogs were also killed, suspected of being witches' "familiars" or demonic assistants.) The furor spread regionally, and more elite people began to fall under charges of witchcraft. Most shockingly, Mary Phips, the wife of the Massachusetts governor, was accused, leading William Phips to intervene. Court proceedings stopped, and Massachusetts officials repudiated spectral evidence as inadmissible. Belief in witches and the devil did not go away, but Salem became the last mass witchcraft prosecution in American history.

New England's wars with Indians and the French became intertwined with the imagery and anxiety of the witchcraft panic. The devil was often described as a "black man" by the accusers, but to the English, "black" did not necessarily mean African—it could also mean Indian. Mercy Short, for example, was captured by Abenaki Indians in an attack on Salmon Falls, Maine, in early 1690. Her parents and several siblings perished in the raid, and Short witnessed torture and executions during her captivity. In 1692, when she began reporting assaults on her by the devil, she described the evil enemy as a "short and black man . . . not of a negro, but of a tawney, or an Indian color." Along with witches' specters, who urged her to sign a covenant with the devil, she saw "French Canadians and Indian sagamores among them, diverse of whom she knew." The devil's crew showed her a Catholic devotional text they used at their meetings.[4]

War with France and its Indian allies and the debacle at Salem helped to convince the devout that New England was in a spiritual crisis. Puritan ministers warned congregations that pervasive immorality and lukewarmness risked bringing the judgment of God on their society. New England's seaport towns saw more and more immigrants who did not seem to care about the original Puritan mission. Harvard College, founded in the 1630s as a training school for Puritan ministers, maintained its Christian commitment in the early 1700s, but was increasingly marked by what proponents called "rational" theology and anti-Calvinism. Prospective Congregationalist ministers at Harvard now learned that a just and loving God must give all people a chance to be saved, instead of being consigned to the fate God assigned to them. Yale College was founded in 1701 in Connecticut by ministers hoping to make it a bastion of traditional Calvinist theology.

Seventeenth-century Puritans tended to focus on ethical problems and moral reform, with hope of cultivating an ideal godly society. In the early 1700s, the emphasis of preaching shifted toward people's inability to change their ways without a dramatic infusion of the Holy Spirit. Pastors called on their congregations to pray for an outpouring of the Spirit. As Jonathan Edwards's grandfather Solomon Stoddard put it, "The Spirit of the Lord must be poured out upon the people, else religion will not revive." Stoddard was the key early revivalist pastor in New England, and he saw a number of "harvests" in his ministry, well before the outbreak of the Great Awakening. New England witnessed a significant regional revival in 1727 in response to a violent earthquake. But the 1734–35 revival led by Jonathan Edwards, in Stoddard's former Northampton, Massachusetts, church, is generally viewed as the first major event of the Great Awakening.[5]

One of the reasons for considering Northampton as the beginning of the Great Awakening was the sheer scope of the new revival. Edwards recorded that "there was scarcely a single person in the town, either old or young, that was left unconcerned about the great things of the eternal world." Edwards's compelling account *A Faithful Narrative of the Surprising Work of God* was published in London. Printed accounts of revival were one of the primary ways that those involved with the Great Awakening gained a sense of participating in a transatlantic work of God.

George Whitefield, the greatest itinerant preacher of the awakenings, was also a master of print and publicity. Whitefield was the single most important link of all the Anglo-American revivals. Converted at the University of Oxford under the influence of Methodist leaders John and Charles Wesley, the Anglican (Church of England) Whitefield soon became a fabulously successful itinerant preacher. He combined a personal background in the theater, innate talent for public speaking, and passionate Calvinist convictions to become the most dazzling preacher of the era. Crowds in the tens of thousands of people assembled to hear him preach all over Britain and America. (Critics always questioned those numbers, which Whitefield sometimes reduced in later estimates.) He forged a network of evangelical allies and supportive printers. Among the latter, perhaps none became as close to Whitefield as the non-evangelical Ben Franklin of Philadelphia, whose own renown was enhanced by his decades-long partnership with Whitefield.

Whitefield and Franklin had a warm if peculiar friendship, given that they had no "religious connection," as Franklin put it in his autobiography. Franklin saw Whitefield as a major opportunity in his publishing business, selling many Whitefield imprints, as well as some by Whitefield's opponents. By 1742, Franklin was even selling images of Whitefield alongside a number of imported goods from London. One of his newspaper ads listed such "fine mezzotinto and grav'd pictures of Mr. Whitefield" as well as fountain pens, brass ink bottles, pocket compasses, and other consumer goods.[6]

Many aspects of Whitefield's theology and methods struck critics as dangerous. He encountered opposition from a number of Anglican ministers and officials in England and the colonies, many of whom saw him as an "antinomian," or someone who preached lawless chaos. Whitefield's primary theological emphases were the "new birth" of salvation, and the work of the Holy Spirit. Anglican critics insisted that infants were "born again" at baptism, but Whitefield and his evangelical allies taught that the new birth was a discernible, wrenching experience that each individual must undergo before she or he could have a reasonable assurance of salvation. Whitefield believed that the Holy Spirit had to bring about conversion, for lost and corrupt people would not choose to be saved on their own. The Holy Spirit would continue to lead believers, even giving them detailed guidance about passages of Scripture, if a person would only pray and listen. His antagonists saw this confidence as dangerous individualism, threatening the authority of churches and ministers, some of whom Whitefield and the new evangelicals regarded as unconverted.

Whitefield saw his greatest preaching successes during a fall 1740 tour of New England. As was his habit, Whitefield started off his visit by meeting with the resident Anglican commissary, Timothy Cutler, a former Yale rector who had converted to Anglicanism in the 1720s. Cutler wanted to know why Whitefield, who remained an Anglican, cooperated with all Protestant denominations. Whitefield replied that he "saw regenerate souls among the Baptists, among the Presbyterians, among the Independents, and among the Church [Anglican] folks, — all children of God, and yet all born again in a different way of worship." In an era of intense intra-Protestant strife, this kind of interdenominational cooperation was unusual. It gave Whitefield many more supporters than a more exclusionary minister would have enjoyed. His interdenominational bent also made him many enemies.[7]

Those touched by Whitefield's ministry ran the gamut from elite politicians to servants, slaves, and Native Americans. Whitefield once met with Massachusetts's governor, and then immediately preached to a "great number of Negroes on the conversion of the Ethiopian [Acts 8], (at which the poor creatures, as well as many white people, were much affected)." Calling the blacks in his audience "poor creatures" signals Whitefield's paternalistic attitude toward African Americans. On one hand, Whitefield gave blacks personal attention at a time when many whites worried that Christianizing them (especially slaves) might give them subversive notions about liberty. On the other hand, Whitefield never repudiated slavery, and he went on to become a slave owner himself, and even agitated for the introduction of slavery in Georgia, a colony where slavery was originally prohibited.[8]

As congenial as Whitefield found New England's Puritan legacy, he was concerned by the resistance he encountered among Congregationalists at places such as Harvard College. In published statements that would come back to haunt him, Whitefield said that Harvard was spiritually negligent, with discipline at "too low an ebb," while students and professors chased after faddish books. By the end of his New England tour, he had determined that the "generality of preachers talk of an unknown, unfelt Christ. And the reason why congregations have been so dead, is because dead men preach to them." Even some of his more moderate supporters were turned off by such judgments.[9]

Whitefield's concern about unconverted ministers became a hallmark of the radical wing of the evangelical movement. Historians have often spoken of the debates over the Great Awakening as dividing "Old Light" critics from "New Light" supporters of the revivals, but reactions to the Great Awakening actually ran along a continuum from staunch opposition, to cautious support, to radical zeal. Moderate evangelicals were happy to see great numbers of conversions, but they worried that extremists would disrupt the churches and jeopardize pastors' traditional authority. Whitefield and his key pastoral ally Gilbert Tennent of New Jersey—whose most famous sermon was "The Danger of an Unconverted Ministry" (1740)—helped to create the radical impulse by their talk of unregenerate pastors. Many of America's denominations assumed a parish model, in which a person attended the nearest church of the denomination with which they identified. Tennent and Whitefield fostered a new market-mindedness among American churchgoers. If you did not like your parish church, or if you suspected your pastor was unconverted, then you had the right to seek fellowship elsewhere.

Some radical evangelicals took their zeal, and their criticism of pastors and churches, further than Whitefield and Tennent intended. While Whitefield was comfortable with a certain level of spiritual fervor in his meetings, the radicals saw wondrous, egalitarian scenes in their meetings unlike any others in eighteenth-century America. Whitefield's assistant Daniel Rogers had worked as a tutor at Harvard but left to join the itinerant's traveling cohort in 1740, and soon he experienced the new birth. Rogers went on to lead his own round-the-clock revivals in his hometown of Ipswich, Massachusetts. In those meetings, Rogers not only permitted but affirmed the exhortations of female converts whom he regarded as filled with a spirit of "prophecy." At a New Year's assembly in 1742, Rogers recorded that the Spirit of God came as a "spirit of supplication and intercession and prophecy, by which I here mean a person speaking the truths of the Word or gospel by the immediate help—or influence of the Spirit of God." He said that this spirit was in a woman named Lucy Smith, who apparently addressed the meeting for two hours.[10]

Bathsheba Kingsley of Westfield, Massachusetts, even went a step further than Lucy Smith and began itinerating as an evangelical preacher. Having received "immediate revelations from heaven" to do so, Kingsley stole a horse and rode through the region proclaiming the gospel. She repented for her indiscretions before the Westfield church in 1741, but in 1743 she was back in trouble, appearing before a ministerial council that included Jonathan Edwards. She told the ministers of her intimate relationship with God, and how she was often "caught up" in the Spirit, receiving dreams and spiritual impressions as guidance. Edwards noted with dismay that she rambled about telling people of her revelations, but Kingsley asserted that she was a "proper person to be improved for some great thing in the church of God; and that in the exercise of some parts of the work of ministry." The council agreed that she had "almost wholly cast off that modesty, shamefacedness, and sobriety and meekness, diligence and submission, that becomes a Christian woman in her place." Edwards called her a "brawling woman." Not wanting to deny the reality of the Spirit's work in women's lives, however, the council did not punish her severely, only insisting that she stop assuming pastoral authority, and that she limit her testimony to private settings.[11]

Kingsley's case, and Lucy Smith's prophesying, remind us that one hundred years after Anne Hutchinson's trial, New Englanders were still wrestling with the tensions created by individual Christians' experiences in the Spirit. Moderate evangelicals had a high view of clerical authority and decorum, which meant that pastors controlled the right of public speaking and testifying in meetinghouses. Yet the moderates also believed that individuals—women or men; rich or poor; white, black, or Indian—could relate to God directly by the Holy Spirit, who dwelled in the bodies of believers. In theory, a pastor might know a great deal about the Bible and theology, yet he might have missed the most important thing—the new birth. A poor woman, man, or child might have experienced the new birth and know God in a more immediate way than the unconverted pastor. This created space for people like Smith and Kingsley to speak publicly, regardless of how it might violate conventional church boundaries. Moderate evangelicals did not believe a true work of the Spirit would disrupt traditional, biblical order in the church. Radicals like Daniel Rogers believed that the awakenings were inaugurating a new era of the Spirit, in which even women might prophesy.

The radical evangelicals also testified to a range of transcendent, mystical experiences in the Spirit, including dreams, spirit journeys, trances, fits, miraculous healings, and in some rare cases, speaking in "tongues," or the language of the Spirit. It is difficult to know just how common these experiences were, as we may assume that many of them were not recorded for posterity. But these spiritual manifestations became key tests for a person's reaction to the Great Awakening. Radicals pointed to them as confirmation of the Spirit's presence; moderates regarded them warily and downplayed their significance; antirevivalists seized upon these experiences as evidence of the revivals' illegitimacy. Hannah Heaton's vision of Jesus as a "lovely god-man," then, was hardly unique. Heaton emphasized that she saw Jesus with the eyes of her soul, yet some even reported seeing Jesus, or the Holy Spirit, with their "bodily eyes." The physical sighting of divine beings was a species of vision that only the most radical evangelicals were willing to accept.[12]

The Great Awakening's ferment spawned hundreds of Separate congregations, some of them basically informal prayer meetings (like that of the Westerly Narragansetts), some officially breaking away from sanctioned churches and opening one of their own. But people could not open their own churches in New England without government permission, so Separate churches and pastors were subjected to fines and harassment. Many of them did not last long. Separate leaders generally upbraided their existing pastor for not adequately supporting the revivals, or for banning popular itinerant preachers from their pulpits. They also worried that churches had been admitting unconverted persons to full church membership. In Norwich, Connecticut, moderate evangelical pastor Benjamin Lord endured a separation in his church in 1745, when some thirteen members, including future Baptist minister Isaac Backus, withdrew from his church. Those who left explained that they did not regard Lord as supportive of the awakenings, and that the church did not require a testimony of conversion for admission to membership. Some resented Lord's prohibition of itinerating Separate preachers. One of the withdrawing members, Mary Lathrop, declared that the scrupulous members had a right to seek out the best church for them. "By covenant I am not held here any longer than I am edified," she asserted.[13]

Following his withdrawal from the established church, Isaac Backus (like many Separates) began to have doubts about the long-standing practice of infant baptism. Baptizing infants had been the predominant Christian practice for more than a millennium, but certain Protestants on the Continent and in England had become "Anabaptists," or just Baptists, believing that only converted adults were proper candidates for the ritual of baptism. Baptizing infants had been understood to give children quasi-official status in the churches of New England, but not full membership. By the mid-1600s, the growing number of baptized but unregenerate parents in New England had led to the Halfway Covenant (1662), under which unconverted parents could have their own children baptized. But to Baptist critics, infant baptism compromised the "purity" of the churches. In 1751 Backus came under the influence of a number of baptistic Separates, who convinced him that the scriptural norm was believer's baptism by immersion in water. Backus repudiated his own baptism as an infant and received believer's baptism. In Baptist practice, only those who could give a clear conversion testimony would receive baptism, which served as the gateway to membership.

Backus and other converts helped to inaugurate a new evangelical Baptist movement in America. English and Continental Baptists had been present in America since the early colonial period, but the Separate Baptists had little connection to those existing churches. New England Baptists planted churches in the backcountry, and they made significant inroads in the Carolinas and Virginia starting in the 1750s. Anglican missionaries reported with dismay the churning religious diversity of the American hinterlands. Charles Woodmason served the Anglican churches of the southern backcountry in the 1760s, and he found that although Anglican parsons were rare, the people were "eaten up by itinerant teachers, preachers, and imposters from New England and Pennsylvania—Baptists, New Lights, Presbyterians, Independents, and a hundred other sects." His denominational rivals played tricks on him, once setting fifty-seven dogs to fighting outside the meetinghouse while he was trying to preach. Some accused Woodmason of being a Jesuit.[14]

The rising religious pluralism spawned by the Great Awakening, in the face of continued state support for particular denominations, set the stage for a Revolutionary-era campaign for religious liberty. Separates and Baptists did not like having to pay religious taxes to support churches they did not attend. In many colonies it was difficult to obtain formal permission to preach or start a new church if you were not a clergyman associated with the official denomination (Anglican in the southern colonies, Congregationalist in New England). Already by the late 1740s, Connecticut Separates were calling for "universal liberty" of conscience for all Protestants in the colony, and an end to persecution of the Separates. A massive outcry by evangelicals helped win full liberty of conscience in Virginia in the 1780s. New England would take the longest of all America's regions to embrace religious liberty, as some northeastern states maintained their established churches well into the nineteenth century.[15]

As evangelical faith spread south—into the least-churched part of the mainland colonies—ministers had to deal more directly with the large African population and the cruel realities of slavery. George Whitefield had addressed the slavery issue in a 1740 letter to southern slave masters, in which he charged that "God has a quarrel with you for your abuse of and cruelty to the poor negroes." Whitefield declined, however, to address the question of whether it was morally permissible for Christians to own slaves. Several years later he answered the question by becoming a slave owner. Whitefield set a pattern that became common among moderate evangelicals, who raised questions about the practices of slavery and the slave trade but did not denounce the institution itself. Jonathan Edwards, Whitefield, and other key leaders of the Great Awakening owned slaves.[16]

As we have seen, slaves came from Africa with their own religious beliefs, and most of them did not come with much background in Christianity. When they did, that background was generally Catholic. Whitefield and other evangelicals sought to convert slaves and free blacks to Protestant Christianity, and made some modest inroads among them. Perhaps the greatest successes came among slaves in the Caribbean, by the efforts of Moravian missionaries. These German Pietist evangelicals, pioneers in eighteenth-century global missions, were the most intentionally interracial in their church practices, yet even some Moravian leaders became slave owners.

The Moravians also raised up remarkable Afro-Caribbean leaders, including Rebecca Protten of the island of St. Thomas. Protten combined her passion for the Moravian faith and her creole facility with different languages to become a trailblazer among Afro-Caribbean women. Protten married a German Moravian missionary, to the consternation of white planters. She eventually returned to Europe with her husband, who died en route. In Germany, Moravian leaders found her another husband, Jacob Protten, a man of mixed-race ancestry from Africa's Gold Coast. The Moravians also ordained Rebecca as a deaconess, giving her formal ministry responsibilities in the church. She must have been one of the first black women ordained to any church office in the history of western Christianity, "signaling the power of this form of evangelical religion to take any and all into its bosom." Rebecca and Jacob moved to the slave trading port of Christiansborg, on the Gold Coast, where she died in 1780.[17]

Whatever its limitations with regard to slavery and ethnic equality, evangelicalism literally gave voice to many African Americans and Afro-Caribbean people. A number of the earliest African American published authors were evangelicals, as were many early black and white antislavery advocates. Phillis Wheatley of Boston was the first published female African American, her first stand-alone poem appearing in 1770 on the occasion of George Whitefield's death in Newburyport, Massachusetts. She won her freedom from slavery in 1773, and although some of her writing accepted slavery as part of God's providential plan for saving the souls of Africans, in one pointed letter to evangelical Native American leader Samson Occom, she took exception to slavery and the "modern Egyptians" in the British empire who bolstered it.[18]

That Wheatley's poem on Whitefield was published in London and in multiple American editions hints at how intertwined religion, publishing, and commerce were in the colonial Atlantic world. The Great Awakening secured those connections unlike any other event. Whitefield set the pattern: not only did he partner with a transatlantic network of publishers, but he sought to bring evangelical printed materials into every locale he visited. When he came to America in fall 1739, he carried boxes full of standard texts of evangelical and Puritan spirituality, including hymns by English evangelical writer Isaac Watts. Antagonists like Boston's Timothy Cutler attributed Whitefield's broad influence to his traveling and preaching, as well as his flood of publications, which were "reprinted and eagerly bought" by Bostonians. Cutler insisted that antirevivalist Anglicans must fight the "enthusiastic notions very much kindled among us and like to be propagated by his writings, dispersed everywhere, with Antinomianism revived." Those notions must be countered with solid Anglican texts, Cutler advised London authorities.[19]

Whitefield's published journals and sermons took on a life of their own, spreading revival even in his absence. A group of pietist Christians in Hanover, Virginia, heard about Whitefield's ministry in the early 1740s. Their revival meetings, led by a converted bricklayer named Samuel Morris, flourished when he obtained copies of Whitefield sermons published in Glasgow in 1741, brought to Virginia by a Scottish immigrant. Morris simply began preaching the Whitefield sermons himself. "I invited my neighbors to come and hear it," Morris remembered, "and the plainness, popularity, and fervency of the discourses, being peculiarly fitted to affect our unimproved minds, and the Lord rendering the Word efficacious, many were convinced of their undone condition, and constrained to seek deliverance." Morris and his followers soon built their own meetinghouse for reading sermons.[20]

Religious topics had long commanded a top position in the Anglo-American book trade, but Whitefield dramatically increased the scale of printing in both Britain and America. In each year from 1739 to 1745, Whitefield was the most-published author in the colonies. From 1738 to 1741, the output of the colonial presses increased 85 percent, with almost all of the growth coming from imprints by or about Whitefield. Similarly, in 1740 thirty-nine separate publications by or regarding Whitefield appeared from American publishers, which accounted for almost a third of their entire catalog that year.[21]

Not only were revival publications good business, but they played a critical role in conveying the impression that there was an unprecedented, cohesive awakening spanning the Atlantic. Writers and printers also tried to set boundaries between appropriate revival fervor and the ostensible frenzy of the radicals. Boston's Thomas Prince published the revivalist newspaper *The Christian History* for two years starting in 1743. The moderate Prince's timing was off, however, because by that stage of the revivals, only the radicals were still seeing

success in New England, and Prince was not eager to give attention to their tri-
umphs. Accordingly, Prince struggled to find any news of moderate revivals to
cover for the first half-year of *The Christian History*. When he did finally publish
a new narrative from New England, it focused on Joseph Park's Rhode Island
revival, which featured a number of conversions among Indians and blacks. But
the account gave credit to arch-radical James Davenport's preaching in spurring
the awakening.[22]

Davenport had only months earlier participated in the most notorious episode of New England's awakenings, a book- and clothes-burning at the New
London, Connecticut, waterfront. He first called on his followers to burn du-
bious religious books, including works by moderate evangelical leaders such as
Boston's Benjamin Colman. Then he turned his eye on the fancy clothes he
saw in the New England port town, and soon "a lofty pile of hoop petticoats, silk
gowns, short cloaks, cambrick caps, red heeled shoes, fans, necklaces, gloves,
and other such apparrel" was prepared for the flames. Davenport pulled off
his own pants and threw them on the smoldering stack, but one courageous
woman thought this was outrageous, so she snatched his pants from the fire and
threw them "into his face." The crowd sided with the woman, and the incident
became a major humiliation for Davenport. To revival critics, it became em-
blematic of what the awakenings were really about: foolish chaos.[23]

For Thomas Prince, even having to mention Davenport's name was painful.
Critics lambasted Prince for the piece, saying that the real design of the paper
was to "maintain and propagate a spirit of disorder, enthusiasm and separation
in the land." How could Prince publicize a Davenport-influenced event, when
Prince had already joined moderate evangelical pastors in denouncing the radical preacher as unfit to speak in the region's churches? Prince did not attempt
to respond, but he soon published an account of an awakening in Wrentham,
Massachusetts, which the contributors noted was free of "trances, visions, revelations," censoriousness, or reckless exhorters.[24]

Regardless of the moderate evangelicals' struggles, the revivals went on, as did
missions work among Native Americans. That work had been hamstrung by the
vicious wars of the seventeenth and early eighteenth centuries, but the Great
Awakening reignited evangelicals' commitment to reaching Native Americans
with their gospel. In 1741, Presbyterian missionary Azariah Horton, operating
under the auspices of the Society in Scotland for Propagating Christian Knowledge, began working among Montauk and Shinnecock Indians on southern Long Island, New York. A Scottish evangelical magazine, the *Christian*

Monthly History, subsequently published Horton's accounts of his ministry, further sealing the transatlantic cohesion of the revivals that evangelical publications fostered.

As Horton preached and visited "from Wigwaam to Wigwaam," he found that Indian women ("Squaws") showed the most spiritual interest. One woman told him how she had come under conviction of sin but that "the Lord Jesus appeared to her exceedingly lovely; and that the load of guilt she felt before, was now gone." One of the few Indian men to whom he ministered was on his deathbed, but he claimed that he "saw Christ, and hoped that he should go to a good place." Even here the radical-moderate tension concerned Horton, who clarified that he did not suppose that this man "saw Christ with his bodily eyes," but instead meant he saw Jesus with his heart. By 1743, Horton became concerned about the influence of radical exhorters who were "strengthening the interest of Satan." Horton wrote this the same day as James Davenport's book-burning in New London. Horton and Davenport were both natives of Southold, Long Island, and Long Island became one of the key battlegrounds between moderates and radicals for both white and Indian adherents.[25]

Jonathan Edwards also took up the banner of Indian missions when he was dismissed from his Northampton congregation in 1750 in an ugly controversy over its policy on admission to the Lord's Supper. From the early days of his pastoral career, he had expressed negative sentiments about the Indians' spiritual state, assuming that they were bereft of true religion, and unwittingly under the sway of Satan. "The devil sucks their blood," he said, and outside of accepting Christ, they could only expect condemnation in eternal hell. If Edwards's views sound strident to modern ears, it may help to remember that he had an aunt and two cousins killed in a notorious 1704 Kahnawake Indian raid on Deerfield, Massachusetts. His early pastoral career coincided with Father Rale's War in northern New England. But Edwards also had reasons to take a more positive view of Native American potential, especially because of converts made by his disciple, missionary David Brainerd. Edwards edited and published Brainerd's diary, which became one of the most influential missionary accounts in Anglo-American history. Edwards did not hesitate to affirm the sincere faith of Indian converts under Brainerd's watch. One Native American woman evidenced, in trademark Edwardsian terms, "a true spiritual discovery of the glory, ravishing beauty, and excellency of Christ."[26]

When Edwards and his family relocated to the mission at Stockbridge, Massachusetts, his sermons seemed rhetorically simpler than those at Northampton, but they remained theologically consistent. Unlike the views of Jesuit missionaries in New France regarding Indian spiritual practices, Edwards did not see any glimmers of Christianity in native religion, but he did insist that all people were equal in sin and their need for salvation. He told the Stockbridge Indians that the English "are no better than you in no respect." New Englanders knew the gospel, but they had sinfully neglected to bring it to the Indians. Many whites in America called themselves Christians, but in reality they had "wicked hearts and live wicked lives, are the devil's people as well as the heathen. They are on the devil's side, not on [Christ's] side," he confided to them. The pastor denounced Dutch and English traders who preferred to keep Indians illiterate, and thereby easily duped, as well as the French Catholic missionaries who would not give proselytes the Bible in the vernacular. To be fair, Edwards did not seek to learn the Stockbridges' language, either.[27]

The most influential Native American evangelical convert in the eighteenth century was Mohegan pastor Samson Occom, who emphasized his background in "heathenism" prior to the coming of the Great Awakening revivalists. New Englanders had actually made a number of efforts, at Mohegans' and other Indians' request, to bring Christian education into their communities before the revivals, but Occom would recall the coming of James Davenport and other English pastors as a major break with the past. God used the awakeners' preaching "to bless and accompany with divine influences, to the conviction and saving conversion of a number" of Mohegans, Occom said. Occom went through a six-month conversion ordeal before making his "discovery of the way of salvation through Jesus, [being] enabled to put my trust in him alone for life and salvation."[28]

Occom began itinerating among the Mohegans, and Lebanon, Connecticut, minister Eleazar Wheelock took him on as a student. For decades Wheelock worked on abortive plans to start an evangelical Indian school, and Occom became his star pupil and key exhibit for the promise of Native American education. In the late 1740s, Occom moved to Montauk, Long Island, serving as a teacher and (unordained) pastor to area Indians, some of whom had become disaffected from missionary Azariah Horton. Occom wrote that "Enthusiastical Exhorters" from New England had abetted their falling away. Although Occom positioned himself against radical Separatism, he fostered a kind of de facto Indian Separatism of the kind seen under Samuel Niles's ministry in Rhode Island. Horton became discouraged with Indians' preference for Native American pastors, and soon requested a transfer to an Anglo congregation in New Jersey.[29]

In Horton's absence, Occom emerged as the key evangelical Indian pastor in New England, traveling between Indian settlements on Long Island and in New England. He began receiving a stipend from the Society in Scotland for Propagating Christian Knowledge, Horton's sponsoring agency. White-led ecclesiastical bodies were hesitant to ordain him, so he did not receive this recognition until a decade after he became the leading Native American minister on Long Island. In the 1759 ordination sermon, Samuel Buell, an influential white pastor on Long Island, compared Occom's ministerial successes to happenings in the Seven Years' War, which was reaching its height in North America. Both developments suggested that the prophesied "Latter-Day Glory" was dawning, Buell proclaimed. Missionary successes and the military defeat of Catholic powers brought thoughts of the last days to the minds of evangelicals.[30]

In spite of this recognition, Occom continued to feud with white pastors such as New London minister David Jewett, who in 1765 initiated a host of charges against Occom, trying to deprive him of missionary support. Ultimately Occom was forced to apologize for getting involved in political wrangling over a Mohegan land controversy in Connecticut. Although the Indian pastor's reputation was now damaged, Wheelock still thought he would be valuable as a fundraiser for the Indian school project. In 1765 Wheelock sent Occom to England for what became a lucrative three-year tour there. But upon his return, Occom found his wife and children nearly destitute, even though Wheelock had promised to look after them. Renewed charges of drunkenness and other sins flew against the Indian pastor. In a final indignity, Wheelock gave up on the plan for the Indian school, relocating the project to New Hampshire, where it became Dartmouth College and focused on white pupils. The disgusted Occom broke with Wheelock, writing that he was "jealous that instead of your seminary becoming Alma Mater, she will be too Alba Mater [white mother] to suckle the Tawnies." Using characteristic anti-popery language, Occom said that the school was "already adorned up too much like the Popish Virgin Mary." Wheelock had sent him as a "gazing stock" to England, only to betray the cause of Christian education for Indians upon his return. Occom and other evangelical Indians decided to relocate in the 1780s to a new Native American settlement, Brothertown, in New York. Although Brothertown was not that successful at attracting mass Indian relocation, many of its leaders had once attended Wheelock's Indian school.[31]

Occom and Wheelock's difficult relationship suggested both the promise and limitations of evangelicals overcoming ethnic boundaries in the era of the Great Awakening. The evangelical message held seeds of radical equality: whether whites, blacks, Indians; slave or free; male or female; educated or uneducated; all stood equal before the cross of Christ. All believers could commune with directly with God, through the Holy Spirit. In episodes from female exhorters to early antislavery sentiments, these egalitarian impulses surged at times, and often fell away again. But as a catalyst for potential social change and democratic notions, the Great Awakening had few equals in early American history.

The religion of the Great Awakening crystallized changes in commerce and print, too. Whitefield and his followers forever clinched the Anglo-American connection between faith and publishing. In the process Whitefield himself became the most famous man in the colonies, putting an indelible imprint on early American culture, trade, and religion. But for converts like Samuel Niles, Hannah Heaton, and Samson Occom, the significance of the Great Awakening was not in social power, nor in cultural change. It was in the individual's ability to find a right standing before God. The experience of the new birth put many, though certainly not all, on a road of lifelong devotion to the precepts of evangelical faith. That kind of faith would have enduring consequences in American history.

Moravian Baptism, from *Short Account of the United Brethren Church* (1762).
Photograph copyright 2014 by Hansmuller, Wikimedia Commons.

───────────●───────────

ITINERANT PREACHER GEORGE WHITEFIELD MINISTERS TO AFRICAN AMERICANS AND WOMEN IN PHILADELPHIA (1740)

From George Whitefield, *A Continuation of the Reverend Mr. Whitefield's Journal,
After His Arrival at Georgia* (London, 1741), 36–38.

Conversed also with a poor Negroe Woman, who has been visited in a very
remarkable Manner. GOD was pleased to convert her by my Preaching the last
Fall; but being under Dejections on *Sunday* Morning, she prayed that Salvation might come to her Heart, and that the LORD would be pleased to manifest himself to her Soul that Day. Whilst she was at Meeting, hearing one Mr.
M—n, a Baptist Preacher, whom the LORD has been pleased lately to send
forth, the Word came with such Power upon her Heart, that at last she was
obliged to cry out; and such a great Concern also fell upon many in the Congregation, that several betook themselves to secret Prayer. The Minister stop'd,

"Phillis Wheatley, Negro servant to Mr. John
Wheatley, of Boston" (1773). Courtesy of the
Library of Congress.

and several persuaded her to hold her Peace: But the Glory of the Lord shone
so brightly round about her, that she could not help praising and blessing GOD,
and telling how GOD was revealing himself to her Soul. After some Time, she
was taken out of the Meeting-House; but she fell upon her Knees, praising and
blessing GOD. She continued in an Agony for some considerable Time; and
afterwards came in and heard the Remainder of the Sermon.—Many since this,
have called her mad, and said she was full of new Wine: But the Account she
gave me was rational and solid, and I believe in that Hour the LORD JESUS took
a great Possession of her Soul. Such Cases indeed have not been very common:
But when an extraordinary Work is carrying on, GOD generally manifests himself to some Souls in this extraordinary Manner. And I doubt not, but when the
poor Negroes are to be called, GOD will highly favour them, to wipe off their
Reproach, and to shew that *he is no Respecter of Persons, but that whosoever
believeth in him shall be saved.*

Preached in the Morning about eleven to 6 or 7000 People. Had great Freedom of Spirit, and cleared myself from some Aspersions that had been cast upon

my Doctrine, as tho' it tended to *Antinomianism*. But I abhor the Thoughts of it; and whosoever entertains the Doctrines of Free-Grace in an honest Heart, will find, they will in their own Nature cause him to be fruitful in every good Word and Work.—Many expressed how the Power of GOD was amongst them; and I believe GOD has much People in *Philadelphia* City. The Congregations are very large and serious, and I have scarce preached this Time amongst them but I have seen a stiring amongst the dry Bones.—At five in the Evening I preached again with the like Power, but rather to a larger Audience; and after Sermon rode ten Miles to a Friend's House, that I might be in readiness to preach according to Appointment the next Morning.—How differently am I treated from my Master? He taught the People by Day, and abode all Night upon the Mount of Olives. He had not where to lay his Head: But go where I will, I find People with great Gladness receiving me into their Houses.—*Lord, I lack for nothing: O prepare me for a Suffering Time, and make me willing, naked, to follow a naked Christ. Amen. Amen.*

PENNYPACK AND PHILADELPHIA

Friday, May 9. Preached at *Pennypack*, about three Miles Distance from the House where I lay, to about 2000 People. Eat a little Dinner. Came to *Philadelphia* about two in the Afternoon.—Agreed with Persons to build my Negroe Schools on the Land which I have lately purchased; preached in the Evening with great Freedom and Power; and afterwards began a Society of young Men, many of whom I trust will prove good Soldiers of JESUS CHRIST. *Amen, Lord Jesus, Amen and Amen!*

Saturday. May 10. Tho' GOD has shewn me Things already in this Place, yet to To-day I have seen greater. I preached twice with Power, and to larger Congregations than ever: And in the Evening went to settle a Society of young Women, who I hope will prove wise Virgins.—As soon as I entered the Room, and heard them singing, my Soul was uncommonly delighted. When the Hymn was over, I desired to pray before I began to converse: But, contrary to my Expectations, my Soul was so carried out that I had not Time to talk at all. A wonderful Power was in the Room, and with one Accord, they began to cry out and weep most bitterly for the Space of half an Hour. They seemed to be under the strongest Convictions, and did indeed seek JESUS sorrowing. Their Cries might be heard a great Way off. When I had done, I thought proper to leave them at their Devotions. They continued in Prayer (as I was informed by one of them afterwards) for above an Hour, confessing their most secret Faults: And at length the

Agonies of some were so strong, that five of them seemed affected as those that are in Fits.—The present Captain of our Sloop going near the Water-side, was called into a Company almost in the same Circumstances; and at Midnight I was desired to come to one who was in strong Agonies of Body and Mind, but felt somewhat of Joy and Peace, after I had prayed with her several Times. Her Case put me in Mind of the young Man whom the Devil tore, when he was coming to JESUS. Some suchlike bodily Agonies, I believe, are from the Devil; and now the Work of GOD is going on, he will, no doubt, endeavour by *these* to bring an evil Report upon it.—*But, O lord, for thy Mercy's Sake, rebuke him; and tho' he may be permitted so bite thy Peoples Heel, fulfil thy Promise, and let the Seed of the Woman bruise his accursed Head. Amen. Amen!*

ANGLICAN MINISTER THOMAS BARTON DESCRIBES HIS MINISTRY TO THE DIVERSE POPULATION OF PENNSYLVANIA (1764)

From William Stevens Perry, ed., *Historical Collections Relating to the American Colonial Church, vol. 2—Pennsylvania* (Hartford, Conn., 1871), 366–70.

Mr. BARTON *to the Secretary.*
(EXTRACT.)
Lancaster in Pennsylvania, Nov[r] 16th, 1764.
REV[D] SIR,

This mission then takes in the whole of Lancaster county (80 miles in length and 26 in breadth), part of Chester County and part of Berks, so that the circumference of my stated mission only, is 200 miles. The County of Lancaster contains upwards of 40,000 Souls; of this Number not more than 500 can be reckon'd as belonging to the Church of England; the rest are German Lutherans, Calvinists, Mennonists, Moravians, New Born, Dunkars, Presbyterians, Seceders, New Lights, Covenanters, Mountain Men, Brownists, Independents, Papists, Quakers, Jews, &c. Amidst such a swarm of Sectaries, all indulged and favored by the Government, it is no wonder that the National Church should be borne down. At the last Election for the county to choose Assemblymen, Sheriff, Coroner, Commissioners, Assessors, &[c]., 5000 Freeholders voted, and yet not a single member of the Church was elected into any of these offices. Notwithstanding these and the like discouragements, I have the satisfaction to assure the Hon[ble] Society that my people have continued to give proofs of that submission and obedience to civil authority, which it is the glory of the Church of England to inculcate; and whilst faction and party strife have been rending the province to pieces, they behaved themselves as became peaceable and dutiful subjects, never intermeddling in the least. Suffer me to add, Sir, that in the murder of the Indians in this place and the different insurrections occasioned by this inhuman act, not one of them was ever concerned. Justice demands this testimony from me in their favour; as their conduct upon this occasion has gained them much credit and honour. Upon the whole, the Church of England visibly gains ground throughout the province. The mildness and Excellency of her Constitution, her moderation and charity, even to her Enemies, and (I hope I may be indulged to say), the indefatigable labours of her Missionaries, must at length recommend her to all except those who have an hereditary prejudice and aversion to her. . . .

The Presbyterians are in much disrepute with all the other Sects and seem to be at a stand. They gain no accessions except from the Importations of their own Society from the North of Ireland, and yet what is strange Numbers of their young Men are daily emancipated by the Colleges of New England and the Jersey who are Licens'd by their Presbyteries, and sent by scores into the world in search of a Flock. But they are a people who are unsteady and much given to change, fond of Novelty, and easily led away by every kind of Doctrine. This disposition will ever be a bar to their encrease. The Seceders are making great Havock among them and are proselyting them by thousands to their opinions. These last, however, are a set of Men who under a Monarchial Government I think cannot subsist long. Their interest upon their own principles must undoubtedly destroy itself.

The Church of England then must certainly prevail at last. She has hitherto stood her Ground amidst all the rage and wildness of fanaticism; and whilst Methodists and New Lights have roamed over the Country, "leading captive silly women" and drawing in thousands to adopt their strange and Novel doctrines the Members of this Church (a few in Philadelphia excepted) have "held fast the professions of their faith without wavering," and if deprived, as she is, of any legal establishment in her favour, and remote from the Immediate Influence and direction of her lawful Governors the Bishops, she has stood unmoved and gained a respectable footing, what might be expected if these were once to take place?

The Establishment of Episcopacy in America has been long talked of and long expected; and I humbly beg the Hon'ble Society's pardon if I should take the liberty to observe that this could never in any former time be introduced with more success than at present. Many of the principal Quakers wish for it in hopes it might be a check to the growth of Presbyterianism, which they dread, and the Presbyterians, on the other hand would not chuse to murmur at a time when they are obliged to keep fair with the Church whose assistance they want against the Combinations of the Quakers who would willingly crush them. I hope to be indulged if with all humility I should further observe that it is thought the lands lately belonging to the Romish Clergy in Canada, are sufficient to support a Bishop in America, and a number of Missionaries in the new Conquests without adding to the burden of the Mother Country; and that His Majesty if properly applied to would be graciously pleased to appropriate them to this use. These things perhaps have been already mentioned to and considered by the Society. But the Affection which I bear to the Church of England would not suffer me to omit any hint that I thought might be an advantage to her.

As it will be my highest ambition in life to spend and be spent in promoting the Kingdom of Christ, I shall think it the duty and Glory of my office whenever a door is opened to preach the "Glad tidings of Salvation" to the unenlightened Heathen around me. But the time for doing this seems yet at a distance. The Indian war still rages; and the fierceness and barbarity of these faithless wretches at present strike a dread and terror upon any attempts of this kind. Colonel Boquet is now at the Head of a large Body of Troops in the heart of their Country; and it is hoped will reduce them to such terms as they will not for the future dare to violate. Whenever this is done, Missionaries may be able, under the influence and direction of Heaven to bring Numbers of these poor Infidels to the knowledge of the true God and to embrace the Gospel of his Blessed Son. Notwithstanding the hardships and difficulties that must unavoidably attend this great work I shall never refuse to bear my part in it when prudence and a prospect of success shall invite to it. I have already a very laborious part in the Vineyard as will appear from the following view of the different Churches under my pastoral care.

The town of Lancaster contains about 600 houses, and is a very respectable and wealthy place. It has a large and elegant German Lutheran Church, a Calvinist Church, a Moravian Church, a Quaker Meeting, Presbyterian Meeting, a Popish Chapel, constantly supplied by Jesuitical Missionaries, besides the Church under my care which is a Stone Building with a handsome Steeple and neatly finished within. . . .

At these Churches I officiate Sunday about alternately, and have never to my knowledge been absent once, even in the severest weather except detained by sickness, to which I was always happy enough to be a stranger till of late. I have baptized within this twelvemonth 115 Infants, 12 White Adults and 2 Black ones. Four or five of these were Converts from Quakerism. The rest were such whose parents had belonged to the Church, but dying early they neglected this

Sacrament till roused to consider the great necessity of it. They all came to the Font well prepared, and were able to give a good account of their Faith. The Catechetical Instructions to my young people are never omitted; and here I have the pleasure to acknowledge the receipt of the Catechisms sent for their use, for which in their name I return many thanks. They were very acceptable, and I am persuaded will be useful. . . .

Besides these stated duties I am often called 10, 15, or 20 Miles to visit the sick, bury the dead, &c., which greatly adds to my fatigue. My Itinerancy also bears heavy upon me in my present state of health. . . .

PHILLIS WHEATLEY ON SLAVERY (1774)

From Phillis Wheatley to Samson Occom, Feb. 11, 1774, from *Boston Post-Boy*, Mar. 14, 1774, p. 3.

Reverend and honored Sir,

I have this Day received your obliging kind Epistle, and am greatly satisfied with your Reasons respecting the Negroes, and think highly reasonable what you offer in Vindication of their natural Rights: Those that invade them cannot be insensible that the divine Light is chasing away the thick Darkness which broods over the Land of Africa; and the Chaos which has reigned so long, is converting into beautiful Order, and reveals more and more clearly, the glorious Dispensation of civil and religious Liberty, which are so inseparably united, that there is little or no Enjoyment of one without the other: Otherwise, perhaps, the Israelites had been less solicitous for their Freedom from Egyptian Slavery; I do not say they would have been contented without it, by no Means, for in every human Breast, God has implanted a Principle, which we call Love of Freedom; it is impatient of Oppression, and pants for Deliverance; and by the Leave of our Modern Egyptians I will assert, that the same Principle lives in us. God grant Deliverance in his own way and Time, and get him honor upon all those whose Avarice impels them to countenance and help forward the Calamities of their Fellow Creatures. This I desire not for their Hurt, but to convince them of the strange Absurdity of their Conduct whose Words and Actions are so diametrically opposite. How well the Cry for Liberty, and the reverse Disposition for the Exercise of oppressive Power over others agree,—I humbly think it does not require the Penetration of a Philosopher to determine.

THE ANGLO-AMERICAN BACKCOUNTRY

In the 1750s, the trans-Appalachian backcountry became the focus of growing tension over land claims between Britain, France, and Native Americans. Appalachia and the Ohio River Valley stood in between the growing British and French colonies, and the allegiance of Native American groups also lay in the balance. English traders led by the prominent negotiator George Croghan established a British presence at Pickawillany, on the Miami River in present-day Ohio, but New France authorities forbade the English from intruding on what they regarded as their territory.

In 1752, New France's governor, the Marquis Duquesne, commissioned a joint expedition with Ottawa allies to destroy Croghan's post. The French force wrecked the village, killing a number of Croghan's traders and taking trade goods to the French fort at Detroit. The Indian warriors killed, boiled, and cannibalized Memeskia, a Miami leader and ally of the English, as a warning to the region's Native Americans that they should stop working with British traders. Duquesne soon ordered the construction of a string of outposts from Lake Erie to Fort Duquesne, situated at the forks of the Ohio in western Pennsylvania. Later this fort would become one of the key points of conflict in the great war for imperial control of North America. The backcountry became the decisive zone of conflict in the latter decades of the American colonial era.[1]

The number of Africans, British, and Europeans continued to expand in the eighteenth-century English colonies, which partly accounted for settlers' increasing proximity to Native Americans and the French. As we have seen, the number of slaves dwarfed the total of European immigrants to the Americas:

some 219,000 slaves disembarked in mainland North America from 1701 to 1775, which was eclipsed by the almost two million slaves who came to the Caribbean islands during the same period. Among Europeans coming to the mainland, the English and Welsh fell behind in the eighteenth century, and Scots, Scots-Irish, and Germans came to the fore. Perhaps 350,000 English and Welsh settlers came to North America in the seventeenth century, while only about 73,000 came during the first three-quarters of the eighteenth. Ireland supplied about 115,000 immigrants in the period 1700–1780, with most of them Scots-Irish people coming from Ulster, or Northern Ireland. Scotland produced another 35,000 emigrants during that time. At least 85,000 German-background immigrants came during the century's first eight decades.[2]

The vast majority of the African emigrants were forced and unfree, but a number of the European emigrants also came under some terms of indentured servitude, or as convicts. The Caribbean planters turned mostly to slaves for workers, but mainland farmers and other industries still needed both slaves and servants in the eighteenth century. Improved transportation and increasing demand meant that record totals of slaves, servants, convicts, and free emigrants were coming to the American colonies. Around 100,000 of the European emigrants in the first three-quarters of the eighteenth century were indentured servants, including some felons who had been assigned to bound labor in the colonies.[3]

Indentured servitude offered the prospect of transport to the colonies, where one might acquire land if you lived out your term of service. But many servants complained about dishonest brokers, harsh treatment, and dashed hopes. Many endured experiences like those of Maria Barbara Kober, a German emigrant from Schwaigern (in modern southwestern Germany). In spring 1738 she left with her new husband and baby, en route to Philadelphia. On the journey from Rotterdam to England's southern port of Cowes, the Kobers' infant died. The journey from England to Philadelphia took sixteen weeks. When they arrived, the Kobers looked for means to pay off the debts incurred because of the passage, and Maria indentured herself to a family outside of the city. This meant that she had to leave her husband behind in Philadelphia, and she worked for four years as a servant without a word from him. (Her husband had actually died not long after she left.) She looked for him in the city following her release, but unable to find him or steady work, she returned to her master's family.[4]

Other immigrants to America from Europe came under different kinds of duress. The most common kind of forced European immigrant was the convict. From 1718 to 1775, Britain deported some 50,000 criminals to North America, and more than half of the English immigrants during that time were convicts. By far the most common destination for these white criminals was the Chesapeake. The treatment of convict workers was similar to that of slaves, as they crossed the Atlantic bound in chains. In America, they were sold at auction and typically used as farm workers. Unlike slaves, they were not bound in perpetuity, normally serving sentences of seven or fourteen years. Their shorter terms accounted for their relatively cheap price, which was about a third of the cost of a slave.[5]

The Scots and Scots-Irish immigrants filling the new settlements of the backcountry came from three distinct sources. The smallest group were the Lowland Scots, but they were more prosperous and educated than most other British immigrants. Most of them had some connection to the Chesapeake tobacco trade. By the 1760s, tobacco accounted for 80 percent of all Scottish imports from America. Many new Scottish immigrants were like John Henry, father of the Patriot leader Patrick Henry. John Henry journeyed to Hanover County, Virginia, in 1727, some sixty miles inland from the colonial capital at Williamsburg. Henry had attended (but did not graduate from) the University of Aberdeen, and came to Hanover due to a connection with a wealthy tobacco farmer there. Patrick Henry's uncle and namesake, Patrick, was an Aberdeen-educated Anglican minister who also immigrated to Hanover County, where he became the rector of St. Paul's Anglican parish.[6]

Highland Scots, from the north and west of Scotland, came in bursts across the eighteenth century, motivated by political turmoil and economic unrest. The suppression of Jacobite rebellions in 1715 and 1745 (Jacobites wished to return the Stuart line to the British throne, and the Scottish Highlands were a Jacobite stronghold) dispersed many Highlanders within Britain and across the ocean. Especially after the 1745 revolt, English authorities sought to break up the old Highland clan system and seized the lands of clan leaders. Clusters of Highland settlement sprung up from Georgia to Prince Edward Island in Canada. Many Highlanders were infected with a "spirit of emigration," disdaining to seek refuge among the Lowland Scots and preferring to seek opportunity in the colonies. One observer reckoned that the Highland emigrants "launched into a new world breathing a spirit of liberty and a desire of every individual becoming a proprietor, where they can imagine they can still obtain land for themselves and their flocks of cattle at a trifling rent or of conquering it from the Indians with the sword."[7]

Many Scots had immigrated to Northern Ireland, or Ulster, in the seventeenth century, only to have their children and grandchildren immigrate to America in the early eighteenth. Financial problems and conflict with the Catholic Irish prompted some 100,000 "Scots-Irish" to come to the colonies from 1718 to 1775. They represented the single largest ethnic migration from Britain to the colonies in the eighteenth century. They brought with them an intensifying commitment to the Reformed Presbyterian faith, and shared in the revivals of the Great Awakening.

Famine conditions in Ireland in the 1720s prompted satirist Jonathan Swift to pen his "Modest Proposal," in which he suggested that the Irish could solve all their problems by eating their children. The women and men of Ulster had little time for macabre joking, however, as terrible harvests and the unreliable nature of the region's linen trades turned their eyes across the ocean. Unlike convicts, slaves, or indentured servants, most of the Ulster immigrants had some financial means. Many paid for their Atlantic passage, and came with their families. Many of them—especially Presbyterians—resented the disadvantages that non-Anglican Protestants endured in the officially Anglican north of Ireland. Observers noted that it was the "hardships and oppressions which the Protestant Dissenters laboured under" that led great numbers to transport "themselves to the American Plantations."[8]

As with many immigrants, the Ulster Scots followed in paths cut by earlier commercial and religious pioneers. Many in Ulster already had ties to the Middle Colonies. The town of Derry in Ulster had vital trading connections to Pennsylvania, importing a great deal of flaxseed grown there. Northern Ireland also exported vast amounts of linen to the colonies, much of which was fabricated from American flaxen fiber. The British delivered some 60,000 yards of linen to the colonies in 1706, a total that rocketed to 400,000 yards in 1741. A number of Ulster settlers, many of them Quakers or Presbyterians, had already left for Pennsylvania or East Jersey by the end of the 1600s. Presbyterian pastor Francis Makemie, regarded as the father of American Presbyterianism, began ministering to English, Scottish, and Welsh Presbyterian families in the Chesapeake in the 1680s.[9]

By the mid-1700s, Ulster Scots represented a dominant presence in the Presbyterian churches of the Middle Colonies. As Presbyterian pastor Samuel Blair (who was from Ireland himself) noted in 1744, "all our congregations in Pennsylvania except two or three chiefly are made up of people from Ireland." The earliest immigrants congregated in frontier settlements like Donegal, named for an Irish town. Most grew flax for trade, as well as subsistence crops. They could acquire acreage on the frontier, but many had little besides land. One early Scots-Irish settler, Joseph Cochran, listed a Bible, "old bedding," and "iron utensils" among his only worldly goods. These colonists made their own clothes and built their cabins from logs. The early Scots-Irish communities were rife with unregulated violence and conflict with Indians, who were often their

closest non-Irish neighbors, and who often used desirable tracts of land. Part
of the appeal of Presbyterian religion, which slowly built a solid institutional
presence among the Scots-Irish through the middle decades of the 1700s, was
that it gave the immigrants a semblance of order in this dangerous, disorienting
world.[10]

Roughly the same number of German immigrants as Ulster Scots came to
America during the eighteenth century, about 100,000. Like the Ulster immigrants, most of the Germans came through Middle Colonies ports, especially
Philadelphia. Religious and political conflict, as well as economic dislocation,
drove many Germans to move, particularly from the Rhineland of southwestern Germany. Most of the Germans were Protestants, and many were affiliated
with sectarian and pacifist movements, such as Moravians, Mennonites, and
Amish, who were drawn to Pennsylvania's tradition of religious freedom. They
fueled the remarkable religious and ethnic diversity of the eighteenth-century
Middle Colonies. Few in the colonies were comfortable with this kind of diversity, and expressions of mistrust about the Germans, Irish, and other groups
became common. Swiss settler Esther Werndtlin was appalled by the pluralism
she observed in Pennsylvania in 1736, writing that "the religions and nations are
innumerable, this land is an asylum house for all expelled sects, a refuge for all
delinquents of Europe, a confused Babel, a receptacle for all unclean spirits, a
shelter of devils, a first world, a Sodom." Most early modern Europeans had a
high view of their ability to apprehend religious truth, through the Bible and
the illumination of the Holy Spirit, so a multiplicity of sects could signal degen-
eracy as much as healthy diversity.[11]

German ethnic identity often united the immigrant communities in the
Middle Colonies, but sectarian differences could sunder ethnic ties. The pacifist groups, in particular, often felt themselves besieged not only by Anglo-
American colonists and Indians, but also by mainstream Lutheran and Reformed Germans. They readily employed the rhetoric of martyrdom to help
define their besieged American self-understanding. One Mennonite wrote a
typical verse of martyrdom in the Bible he brought from Germany to Pennsylvania:

The martyr's role is wholly gain
In contrast to hell's frightful pain;
That role is brief, whereas 'tis sure
That hell forever will endure.

He who holds Jesus in his heart,
Though troubles be his earthly part,
To heaven's joys goes happily
To live through all eternity.

Such sentiments helped persecuted Germans filter their experiences of leaving Europe and making new homes on the American frontier. The German Christians circulated countless German-language imprints, hymn books, and prayer guides that emphasized the sufferings expected by Christ's peaceful witnesses.[12]

Some radical groups from the Continent found space in eighteenth-century America to create experimental spiritual communes, ones that seemed to flourish in the "wilderness" setting of the backcountry. In the 1690s, dozens of German Pietist followers of Johannes Kelpius founded the Woman in the Wilderness community to the west of Philadelphia. But this commune, like a number of others, floundered after the passing of its leader. In the 1730s, a similar group led by Conrad Beissel—who had heard about the Woman of the Wilderness before leaving Germany—established the Ephrata cloister in Lancaster County, Pennsylvania. Like Moravian radicals, the Ephrata group emphasized the feminine qualities of the divine. Beissel focused on the figure of the virgin Sophia, the female embodiment of God and the source of godly wisdom. The Ephrata pilgrims enacted programs of fasting, celibacy, and self-denial, and operated an influential printing press to distribute their teachings and hymns. Beissel directed an intensive singing school, through which the community might literally manifest the harmony of the Holy Spirit (who was often cast in female qualities). They pursued "the holy dove," Beissel wrote, "which has . . . unsealed the gates of the secret and hidden wisdom and has come forth to us and opened us a glimpse of the secret of Paradise." The "Babel church" of Europe, Beissel asserted, had lost touch with that revelatory source of wisdom.[13]

Beissel affected the style of a prophet, preaching with his eyes closed and Bible shut, ostensibly to open himself to the leading of the Spirit. One chronicler of Ephrata averred that during his addresses to the commune, "wonderful mysteries were often revealed through him of which he himself had before been ignorant." By the late 1720s, Beissel had repudiated infant baptism and received re-baptism himself from a German Baptist (or "Dunker"). He also repudiated Sunday as the Christian Sabbath, and taught that the Saturday Sabbath remained compulsory for Christians. Beissel insisted that sex of any kind was profane, and that true saints should maintain celibacy, even in marriage.

His teachings drew a number of followers to Ephrata, including several married women whose enthusiasm for Beissel and celibacy did not sit well with their husbands. One of his most prominent converts was Maria Sauer, the spouse of the Germantown, Pennsylvania, printer Christopher Sauer. The cloister's printing operation was among the most elaborate in colonial America, publishing an array of texts, including German translations of John Bunyan's *The Pilgrim's Progress* and the Quaker Anthony Benezet's antislavery *Observations on the Enslaving, Importing, and Purchasing of Negroes*. Fueling the desire for martyrology in the region, they produced a vast 1,512-page edition of the Dutch *Martyrer-Spiegel*, the largest printed item in America prior to the Revolution. Ephrata struggled in Beissel's waning years, and began to dissolve after his death in 1768.[14]

The backcountry presented religious opportunities for sectarians, evangelists, and missionaries alike. The growing white populations of the backcountry needed churches and pastors. The denominations that won the battle for the backcountry—especially the Baptists and, following the Revolution, the Methodists—became America's largest Protestant groups. The Separate Baptists of New England took the lead in evangelizing not only their own region's interior, but also that of the southern colonies. The key leaders in the southern missionary effort were Baptist convert Shubal Stearns and his brother-in-law Daniel Marshall, who itinerated from Connecticut, through Virginia's Shenandoah Valley, and into central North Carolina. At Sandy Creek, North Carolina, they formed a Baptist church in 1755 from which the Separate Baptist movement radiated throughout the southeast. Within seventeen years, the Sandy Creek Baptists had planted forty-two additional churches across the southern backcountry. Anglican itinerant Charles Woodmason noted with dismay in 1765 that the Baptists were "the most numerous and formidable body of people which the [Anglican] Church has to encounter with, in the interior and back parts" of the South.[15]

Women played a prominent role in all evangelical churches, but not often in such a formal way as in the Separate Baptists' congregations. Many Separate Baptists ordained women as deaconesses, and some even chose women eldresses. These women played a quasi-pastoral role in the churches, especially for the female believers, whom the eldresses taught, baptized, and represented before the elders of the congregation. Shubal Stearns's sister Martha Marshall commonly spoke to mixed audiences of men and women, sometimes reducing "a whole concourse into tears by her prayers and exhortations." Daniel Marshall's sister Eunice likewise exhorted publicly. Like many Baptist itinerants,

Eunice Marshall ran afoul of local authorities on at least one occasion and landed in jail for her subversive preaching, even though she was pregnant at the time.[16]

Prior to their move to North Carolina, Martha and Daniel Marshall spent a year in the Mohawk mission village of Onaquaggy, on the Susquehanna River in Pennsylvania. For them and many evangelicals, missions to the Native Americans of the interior remained an attractive, if daunting prospect. As we have seen, Jonathan Edwards ministered to Indians at Stockbridge, Massachusetts, following his expulsion from his Northampton congregation. But Edwards's disciple David Brainerd made a greater impact on the Anglo-American view of Indian missions, primarily through Brainerd's journal, which Edwards edited for publication. Brainerd struggled to find the right outlet for ministry until 1745, when he began working among Delaware Indians in rural New Jersey. Aided by his Native American translator, Moses Tattamy, Brainerd saw dozens of conversions at his Crossweeksung mission.

Brainerd's intense piety drew his attention farther afield, however, to the Indians of the Pennsylvania backcountry. He went to the Indian town of Shamokin, where he conversed with a Delaware "king" about his faith, but Brainerd determined that "the devil reigns in the most eminent manner in the town." Brainerd was not the only white traveler to have this reaction to the multiethnic trading and diplomatic center at Shamokin. When Moravians Martin and Anna Mack set up a mission there in 1745, many Indians ridiculed them. Soon they had to confront a group of drunk Indians who intruded into their hut, and who "looked very dismal and roared like the very beasts." After only about six weeks there, the dismayed Macks went back to the Moravian town of Bethlehem. Martin reckoned that Shamokin was the "very seat of the Prince of Darkness." Missionaries found their greatest success among Indians living closest to white settlements, many of whom had already suffered deep disruptions because of their encounters with European colonists.[17]

In spite of his troubled reaction to Shamokin, David Brainerd moved on to Juniata Island, at the confluence of the Juniata and Susquehanna rivers in Pennsylvania. There he observed a Delaware ritual that culminated in the sacrificing of ten deer. Shamans on the island were working to discern the reasons for epidemic diseases that were ravaging the native people of the area. Brainerd wrote that they made "all the wild, ridiculous, and distracted motions imaginable; sometimes singing, sometimes howling . . . grunting, puffing, etc." But Brainerd also met a Delaware prophet with whom he felt a strange kinship. After an initial encounter in which the prophet, wearing a wooden mask, shook a tortoise-shell rattle in his face, the two settled down to discuss spiritual matters.

They exchanged views on faith, and the prophet affirmed some of Brainerd's Christian convictions, while denying others. Brainerd appreciated the way that the man was trying to call his people back to traditional Indian ways, and to reject the corruptions of European trade goods, especially alcohol. "There was something in his temper and disposition that looked more like true religion than anything I ever observed amongst other heathens." Sometimes Brainerd wondered how God could ever break through to Native Americans, but at Juniata he saw a glimmer of hope.[18]

From eighteenth-century Georgia to Nova Scotia, white settlement in the Anglo-American backcountry was growing, and it was not entirely a result of the available (or Indian-held) land that seemed to promise wealth. Colonial governors and British officials also saw the settlement of German and Scots-Irish people on the trans-Appalachian frontier as a component of imperial policy, securing that region for Britain. As the colonies repeatedly faced wars and uprisings with Native American groups, from the Tuscarora War in Carolina in 1711 to Father Rale's War in northern New England in the 1720s, leaders believed that they were at risk of a pan-Indian revolt, inspired by French and/or Spanish intrigues and anger among Indians over British seizure of their lands. The British colonists also feared that the backcountry could become a haven for runaway slaves. Settling sympathetic white Protestant colonists in the backcountry could help stabilize the region and keep it more firmly under the umbrella of British authority.

Virginia officials were especially active in recruiting European settlers to the frontier. In the early 1730s, the governor there issued land grants totaling 385,000 acres in the Shenandoah Valley. They mandated the recruitment of families to settle the lands as part of the terms of the grants. Most of the families recruited were from the German Palatinate or Northern Ireland. The governor explained that it was in the king's interest to "encourage such settlements, since by that means we may in a few years get possession of the [Great] Lakes, and be in a condition to prevent the French surrounding us by their settlements." But the governor acknowledged that any frontier residents lay "exposed to the barbarous insults of [the] Indians, and the foreign nations they call in to their aid." More settlers could form a potent barrier against such threats.[19]

One German settler who came to the Shenandoah Valley was Jost Hite, who had originally relocated from Germany to England in 1709, part of an exodus of thousands fleeing the devastation wrought by the War of Spanish Succession. Within a year, Hite and 2,500 other Germans left England for New York under an agreement that the immigrants would work to produce naval stores such as pitch and tar to pay off the cost of their Atlantic voyage. New York's governor also had notions of settling the German refugees on the borders of the colony, to serve as protection against the French and their Indian allies. These projects never panned out, and Hite subsequently married and moved to Pennsylvania. Around 1730, he began hearing that Virginia had "proposed to give encouragement for the settlement of the frontiers of that colony which were much exposed to the incursions of the Indians and other enemies." Soon Virginia granted Hite 140,000 acres in the Shenandoah region, with the stipulation that he needed to recruit a family per every thousand acres. Hite personally acquired five thousand acres at Opequon, building a distinctively German home there that also functioned as a tavern. He also built a mill on Opequon Creek, and he and his neighbors petitioned Orange County, Virginia, authorities to construct a public road between the mill and a nearby ford on the Shenandoah River. Early Opequon was dominated by German and Scots-Irish settlers, who grew European grains, but little tobacco. Because of this agricultural focus, and the settlers' modest means, slavery played a marginal role in the Shenandoah. Conflict over Native Americans' land always loomed as a possibility for settlers like the Hites, as the Six Nations Iroquois considered the Shenandoah their territory and the whites as interlopers.[20]

Georgia was a latecomer to the British imperial settlement of North America, and more than any other it fit the model of a buffer colony of white European Protestants. Or at least that was the Georgia trustees' original vision. A group of London-based philanthropists, led by General James Oglethorpe, sponsored the venture. British leaders had been discussing the founding of a colony south and west of the Savannah River (South Carolina's western border) since the 1710s, when continued concerns about Spanish and French expansion, and the ravages of the Yamasee War, convinced many that the English needed to control these interior lands before a Catholic power did. Anxieties about Catholic expansion went higher when the French founded Fort Toulouse in present-day east Alabama in 1717, and the port city of New Orleans in 1718. Georgia's trustees hoped that they could counter Spain and France while also providing an outlet for Britain's landless poor, and for refugees displaced by Europe's wars of religion and empire.

In 1733, Oglethorpe founded Savannah on a bluff not far from the mouth of the river. Further south, at the mouth of the Altamaha River, he placed a settlement of Highland Scots at Darien. And up the river from Savannah, he established the village of Ebenezer for the Salzburgers, a group of German Lutherans forced to relocate from the Continent because of their Protestant faith. Because Oglethorpe and the trustees were seeking to foster a colony dominated by modest white farmers, they took the unprecedented step of banning slaves from Georgia. They discouraged the production of rice, the staple crop of South Carolina's plantations, and instead envisioned Georgia becoming a competitor in goods commonly imported to Britain from the Mediterranean, such as wine, olives, coffee, and silk. But none of these goods ever flourished in Georgia, and pressure grew in the 1730s to rescind the policy on slavery.[21]

In retrospect, Georgia's ban on slaves was fated to fall, because it emerged not from any hard conviction about slavery's immorality, but instead from an idealistic view of beneficial white settlement. The ban was difficult to enforce, and many came to believe that unless Georgia pursued the paths of white prosperity adopted by its southern and Caribbean counterparts, the colony could not thrive. One influential proponent of this view was evangelist George Whitefield, who located his Bethesda orphanage near Savannah, and who wanted to establish plantations at Bethesda in order to fund operations there. He also believed that white Christians had a moral responsibility to evangelize slaves, and he did not see any necessary contradiction between proselytizing African Americans and owning them as slaves. In 1751, trustees permitted white Georgians to import and own enslaved people. Over the next quarter-century before the Revolution, Georgia, with its Anglo and African populations clustered near the coast and up the Savannah River, came to mimic South Carolina's demographics and economy. Many new settlers came from South Carolina, hoping to develop rice and indigo operations along the seacoast.

African Americans did not come to the trans-Appalachian backcountry in great numbers, partly because of the rarity of plantation agriculture there. But blacks did play a role in backcountry society, and whites entertained fears about the mountains as havens for slave maroons, or runaways. One of the most fascinating backcountry residents of Virginia was Edward Tarr, or "Black Ned," who had purchased his freedom in Pennsylvania. In 1754 he bought land in Augusta County, Virginia, making him the first African American real estate owner west of the Blue Ridge mountains. From his background as a slave, Tarr had gained blacksmithing skills, and he also spoke German, which was unusual for any American slave, but useful for Tarr in his backcountry setting. Also unusual was Tarr's marriage to a white woman, with whom he lived in Augusta County.[22]

Tarr had fallen under the influence of Moravian preachers in Pennsylvania while still a slave, and in 1753 a group of Moravian travelers encountered Ned and his wife in Virginia and recorded the episode. One of the Moravians needed his horse re-shod, so they visited Tarr, "the only smith in these parts. . . . The negro and his wife, who was a Scotch woman, were very friendly," the Moravian recalled. They asked that when the Moravians passed through again, they would stop and preach, "for they loved people who spoke of the Saviour. The negro understood German well." Although Tarr never formally became a Moravian, he owned a Moravian book of sermons and welcomed their itinerant ministry. (Like other people of African background, he may have also appreciated the Moravians' relatively egalitarian racial views.) Tarr likely attended the Presbyterian church of Alexander Craighead, who like the blacksmith relocated to Augusta County in the early 1750s. Tarr joined Timber Ridge Presbyterian Church, and in 1753 he and other church members signed a document calling for a new pastor of the church, and pledging ten shillings a year toward the minister's salary.[23]

In 1761, Tarr's standing in Augusta County came into serious question, when a former white resident of the county presented a claim that he owned Tarr, having purchased him from a relative of Tarr's former master. Tarr was apparently prepared for this eventuality, as he presented a raft of documents demonstrating that he was legally free. County judges were inclined to believe Tarr, but also to give his accuser a hearing. In what must have been a galling development, the judges made Tarr post five hundred pounds sterling as security to guarantee his appearance at a hearing. Tarr posted bond and did indeed appear. His accuser did not, so Tarr remained a free man. The county magistrates identified Tarr as a "Negro Man . . . who has resided in this County for Ten years last past and is a Freeholder." Although some affluent whites in the trans-Appalachian backcountry owned slaves, and the legal status of free blacks like Tarr was tenuous, Tarr found a niche to reside as a respected "freeholder"—a member of community and church—even in late colonial Virginia.[24]

Beginning with the Glorious Revolution, Britain engaged in a series of wars with France and Spain, conflicts that the Peace of Utrecht (1713) technically put on hold for a quarter century. But colonial expansion and ongoing Protestant-Catholic tension meant that localized conflict was more likely to continue in the North American colonies than in Europe itself. In the early 1720s, British and French hostilities in New England focused on Jesuit missionary Sebastien Rale. Rale had long worked among the Abenakis of Maine, and as British settlers continued to establish settlements in northern New England, Rale encouraged the Abenakis to push back in defense of their lands. He wrote a letter to British officials and denied that the growing tension was his fault: "'tis you English, you seize our lands against our will. . . . Shall [the Abenakis] be cheated, driven from their lands and prayers, and shall not I counsel and defend them?" Massachu-

Germantown, Pennsylvania, Mennonite Meetinghouse, built 1700, photograph
circa 1900 to 1906, courtesy of Library of Congress, Prints and Photographs Division,
Detroit Publishing Company Collection.

setts put out a hundred-pound bounty for the Jesuit, and in 1724 New England
troops attacked his mission village at Norridgewock, shot and scalped Rale, and
brought his scalp along with those of dozens of natives back to Boston.[25]

Just as New France seemed a menacing presence to northern British colonists, Spanish possessions in Florida and the Caribbean aggravated British colonists in the South. The Spanish resented the founding of Georgia, a territory
that they still claimed. Tensions between Georgia and Florida turned into open
conflict in 1739, with the outbreak of the War of Jenkins' Ear, named for an
unfortunate British captain who had his ear cut off by Spanish attackers near
Florida in 1731. Jenkins reportedly kept the ear and displayed it when testifying
before Parliament in 1738. Britain and Spain went to war again in 1739, with
action spanning the Gulf of Mexico, and major British assaults on Caribbean
Spanish ports, including Portobelo and Cartagena.

Georgia entered the war when James Oglethorpe raised an expedition against
St. Augustine, Florida, in 1740. Oglethorpe had hoped to recruit a massive force

built largely on recruits from South Carolina, but that colony was still reeling from the Stono Rebellion and was not inclined to offer much support, especially in the form of the hundreds of armed slaves the general had requested. Moreover, Oglethorpe had asked for two thousand Native American recruits, but got just five hundred Creeks and Cherokees. Undeterred, Oglethorpe brought about 1,600 men to Florida, but they bogged down in the swampy terrain around St. Augustine. Finding that they could not launch an effective siege against the town's fort, Oglethorpe had to retreat. One of the British captains in the botched campaign called it an "ill-concerted and worse conducted attack."[26]

The Spanish retaliated against Georgia and Oglethorpe in 1742, overrunning British coastal defenses at St. Simons Island, south of Darien. But in multiple engagements in July 1742, Oglethorpe's defensive forces, including numbers of Highland Scots and Creek Indians, decimated the Spanish invaders, who retreated from Georgia. Oglethorpe's friend and ally George Whitefield compared the defense of Georgia to the Old Testament's accounts of Israel's victories over the Canaanites. Oglethorpe attempted yet another campaign against St. Augustine in 1743, and although this one was more damaging to the Spanish in the area, he still failed to conquer the town itself.[27]

Places on the imperial periphery, from Georgia to Nova Scotia to George Croghan's Pickawillany, became the focus of back-and-forth aggression between Europe's powers in the mid-eighteenth century. The stage was being set for a major clash pitting Spain and France against Britain for control of North America and the Caribbean. In the far northeast, the French and British exchanged hostilities over their respective outposts at Canso and Louisbourg. The French had begun building the Louisbourg fortress on Cape Breton Island in 1720, with the intent of protecting the region's valuable fisheries and the entrance to the Gulf of St. Lawrence. The French used Louisbourg as a base for attacks on the British posts at Canso and Annapolis Royal, Nova Scotia, in 1744. The French and their Mi'kmaq allies made four failed attempts on Annapolis Royal over the next three years. Reports of scalp-taking by the Indians led Massachusetts to declare war on the Mi'kmaqs and issue a scalp bounty on them: one hundred pounds sterling for the scalp of an adult male Mi'kmaq, fifty for those of women or children.[28]

Massachusetts summoned a force of four thousand men to assault Louisbourg in 1745. Assisted by a British fleet out of the Caribbean, the colonial troops were led by William Pepperrell, a close associate of evangelist George Whitefield, who counseled Pepperrell about the campaign. Pastors called on those left behind to pray for the defeat of the French and Catholic power, and the New England troops conquered the fortress with surprising ease. It was Britain's most important victory in the North American side of King George's War (1744–48), or the War of the Austrian Succession. New Englanders, who were still bickering over the divisions caused by Whitefield and the Great Awakening, found in the Louisbourg campaign an opportunity for harmony. Northampton's Jonathan Edwards, who had a number of men from his congregation join Pepperrell's army, regarded the victory as "a dispensation of providence, the most remarkable in its kind, that has been in many ages." He rejoiced that "we live in an age, wherein divine wonders are to be expected."[29]

Final resolution between Britain and the Catholic empires in America was frustratingly elusive, however. Louisbourg itself was given back to the French in the European treaty of Aix-la-Chapelle in 1748. Europe's powers might declare formal peace, but how could they resolve the raw hostilities in America, which were always complicated by uncertain borders and complex alliances with Native Americans? The destruction of Pickawillany and New France's insistence on building new forts in the Ohio River valley escalated the anxiety among British colonial leaders. France and Spain, they feared, could easily exploit Native Americans—and perhaps even slaves—to tighten a noose of Catholic power around Britain's mainland and Caribbean colonies. In the mid-1750s, British authorities would attempt to resolve this tension, seeking to decisively expel the French from the backcountry. This desire would precipitate the Seven Years' War.[30]

A ST. ANDREW'S DAY FESTIVAL, HANOVER, VIRGINIA (1736)

From *Virginia Gazette* (Parks), Nov. 26, 1736, p. 4.

We hear, from *Hanover* County, that on *Tuesday* next, (being St. *Andrew's* Day,) some merry-dispos'd Gentlemen of the said County, design to celebrate that Festival, by setting up divers Prizes to be contended for in the following Manner, (to wit,) A neat Hunting-Saddle, with a fine Broad-cloth Housing, fring'd and flower'd, etc. to be run for (the Quarter,) by any Number of Horses and Mares: A fine *Cremona* Fiddle to be plaid for, by any Number of Country Fiddlers, (Mr. *Langford's* Scholars excepted:) With divers other considerable Prizes, for Dancing, Singing, Foot-ball-pay, Jumping, Wrestling, etc. particularly a fine Pair of Silk Stockings to be given to the *handsomest Maid* upon the Green, to be judg'd of by the Company.

THE WOMEN'S ORDER OF THE EPHRATA CLOISTER (1745)

From Julius Friedrich Sachse, *The German Sectarians of Pennsylvania, 1742–1800* (Philadelphia, 1900), 193–98.

"What shall we say more of the quiet and justly in God enamoured souls, how they arrange their lives and conduct, so as to please only and alone their King of Heaven, whose kingdom is not of this world. Therefore our life and conduct cannot agree or conform to the world, whether it be in eating and drinking,—sleeping or waking,—in clothing or other requisite things pertaining to the natural life. Thus we have taken it into hand to deny and refute such engagements, and have schooled ourselves to be moderate in our eat and drink, and subsist upon little, and that with scant preparation, not according to the usual desire of nature, but merely reflecting upon the necessity of human frailty, so that the spirit may the more readily accomplish its divine task. Our sleep we have also arranged so that we can without great difficulty keep the time of our midnight vigil. Thus we make no further preparation when retiring to rest, than to lay down in the clothing or habits we wear during the day. Our couch is a bare bench, the pillow, a small block of wood or small straw pillow,— more frequently neither,—in this matter every one has their option.

"O! blessed souls, who are thus enriched by the King of heaven, that they be worthy to go out with him before the city and help carry his ignominy until death. Souls which the Lord at the proper time will exalt and set in honor in the house of our God."

"Now follows our daily school practice and labors before God that we can bring our bodies under earnest subjection, so that the spirit may not be pained or hindred in its daily routine, therefore we regulate all our work so as to mortify the body under the spirit and bring it under bit and bridle, so that we can control it and guide it to the proper uses of the spirit.

"As we have first renounced all vanities of the world, our future conduct will be guided according to the discipline of the body. We will begin by contracting to the utmost our eating and drink, sleep and waking. So that our whole life and conduct be that of a suffering and dying pilgrim upon earth, for which reason we have divorced ourselves from the ways and customs of this world, and daily and hourly learn the manner and laws of our crucified Jesus, who instructs us in all things and taught us abnegation of self, and to take up the cross and follow him.

"Then again it is to be mentioned what is requisite to keep duly and properly within bounds. Firstly, it is meet that we keep proper order with our eating. As it is set inevitably that there is to be but one meal a day, it will be held in the evening, and great stress is laid that the entire Society assemble at it. It may happen during the day that one perhaps takes a bite of bread, owing to our weakness, this is not prohibited to such as feel the necessity of it. Let them partake of the same as a special gift, and acknowledge themselves a debtor unto God, and pray for him to grant the strength yet wanting.

"What further concerns our virginal discipline, before the meal, all shall be served, and none shall have the right to exercise their own will, but show due respect. Whatever else takes place is an exception and not within the rule of discipline.

"Concerning our sleeping and waking, which is also within divine and regular bounds. Six hours are designated for spiritual and bodily rest, the remaining hours of the night we spend in dutiful spiritual and bodily exercises, for these six hours are kept with great strictness. For this purpose, one sister is ordered to see to the awaking of the whole society; when the time for sleep has expired, she is to light the candles and lamps in every room to awaken the sisters from their sleep. This order is changed weekly from one class to another. The six hours of rest, can be passed by each soul as she pleases. She can either sleep or stay awake, for they are given over to her welfare. The remaining time, however, comes under our virginal rule of discipline, which we have already said is to be passed in dutiful exercises.

"What then further concerns our intercourse with and toward one another, is this: It is to be striven in all seriousness and diligence, that our life be modest, quiet, tranquil and retired, so that each becomes an example for the other, and exemplifies the secret course of life and communion with God. All levity and needless gossip with one another, or light laughter, is not to be thought of, nor shall it occur in this spiritual society. Therefore it is unnecessary to make much of this rule, as it is not considered and much less likely to occur.

"It is further to be said of the mood of the hearts and souls who have sacrificed their whole life unto God, and live for him in the silent contemplation of their heart, and walk in his ways.

"Should it happen in our spiritual society that we have to go out among mankind, be it as a visit, or to follow the natural inclination of our mind, to call on friends or relatives. It is known to God how it all causes pain to both heart and spirit. There is no greater pain than this as it is all so contrary to our virginal discipline and can never agree with it, when it is done by reason of the weakness of the spirit, and not according to our rule, therefore we count it a disgrace when it occurs, etc.

"According to our virginal discipline no visits can be permitted except such as are called for by an urgent necessity and if it were possible to be relieved entirely, it would be to our pleasure, then we could live entirely to the duties of our calling. But so long as circumstances that such is to be in our Society, that for spiritual and corporeal reasons cannot be obviated, it is requisite that we bring them under order and within bounds, so that the desire lead not our perverse nature into temptation under the pretext of performing spiritual duties. Therefore proper precautions are to be taken, etc.

"Now it is ordered that the sister selected as the overseer of her class is to be the absolute ruler and guide, governing herself so that the souls who stand before God and have been placed under her charge by the superior of the whole society are equally treated; that to none is given too much or too little; and when anything happens, no matter in which class, if one or another has any desire to go out the sister overseer, as the supervisor, is to well interrogate the souls of their desire for the proposed visit and learn whether their desire be a dutiful one of the mind or one of our perverted nature, which generally emanates from the uncontrolled will, not yet brought into subjection under the holy will of God and our discipline, etc.

"Concerning the sisters who are chosen as overseers, they are well to instruct the souls and daily and hourly remind them of their hidden walk in the faith of God, and to steadily maintain that intercourse until our labor and trouble have reached a blessed end, and seek to discourage all unnecessary goings out to visit natural friends or acquaintances; further, to instruct and remind them that the tongue of truth hath taught and said that whosoever doth not give up father, mother, brother and sister, yea even his own life, cannot be my scholar nor follower.

"It is to be noted that when one or another sister in a class finds that she wants to go out, be it either by duty or permission, she is to know that such is not to be according to her desire, but only after a previous application to the overseer of her class, who can investigate whether to grant or refuse and act as she thinks best the matter will stand before God, assuming that the monitors will so shape their lives that they prove a bright example to their subordinates, who shall have confidence in their monitor, etc.

"First of all, in every class of sisters who live together a certain one shall be an overseer or monitor, who shall have supervision over all matters, opportunities and conditions as they present themselves. What her duties are to be will be briefly stated: Be it known that such a sister is to strive in all earnestness that her life and walk be without fault or blemish in the society, and she must be in unity and full accord with the spiritual and personal poverty and deprivation whereby our laudable community is blessed by God, etc.

"To such a sister all power may be given, and she is to use her best endeavor for the souls and take heed of the outside trifles, such as the carrying of wood, kindling the fires, drawing water, lighting the lights. The time of awakening is to be well noted, and the rule for locking and securing the door is to be well seen to, so that all unseeming egress and incoming may be stopped. Then the society can all the more easily walk within the confined discipline of the rule of the spirit."

A PROPOSAL FOR A GERMAN- AND SWISS-POPULATED COLONY IN WESTERN VIRGINIA (1730)

From Charles E. Kemper, ed., "Documents Relating to a Proposed Swiss and German Colony in the Western Part of Virginia," *Virginia Magazine of History and Biography* 29 (1921): 184–86, 187.

"Whereas the British Subjects hitherto setled in the Several Colonies upon the Sea Coast of the North Continent of America have not yet been able to extend any of their Settlements beyond the great Ridge of Mountains which divide those Inhabitants from the Lakes and Branches of the River Messussippi, by which means the French Indian Traders from Canada have for ten Years without Interuption Caried on a Commerce with the Western or Naked Indians upon the Lakes and behind the British Colonies on Lands and Territories which of Right belong to the Crown of Britain. And whereas the underwritten Thomas Gould of London, Merchant, John Ochs, Jacob Stober and Ezekiel Harland have by their humble Petition to the Lords Commiss^rs for Trade and Plantations dated _____ besought their Lordships favour to obtain a Grant from his Majesty of a certain Tract of Land extending from behind the great Mountains in Virginia beginning at the two headed Mountain in breadth two Hundred Miles North, bounded to the East by the West line of Pensylvania and to the West by the River Messussippi upon which they undertake to Settle one hundred Families within three years from the date of such Grant on pain of Forfeiture and by their Acquaintance in Switzerland and other parts of Germany to bring over such a number of Industrious Protestants at their own proper Charge to become faithful Subjects of his Britannick Majesty and Setlers on the Tract of Land aforesaid as will not only form a strong and sufficient Barrier to all the British Colonies aforesaid against any opposite Interest or Enemy whatsoever but will also secure the Trade Friendship and Correspondence of the said Western or Naked Indians, by means whereof the Exportation of Course Woolings and large Quantities of other British Manufactures will be vastly Increased, as well as the product of Silk Hemp, Flax, Pot-Ash and Wines greatly encouraged, to favour the ballance of Trade on the part of Great Britain, And as a Testimony that the said Petitioners have no private End or Interest in view but what is founded upon and perfectly Consistent with the Laws Liberties Trade and Prosperity of Great Britain, They are not only willing but earnestly desire that their Patent or Grant from the Crown may be limitted in the following Particulars or in such others of the like Nature as his Majesty in his Royal Wisdom shall think fit to ordain.

1. That all persons whatsoever going over to Inhabit and Settle on the said Tract of Land to be called the Province of Georgia or such other name as his Majesty shall think fit, be thereupon Intituled to the same Common Rights Liberties and Priviledges as British Subjects in America do or ought to enjoy." . . .

5. That an Unlimited Liberty of Conscience be established in the said Province and an equal Priviledge allowed to the Publick Profession of all Religions excepting Heathenism Jews and Papists who are to be utterly disqualified and for ever excluded from holding any office of Trust or Profit in that Province and all Professors or other Practitioners in Physick or Law shall be obliged to apply for and Receive a License from the Supream Provincial Court and Authority before their Admission to Practice in their respective Profession.

St. Augustine, Florida. From *Description de l'univers, contenant les differents systemes du monde* (1686). Courtesy of the John Carter Brown Library at Brown University.

6. That all Commerce or Traffick of any kind whatsoever with the subjects of any European Foreign Nation be strictly Prohibited and that the party Convicted of offending herein whether it be in the Woods or amongst the Settlements of such Foreigners shall be fin'd one hundred Pounds Sterling. . . .

SPEECH OF JAMES OGLETHORPE ON THE FOUNDING OF THE GEORGIA COLONY (1733)

From Peter Force, ed., *Tracts and Other Papers Relating Principally to the Origin* (Washington, D.C., 1896), 1: 13–15.

I should think myself very much wanting in justice and gratitude, if I should neglect thanking your Excellency, you Gentlemen of the Councel, and you Gentlemen of the Assembly, for the assistance you have give to the Colony of Georgia. I have long wished for an opportunity of expressing my sense of the *universal zeal*, which the inhabitants of this Province have shewn for assisting that Colony; and could not think of any better opportunity, than now the whole Province is virtually present in its General Assembly. I am, therefore, Gentlemen, to thank you for the handsome assistance given by private people, as well as by the public. I am to thank you, not only in the name of the Trustees, and the little Colony now in Georgia; but in behalf of all the distressed people of Britain and persecuted Protestants of Europe, to whom a place of Refuge will be secured by this first attempt.

Your charitable and generous proceeding, besides the self-satisfaction which always attends such actions, will be of the greatest advantage to this Province. You, *Gentlemen,* are the best judges of this; since, most of you have been personal witnesses of the dangerous blows this country has escaped from French, Spanish, and Indian arms. Many of you know this by experience, having signalized yourselves personally; either, when this Province by its own strength, and unassisted by every thing but the courage of its inhabitants, and the providence of God, repulsed the formidable invasions of the French; or, when it defeated the whole body of the southern Indians, who were armed against it, and invaded the Spaniards, who assisted them. You, *Gentlemen,* know there was a time, when, every day brought fresh advices of murders, ravages, and burnings; when, no profession or calling was exempted from arms; when, every inhabitant of the Province was obliged to leave their wives, their families, their useful occupations, and undergo all the fatigues of war, for the necessary defence of the country; and, all their endeavors scarcely sufficient to defend the western and southern frontiers against the Indians.

It would be needless for me to tell you, who are much better judges, how the increasing settlements of the new Colony upon the Southern frontiers, will prevent the like danger for the future. Nor need I tell you, how much every plantation will increase in value, by the safety of the Province's being increased, since the Lands to the southward already sell for above double what they did when the new Colony first arrived. Nor need I mention the great lessening of the burthen of the people, by the increasing of the income of the Tax, from the many hundred thousand acres of land, either taken or taking up on the prospect of future security. The assistance the Assembly have given, tho' not quite equal to the occasion, is very large, with respect to the present circumstances of the Province; and, as such, shews you to be kind benefactors to your new-come countrymen, whose settlements you support; and dutiful subjects to his Majesty, whose revenues and dominions, you by that means increase and strengthen.

As I shall soon return to Europe, I must recommend the infant Colony to your farther protection; being assured, both from your generosity and wisdom, that you will in case of any danger and necessity, give them the utmost support and assistance.

THE EARLY AMERICAN WEST

The French founded the village of New Orleans in 1718, at Bayou St. John, which flowed between the Mississippi River and Lake Pontchartrain. The Company of the West, which had received a charter to develop Louisiana in 1717, decreed that La Nouvelle Orléans would be founded somewhere on the river. The town could have ended up any number of places, from Fort Maurepas (Biloxi) on the Gulf coast, to an upriver settlement at Bayou Manchac, near present-day Baton Rouge. The low-lying location they picked, however convenient for trade and sheltered from attacks by the Spanish or British, was unsafe from deluges and hurricanes. Indeed, New Orleans flooded in 1719 and stayed underwater for six months.

The French envisioned Louisiana as a tobacco colony, but tobacco does not grow in swamps. Nevertheless, through skillful political maneuvering, the city's founder, the Sieur de Bienville, managed to locate it at Bayou St. John. Bienville worked hard to recruit French settlers with the promise of abundant land and cheap slaves. The riverine outpost became a slave village almost overnight. By 1721, some 1,200 people lived in New Orleans. Half of them were slaves, mostly African, but there were a few Native Americans too. Two-thirds of the free households in town owned a slave—the broadest pattern of slave owning that the city would ever know.[1]

The west—the Mississippi River and beyond—has typically not figured much in histories of colonial America. This omission is short-sighted, and is prompted by our collective fascination with the thirteen British colonies that declared independence in 1776. But when you set aside the anticipation of the Revolution, there are many important stories to tell about developments from New Orleans, up the Mississippi River valley, out onto the Great Plains and across the Spanish and Native southwest, to the Pacific coast and even to Alaska. If all we consider is population, there are notable contrasts: there were perhaps twice as many people living in the Great Plains (some 189,000) in the year 1700 than in New England (92,000). Even further west, where native peoples remained somewhat protected from European diseases, the population numbers were more impressive: some 221,000 people may have lived in California in 1700, and another 175,000 in the Pacific Northwest. This compares to about 53,000 people living in the Middle Colonies, and about 50,000 living in the lower South mainland colonies as of the turn of the eighteenth century. All told, people of European and African descent may have accounted for only about 15 percent of the North American population in 1700. But as European imperial settlements moved into the interior, and into California, over the course of the eighteenth century, tragic rounds of epidemic disease, war, and dislocation would follow. The native population at the time of Thomas Jefferson's election as president in 1800 was probably reduced by a quarter of that in 1700. By 1800, European and African peoples accounted for a stunning 85 percent of the North American population, a population reversal unsurpassed in human history.[2]

The Great Plains, the immense grassland area between the Mississippi River valley and the Rocky Mountains, was controlled by Native American tribes from Caddoan-speaking Wichitas in the south to Siouan-speaking Lakotas in the north. Many hunted buffalo (bison), America's largest mammals, which could weigh more than a ton. These animals, which numbered in the tens of millions in the early colonial era, adapted well to the arid grasslands of the plains, and supplied native people with meat, clothing, and other goods. Plains Indians attached spiritual significance to the buffalo and other animals, often including items from successful hunts in the sacred packets known as medicine bundles. A nineteenth-century observer of a Pawnee ritual said that the tribe's medicine bundle contained "a buffalo robe, fancifully dressed, skins of several fur-bearing animals, as the beaver, mink, and otter, the skull of a wildcat," stuffed bird skins, scalps and arrows taken from enemies, ears of corn, and "a few wads of buffalo hair." The Pawnees kept the bundle suspended from the roof of their lodge, beneath which was a seat of honor. The bundle needed delicate handling, lest spirits associated with corn or the buffalo send a blight or frustrate the hunt.[3]

Of all the European powers, the French generally maintained the best relations with the Plains Indians. Outside of Canadian New France, the French tended only to trade with Indians, and did not try to establish many farms on their land. Much of the French-Indian contact came via the *coureurs de bois*, young Frenchmen who often operated far into the interior, making their own trade business and often establishing relationships and even marriages with Indian women, in order to secure commercial footholds. The children of these relationships, the *métis*, also facilitated French-Indian commerce and alliances.

Indians in the Mississippi River valley often sought partnerships with the French, knowing that access to French goods—especially firearms—could help them consolidate power in their own regions. The Quapaws of present-day Arkansas, for example, visited French stations asking for more commerce, and they hunted more deer and bison in order to exchange their hides for European trade goods. But contact with the French precipitated the typical tragic decline of the Quapaw population (which had begun before they even met French traders and missionaries in person). Their numbers went from about five thousand in the 1680s to two thousand by the turn of the eighteenth century. One priest recorded that entire villages were wiped out from disease and war, with former thriving villages now dotted mostly by graves. By 1800 the Quapaws had dropped below one thousand people. In spite of these losses, the Quapaws showed little substantial interest in French Catholic missionary overtures. Instead, they tended to treat the priests like a different class of trader. They welcomed the priests and included them in calumet (ceremonial pipe) rituals, but few seemed to embrace Christianity.[4]

Other Indians did show signs of an indigenized Christian faith, however. A breakthrough among Illinois Indians came in 1693 when Marie Rouensa, the teenage daughter of a Kaskaskia chief, converted to Catholicism, precipitating the subsequent conversion of her parents and many others at the Kaskaskia mission, leading to more than two hundred baptisms in an eight-month period. The Jesuits followed these conversions with years of intensive study and translation of Catholic texts into Miami-Illinois, an Algonquian language spoken by the mission Indians, who were indispensable assistants in that translation effort. The resulting first lines of the *Credo*, or the Apostles' Creed, had a distinctive Illinois cast: "I believe in the great spirit who is the father, all powerful, who creates the sky and the earth. I believe in his only son, our chief, Jesus Christ . . . " Many key Christian terms, from "Lord" to "Trinity," had no direct parallel in Illinois, however. Although missionaries could never be sure that native converts were internalizing Catholic orthodoxy, the missions did produce some striking results. An Illinois delegation visiting New Orleans in 1730 impressed Catholic observers with their rigorous piety. A Jesuit noted that they went to mass every morning and said the rosary every evening. The city's Ursuline nuns joined the Illinois in a responsive Gregorian chant, during which the nuns "chanted the first Latin couplet, . . . and the Illinois continued the other couplets in their language." The leaders of the delegation presented the French governor with two calumets, one reflecting the common commitment of the French and the Illinois to Catholicism, the other their diplomatic and military ties.[5]

Despite their advantages, the French had their share of struggles and violence with Indians. The French founded Detroit in 1701 with a hope of making it a regional trade hub, and the fort's founder, Antoine de Lamothe Cadillac, invited a number of friendly Indians, including Ottawas and Potawatomis, to resettle in the area. This effort met initial success, as some six thousand Indians moved to the region within a few years. But then Cadillac offered to have Fox Indians move there, as well, who were traditional enemies of the area's Indians as well as the French. When Cadillac left for Louisiana, a vicious conflict erupted between the Foxes and the French, Potawatomis, and the Ottawas. In 1712, the Foxes and their allies attacked Detroit, and the French and their Indian allies struck back, killing many Fox warriors as they tried to escape and enslaving many of the Fox women and children, selling them to French farmers. The French continued sporadic war with the Foxes until 1730, when they finally determined to put an end to the tribe. In northeastern Illinois, allied French, Potawatomi, Illinois, and other native forces descended on a Fox fort. The Foxes tried to surrender, but the French would not allow it. Just as they had eighteen years before, the Foxes attempted to escape, but the French and Indian forces cut them down, killing some five hundred men, women, and children. What once had been a formidable tribe was now reduced to less than 150 people, yet the French governor still ordered his men to "kill them without thinking of making a single prisoner, so as to not leave one of the race alive in the upper country." Tiny numbers of the Foxes managed to survive in Wisconsin and Iowa, however.[6]

As the French in the lower Mississippi valley spread their tobacco farms up the Mississippi and took native land, they clashed with the Natchez Indians at almost the same time they attempted to wipe out the Foxes. Although the French settlers and their African slaves were outnumbered by the local Indians around Fort Rosalie (founded 1716), the fort's commander "insulted and infuriated the very people he should have been handling gently," noted a French observer. As the French kept pressuring the Natchez to cede their lands, Natchez leaders launched a surprise attack on the European colonists. One of the Natchez chiefs reasoned that

> the wares of the French yield pleasure to the youth; but . . . to what purpose is
> all this, but to debauch the young women, and taint the blood of the nation,

and make them vain and idle? . . . Before the French came amongst us, we were men, content with what we had, and that was sufficient: we walked with boldness every road, because we were then our own masters: but now we go groping, afraid of meeting thorns, we walk like slaves, which we shall soon be, since the French already treat us as if we were such. . . . For the least fault of our young people, they will tie them to a post, and whip them as they do their black slaves . . . why then wait we any longer? Let us set ourselves at liberty.

The Natchez attacked Fort Rosalie in late 1729, killing more than two hundred whites, amounting to a tenth of Louisiana's European settlers. Ominously, hundreds of slaves allied with the Natchez in the revolt. As with the Foxes, the French allied with other natives, in this case the Choctaws, in order to rout the Natchez and their African allies. The remaining Natchez melded into Chickasaw villages. The Chickasaws were allies of British traders, so the French went to war with them as well, commissioning Choctaw and Quapaw allies to take Chickasaw scalps and redeem them for cash. The French secured the return of many enslaved people who had fought alongside the Natchez. They sent some of them to be tortured and burned alive by the Choctaws.[7]

French Louisiana had imported about six thousand Africans over the course of the 1720s. Many of these died en route or after arrival, and the black population in Louisiana was only four thousand in 1731. Nevertheless, Louisiana had become a slave society, with blacks counting for 60 percent of the population. The enslaved people—mostly males—worked on farms, transported goods on the river, and bolstered New Orleans's infrastructure of levees and canals. City officials assigned some black workers to "cut down the trees at the two ends of the town as far as Bayou St. John in order to clear this ground and to give air to the city." Although slave masters experimented with cultivating tobacco, indigo, and rice, they struggled to seize upon a cash crop that would make the colony profitable.[8]

The large slave population led French authorities to produce Louisiana's 1724 *Code Noir*, statutes based on a similar code from 1685 in Sainte-Domingue, which established policies for the treatment of slaves. It encouraged masters and ministers to provide religious instruction to slaves, but it also outlined a range of restrictions and punishments for the colony's enslaved people, including the threat of dismemberment or execution for striking a free person, or for repeatedly running away. Although some slaves in New Orleans did receive Catholic instruction, one priest wrote that most black and Indian slaves in the colony "die without baptism and without any knowledge of the true God." The masters, the priest wrote, "think only of deriving profit from the work of these poor wretches without being touched by concern for their salvation."[9]

The *Code Noir* also forbade sexual relations between whites and blacks ("les Noirs"), whether slave or free. This stood in contrast to the relative freedom of French men to marry Indian women throughout the French colonies. Some French authorities and clerics encouraged French traders and farmers to marry native women, especially since female French settlers were in such short supply. One missionary argued in the 1710s that unmarried French men tended to live in exploitative relationships with Indian women as concubines, fostering irreligion and lassitude. Throughout the seventeenth century, other figures in New France had similarly speculated that if *coureurs de bois* would marry Indians, it would stabilize relations between the French and native trade partners. In general, Catholic missionaries took a more favorable view of Indian-French marriages than did secular officials. Nevertheless, French-Indian relationships bolstered trade alliances, while the offspring of French-African relationships seemed to threaten the integrity of the white-black color line that undergirded racial slavery. Thus, cross-racial unions may have been more helpful to trade-based segments of colonial economies than plantation-based ones.[10]

In spite of France's internal troubles with the Indian and African people of Louisiana, the Spanish were concerned about the French presence and made their own renewed efforts at colonizing the southwest. As in New Mexico in the seventeenth century, missionary priests did much of the early work in colonial Texas, where the Spanish opened missions among the Hasinai confederacy of Caddo Indians (misnamed the "Tejas") in east Texas in the 1690s. The Spanish came in such small numbers that they risked being overrun by the Hasinais, but they may have gained unwitting aid from the religious symbols they brought with them, especially their banners of the Virgin Mary. To the Spanish, these images signified the link between Spanish imperial power and Catholicism, but to the Indians, who associated women with peace, they indicated that the Spanish did not mean to make war. The Spanish included images of Jesus and the cross in their iconic repertoire, of course, but the royal standard featuring Mary was ubiquitous, especially in their rituals of meeting with the Hasinais. The Hasinais identified the Spanish with the Virgin: one French missionary related that a Hasinai tried to describe the Spanish to him by drawing a sketch of a "painting that he had seen of a great lady, who was weeping because her son was upon a cross." The initial goodwill between the Spanish and Hasinais was wrecked by epidemic disease and repeated assaults on Hasinai women by soldiers, and within three years the Indians ordered the Spanish and their missionaries to leave, which they did.[11]

By the 1710s the Spanish were back in Texas, establishing a presidio and mission at San Antonio in 1718, the same year as New Orleans's founding. One Spanish missionary described the original settlers of San Antonio as a motley group of "mulattoes, lobos, coyotes, and mestizos, people of the lowest order, whose customs are worse than those of the Indians." The Spanish opened four more missions near the town by 1731. The Franciscans normally had between two and six hundred "neophyte" Indians, mostly Coahuiltecans, residing in the missions. Priests worked with the Indians to teach them Catholic doctrine and practices, and to encourage them to live as European-style farmers. San Antonio's strategic location also made it vulnerable to Indian raids, especially by Lipan Apaches.[12]

War with Comanches led the Apaches into an alliance with the Spanish in the 1750s, and in 1757 the Spanish established an Apache mission at San Saba, 135 miles northwest of San Antonio and deep in Comanche territory. The Comanches saw the mission as a direct intrusion on their land, and they launched a devastating assault on it in 1758. Thousands of warriors, carrying French muskets, burned the mission and shot many of the residents, including two priests. They beheaded one of the priests and placed his body on the church altar. A similar incident transpired in 1766 at the unauthorized Franciscan mission at San Lorenzo, ninety miles south of San Saba. Most Apaches realized that trying to find protection under Spanish authority was futile, so they retreated to the margins of the Great Plains. Texas was not much of a refuge for Spaniards, either, and by 1760, about 1,200 Spanish settlers lived in Texas, half of them at San Antonio.[13]

Indians often fell under immense duress because of European diseases, but in the Great Plains, European contact could also bring new sources of strength and power. Among the most significant arrivals were horses, which were not native to the Americas, but which quickly became an integral part of Apache and Comanche societies. Horses, well adapted to the Plains — not least because they could graze on the bountiful grasses — extended these groups' ranges for hunting, commerce, and war making. The Apaches emerged first as the dominant horse culture of the southern Great Plains by the early eighteenth century (reflected in raids on places like early San Antonio). The Comanches made the horse even more central to their nomadic culture, and by the mid-eighteenth century they had supplanted the Apaches as the hegemonic Indian power of the southern Plains. By the late eighteenth century, Comanches had forged a "multifaceted trade empire" that could easily compete with Spanish power and other Indians across the Plains.[14]

Comanches conducted extensive raiding operations, stealing both livestock and humans. A Franciscan priest in 1751 observed the Spanish trade with the Comanches in Taos, noting with dismay the "trade and barter with these barbarians in exchange for deer and buffalo hides, and what is saddest, in exchange for Indian slaves, men and women, small and large, a great multitude of both sexes." Of course, the Spanish empire had a long tradition, dating back to Bartolomé de las Casas, of criticism of such practices as buying war captives as slaves. But officials justified the practice by suggesting that the slaves would otherwise be executed by the Apaches or Comanches, and that they might find baptism and salvation among the Spanish. Displaced from their home tribes and victimized multiple times over, the *genizaros*, as they were called, could be subjected to the worst kinds of abuses. One missionary in 1761 claimed that teenage girls and adult slave women were often publicly raped before both Spanish and Indian audiences before the "barbarians" turned them over to Spanish buyers. The slaves would work on New Mexican farms or in homes; some would be sent to labor in Mexican silver mines.[15]

The growth of French settlement put the Comanches in a stronger position against the Spanish, for if the Spanish tried to limit or ban the trade of guns or livestock, the Comanches could turn to French traders for supplies. Along the Arkansas River, flowing from present-day Colorado to Arkansas, where it met the Mississippi, the Comanches traded with the French for "rifles, gunpowder, bullets, pistols, sabers, coarse cloth of all colors, and other inexpensive merchandise, for skins of deer and other animals, horses, mules, burros, and a few Indian captives whom the Comanches have taken as prisoners from other tribes." The Spanish worriedly observed these trends, and needed to accommodate the Comanches in trade, even as Comanches raided Spanish farms and ranches. The Comanches split into western and eastern branches over the eighteenth century, the former more focused on trade, and the latter (centered in Texas) more on raiding. The Western Comanches, in spite of their nomadic habits, established a major trade center in the Big Timbers region of southeastern Colorado, which drew European and Indian visitors from across the Great Plains. This site symbolized their dominance until the late 1770s, when Spain—ever frustrated by Comanche raids—launched a war against the Western Comanches, who were also decimated by a massive smallpox epidemic in 1780–81. The Comanches and Spanish made peace in 1786, however, and the Big Timbers center revitalized. By the end of the eighteenth century, traders from the United States began to enter the Western Comanches' commercial orbit—American traders would supplant the Comanches as the key commercial force in the southern Plains during the antebellum period.[16]

In the northern Great Plains, the French expanded their trade networks into

Sioux territory by the late 1600s. The French and other Europeans still held out hope for a water passage to the Pacific, so in 1731 French authorities sent Pierre Gaultier de Varennes de La Vérendrye in search of this route. He also sought to broker peace between the Sioux, the French, and France's Indian allies (such as the Crees), but pressure from other Indians and financial opportunities led La Vérendrye to get involved in the capture and trading of Sioux slaves. In 1734 La Vérendrye purchased a slave of his own from Crees in return for some clothes, tools, and ammunition. The Sioux, enraged by the French traffic in slaves, attacked a group of La Vérendrye's men at Lake of the Woods, on the modern Canada/Minnesota border. They killed twenty-one, including one of La Vérendrye's sons and a Jesuit missionary. The Sioux beheaded the French, including La Vérendrye's son, mutilating his body and decorating it with porcupine quills.[17]

Hoping to find allies against the Sioux (and still hoping to find the Northwest Passage), La Vérendrye traveled in fall 1738 with hundreds of Assiniboines to the Mandan villages and trade center on the Missouri River near present-day Bismarck, North Dakota. The Mandan villages had apparently never seen a European visitor, but (like the Comanche center to the south) they were a vital hub of the Plains Indians' world. In spite of their isolation from Europeans, the Mandans already possessed some British and Spanish trade goods, acquired from other Indians who operated in networks far to the east and south. The Mandans had built five "forts" and perhaps as many as 130 lodges, each of which housed ten to twelve people. There were probably about six thousand people living in the villages. Although the villages were more scattered than European-style cities, the Mandan center had about as many residents as Charles Town, South Carolina, and Newport, Rhode Island, the fourth and fifth largest towns in English America at the time. The Lewis and Clark expedition, also looking for the Northwest Passage, would visit the Mandan villages in 1804, but by that time the Mandan center had fallen into serious decline as compared with the formidable place La Vérendrye encountered.[18]

It is striking how long European and European-American misinformation about the geographic basics of the American interior persisted, and how that misinformation shaped policy making and war. From Cortés to Thomas Jefferson, the false hope for the water route to the Pacific and the East Indies inspired Spanish, French, British, and American explorations and conflicts on the North American continent. Many in the French government, for example, remained convinced in the mid-eighteenth century that the British were still working to discover the Northwest Passage, and that if they did, it could disrupt the imperial and commercial balance of power in Europe. Such fears made the outbreak of new imperial conflict in North America, which did come in 1754 with the Seven Years' War, even more likely.[19]

If our typical focus on the English colonies and the coming of independence lead us to neglect places like the Mandan villages, that same focus—and a tendency to end the colonial era in 1763 or 1776—has obscured colonial development in Pacific America. Perhaps the most obscure among all European colonizers have been the Russians, who left no enduring settlements in the contiguous forty-eight states, but whose presence in the Pacific region was of considerable concern to the Spanish, British, and Native Americans of the northern Pacific and Alaska. As with the French in the east, the fur trade pushed Russian exploration into Alaska and the Aleutian islands. By the mid-eighteenth century, Russian fur traders had devastated the sable and sea otter populations in Russia's Siberian northeast, leading them to seek pelts in Alaska.

In 1763, four Russian ships visited the Aleutian islands of Umnak and Unalaska. When the traders demanded tribute from the Aleuts living there, the Aleuts attacked the Russians, killing hundreds and burning their ships. The Russian captain retaliated, summarily executing many Aleuts by fire and sword. "The slaughter was so atrocious," Aleuts recalled, "that the sea around the islet became bloody from those who threw themselves or were thrown into it." In 1784, Russians established their first permanent Alaskan settlement at Kodiak Island. In 1794, 331 male Russians lived in the area, along with a tiny number of Russian women. Ten Russian Orthodox missionaries also came to Kodiak. One observer of the Russian missions work proposed that "the Russians' desire for great profits served as a means for spreading the principles of Christianity among the Aleuts." But the Aleuts' population went into the familiar pattern of decline, falling from perhaps twenty thousand at contact to two thousand by 1800.[20]

Small though the Russian presence may have been, it prompted Spanish expansion along the Pacific coast, especially in California. A book titled *Muscovites in California* (1759), written by a Franciscan missionary to Mexico, typified Spanish fears about Russian incursions in the region. Even though missions had declined in importance in other parts of New Spain, Franciscans again led the Spanish efforts at colonizing "Alta California," which began in 1769, resulting in a chain of mission settlements from San Diego to San Francisco. In 1770, they established a presidio at Monterey and the nearby Mission San Carlos Borromeo. One Spanish explorer explained that Monterey would "defend us from attacks by the Russians": a delusional sentiment (Russians were hardly thinking of menacing the Spanish in California), but one that illuminates the imperial impetus behind the California missions. Leading the Franciscans was Junípero Serra, a former philosophy professor given to intense practices of mortification and piety, including self-burning and self-flagellation. Serra had nearly been assigned to Texas's San Saba mission in 1758, which surely would have sent him to his death. But now he pioneered Spanish work among the California Indians.[21]

Alta California at the time of Spanish colonization probably had more than 300,000 Indians living within the borders of the modern state. The Indians' villages were generally autonomous and had differing customs and dialects, making united native resistance against the Spanish difficult. Nevertheless, coercive and predatory behavior by many of the Spanish led to resentment against the colonizers. Ipais attacked and burned the San Diego mission in 1775, destroying the church's icons. Father Luis Jayme, one of the missionaries, had baptized almost two hundred Indians, but now Ipai attackers stripped him naked, crushed his skull, and disemboweled him. Serra thought that God would use Jayme's martyrdom to bring more Indians to Christ. Spanish authorities rounded up many Indians, however, subjecting them to whippings of fifty lashes or more in order to gather confessions about the uprising. A Spanish governor told a group of Ipai prisoners, "I must know everything," and that he had "a medicine to make them tell the truth . . . my medicine is punishment."[22]

In spite of the tensions endemic to the missions, the Spanish were able to retain thousands of Indian neophytes in them. There was a great deal of racial intermixing in New Spain among Spaniards and Indians, but still the Spaniards in Alta California maintained a twofold distinction between those they labeled *gente de razón* (people of reason) and *gente sin razón*. One Franciscan commented that he knew of no "nation so stupid, of such contracted ideas, and weak in both body and mind, as the unhappy Californians. Their characteristics are stupidity and insensibility, want of knowledge and reflection . . . in fine, a most wretched want of everything which constitutes the real man and renders him rational, inventive, tractable, and useful to himself and society." Although some Christianized Indians could cross over into the *gente de razón*, in general the terms of people with, and without, reason were synonymous with Spanish and Indian. The missionaries worked to mold the neophytes into Christians, as well as to teach them the Spanish language and European-style agriculture.[23]

Serra and the Franciscans envisioned the missions as bastions for neophytes, sheltered from the corrupting influences of Hispanic soldiers and traders, yet supplied with sufficient food and goods to allow them to practice their new

Christian faith in health. The priests tried to maintain disciplined adherence to the mass, and other sacred occasions, making attendance at services mandatory. They would call roll at mass, and each of the neophytes would come to the priest and kiss his hand as his or her name was called. The Franciscans punished Indians for absence from service, as well as for other signs of rebelliousness or sexual immorality. But they also were vigilant to stop instances of soldiers preying sexually on Indian women or boys, or living with Indian women as concubines. Their insistence on protecting vulnerable Indians from the Spanish put Serra and the Franciscans at odds with many of Alta California's civil officials. Although missionaries were losing authority in other parts of Spain's empire, Serra successfully campaigned for the Franciscans alone to exercise discipline over the mission Indians. A 1773 regulation made it clear that the "management, control, punishment, and education of baptized Indians pertain exclusively to the missionary Fathers."[24]

California Indians were faced with a difficult choice, as the missions offered short-term protection and sustenance. One Franciscan noted that "the foremost sermon with which these unfortunate savages can be reduced to our Holy Faith . . . is food, and clothing." But those who lived at the missions also died of disease at terrible rates. Infant mortality rates were high, women's fertility rates were low, and epidemic disease, including dysentery, influenza, and tuberculosis, was ever present. Venereal disease, especially syphilis and gonorrhea, was also common and added to problems of low fertility. The exact diagnoses and sources of these infectious maladies remain unknown, but the Spanish routinely commented on syphilitic symptoms, which one observer noted was "common among the Spanish and the Indians and causes even greater devastation, because absolutely no medical measures are taken to prevent it. The usual results are spots on the skin, horrible rashes, persistently running sores, painful aches in the bones, throat infections, loss of the nose, deformities and death." Many Indian children were born with syphilis.[25]

Still, the Franciscans hoped that prior to death the Indians could learn of Jesus and his ways. They were bolstered by the tradition that a seventeenth-century Franciscan nun, María de Jesús de Agreda, had been mystically transported to New Mexico and California to deliver the gospel to the Indians during her life. Similar reports circulated that Saint Francis himself, and missionaries of his order, had miraculously visited California centuries earlier. One old Indian woman reportedly told one of the new priests that her father once told her that "a priest who wore the same habit as we, had come into this land, not traveling on horseback or on foot, but flying . . . remembering this caused her to be a Christian." But the practical challenges of evangelism and indoctrination were formidable. Priests struggled to learn Indian dialects. They put their hope in teaching native children Spanish and using them as interpreters, but disease often felled the children before they could be of much help.[26]

Because of the linguistic difficulties, and because many missionaries had little confidence in natives' intellectual abilities, priests leaned heavily on the art and icons of Catholic devotional culture to instruct and retain baptized Indians. Serra was particularly keen on obtaining devotional art for the missions, making regular requests for art to Mexican church officials, in addition to requests for mundane supplies. In 1774 alone, Mission San Carlos obtained a painting of its patron, Saint Charles Borromeo, as well as images of Saint Bonaventure, Saint Louis, and the death of Saint Joseph. They also received engravings of a sorrowful Virgin Mary, Jesus on the cross, and a tree symbolizing the Franciscan order, in addition to a host of prints representing various popes and saints. The mission hung two paintings, *The Horrors of Hell* and *The Glory of Heaven*, opposite one another, in order to contrast the stakes of the Indians' choice between Christ and the devil. *The Horrors of Hell* showed the damned in the "jaws of a dragon" and devils torturing their victims with pitchforks and spears. *The Glory of Heaven*, which still hangs at the mission today, represented a range of biblical characters and angels, and some of the martyrs in the painting appear to be Indians, both by skin color and by attire.[27]

The extent to which California mission Indians internalized Catholic doctrine is hard to discern. Some surely imbibed Franciscan orthodoxy wholesale; others appreciated the potential value of the Christians' spiritual and material power; others undoubtedly complied with the friars' basic expectations in order to receive food and shelter, but quietly rejected their evangelistic message. In many reports, however, the missionaries trumpeted the successes in California. Serra wrote in 1774 from Mission San Carlos that "where but yesterday there had never been pronounced the name of God nor of Jesus Christ, [there are] more than two hundred souls, counting Christians and catechumens. . . . Three times a day they eat from what we provide them; they pray, sing, and work."[28]

In spite of such optimistic reports, friars seemed aware that mission communities were unstable, and that Indian inhabitants might show their frustration in methods ranging from leaving the mission to outright rebellion. The latter was uncommon, perhaps because whatever the Indians' grievances, those who lived at the missions were still dependent on Spanish supplies. More devout neophytes would not have considered lashing out against them, in any case. The missionaries employed certain Indians as assistants, giving the converts a kind of authority within the mission station. Even this practice entailed danger for the Spanish, as native assistants sometimes engaged in plots against the missions. At

Mission San Gabriel, a native helper named Nicolás José received baptism in 1774, and for a decade served in a variety of church capacities, such as godparent and marriage witness. In 1785, however, Spanish authorities preemptively arrested twenty-one San Gabriel Indians to stop an uprising, and some suspects identified Nicolás José as the ringleader of the plot. He was reportedly angry that the Spanish would not permit the annual fall Mourning Ceremony, in which natives honored those who had died during the year. (Nicolás José himself had lost two wives in succession to death in the 1780s.) Some at San Gabriel still saw this ritual as the moment when those who had passed away would gain entrance into the land of the dead. For his alleged crimes, Nicolás José was banished from the mission, sentenced to six years' hard labor at San Francisco's presidio.[29]

Threatened and actual Indian revolts scarred European settlements from California to New England. Back in New Orleans, the 1729 Natchez rebellion forced the French to rethink the whole character of the Louisiana colony. The dangers of extending plantation agriculture into the interior, and the instability of tobacco cultivation in the Mississippi delta, led the French largely to give up on that crop, which was partly replaced by dye-making indigo. The curtailment of the plantations effectively stopped slave imports, and cut adrift many of the slaves already in Louisiana. They helped fashion New Orleans into a sort of African market town, with many free and enslaved blacks engaged in licit and illicit commerce. New regulations in the 1740s and 1750s sought to control the slaves' business pursuits and nocturnal ramblings. Slaves now needed a permit to carry weapons and were ordered to observe a nighttime curfew. Officials warned against rural slaves entering New Orleans in the evening, for fear that they "commit every kind of malfeasance," including tavern-hopping.[30]

As elsewhere, missionaries joined in the effort to Christianize and civilize New Orleans, but some of them fell prey to the financial and social intrigues endemic to the town. New Orleans's founder, the Sieur de Bienville, worked closely with Jesuit priests, selling them large tracts of land upriver from New Orleans, which they used as a lucrative indigo plantation. But the Jesuits fell out of favor in France, where officials suppressed the order in the 1760s in a fit of resentment and suspicions that the missionaries were consumed with greed rather than piety. Paris authorities ordered the seizure and sale of Jesuit properties, and the destruction of their mission churches. In 1763, city officials auctioned off the Jesuit plantation to eager local buyers, leaving Capuchins as the city's predominant male clergy.[31]

Ursuline nuns and missionaries, who maintained a distinctive ministry to women, made an indelible impression on New Orleans's early religious culture. The Ursulines operated New Orleans's hospital, but they also sought to educate French, Native American, and African women in Catholic piety and doctrine. Twelve Ursulines came to New Orleans in 1727, founding a girls' school and a lay women's confraternity whose members ranged from plantation wives to poor widows. By the 1730s, women and infant girls represented about half of those Africans baptized as Catholics in New Orleans, even though females represented only about 40 percent of the enslaved population there. Nanette, one of the baptized slaves, worked in the home of Marie Payen Dubreuil, a confraternity member (as was Dubreuil's daughter-in-law). Nanette came to New Orleans from West Africa—she was likely a Wolof from Senegambia, where she probably first encountered French Catholicism. Women from this West African region often took on leading devotional and proselytizing roles in local African cults, roles that may have made the female confraternity's overtures to Nanette seem familiar. Nanette went on to have four daughters who also received Catholic baptism. Although African men received baptism in growing numbers, too, the Ursulines' efforts and those of Catholic laywomen to evangelize slave women bore significant fruit, giving a disproportionately African female cast to early New Orleans Catholicism.[32]

As New Orleans's Afro-French culture continued to grow, it (like so much of North America) could not avoid the implications of the climactic contest for empire, the Seven Years' War, which engulfed the continent in the 1750s and 1760s. Jamaican privateers blockaded New Orleans, which French authorities had long since determined was not worth keeping. In 1762, the French king quietly ceded Louisiana to the Spanish, news that did not reach New Orleans until well after the peace treaty of 1763 ended the war. The coming of new Spanish rulers and trade regulations irritated the city's creole elites, whose frustration crested in 1768 when they rallied French, German, and newly arrived Acadians (expelled from Nova Scotia by the British) in New Orleans and threatened the Spanish governor with rebellion. The governor abandoned the colony and headed for Havana, and the Spanish did not reassert control until summer 1769, when a detachment of two thousand Spanish soldiers arrived in New Orleans, resulting in the arrest of many of the rebels and the execution of five. These were all signs of the bewildering turns of imperial fortune resulting from the Seven Years' War. Although Louisiana would remain in Spanish and French hands for another four decades, the war seemed to give eastern North America decisively to the British.[33]

TRAVELS OF FATHER JAMES GRAVIER FROM THE ILLINOIS COUNTRY TO THE MOUTH OF THE MISSISSIPPI RIVER (1701)

From John Gilmary Shea, ed., *Early Voyages Up and Down the Mississippi* (Albany, N.Y., 1861), 125–30.

About noon we discovered four periaguas [canoes] of Akanseas; when my canoe got near land, an old man came into the water and carried me ashore on his shoulders. The chief made me sit down on a great bearskin, and the French on osier branches, which he made his young men cut. He presented me two piakimina cakes, which I distributed among the French; and afflicted as I was that they did not understand me, wishing to speak to them of God, I retired to pray for them, while the kettles were boiling. They served me a plate of sagamity of small Indian corn, and another of small corn whole, seasoned with excellent squash. I made a little present to the chief of the band, and on the 30th we went and cabined a league lower down, half a league from the old village of the Akansea, where they formerly received the late Father Marquette, and which is discernible now only by the old outworks (*dehors*), there being no cabins left.

On the 31st, about 9 A.M., we arrived at the village of the Kappa Akansea, who are at 24 deg., according to Father Marquette's estimate. The village is half a league from the water's edge. Mr. de Montigny planted a cross on the hill, which is very steep, and forty feet high. After saluting the cross and chanting the Vexilla Regis with the French we notified the Akansea by three guns, and in less than half a quarter of an hour at most, two young men appeared sword in hand, followed close by the chief of the Kappas and the chief of the Tourima, and twenty or thirty well made young men with their bows and arrows. Some had swords, and two or three English guns, given to them last year by the man who brought them a lot of merchandise to alienate them from the French, and especially from the missionaries, whom he had an aversion against, boasting that he would put the first he met in irons and put them to death. The French who took him where with to make him a pair of handcuffs with irons, and prevented his doing all the harm he proposed to do. He had already two concubines at the Kappas.

To resume; the chiefs invited me to go to their village, which consists of forty cabins. A part of the French accompanied me there, while the others guarded the canoes at anchor. They took me to the cabin of the chief, who made me sit down on a mat of dressed canes, and at the same time put on the fire a kettle of small Indian corn, seasoned plentifully with dried peaches. They brought me from another cabin a large platter of ripe fruit of piakimina. It is pretty much like the French medlar. The platter was presented to the chief to hand to me. As it is the most excellent fruit the Indians have from the Illinois to the sea, the chief did not fail to begin his feast with it. After tasting a little I passed the dish to Brother Guibert and the French who sat opposite me. I did the same with the sagamity. I remarked that all who entered the cabin stood at the door, and advanced only when the chief told them to do so and sit down. There was a Metchigamikoüé woman there, who acted as my interpreter, and confirmed the story of Father de Limoges' capsizing and loss of all he had. She game him her provision of Indian corn and squashes to carry him as far as the Natchez, and the chief gave him an earthen pot, after regaling him as well as he could. I asked him whether he recollected to have formerly seen a Frenchman dressed in black, attired like me, in their village. He replied that he recollected it well, but that it was so long ago that he could not count the years. I told him that it was more than twenty-seven years. He added that they danced at the Captain's calumet to him, which I did not at once understand, supposing that he spoke of the calumet of Illinois, which the Kaskaskias had given Father Marquette to carry with him on the Mississippi as a safe guard; but I found in the Father's journal that they did in fact dance the calumet to him. He then had me asked in how many days I would start, and having told him that I had come ashore merely to salute him in his cabin, and that I was going to embark, he begged me to remain at least one day, to have provisions prepared, and that all the young men of his village were very glad to see me. I replied to his compliment and stated that I was in haste to get to my journey's end. I had previously inquired whether there were any sick; my interpreter informed me that there were none. At last, after a good deal of going and coming, and many consultations with his people, the chief of the village asked me to stay till the next day, because he wished to dance the chief's calumet with his young men to me. As this is a special honor which is done but rarely, and only to persons of distinction, I thanked him for his good will, saying that I did not esteem myself a captain, and that I was starting immediately. My answer pleased the French, but it was scarcely agreeable to all the others, who by doing me this honor home to draw presents from me. The chief conducted me to the water's edge, followed by all his people, and they brought me a quantity of dried peaches, piachimina, and squashes. I made a present to the chief of a little lead and powder, and a box of vermillion to daub his youth, and some other trifle which he was much pleased with, telling him that I thanked him for the service he had rendered Father

Limoges. After I embarked they fired four guns, to which the people with me responded. Two leagues from the village there is a little river, on which they go in canoes in the spring, behind the hills, to their cabin doors.

As I have here mentioned the calumet, you will be pleased to have me tell you something of it here. There is nothing among these Indians more mysterious or commendable. No such honor is paid to the crowns and sceptres of kings as they pay to it. It seems to be the god of peace and war, the arbiter of life and death. To carry and show it enables you to march with assurance amid enemies who in the heat of the combat lay down their arms when it is shown. It was on this account that the Illinois gave one to the late Father Marquette as a safeguard among the nations of the Mississippi, through whom he was to pass on his voyage going to the discover of this river and the nations dwelling on it.

There is a calumet for peace and one for war, which are distinguished simply by the colour of the feathers with which they are trimmed. The red is a mark of war; they use it to also settle their disputes, to confirm alliances and to speak to strangers. It is a kind of pipe to smoke tobacco, made of a red stone polished like marble and pierced so that one end serves to receive the tobacco and the other fits on the handle. This is a hollow piece of wood, two feet long, and as thick as an ordinary cane. It is by reason of this that the French have styled it Calumet, corrupting the word, *Chalumeau*, because it resembles a pipe, or rather a long flute. It is embellished with the head or neck of various birds, whose plumage is very beautiful. They add also large red or green or other coloured feathers, with which it is all trimmed. They esteem it especially because they regard it as the calumet or piper of the fun, and in fact they proffer it to him to smoke when they wish to obtain calm, rain or fair weather. They would scruple to bathe in the beginning of hot weather, or to eat new fruits till after they had danced the calumet, that is to say, the chief holds it in his hands singing airs, to which the others respond, dancing and making gestures in time with the sound of certain instruments of the fashion of small drums.

A NATCHEZ INDIAN LAMENTS THE COMING OF THE FRENCH (CIRCA 1720S)

From Antoine-Simon Le Page du Pratz, *The History of Louisiana* (London, 1774), 41.

"Why," continued he, with an air of displeasure, "did the French come into our country? We did not go to seek them: they asked for land of us, because their country was too little for all the men that were in it. We told them they might take land where they pleased, for there was enough for them and for us; that it was good the same sun should enlighten us both, and that we would walk as friends in the same path; and that we would give them our provisions, assist them to build, and to labour in their fields. We have done so; is this not true? What occasion then had we for Frenchmen? Before they came, did we not live better than we do, seeing we deprive ourselves a part of our corn, our game, and fish, to give a part to them? In what respect, then, had we occasion for them? Was it for their guns? The bows and arrows which we used, were sufficient to make us live well. Was it for their white, blue, and red blankets? We can do well enough with buffalo skins, which are warmer; our women wrought feather-blankets for the winter, and mulberry-mantles for the summer; which indeed were not so beautiful; but our women were more laborious and less vain than they are now. In fine, before the arrival of the French, we lived like men who can be satisfied with what they have; whereas at this day we are like slaves, who are not suffered to do as they please."

LOUISIANA'S *CODE NOIR* REGULATES RACE AND RELIGION (1724)

From B. F. French, *Historical Collections of Louisiana* (New York, 1851), 89–90, 92–93.

BLACK CODE OF LOUISIANA

I. Decrees the expulsion of Jews from the colony.

II. Makes it imperative on masters to impart religious instruction to their slaves.

III. Permits the exercise of the Roman Catholic creed only. Every other mode of worship is prohibited.

IV. Negroes placed under the direction or supervision of any other person than a Catholic, are liable to confiscation.

V. Sundays and holidays are to be strictly observed. All negroes found at work on these days are to be confiscated.

VI. We forbid our white subjects, of both sexes, to marry with the blacks, under the penalty of being fined and subjected to some other arbitrary punishment. We forbid all curates, priests, or missionaries of our secular or regular clergy, and even our chaplains in our navy to sanction such marriages. We also forbid all our white subjects, and even the manumitted or free-born blacks, to live in a state of concubinage with blacks. Should there be any issue from this kind of intercourse, it is our will that the person so offending, and the master of the slave, should pay each a fine of three hundred livres. Should said issue be the result of the concubinage of the master with his slave, said master shall not only pay the fine, but be deprived of the slave and of the children, who shall be adjudged to the hospital of the locality, and said slaves shall be forever incapable of being set free. But should this illicit intercourse have existed between a free black and his slave, when said free black had no legitimate wife, and should said black marry said slave according to the forms prescribed by the church, said slave shall be thereby set free, and the children shall also become free and legitimate; and in such a case, there shall be no applications of the penalties mentioned in the present article.

VIII. We forbid all curates to proceed to effect marriages between slaves without proof of the consent of their masters; and we also forbid all masters to force their slaves into any marriage against their will.

IX. Children, issued from the marriage of slaves, shall follow the condition of their parents, and shall belong to the master of the wife and not of the husband, if the husband and wife have different masters.

X. If the husband be a slave, and the wife a free woman, it is our will that their children, of whatever sex they may be, shall share the condition of their mother, and be as free as she, notwithstanding the servitude of their father; and if the father be free and the mother a slave, the children shall all be slaves.

XI. Masters shall have their Christian slaves buried in consecrated ground.

XII. We forbid slaves to carry offensive weapons or heavy sticks, under the penalty of being whipped, and of having said weapons confiscated for the benefit of the person seizing the same. An exception is made in favor for those slaves who are sent a hunting or a shooting by their masters, and who carry with them a written permission to that effect, or are designated by some known mark or badge.

XIII. We forbid slaves belonging to different masters to gather in crowds either by day or by night, under the pretext of a wedding, or for any other cause, either at the dwelling or on the grounds of one of their masters, or elsewhere, and much less on the highways or in secluded places, under the penalty of corporal punishment, which shall not be less than the whip. In case of frequent offences of the kind, the offenders shall be branded with the mark of the flower de luce, and should there be aggravating circumstances, capital punishment may be applied, at the discretion of our judges. We command all our subjects, be they officers or not, to seize all such offenders, to arrest and conduct them to prison, although there should be no judgment against them.

XXVII. The slave who, having struck his master, his mistress, or the husband of his mistress, or their children, shall have produced a bruise, or the shedding of blood in the face, shall suffer capital punishment.

XXVIII. With regard to outrages or acts of violence committed by slaves against free persons, it is our will that they be punished with severity, and even with death, should the case require it.

XXIX. Thefts of importance, and even the stealing of horses, mares, mules, oxen, or cows, when executed by slaves or manumitted persons, shall make the offender liable to corporal, and even to capital punishment, according to the circumstances of the case.

XXX. The stealing of sheep, goats, hogs, poultry, grain, fodder, peas, beans, or other vegetables, produce, or provisions, when committed by slaves, shall be punished according to the circumstances of the case; and the judges may sentence them, if necessary, to be whipped by the public executioner, and branded with the mark of the flower de luce.

XXXI. In cases of thefts committed or damages done by their slaves, masters, besides the corporal punishment inflicted on their slaves, shall be bound to make amends for the injuries resulting from the acts of the said slaves, unless they prefer abandoning them to the sufferer. They shall be bound so to make their choice, in three days from the time of the conviction of the negroes; if not, this privilege shall be forever forfeited.

XXXII. The runaway slave, who shall continue to be so for one month from the day of his being denounced to the officers of justice, shall have his ears cut off, and shall be branded with the flower de luce on the shoulder: and on a second offence of the same nature, persisted in during one month from the day of his being denounced, shall be hamstrung, and be marked with the flower de luce on the other shoulder. On the third offense, he shall suffer death.

13

THE SEVEN YEARS' WAR

In 1753, British and French forces wrestled to control the spot where the Allegheny and Monongahela rivers converged, in western Pennsylvania, forming the Ohio River. This place became an epicenter in the larger imperial clash between France and Britain, and their respective Indian allies, to control eastern North America. The Marquis de Duquesne in 1753 sent a couple thousand French troops on an exhausting campaign to establish a string of outposts from Lake Erie to the forks of the Ohio. About a quarter of the overworked, sickly men died on the expedition, but it put the British—and the region's Indians—on notice that the French meant to dominate the area. Native traders, sensing a shift in the balance of power, began drifting away from the British. Virginia's lieutenant governor, Robert Dinwiddie, tasked eight men, led by twenty-one-year old George Washington, to confront the French and tell them to leave.[1]

On the way to Lake Erie, Washington stopped to observe the forks of the Ohio, where he "spent some Time in viewing the Rivers, & the Land in the Fork, which I think extreamly well situated for a Fort; as it has the absolute Command of both Rivers." Moving up to Fort Le Boeuf, near the lake, Washington presented his request to commandant Jacques le Gardeur de Saint-Pierre, a veteran of French imperial ventures among the Cree and Sioux tribes of the northern Great Plains. Saint-Pierre politely hosted Washington and his men, but made clear that he had no intention of withdrawing. "I do not believe myself obliged to submit," Saint-Pierre wrote, "no matter what your instructions may be, I am here by virtue of my General's orders, and I beg you not to doubt for one instant that it is my unshaken resolve to comply with them with all the exactitude and firmness that one would expect of the best officer." Washington could no nothing but trudge back to Williamsburg.[2]

Still, Britain's Ohio Company sought to counter the French by establishing a fort at the forks of the Ohio. Virginia's George Mason had arranged for the purchase and importation of twenty swivel guns for it in the summer of 1753. In the spring of 1754, a small British force began construction at the forks, but hundreds of French soldiers arrived and forced them to surrender. The French razed the British edifice and built the log-and-earth Fort Duquesne on the spit of land between the Allegheny and the Monongahela. At 160 feet across at its widest, Duquesne would become one of the most imposing structures in the North American interior. It was circled by a dry moat, and had enough room inside for a parade ground, a blacksmith's shop, a hospital, and a bakery.[3]

Robert Dinwiddie sent Washington back into western Pennsylvania in 1754 with a ragged force of 160 men. The French sent Ensign Joseph Coulon de Villiers de Jumonville with several dozen men to challenge Washington and ascertain his intentions. Securing the help of a Seneca leader and guide named Tanaghrisson (whom the English called the "Half King"), Washington located and surrounded the French detachment. A fifteen-minute firefight ensued before the French surrendered. During the negotiations for the terms of capitulation, Tanaghrisson approached the wounded Jumonville and said "Tu n'es pas encore mort, mon père" (Thou art not yet dead, my father). With this, Tanaghrisson raised his hatchet and sunk it into Jumonville's skull. As one contemporary account recorded it, the Half King "then took out [Jumonville's] Brains and washed his Hands with them and then scalped him." Tanaghrisson's men set upon the injured French, killing, scalping, and stripping each of them. One was decapitated, his head posted on a stake. Washington, stunned but unable to stop them, put the remaining French captives under guard and scurried away.[4]

The French interpreted the killing of Jumonville and his men as murder, and sent a massive force of French and Indian troops to attack Washington. The Virginians retreated to a ramshackle camp at Fort Necessity, where incessant rains swamped the men's tents even before the French assault commenced on July 3, 1754. As the English fighters huddled in mud-filled shallow trenches, the French poured musket fire down the hillsides into Fort Necessity. They were joined by fighters who had been traditional allies of the British: Shawnees, Delawares, and Mingos. Before he surrendered, a third of Washington's men were dead or wounded. The formal capitulation, drawn up by the French, blamed Washington for the "assassination" of Jumonville, an unwitting admission that would fan the flames of war in Quebec and Paris.[5]

Alarmed by the burgeoning conflict, British general Edward Braddock in 1755 assembled a force of 2,500 regular soldiers and colonial militiamen, planning for a complex invasion of western Pennsylvania. An eager Benjamin

Franklin put out a call for Pennsylvania farmers to send wagonloads of supplies for the grand campaign, for which they would receive compensation. Franklin warned that "if you do not this Service to your King and Country voluntarily, when such good Pay and reasonable Terms are offered you, your Loyalty will be strongly suspected; the King's Business must be done; so many brave Troops, come so far for your Defence, must not stand idle, thro' your backwardness to do what may be reasonably expected from you; Waggons and Horses must be had; violent Measures will probably be used." Pennsylvania's farmers took the hint and complied in abundance, sending not just horses and wagons but smoked meats, rum, brandy, tea, coffee, and other supplies for the road. Franklin recalled warning Braddock about the "ambuscades of Indians, who, by constant practice, are dexterous in laying and executing them." Braddock smiled "at my ignorance," Franklin wrote, and said that "these savages may, indeed, be a formidable enemy to your raw American militia, but upon the king's regular and disciplines troops, sir, it is impossible they should make any impression."[6]

Braddock was tragically mistaken. Within ten miles of Fort Duquesne, Braddock's weary army fell into a French and Indian ambush. Using unconventional tactics—hiding behind cover along the road—the Native Americans and French troops unleashed destruction on Braddock's force, wounding or killing more than half of his soldiers and officers. Braddock himself lay among the dead. George Washington twice had horses shot out from under him; he was haunted by memories of the debacle and retreat: "the dead—the dying—the groans—lamentation—and cries along the road of the wounded for help . . . were enough to pierce a heart," he recalled. For the moment, the French and their Native American partners had taken command of the war in North America.[7]

The British and the French realized that Native Americans remained a seminal force in the North American interior, whatever their weakened state due to European disease and land incursions. Especially in those areas in between French and British colonial possessions, Indian allegiances would be decisive. One English trader wrote in 1755, the year of Braddock's debacle, that "the prosperity of our colonies on the continent will stand or fall with our interest and favor among [the Indians]. While they are our friends, they are the cheapest and strongest barrier for the protection of our settlements; when enemies, they are capable of ravaging in their method of war, in spite of all we can do." Many tribes remained riven by disputes and were alienated from other Native American powers. Those who could muster intertribal and regional alliances stood strongest. The Comanches in the southwest, and the Six Nation Iroquois of the Great Lakes, were two of the most formidable such groups during the eighteenth century.[8]

The Iroquois—an alliance that added the Tuscaroras as a sixth member in 1722—had long used diplomacy, trading, and war to balance their interests among the British, French, and non-Iroquois natives. As early as 1676, New York governor Edmund Andros convinced Iroquois leaders to assist the New England colonies in defeating the allied forces of King Philip, or Metacom, who had brought England's northeastern colonies to their knees. A Mohawk-led attack on Metacom's warriors in early 1676 represented a terrible blow, helping to end King Philip's War six months later. In the 1670s, Mohawks and other Iroquois allies engaged in extensive "mourning wars," taking Algonquian and Susquehannock captives and adopting them into their own societies. In these conflicts, the Iroquois tribes bolstered their own populations and resources through Indian captives and English materiel. During a long-standing period of diplomatic peace between Britain and France from 1713 to 1744, Iroquois member nations tended to partner with the French in campaigns against enemy Native Americans, such as wars against the Fox in the upper Midwest from the 1710s to the 1730s. When war between Britain and France resumed in 1744, the Iroquois nations worked to do nothing that would pit member groups against each other, or that would fully align the confederacy with either France or Britain. The Onondaga Council asserted that "it was one matter for Europeans to go to war, since they had kings who ordered their subjects when to make war and when to stop for peace, and their subjects had to obey. It was not so with them. They have no king, every Indian was his own master, so if they should once enter into a war with one another, there could be no such thing as to come to a peace, but the war must continue forever."[9]

Iroquois leaders did occasionally enlist on the side of the British or French in war, but tried not to do so within Iroquois territory, or in a manner that would align them against other Iroquois confederates. The Senecas, including George Washington's ally Tanaghrisson, were a growing presence within the Ohio River valley and thus were inevitably touched by the conflict there in the 1750s. But Tanaghrisson scrupulously directed his hostilities toward the French, not the Canadian Iroquois allies of the French. Tanaghrisson and his warriors did not participate in the defense of Fort Necessity, so they avoided a direct clash with the Canadian Iroquois there.[10]

The Seven Years' War actually lasted nine years—from the killing of Jumonville in 1754 to the official peace in Paris in 1763. At the outset, the Iroquois and other

Indians tended (Tanaghrisson and other British allies notwithstanding) to side with the French, drawing on a long understanding that the French were more accommodating and less inclined to seize Native American lands. The British invested heavily in Indian diplomacy and gift-giving, too, but the small population of New France mandated that the French be cooperative with Indians. One French observer lamented how long it took Indian diplomats to "make up their minds. It requires authority, brandy, equipment, food and such. The job never ends and is very irksome." One Iroquois leader explained the advantages of siding with the French in 1755, asking his fellow Indians if they were "ignorant of the difference between our Father [the French] and the English? Go and see the forts our Father has created, and you will see that the land beneath their walls is still hunting ground . . . whilst the English, on the contrary, no sooner get possession of a country than the game is forced to leave; the trees fall down before them, the earth becomes bare." Working with the French entailed more benefits and less sacrifice for native groups.[11]

The shock of Braddock's demise encouraged Shawnees and Lenni Lenapes in the Ohio valley to begin attacking British frontier settlements. Many of the settlers were newer arrivals from Northern Ireland or Germany, but now they abandoned their cabins and retreated back toward Philadelphia. Benjamin Franklin came to Bethlehem, Pennsylvania, in 1756, seeking to bolster the colony's frontier defenses. Franklin wrote, "As we drew near [to Bethlehem], we met a Number of Waggons, and many People moving off with their Effects and Families from the Irish Settlement and Lehi Township, being terrified by . . . the Burnings and Murders committed in the Township on New Year's Day. We found this Place fill'd with Refugees, the Workmen's Shops, and even the Cellars being crouded with Women and Children; and we learnt that Lehi Township is almost entirely abandoned by the Inhabitants." Similar scenes of terrified refugees transpired further south. Across the Blue Ridge Mountains at Winchester, Virginia, the road was impassable because of "the crowds of people who were flying, as if every moment was death." Virginia's legislature instituted a new round of payments for Indian scalps. Dozens of Iroquois warriors participated in raids on the Pennsylvania and Virginia frontiers, yet the league still resisted a formal alliance with the French.[12]

War between Catholic and Protestant powers, as well as the horrors on the frontier, prompted many American colonists to frame the Seven Years' War in religious categories, even though the conflict originated in imperial competition and economic concerns. Samuel Davies, one of the leading ministers of the Great Awakening in Virginia, addressed Virginia militiamen in 1755, warning, "Our territories are invaded by the power and perfidy of France; our frontiers ravaged by merciless savages, and our fellow-subjects there murdered with all the horrid arts of Indian and Popish torture." The army of brave General Braddock, he lamented, was routed by a much smaller force of "dastardly, insidious barbarians." Now the "blood-thirsty savages" had fallen on frontier settlers, using on them "the most unnatural and leisurely tortures." He mused whether human nature could "bear the horror of the sight! See yonder! The hairy scalps, clotted with gore! The mangled limbs! The ript-up women! The heart and bowels, still palpitating with life, smoking on the ground!" These Indians, Davies thundered, were not "men; they are not beasts of prey; they are something worse; they must be infernal furies in human shape." Behind these devils stood the demonic spirit of France's "Popish slavery, tyranny and massacre." Citing an admonition from the prophet Jeremiah, Davies insisted that under the threat of such terrible foes, "cursed be he that keepeth back his sword from blood."[13]

In spite of British rage against the French and their Indian compatriots, the years 1754–57 were favorable ones for the French side. In 1757, French general Louis-Joseph Montcalm prepared for a major assault on Fort William Henry, which the British erected at the southern end of New York's Lake George. Although Montcalm was uncertain about using Indian warriors in the attack, word had filtered far into the western frontier about French successes, drawing some two thousand Native Americans, from Fox fighters of the upper Midwest to Catholic mission Indians from Canada. Montcalm realized that one could not really turn away such allies "in the midst of the American woods," so he agreed to use them in the attack on Fort William Henry. An advance party of Indians surprised some American provincial troops in late July, killing and capturing many.[14]

The full assault on Fort William Henry began in early August 1757, and after days of withering bombardment, the British garrison surrendered. Montcalm offered conventional terms, including a prisoner exchange; he did not consult with Native American leaders, who expected to take plunder and captives. This misunderstanding precipitated what became known as the Fort William Henry "massacre," as Indians entered the fort and assaulted British troops, taking a number of scalps. Other British troops were waiting nearby to march to another British fort, and some of the warriors also attacked these, taking supplies and captives, especially the women, children, and African Americans they discovered among Fort William Henry's expelled residents. As chaos descended on the column, Indians began tomahawking American provincials. The French troops tried to stop them, but may have unintentionally caused more American colonists to die, as the Native Americans may have preferred to take scalps if they were to be denied their captives. About 185 troops, servants, women, and children perished in the episode, and perhaps as many as 500 were taken as prisoners. A similar number escaped to French protection. Native fighters were disgusted by the French attempt to deny them what they saw as the just rewards of their service. Most simply left, taking supplies, captives, and scalps with them. (In a bitter irony, many of the captives were carrying smallpox, which undoubtedly contributed to a massive epidemic in the coming years that spread through many tribes of the Great Lakes region.) Most Indians, already hesitant about a full-fledged French alliance, determined after the Fort William Henry disaster that they would no longer assist the French. Some would go on to help the British, even though the massacre became a focal point for the kind of British anti-Indian hatred that Samuel Davies's sermon illustrated.[15]

Native American frustration with the French, combined with more effective British leadership, turned the course of the war. William Pitt became the new leader of the British administration in London, and he launched a decisive and expensive campaign to defeat the French in America. Raising new taxes and borrowing millions of pounds, Pitt guaranteed that the colonial assemblies would receive complete reimbursement for all the soldiers and supplies they provided in the war effort. This made the colonists much more responsive to British demands for help. The British also began fighting most of the war's battles with regular army forces (many of them recruited from the colonies, however), instead of less disciplined colonial militias. The British also secured well-timed assistance from Cherokees moving up from the south, who held France's former Indian allies in check. The Cherokees set the stage for a renewed British campaign against the French in western Pennsylvania, too, as the Indians conducted at least seventeen raids against Fort Duquesne in mid-1758. (Back in South Carolina, the Cherokees soon battled against the British—sometimes against the very soldiers they had helped in Pennsylvania—in a vicious war from 1759 to 1761.) Faced with abandonment by Indian allies, dwindling supplies, and an approaching British army, the French evacuated Fort Duquesne and blew it up. The British renamed the site Pittsburgh, and built a much larger fortress there than France's.[16]

Even though Native American support for the French had diminished, British authorities still harbored deep suspicion of any prospective native allies for the French. This antagonism helps explain the otherwise pointless 1759 raid by Robert Rogers's "rangers," regular army recruits from New England, against the village of St. Francis, a Jesuit mission among Abenakis close to the St. Lawrence River. Urged to "remember the barbarities that had been committed by the enemy's Indian scoundrels on every occasion," the rangers burned the entire village and killed many, including elderly Abenakis, women, and children. One Highland Scot ranger recalled that "those whom the flames did not devour were either shot or tomahawked." The ranger concluded that "the inhumanity of these Savages was rewarded with a calamity, dreadful indeed, but justly deserved."[17]

The St. Francis mission had little strategic value, but Quebec City, the capital of New France, was the most desired target for the British in the war. Following the British (re)capture of Louisbourg in 1758, British general James Wolfe sailed 141 warships and 9,000 soldiers up the St. Lawrence to Quebec in 1759. New Englanders believed that the clash for Quebec had great spiritual significance: one Massachusetts pastor quoted Moses from the Old Testament when he told militiamen on their way to Canada that "The Lord your God is he that goeth with you, to fight for you against your enemies, and to save you." The French general Montcalm had bolstered the walled city's defenses so that it was impossible for Wolfe's army to attack the city directly. (Wolfe was also enduring terrible pain and fever induced by a case of the "gravel," or kidney stones, as he contemplated how to defeat the French.) In September, Wolfe decided on a bold if risky maneuver in which transport ships raced past the city's guns under the cover of night and deposited troops on the bank of the river. There they had to scale 150-foot cliffs to reach the west side of the city walls, at an area known as the Plains of Abraham. Montcalm woke up the morning of September 13, 1759, to the sight of more than four thousand British troops stationed a thousand yards from the city's walls.[18]

Montcalm unwisely decided to leave the city to attack Wolfe's army right away. The half-hour battle turned into a rout of the French, and New France's capital fell into British hands. (Both Montcalm and Wolfe suffered mortal wounds during the fight.) British colonists in America—who had been trying since the 1690s to conquer Quebec—reacted in typical fashion. One broadside poem exulted that

> The Savages lay down their arms.
> The French do cease to raise alarms.
> Now Canada is fallen down
> Before the troops of George's crown.
>
> The time will come, when Pope and Friar
> Shall both be roasted in the fire;
> When the proud Antichristian Whore
> Will sink, and never arise more.

When three coordinated British armies defeated Montreal in September 1760, New France had fallen completely to the British.[19]

In the last two years of the war in America, British attention shifted to fighting the French and Spanish in the Caribbean. In mid-1762, a British naval force laid siege to Havana, Cuba, the key city of Spanish America and of that empire's lucrative trade in sugar and silver. Epidemic disease and hunger ravaged the Spanish defenses in Cuba, made worse by continuous summer rains. By June, authorities expelled all women from the city, and refugees tramped through knee-high mud, as all able-bodied men from the countryside were ordered to go into the town for its defense. Desperate Spanish, African, and mixed-blood Cubans traded supplies to the British; those caught doing so were summarily executed. Spanish priests, fearing mob violence, could safely bury the executed only at night. As their men also suffered from typhoid or other tropical maladies, the British devised a clever plan to tunnel under Havana's main fort and blow it up from underneath. The plan (improbably) worked, exposing the city to a final assault. Havana, like Quebec before it, fell to the British in August 1762, yielding its fortunes of gold and silver, as well as much of Spain's Caribbean fleet. Again, America's British colonists rejoiced. In faraway Boston, the pastor of the Old South Church was elated that the "great supporters of Antichrist" had fallen before King George's forces.[20]

The Treaty of Paris, which concluded the war in 1763, focused on restoring balance in North America and the Caribbean, and offered generous terms to the defeated French and Spanish. For the geography of the North American British empire (and the as-yet undreamed of United States) the most significant developments were that France ceded Canada to Britain, as well as its claims in the Ohio River valley and Great Lakes. But Britain returned many of the valuable sugar islands, including Martinique, to the French, and Cuba to the Spanish. Spain gave Florida to the British in order to get Havana back. For the time being, France ceded New Orleans and the Louisiana Territory to Spain. Now Britain controlled eastern continental North America, with the Mississippi River separating its lands from Spain's. The Native Americans who lived on much of the land in question were not consulted on these arrangements.

Again, Britain's American colonists celebrated the outcome of the war as an epochal event in British history, and even in the history of Christianity. Benjamin Franklin spoke for many when he said that he happily received word of Canada's defeat, "not merely as I am a colonist, but as I am a Briton." Pastor Thomas Barnard was even more exuberant: "Safe from the enemy of the wilderness," he preached, "safe from the gripping hand of arbitrary sway and cruel superstition; here shall be the late founded seat of peace and freedom. Here shall our indulgent Mother, who has most generously rescued and protected us, be served and honored by growing numbers, with all duty, love, and gratitude, till time shall be no more." The early 1760s were arguably the colonists' highest moment ever of patriotic devotion to "Mother" Britain.[21]

British colonists faced a far more uncertain future than Barnard foresaw, however, and not just because of looming controversy with Britain. The "enemy of the wilderness" broke out in mass rebellion against British power, too. Great numbers of tribes, from Shawnees to the Senecas (an Iroquois League member), launched joint attacks against most of the British forts in the Great Lakes and Ohio River valley. The withdrawal of the French from these regions meant the collapse of the longtime balance between British and French power, a system in which Indians had come to expect generous gift-giving from both sides. With the French gone, British commander Jeffrey Amherst decreed an end to the presents and supplies for natives. Indian leaders began to contemplate how to reclaim power in this new, unsettling environment.

The fall of the old imperial order fed into the growing sense that Native Americans had a common cause against the British. Native "prophets" had already begun to call on Indians to reject the Europeans and turn back to their traditional ways. A Lenni Lenape (Delaware) prophet named Neolin was among the most influential. In a vision, the "Master of Life" told Neolin that he had made the natives' lands for them only, not for whites. They had too long depended on Europeans to supply their needs. If they would trust and obey the Master of Life, they could go back to living without alcohol and guns, and back to hunting wild animals for food. Regarding the French, the Master of Life was more equivocal, for he loved them: "They know me and pray to me, and I supply their wants and all they give you. But as to those who come to trouble your lands, — drive them out, make war upon them. I do not love them [the English] at all; they know me not, and are my enemies." Neolin's teaching spread across many tribes, influencing, among others, Pontiac, the Ottawa war leader who tried to unify the disparate tribes to fight the British, and who hoped to secure the return of the French.[22]

Pontiac's Rebellion precipitated grim rounds of recriminations and terroristic incidents. Allied Indians took four British outposts in mid-1763, and they laid siege to Pittsburgh, although they could not finally conquer its formidable fort. Nevertheless, the terrified inhabitants got constant reports of Indian atrocities, and knew they would be next if Fort Pitt fell. "Every hour we hear of scalping," one person wrote from Pittsburgh in summer 1763. In one German settlement, Indians reportedly attacked a schoolhouse in 1764—a neighbor coming upon the "blood-bath" found "the schoolmaster scalped, with his Bible under his arm" and eight pupils lying dead around him.[23]

Bitter Pennsylvania settlers known as the "Paxton Boys" took out their resentment against a small group of Conestoga Indians, who had tried to maintain neutrality on a tiny reservation in eastern Pennsylvania. Demanding to know "why the Indians were suffered to live peaceably here," fifty riders attacked the Conestogas' village, where the Paxton Boys killed and scalped six Indians, whom they burned along with their homes. The remaining Conestogas had been away in Lancaster, where they were confined for their protection at a jail annex. Two days after Christmas, another Paxton Boys posse rode into Lancaster, broke down the jailhouse door, and murdered six Conestoga adults and eight children. Hundreds of vigilantes descended upon Philadelphia in early 1764, and only the intervention of British troops saved the lives of hundreds of Indian refugees they had apparently targeted. Many white Pennsylvanians were disgusted by the Paxton Boys' actions. Benjamin Franklin issued an (anonymous) imprint, *A Narrative of the Late Massacres*, in which he indicted the "enlightened Protestant" Pennsylvanians' behavior as worse than one would expect from Catholics, "Pagan Negroes," or Muslims. The Conestogas "would have been safe in any part of the known world, — except in the neighborhood of the CHRISTIAN WHITE SAVAGES of Peckstang and Donegal!"[24]

The siege of Fort Pitt in 1763 set the stage for another notorious incident, an attempt by British forces to use infected blankets to spread smallpox among Native Americans. By June 1763, smallpox had broken out among the residents of Fort Pitt. Two Lenni Lenape diplomats visited the fort in late June, and pressed the British officials to surrender the fort. When their request failed, the Indians prepared to leave, but requested provisions for their journey back home. A British trader wrote sarcastically that "out of our regard to them we gave them two blankets and a handkerchief out of the smallpox hospital. I hope it will have the desired effect." Fort Pitt's account books even registered the purchase of items to replace "those which were taken from people in the hospital to convey the smallpox to the Indians." Although British general Jeffrey Amherst seems not to have ordered this crude attempt at biological warfare, in July he mused whether the British could "send the smallpox among those disaffected tribes of Indians? We must, on this occasion, use every stratagem in our power to reduce them." Amherst's colonel Henry Bouquet, stationed at Fort Pitt, promised to investigate the possibility of giving Indians smallpox by means of placing contaminated linens in their hands. Amherst approved of this and any "other method that can serve to extirpate this execrable race." The Shawnees and Lenni Lenapes suffered terribly from smallpox during the siege, but the epidemic seems to have begun months before the blanket delivery.

Both Europeans and Native Americans experienced smallpox epidemics, although some Americans of European descent had survived a case of smallpox as children, giving them lifetime immunity from the fearsome malady. Perhaps most important for the future United States, George Washington had survived a case of the disease, which he contracted as a teenager (three years before Fort Necessity) while on a trip to Barbados. The great pastor-theologian Jonathan Edwards did not survive an inoculation attempt, which felled him in 1758 shortly after he became president at the College of New Jersey at Princeton.[25]

By mid-1764, the Indian rebels, wearied by disease and limited victories, had also begun to run out of supplies. Jeffrey Amherst was recalled to London, and the new superintendent of Indian affairs, William Johnson, renewed the program of gift-giving and trade with the Indians of the Great Lakes. Natives began to pursue trade agreements with Johnson. One Chippewa delegation came from Sault Ste. Marie in summer 1764, bringing with them an English prisoner. The prisoner was gathering firewood one day when he realized that a "rattlesnake" was right next to his legs. As he moved away to retrieve a gun, the Chippewas encircled the five-foot-long snake, which they regarded as a manitou spirit. Crawling along the ground, they spoke gently, blowing tobacco smoke over the snake and addressing it as "Grandfather." They asked that the manitou would watch over their families in Sault Ste. Marie, and that he would "open the heart of Sir William Johnson so that he might show them charity and fill their canoe with rum." Most Indians were satisfied that these sorts of prayers were answered, and Johnson hosted lengthy, expensive summits with Indian leaders, gave out tens of thousands of pounds sterling in gifts, and resumed the trade in ammunition and alcohol. A Chippewa chief commented that when William Johnson assumed control of Indian relations, "the lakes became placid, the storms ceased and the whole face of nature was changed."[26]

The pacified rebels continued to insist that they were not under British rule. The French had never conquered them, one group of chiefs insisted in 1765, and they had no right to give their lands to the British. "If you expect to keep these posts," he warned, "we will expect to have proper returns from you." As for Pontiac, many of his former allies now rejected him as an unreliable troublemaker. He wandered in the Illinois country, until in 1769 he was murdered by a Peoria Indian. Rumors suggested that British officers or merchants had put the killer up to it. When he died, Pontiac was reportedly wearing a French officer's uniform once given to him by the admiring French general, the Marquis de Montcalm. He perished in an Indian village near the French town of Cahokia, the mission erected on the ruins of the Native American metropolis of the twelfth century C.E.[27]

JAMES READ WRITES TO BENJAMIN FRANKLIN ABOUT GEN. EDWARD BRADDOCK'S DEFEAT (1755)

From Alan Houston, ed., "Benjamin Franklin and the 'Wagon Affair' of 1755," *William and Mary Quarterly*, 3d ed., 66, no. 2 (Apr. 2009): 281–82.

FROM JAMES READ

25 July. Reading

Dear Sir, The late accounts of the shamefull Defeat of our Army under General Braddock have given a shock to all this part of the Country. Our Inhabitants are apprehensive of being visited by the Indians: for we have vast barrens and hills to the north west of this town, extending to the Ends of the Province; so that we have but few Inhabitants near us on that side. I hope the Legislature will think seriously of our defenceless State, and enable us to put ourselves into a Condition to drive back our Enemies.

I am deeply grieved for our great Loss in the artillery. I think it irretrievable, and fear much that if his Excellency Major General Shirley should succeed in his attack on fort Niagara, yet it will be retaken by the Enemy with the artillery which we have furnished them with. They have a road lately cut from Fort Du Quesne thro' a fine level Country to Niagara.

I think our Army was full of Reprobates, who never had any serious thought of what they were about; and our Officers were too confident of their own strength, and despised their Enemy. Of the ill Consequences of such self-confidence and Contempt of Enemies you may read in the American Magazine for the Year 1746 p. 296 &c. I believe too we may justly say of them, that they were *mighty to drink Wine Men of strength to mingle strong drink.*

Something surely is wanting to rouse the inhabitants of the Province out of their Lethargy. We have an open Enemy on our borders, and a popish intestine Enemy spread thro' all the Land.

A BRITISH COLONIAL OBSERVER ON THE
FRENCH THREAT IN AMERICA (1755)

From *The New-York Mercury,* Jan. 13, 1755, p. 1.

I Believe no one who considers the late Designs of the *French,* can entertain the least Doubt of their aiming at the Conquest of *North-America.* Their Proceedings are equally perfidious and uniform; nor do they ever lose Sight of the grand Object of their Wishes, the Dominion of the Continent. Their recent Hostilities in the Midst of a profound Peace, have justly alarmed our Mother Country; and the present Preparations made at home to repel their Encroachments, are a fresh Demonstration of the watchful Care and parental Protection of our most gracious Sovereign. In so righteous a Cause, may Heaven bless his vindictive Arms with abundant Success!

Indeed their boundless Ambition, and incessant Machinations to disturb the Peace of the World, are enough to arm all Europe against them. To those who are Enemies to all Mankind, all Mankind ought to be at perpetual Enmity.

In attaching the Indian Natives to their Interest, they spare no Labour, no Costs. The lower Sort of their People, they encourage to intermarry with them, and to teach their Children to hunt, and live after the Indian Fashion. By these Means, they are early inured to Toil and Fatigue, learn all the Stratagems practised in their Method of warring, and inbibe the same cruel and ferocious Disposition.

In their Presents to the Indians they are extremely expensive; and at the same Time fail not to awe them with proper Discipline.

Their Indian Castles they fortify, and supply with Missionaries;—who practise incredible Arts to convert them to Popery.

In our Indians, the Spirit of Defection is daily more and more visible: This is principally occasioned by the bad Management of some of our former Governors, who were chiefly influenced by pecuniary Motives.

Such is the Character of the Enemy that thirsts for our Blood. From these, what Mercy, what Indulgence can we expect? Against these, of what Resistance will our defenceless Situation admit? Should they attack us by Sea, or what is more probable, and has actually been concerted by their Emissaries, with a naval Armament, in Conjunction with a Host of *French* and Indians from *Canada,* into what a universal Consternation would they throw this unfortified

City? Amidst the Shrieks of Women, the Wailings of Children, the hideous Shouts of Savages, and the dreadful Din of Arms, to what Method of Opposition should we betake ourselves? Distracted with Fear, and the Prospect of Death in a thousand Forms, should we not fall an easy Prey to an unrelenting Adversary? And what Heart can conceive, what Language describe the Sequel? Virgins deflowered by merciless Savages: Children pluck'd from the fond Grasp of a screaming Mother, and dashed by Barbarians against the bloody Pavement, less obdurate than the unpitying Murders: The reeking Scalp, strip'd from the hoary Head: Matrons exposed to all the libidinous Fury of a victorious Soldiery: The Wife torn from the Embraces of the Husband, and butchered before his streaming Eyes: A Ruffian's Sword reeking with a Father's Blood, and brandish'd in Triumph before the captive Son: All reduced to infamous Bondage: Our Houses ransack'd and our Treasure plundered: Woe, Despair and Horror, raging in every Quarter: Our Substance abandon'd to Spoil and Outrage: The Temples of our God, and our private Habitations, devoured by one common Flame, and converted into Scenes of horrible Desolation and Slaughter.

This, with all the other nameless Cruelties of War, would doubtless be our Portion, should we fall a Victim to an Enemy, whose tender Mercies are Cruelty. What Heart therefore can help bleeding at the bare Prospect of such complicated Misery? Who would not chearfully contribute to the utmost of his Ability, to put his Country in a proper Posture of Defence? Who would murmur at a Tax, in order to ward off such direful, such unutterable Distress? Valour, I am confident, would not be wanting. We should fight for our Liberty and Property, against the despicable Slaves of an absolute Potentate, who have neither. The awful Consequences of a Defeat, would inspire us with invincible Fortitude. Our priceless Freedom, our inestimable Privileges, our holy Religion, the Justice of our Cause, and the Glory of the *British* Name, would conspire to invigorate our Hearts, and render us couragious and inconquerable. In short, we want nothing but an equal Chance, and the Smiles of Heaven, to give them and ignominious Repulse, and send them counting their Beeds, to the *natale Solum* of their Superstition and Trumperies.

CHEROKEE WOMEN ADDRESS THE WOMEN OF THE IROQUOIS LEAGUE (1758)

From E. B. O'Callaghan, *The Documentary History of the State of New-York* (Albany, N.Y., 1850), 2: 445–46.

At a Meeting of the Cherokee Messengers. . . . As at this present troublesome time we are not sure what are Fate may be, on Day the Sun may shine clear upon us, another Day may be Cloudy and dark. Nevertheless Bretheren let us strongly keep up our mutual Friendship and Agreements we made between us, that if any Tempest should break out upon us, we may after it is passt come together and renew the Covenant now Mutually agreed upon, and reap the Benefits of thereof.

4 Strings

The following is a speech exhortation from the Cherokee Women to the Women of the 6 Nations.

Sisters, As it is our Department to furnish ye Warriors wth provisions whenever they go upon any Exploit, it being our Duty to do so they being our children & brought forth by us We earnestly desire & request of you that you will take good Care of them your way, as we shall do here so as to fitt them out such wth necessaries as Warriors stand in need of so that they man'nt want when they are upon their march, and when you expect them home again you will have such victuals &c ready for them as they may refresh them after a fatiguing march.

Gave a Bunch of white Beads.

Conclusion

The Crisis of the British Empire in America

Mohegan pastor Samson Occom traveled to London in the mid-1760s to raise money for evangelical pastor Eleazar Wheelock's charity school for Indians (later Dartmouth College). His tour was phenomenally successful. English revivalist George Whitefield hosted Occom for much of the visit. Like many colonial visitors, Occom was not quite prepared for the bustling scenes of London, with people everywhere "hollowing, wrestling, talking, giggling, and laughing, and . . . poor beggars praying, crying, and begging upon their knees." One February day in 1766, Whitefield took Occom to see the houses of Parliament. Whitefield chose that day because he also wanted to show his support for his longtime friend Benjamin Franklin, who was to appear before the House of Commons and answer questions about the Stamp Act, the revenue measure that had spawned massive unrest in America.[1]

A new British administration had taken power since the Stamp Act's adoption in 1765. The new leaders were inclined to repeal it because of the economic chaos it had created in America. The well-regarded "Franklin, of Philadelphia," seemed like a good spokesman to address the act's negative effects among the colonists. As part of the four-hour interrogation, members asked Franklin, "What was the temper of America towards Great-Britain before the year 1763?" Franklin said, "The best in the world. They submitted willingly to the government of the Crown, and paid, in all their courts, obedience to acts of parliament. Numerous as the people are in the several old provinces, they cost you nothing in forts, citadels, garrisons or armies, to keep them in subjection. They were governed by this country at the expence only of a little pen, ink and paper. They were led by a thread. They had not only a respect, but an affection, for Great-Britain, for its laws, its customs and manners, and even a fondness for its fashions, that greatly increased the commerce."

MP: "And what is their temper now?"

FRANKLIN: "O, very much altered."

MP: "Don't you think they would submit to the stamp-act, if it was modified, the obnoxious parts taken out, and the duty reduced to some particulars, of small moment?"

FRANKLIN: "No; they will never submit to it."

British colonists' attitude toward London was "much altered," to be sure. The Stamp Act had revealed dangerous fault lines between the empire and America. Those cracks were obscured by the Seven Years' War and the surge of British patriotism that had accompanied it. From the heady days of 1763 to the beginnings of resistance in 1765, antagonism emerged that colonists and imperial officials would never resolve.[2]

A host of factors made American colonial culture ready for resistance and rebellion against Britain. Decades of relatively light imperial governance allowed for the maturation of colonial legislatures and the training of talented local political leaders. Although the frontier still saw many episodes of violence, the colonies' extreme instability of the 1600s had passed, especially in the east coast cities. People from Boston to Charles Town now expected serious treatment as a vital part of the British empire, not the kind of casual abuse (as they saw it) only befitting imperial lackeys. The British American colonies were growing at breakneck speed, too, through natural increase and through voluntary and involuntary immigration. Between 1750 and 1770, the population of England's American colonies doubled from about one million to two million people. Many of these new residents were Scots-Irish and German, enhancing America's multiethnic, non-English qualities. In governance, culture, and population, the British colonies had quietly grown more distant from London, even though the 1750s and 1760s saw a surge of pro-British patriotism.[3]

Disagreements with British authorities had occasionally appeared in the colonies for decades. For example, although colonists congratulated themselves for their valiant contributions to the Seven Years' War and other British conflicts in North America, British commanders found Americans unreliable, at best. James Wolfe, who led British troops at Louisbourg in 1758 and Quebec in 1759, avoided using colonial militiamen whenever he could. "The Americans are in general the dirtiest, most contemptible cowardly dogs that you can conceive," the general wrote. "There is no depending upon 'em in action. They fall down dead in their own dirt and desert by battalions, officers and all. Such rascals as these are rather an incumbrance than any real strength to an army." Colonial troops were likewise disturbed by the British regular army's harsh system of discipline, and by the redcoats' profanity and lewd behavior. But the Seven Years' War provided invaluable wartime experience for future Continental Army commanders, especially George Washington.[4]

Even though the Great Awakening was as much a British phenomenon as an American one, the religious upheavals thirty years prior to the Revolution gave many Americans a taste of resisting government-backed authorities. Evangelicals' attacks on the established churches were also attacks on the power of the state. Hostility toward established clergy, including those of the Church of England, escalated in the 1760s, with rumors that England intended to impose a bishop on the colonies. Occasional rumors that George Whitefield might be this bishop never really tamped down colonists' concerns about Anglican coercion over America's spiritual affairs.

In 1763, a lawsuit brought by Anglican ministers in Virginia allowed young lawyer Patrick Henry to express popular resentment against the clergy, and to connect that resentment to the power of the king. The Virginia parsons appealed a pay cut by the colony to London authorities, and the king's Privy Council overturned Virginia's law. The ministers then sued to recoup lost salary. Henry claimed that London's overriding of a just colonial law set an ominous precedent. In 1763, the same year as the Treaty of Paris, Henry charmed the jury with a denunciation of British power in America. "A King, by annulling or disallowing laws of this salutary nature, from being the father of his people, degenerates into a tyrant, and forfeits all right to his subjects' obedience," he thundered. Some in the courtroom muttered that these were treasonous words, but the jury was convinced, and insulted the litigating Anglican minister by awarding him only one penny in damages.[5]

Henry's pyrotechnics may have reflected a growing dissatisfaction with British officials and British power, but the revolutionary crisis grew out of problems left by the outcome of the Seven Years' War. The war for empire had ended with decisive British victories over France and Spain in America and the Caribbean, but it had cost the empire dearly. Britain amassed a staggering war debt of 137 million pounds, and a number of colonists had profited handsomely from imperial expenditures for supplies. Just the payments on the debt amounted to five million pounds a year, swelling the British national budget, which had typically been around eight million pounds total before the war. The demands of managing the territory taken from France suggested that the expenditures on America would not slow any time soon, particularly after the outbreak of Pontiac's Rebellion. Given the frontier's instability, Britain decided to leave a standing army in America. In the short term, this was a reasonable response to conditions in the colonies. In British and European political thought, however, the presence of a standing army was dangerous—military occupation represented a threat to a free people.[6]

To many British officials, the debt and continuing military needs required an additional move: new taxes on the colonists. And the taxes and imposts already on the books needed stricter enforcement, as lax oversight had allowed colonists to establish elaborate systems of bribery and smuggling to evade duties and regulations, such as the one on colonists' importation of foreign (French) molasses. The 1764 Sugar Act lowered the duty on molasses, but now British officials intended to collect the duty with more intrusive naval inspections, and to end the corrupt practices behind the sugar trades. Those who had profited from the underhanded molasses commerce were outraged, but not all colonists were directly affected by the measure. Benjamin Franklin, for one, thought that modest taxes on luxury items made sense, in light of the challenges posed by the war and administering the colonies. Others believed that the "fatal consequences" of the act would "greatly and essentially" injure the colonies' economic interests. Eight colonial assemblies drew up formal protests against the Sugar Act. Virginia contended in 1764 that "laws imposing taxes on the people ought not to be made without the consent of representatives chosen by themselves." Increasing British intervention clashed with the colonists' enhanced sense of competence to govern themselves.[7]

Nothing could have prepared British officials, however, for the ferocious reaction to the next step in the revenue program, the Stamp Act of 1765. This act placed a tax on nearly every kind of printed good that Americans used. Thus, it affected a high percentage of all the colonists. The *New York Mercury* lamented that the act was "enough to break the heart of a Patriot, who would joyfully pour out his blood, to extricate his beloved country from destruction, to find her fainting and despairing, hourly expecting to be utterly crush'd by the iron rod of power." The newspaper envisioned America's guardian angel exclaiming, "How art thou fallen, murder'd America! . . . Even thy own sons have joined to *stamp* on thy bowels."[8]

In Virginia, Patrick Henry once again rose to frame the question as one of liberty versus tyranny. Henry, who at twenty-nine was a new member of Virginia's legislature, penned the colony's resolutions against the act, arguing that only the colonists' own legislatures had the right to lay taxes on them. Newspapers reported even more inflammatory claims in other resolutions Henry supposedly introduced, including one that declared anyone who defended Parliament's right to tax "AN ENEMY TO THIS HIS MAJESTY'S COLONY." In his speech against the Stamp Act, Henry asserted that where Caesar had his Brutus, and Charles I his Cromwell, Henry "did not doubt that some good American would stand up, in favour of his country." Renewed cries of treason led Henry to grudgingly apologize for his rash words, but the point was made: Henry had raised the possibility of an assassination attempt on King George III.[9]

Other colonies followed Virginia's lead. Rhode Island stipulated that their assembly alone had the right to tax the people of their colony. Parliament's attempt to impose taxes on them was "unconstitutional," they said, "and hath a manifest tendency to destroy the liberties of the people of this colony." An intercolonial Stamp Act "congress" likewise declared in October 1765 that no taxes should be imposed upon colonists "but with their own consent, given personally or by their representatives." They denied that they were represented in the British House of Commons. Some of the stamp agents and royal partisans literally fell under attack when they tried to collect the tax. In Boston in August 1765, a crowd burned an effigy of stamp agent Andrew Oliver and accosted his home, breaking windows and threatening to kill him if they could find him (Oliver had wisely left with his family). The "same factious tumultuary and riotous disposition" spread to Rhode Island two weeks later. "Ruffians" with painted faces used broad axes to wreck the homes of the Stamp Act's defenders in Newport. They smashed the imported china and mahogany furniture they found there, and swigged bottles of Madeira wine. Largely accustomed to managing their own political affairs, and used to easy availability of the commercial products that had transformed British colonial culture, the rioters reflected an unanticipated touchiness about the new policies. Many of the stamp agents, subjected to countless forms of intimidation, resigned their post before the act even went into effect. By fall 1765, colonists had rendered the Stamp Act virtually unenforceable.[10]

New organizations styling themselves the "Sons of Liberty" were behind many of the attacks on the British agents and politicians. Often composed of middling merchants and professionals, the Sons of Liberty gave an organizational framework to the emerging resistance movement. In Norfolk, Virginia, the Sons of Liberty asserted that if they submitted to the Stamp Act, all of their "claims to civil liberty will be lost, and we and our posterity become absolute slaves." North Carolinians likewise pledged to resist the act because they preferred "death to slavery." (Patriots rarely hesitated to use the language of enslavement, even though many of them—especially in the South—were already the masters of real slaves.) The Sons of Liberty often employed religious rhetoric about the Patriot cause, too. A speaker at a Boston assembly compared two of the leading British officials behind the Stamp Act to the diabolical beasts of the Bible's book of Revelation, and equated the stamps with the "mark of the beast."[11]

Under pressure from many British merchants, and bolstered by Franklin's testimony, London authorities repealed the Stamp Act in early 1766. But the basic terms of the dispute between Britain and its American colonies was set. Parliament, in a Declaratory Act accompanying the repeal, insisted that they had "full power and authority to make laws and statutes of sufficient force and validity to bind the colonies and people of America, subjects of the crown of Great Britain, in all cases whatsoever." London would continue to pursue the imposition and collection of taxes on a variety of imported goods that had become commonplace in America's emerging consumer market of the mid-eighteenth century, including glassware, printed materials, molasses, and—most provocatively—tea.[12]

Lest we conclude by suggesting that all of American colonial history was funneling toward the clash between the British administration and east-coast Patriots, we should recall that in many parts of America, the American Revolution and the Declaration of Independence held little short-term significance. In some American places, the Revolution hardly registered at all. In St. Louis, founded on the west bank of the Mississippi in 1764, the greatest intrigue of 1776 had nothing to do with British taxes, but with the marital status of Marie Thérèse Bourgeois Chouteau, who had been living with St. Louis's founder, Pierre Laclède, since her husband abandoned her in New Orleans. Chouteau and Laclède had children together and kept house in St. Louis since the village's founding. Their home included several African and Native American slaves. One of the latter was named Thérèse. To confirm his loyalty to Chouteau, Laclède even deeded his property to his children by her.[13]

This patched-together frontier household came under serious threat when Chouteau's husband René returned to New Orleans after a decade's absence in France. When he found out—perhaps from St. Louis merchants who came downriver to New Orleans—that Marie was living with Laclède, René demanded that she come to New Orleans and resume her place as his wife. He may have believed that he could get access to the property that Laclède had given the Chouteaus. The well-placed René Chouteau got French authorities in Louisiana involved, but officials in upper Louisiana reminded those in New

Orleans that Laclède and his household were having great success in producing both hemp (for ropes) and furs, and sending them down the river to New Orleans. Years passed as bureaucrats and Marie dragged their feet and made unfulfilled promises about complying with requirements of marriage law. René finally died in New Orleans, ending the standoff. He passed away in April 1776, as some 850 miles east, delegates in Philadelphia mulled whether the war between the colonists and the British—which had begun at Lexington and Concord, Massachusetts, a year earlier—should result in American independence.[14]

Some two thousand miles west of St. Louis, shortly before René Chouteau's death, the Spanish established a presidio at San Francisco. Alarmed by reports from the Spanish ambassador to St. Petersburg, Russia, that the Russians had plans to challenge Spain in the Pacific Northwest, the Spanish commissioned an expedition to reconnoiter the San Francisco Bay area in 1775. In March 1776, the party reached Spain's mission and presidio at Monterey, its northernmost California outpost. They proceeded up to the Golden Gate, an opening in the mountain range that lines the coast. One of the priests accompanying the explorers, Pedro Font, called the port of San Francisco a "wonder of nature." As they surveyed the region, they passed through areas inhabited by perhaps sixty small Indian tribes, most composed of about three hundred people or less. These people spoke Costanoan dialects, but their language differences were such that they could often not communicate with even close neighboring tribes. Fray Font noted that the Spanish tried to dialogue with a band of hunters they encountered, but could not understand them. In June, the Spanish erected tents and a temporary altar close to the center of the modern city of San Francisco. Back east in Philadelphia, Thomas Jefferson and the Continental Congress were toiling over the details of the Declaration of Independence.[15]

In August, the arrival of a supply ship allowed the Spanish to begin construction on the mission and presidio. A month later, they held an official ceremony to take possession of the area, with missionaries saying mass and soldiers shooting off cannons. Then in early October 1776, the Franciscans marked the formal opening of the mission. One of the priests wrote that he "sang the mass with the ministers, and at its conclusion a procession was formed, in which an image of Our Seraphic Father San Francisco, patron of the port, presidio, and mission, was carried on a frame." Soldiers fired guns and set off fireworks, and the Spanish feasted. The priest wrote that it was a joyous day for all. "The only ones who did not enjoy this happy day," he noted, "were the heathen." The story of mission, empire, and clashing cultures continued in America in 1776.[16]

Which of the three episodes spanning the continent from east to west—the Declaration of Independence, the travails of the Chouteau family, or the founding of San Francisco—is the most important? A civic-minded response would say the Declaration was the most significant, formative as it was for American national identity, and for America's founding ideal of equality by creation. We might also remember that in the longer term—looking forward to the Louisiana Purchase of 1803, or the Compromise of 1850, which brought California into the United States—America's independence, and its role as a new imperial power, would certainly affect the continent from the Mississippi River to the Pacific Ocean.

From the perspective of each place and people, however, we should hesitate to place one event above the other. Most early Americans spent their time focused on matters of work, commerce, religion, and family, but often found—as Marie Chouteau discovered—that the unpredictable quality of their colonial setting could disrupt those daily rhythms. Moreover, the founding of San Francisco illustrated better than any other moment in 1776 the pervasive themes of early American history: the salience of religion, the impulse of empire, and the ubiquity of conflict between different peoples and cultures. Those clashes were most obvious in the east-coast English colonies in the seventeenth century, but as increasing stability and a more Anglicized culture marked those colonies in the decades prior to the Revolution, violence continued in wars and new settlements on the expanding frontier. For many in early America—even for some who were not especially devout—religion helped make sense of war and change.

The civic mandate of knowing the "basics" of American history would put Jefferson and the delegates at Philadelphia front and center, and that mandate is not wrong. But we must be mindful that there is more to the early American experience than the coming of independence. Colonial American history forms a dizzying kaleidoscope of cultures, faiths, and tragic clashes of incompatible powers. The struggle to balance the aspects of history that made us different, and those facets that made us Americans, is perhaps the greatest challenge facing historians today.

NOTES

INTRODUCTION

1. Like many aspects of early Native American history, the exact meaning of this Chaco Canyon painting is disputed. I will seek to present reasonable, up-to-date interpretations of such matters, but will not burden the text with lists of alternative explanations.

2. Timothy R. Pauketat, *Cahokia: Ancient America's Great City on the Mississippi* (New York, 2009), 27.

3. Carl J. Ekberg, *French Roots in the Illinois Country: The Mississippi Frontier in Colonial Times* (Urbana, Ill., 1998), 55–61.

4. Patricia Cleary, *The World, The Flesh, and The Devil: A History of Colonial St. Louis* (Columbia, Mo., 2011), 31.

5. Steven W. Hackel, *Children of Coyote, Missionaries of Saint Francis: Indian-Spanish Relations in Colonial California, 1769–1850* (Chapel Hill, N.C., 2005), 91–92.

CHAPTER ONE. NATIVE AMERICANS AND THE EUROPEAN ENCOUNTER

1. Heather Pringle, "The First Americans," *Scientific American* 305, no. 5 (Nov. 2011), at http://ezproxy.baylor.edu/login?url=http://search.ebscohost.com/login.aspx?direct=true&db=a9h&AN=66913733&site=ehost-live&scope=site [accessed Aug. 27, 2013].

2. Elena B. Décima and Dena F. Dincauze, "The Boston Back Bay Fish Weirs," in Kathryn Bernick, ed., *Hidden Dimensions: The Cultural Significance of Wetland Archaeology* (Vancouver, B.C., 1998), 157–59.

3. Charles C. Mann, *1491: New Revelations of the Americas Before Columbus* (New York, 2005), 208–9.

4. Sarah C. Sherwood and Tristam R. Kidder, "The DaVincis of Dirt: Geoarchaeological Perspectives on Native American Mound Building in the Mississippi River Basin," *Journal of Anthropological Archaeology* 30, no. 1 (Mar. 2011), at http://www.sciencedirect.com/science/article/pii/S0278416510000620 [accessed Aug. 28, 2013]; Andrew

Lawler, "Does North America Hold the Roots of Mesoamerican Civilization?" *Science* 23 (2011), at http://www.sciencemag.org/content/334/6063/1620.full [accessed Aug. 28, 2011]; Eric A. Powell, "Archaic Engineers Worked on a Deadline," *Archaeology*, May 1, 2013.

5. Neal Salisbury, "The Indians' Old World: Native Americans and the Coming of Europeans," *William and Mary Quarterly*, 3d ser., 53, no. 3, Indians and Others in Early America (July 1996): 439; Ramón Gutiérrez, *When Jesus Came, the Corn Mothers Went Away: Marriage, Sexuality, and Power in New Mexico, 1500–1846* (Stanford, Calif., 1991), 3–8; Mann, *1491*, 200–201.

6. Catherine M. Cameron, *Chaco and After in the Northern San Juan: Excavations at the Bluff Great House* (Tucson, Ariz., 2009), 1–6; Timothy R. Pauketat, *Archaeology of the Cosmos: Rethinking Agency and Religion in Ancient America* (New York, 2013), 65.

7. George M. Wrong, ed., *The Long Journey into the Country of the Hurons*, Father Gabriel Sagard (Toronto, 1939), 186–87; William Engelbrecht, *Iroqouia: The Development of a Native World* (Syracuse, N.Y., 2003), 6.

8. Neal Salisbury, *Manitou and Providence: Indians, Europeans, and the Making of New England, 1500–1643* (New York, 1982), 37–39.

9. Salisbury, *Manitou and Providence*, 37.

10. Denys Delâge, *Bitter Feast: Amerindians and Europeans in Northeastern North America, 1600–1664* (Vancouver, B.C., 1993), 72.

11. Alice Beck Kehoe, *America Before the European Invasions* (London, 2002), 35.

12. David Hurst Thomas, *Exploring Ancient Native America: An Archaeological Guide* (New York, 1999), 142–46.

13. Erik R. Seeman, *The Huron-Wendat Feast of the Dead: Indian-European Encounters in Early North America* (Baltimore, 2011), 64–78.

14. Sheldon J. Watts, *Epidemics and History: Disease, Power and Imperialism* (New Haven, Conn., 1997), 93.

15. Alfred W. Crosby, "Ills," in Alan L. Karras and J. R. McNeill, eds., *Atlantic-American Societies: From Columbus Through Abolition, 1492–1888* (London, 1992), 28.

16. Alice Nash and Christoph Strobel, *Daily Life of Native Americans from Post-Columbian through Nineteenth-Century America* (Westport, Conn., 2006), 223.

17. David S. Jones, "Virgin Soils Revisited," *William and Mary Quarterly*, 3d ser., 60, no. 4 (Oct. 2003): 736–38.

18. Pauline Moffitt Watts, "Prophecy and Discovery: On the Spiritual Origins of Christopher Columbus's 'Enterprise of the Indies,'" *American Historical Review* 90, no. 1 (Feb. 1985): 102.

19. Leonard I. Sweet, "Christopher Columbus and the Millennial Vision of the New World," *Catholic Historical Review* 72, no. 3 (July 1986): 372.

20. Irving Rouse, *The Tainos: Rise and Decline of the People Who Greeted Columbus* (New Haven, Conn., 1992), 12–13.

21. Ramón Pané, *An Account of the Antiquities of the Indians: Chronicles of the New World Encounter* (Durham, N.C., 1999), 26.

22. David E. Stannard, *American Holocaust: The Conquest of the New World* (New York, 1992), 66–67.

CHAPTER TWO. THE SPANISH EMPIRE IN AMERICA

1. Baker H. Morrow, ed., *Harvest of Reluctant Souls: Fray Alonso de Benavides's History of New Mexico 1630* (Albuquerque, N.M., 2012), 22.

2. Morrow, ed., *Harvest*, 35.

3. Ramón A. Gutierrez, *When Jesus Came, the Corn Mothers Went Away: Marriage, Sexuality, and Power in New Mexico, 1500–1846* (Stanford, Calif., 1991), 108–10.

4. Morrow, ed., *Harvest*, 38.

5. Gutierrez, *When Jesus Came*, 121.

6. Andrew L. Knaut, *The Pueblo Revolt of 1680: Conquest and Resistance in Seventeenth-Century New Mexico* (Norman, Okla., 1995), 155–59.

7. Hernán Cortés, *Letters from Mexico*, ed. Anthony Pagden (New York, 1971), 59–60, 63.

8. J. H. Elliott, *Empires of the Atlantic World: Britain and Spain in America, 1492–1830* (New Haven, Conn., 2006), 4–5.

9. Cortés, *Letters from Mexico*, 106.

10. Charles C. Mann, *1491: New Revelations of the Americas Before Columbus* (New York, 2005), 124–29.

11. Enrique Pupo-Walker, ed., *Castaways: The Narrative of Alvar Núñez Cabeza De Vaca* (Berkeley, Calif., 1993), 72.

12. Pupo-Walker, ed., *Castaways*, 73–74; Andrés Reséndez, *A Land So Strange: The Epic Journey of Cabeza de Vaca* (New York, 2007), 174–75.

13. Pupo-Walker, ed., *Castaways*, 108.

14. Mann, *1491*, 98–99; David J. Weber, *The Spanish Frontier in North America* (New Haven, Conn., 1992), 41.

15. Robbie Ethridge, "The Making of a Militaristic Slaving Society: The Chickasaws and the Colonial Indian Slave Trade," in Alan Gallay, ed., *Indian Slavery in Colonial America* (Lincoln, Neb., 2009), 251–52.

16. Edward G. Bourne, ed., *Narratives of the Career of Hernando de Soto* (New York, 1922), 1: 120–21.

17. Bourne, ed., *Hernando de Soto*, 162.

18. Reséndez, *Land So Strange*, 301 n. 4; Franklin W. Knight, ed., *An Account, Much Abbreviated, of the Destruction of the Indies*, Bartolomé de las Casas (Indianapolis, Ind., 2003), xvii–xx, 21.

19. Knight, ed., *An Account*, xxvii–xxviii; David Brion Davis, *Inhuman Bondage: The Rise and Fall of Slavery in the New World* (New York, 2006), 354 n. 49.

20. Knight, ed., *An Account*, 5–6.

21. "Vásquez de Coronado's Letter to the Viceroy," Aug. 3, 1540, in Richard Flint and Shirley Cushing Flint, eds., *Documents of the Coronado Expedition, 1539–1542* (Dallas, Tex., 2005), 260–61; Stan Hoig, *Came Men on Horses: The Conquistador Expeditions of Francisco Vázquez de Coronado and Don Juan de Oñate* (Boulder, Colo., 2013), 58–59.

22. Hoig, *Came Men*, 73–74, 80–86, 89.

23. Hoig, *Came Men*, 110–12.

24. David J. Weber, *The Spanish Frontier in North America* (New Haven, Conn., 1992), 60.

25. Weber, *Spanish Frontier*, 60–63.

26. Weber, *Spanish Frontier*, 70–72.

27. Weber, *Spanish Frontier*, 74–75.

28. Delno C. West, "Medieval Ideas of Apocalyptic Mission and the Early Franciscans in Mexico," *The Americas* 45, no. 3 (Jan. 1989): 305–10.

29. Jerald T. Milanich, "Franciscan Missions and Native Peoples in Spanish Florida," in Charles Hudson and Carmen Chaves Tesser, eds., *The Forgotten Centuries: Indians and Europeans in the American South, 1521–1704* (Athens, Ga., 1994), 276–79, 282, 284, 297; Weber, *Spanish Frontier*, 100–103.

30. Weber, *Spanish Frontier*, 134; Knaut, *Pueblo Revolt of 1680*, 76.

31. Gutiérrez, *When Jesus Came*, 127–28; Weber, *Spanish Frontier*, 134.

32. Knaut, *Pueblo Revolt*, 168.

33. Weber, *Spanish Frontier*, 136; Knaut, *Pueblo Revolt*, 10.

34. Weber, *Spanish Frontier*, 168; Gutiérrez, *When Jesus Came*, 157–158.

35. Jim Norris, "The Franciscans in New Mexico, 1692–1754: Toward a New Assessment," *The Americas* 51, no. 2 (Oct. 1994): 161–62.

36. Letter of Governor Pedro Fermín de Mendinueta, 1773, in Marc Simmons, ed., *Coronado's Land: Essays on Daily Life in Colonial New Mexico* (Albuquerque, N.M., 1991), 120–25.

37. Juan Agustín de Morfi, "Account of Disorders, 1778," in Simmons, ed., *Coronado's Land*, 131–32.

38. Francisco Atanasio Domínguez, *The Missions of New Mexico, 1776*, trans. and ed. Eleanor B. Adams and Angélico Chávez (Santa Fé, N.M., 2012), 39–43.

CHAPTER THREE. THE FRENCH EMPIRE IN AMERICA

1. David Hackett Fischer, *Champlain's Dream* (New York, 2008), 318.

2. *The Voyages of Jacques Cartier*, intro. by Ramsay Cook (Toronto, 1993), 26.

3. *Voyages*, 37.

4. *Voyages*, 77; Denys Delâge, *Bitter Feast: Amerindians and Europeans in Northeastern North America, 1600–64* (Vancouver, 1993), 85–86.

5. Delâge, *Bitter Feast*, 71.

6. Emma Anderson, "Between Conversion and Apostasy: The Religious Journey of Pierre-Anthoine Pastedechouan," *Anthropologica* 49, no. 1 (2007): 19.

7. Anderson, "Between Conversion and Apostasy," 20–22.

8. Anderson, "Between Conversion and Apostasy," 23–25, 28–29.

9. Reuben G. Thwaites, ed., *The Jesuit Relations and Allied Documents* (Cleveland, Ohio, 1897), 6: 177; James P. Ronda, "'We Are Well as We Are': An Indian Critique of Seventeenth-Century Christian Missions," *William and Mary Quarterly*, 3d ser., 34, no. 1 (Jan. 1977): 77.

10. Thwaites, ed., *Jesuit Relations*, 6: 179.

11. Peter A. Dorsey, "Going to School with Savages: Authorship and Authority Among the Jesuits of New France," *William and Mary Quarterly*, 3d ser., 55, no. 3 (July 1998): 402–3, 413; James Axtell, *The Invasion Within: The Contest of Cultures in Colonial North America* (New York, 1985), 81.

12. Delâge, *Bitter Feast*, 168–169; Dorsey, "Going to School," 419.

13. Axtell, *Invasion Within*, 72–73; Thwaites, *Jesuit Relations*, 8: 169.

14. Delâge, *Bitter Feast*, 170–71.

15. Delâge, *Bitter Feast*, 217; Bruce Trigger, *Natives and Newcomers: Canada's "Heroic Age" Reconsidered* (Montreal, 1986), 256; Allan Greer, "Conversion and Identity: Iroquois Christianity in Seventeenth-Century New France," in Kenneth Mills and Anthony Grafton, eds., *Conversion: Old Worlds and New* (Rochester, N.Y., 2003), 184.

16. Natalie Zemon Davis, *Women on the Margins: Three Seventeenth-Century Lives* (Cambridge, Mass., 1995), 77–79; Irene Mahoney, O.S.U., ed., *Marie of the Incarnation: Selected Writings* (New York, 1989), 23, 112–13, 116.

17. Davis, *Women on the Margins*, 96–98.

18. Emily Clark, *Masterless Mistresses: The New Orleans Ursulines and the Development of a New World Society, 1727–1834* (Chapel Hill, N.C., 2007), 51–53.

19. Axtell, *Invasion Within*, 86; Dean R. Snow, Charles T. Gehring, and William A. Starna, eds., *In Mohawk Country: Early Narratives About a Native People* (Syracuse, N.Y., 1996), 17.

20. Thwaites, ed. *Jesuit Relations*, 34: 29; Carole Blackburn, *Harvest of Souls: The Jesuit Missions and Colonialism in North America, 1632–1650* (Montreal, Quebec, 2000), 65–67.

21. Delâge, *Bitter Feast*, 146–47; Mahoney, ed., *Marie of the Incarnation*, 162.

22. Trigger, *Natives and Newcomers*, 290.

23. Greer, *Mohawk Saint*, 52–53.

24. Greer, *Mohawk Saint*, 115–17.

25. Greer, *Mohawk Saint*, 122–24; Mahoney, ed., *Marie of the Incarnation*, 60–61.

26. Greer, *Mohawk Saint*, 142–45.

27. José António Brandao and Michael Shakir Nassaney, "Suffering for Jesus: Penitential Practices at Fort St. Joseph (Niles, Michigan) During the French Regime," *Catholic Historical Review* 94, no. 3 (July 2008): 484.

28. Tracy Neal Leavelle, "Practice," in Amanda Porterfield and John Corrigan, eds., *Religion in American History* (Malden, Mass., 2010), 82–83.

29. Brett Rushforth, *Bonds of Alliance: Indigenous and Atlantic Slaveries in New France* (Chapel Hill, N.C., 2012), 253–54.

30. Rushforth, *Bonds of Alliance*, 270–72.

31. Ian K. Steele, *Warpaths: Invasions of North America* (New York, 1994), 140–41.

32. Steele, *Warpaths*, 143–45; Francis Parkman, *Count Frontenac and New France Under Louis XIV I* (Boston, 1902), 287, 295–96; William Douglass, *A Summary, Historical and Political* (Boston, 1755), 476.

CHAPTER FOUR. VIRGINIA AND THE CHESAPEAKE

1. Charles Deane, ed., *A True Relation of Virginia, by Captain John Smith* (Boston, 1866), 14–15.

2. Theo Emery, "Jamestown Thought to Yield Ruins of Oldest U.S. Protestant Church," *New York Times*, Nov. 13, 2011, at http://www.nytimes.com/2011/11/14/us/ruins-of-oldest-us-protestant-church-may-be-at-jamestown.html?pagewanted=all [accessed Jan. 29, 2014].

3. Peter C. Mancall, *Hakluyt's Promise: An Elizabethan's Obsession for an English America* (New Haven, Conn., 2007), 155.

4. Charles Deane, ed., *A Discourse Concerning Western Planting, Written in the Year 1584 by Richard Hakluyt* (Cambridge, Mass., 1877), 7–8.

5. Deane, ed., *Discourse Concerning Western Planting*, 9–11.

6. Deane, ed., *Discourse Concerning Western Planting*, 74; Mancall, *Hakluyt's Promise*, 62–63.

7. Mancall, *Hakluyt's Promise*, 164.

8. Mancall, *Hakluyt's Promise*, 159.

9. *A Brief and True Report of the New Found Land of Virginia, by Thomas Hariot*, facsimile with introduction by Luther S. Livingston (New York, 1903), n.p.

10. James Horn, *A Land as God Made It: Jamestown and the Birth of America* (New York, 2005), 20–22.

11. John Smith, *The Generall Historie of Virginia* (London, 1632), 48; Horn, *Land as God Made It*, 20, 65–66.

12. Horn, *Land as God Made It*, 13–15.

13. Horn, *Land as God Made It*, 42, 44, 48; James Axtell, *The Rise and Fall of the Powhatan Empire: Indians in Seventeenth-Century Virginia* (Williamsburg, Va., 1995), 35.

14. Robert Gray, *A Good Speed to Virginia* (London, 1609), n.p.

15. Carville V. Earle, "Environment, Disease, and Mortality in Early Virginia," in Thad W. Tate and David L. Ammerman, eds., *The Chesapeake in the Seventeenth Century* (Chapel Hill, N.C., 1979), 108–10.

16. See Karen Ordahl Kupperman, "Apathy and Death in Early Jamestown," *Journal of American History* 66, no. 1 (June 1979): 24–40; Edmund S. Morgan, "The Labor Problem at Jamestown, 1607–1618," *American Historical Review* 76, no. 3 (June 1971): 595–611.

17. William Strachey, *For the Colony in Virginea Britannia* (London, 1612), 1–3.

18. Horn, *Land as God Made It*, 68–69.

19. Ralph Hamor, *A True Discourse of the Present Estate of Virginia* (London, 1615), 63; Horn, *Land as God Made It*, 217–18.

20. Hariot, *Brief and True Report*, n.p.; Lawrence A. Peskin and Edmund F. Wehrle, *America and the World: Culture, Commerce, and Conflict* (Baltimore, 2012), 22; April Lee Hatfield, *Atlantic Virginia: Intercolonial Relations in the Seventeenth Century* (Philadelphia, 2004), 39–40; Horn, *Land as God Made It*, 253; Helen C. Rountree, *Pocahontas's People: The Powhatan Indians of Virginia Through Four Centuries* (Norman, Okla., 1990), 60–62.

21. Horn, *Land as God Made It*, 255; Edward Waterhouse, *A Declaration of the State of the Colony and Affairs in Virginia* (London, 1622), 14.

22. Waterhouse, *Declaration*, 1, 23; Horn, *Land as God Made It*, 264–65, 270, 286; Rebecca Anne Goetz, *The Baptism of Early Virginia: How Christianity Created Race* (Baltimore, 2012), 60.

23. John C. Coombs, "The Phases of Conversion: A New Chronology for the Rise of Slavery in Early Virginia," *William and Mary Quarterly*, 3d ser., 68, no. 3 (July 2011): 359–60.

24. Edmund S. Morgan, "Slavery and Freedom: The American Paradox," *Journal of American History* 59, no. 1 (June 1972): 21.

25. Cynthia A. Kierner, *Beyond the Household: Women's Place in the Early South, 1700–1835* (Ithaca, N.Y., 1998), 10.

26. Bradley Tyler Johnson, *The Foundation of Maryland and the Origin of the Act Concerning Religion* (Baltimore, 1883), 28; John D. Krugler, *English and Catholic: The Lords Baltimore in the Seventeenth Century* (Baltimore, 2004), 119–20; Goetz, *Baptism of Early Virginia*, 134.

27. Krugler, *English and Catholic*, 186–89; Daniel L. Dreisbach and Mark David Hall, eds., *The Sacred Rights of Conscience: Selected Readings on Religious Liberty and Church-State Relations in the American Founding* (Indianapolis, 2009), 103–7.

28. Hatfield, *Atlantic Virginia*, 34–35.

29. Morgan, "Slavery and Freedom," 22; Warren M. Billings, "Sir William Berkeley and the Diversification of the Virginia Economy," *Virginia Magazine of History and Biography*, 104, no. 4 (Autumn 1996): 452–53.

30. "Proclamations of Nathaniel Bacon," *Virginia Magazine of History and Biography* 1, no. 1 (July 1893): 56–61.

31. *A Narrative of the Indian and Civil Wars in Virginia in the Years 1675 and 1676* (Boston, 1814), 26; Goetz, *Baptism*, 131–32.

CHAPTER FIVE. NEW ENGLAND

1. Robert Tracy McKenzie, *The First Thanksgiving: What the Real Story Tells Us About Loving God and Learning from History* (Downers Grove, Ill., 2013), 85–89.

2. *Fox's Book of Martyrs* (Philadelphia, 1856), 392; Francis J. Bremer, *The Puritan Experiment: New England Society from Bradford to Edwards*, rev. ed. (Hanover, N.H., 1995), 3–5.

3. Bremer, *Puritan Experiment*, 37–38.

4. Avihu Zakai, *Exile and Kingdom: History and Apocalypse in the Puritan Migration to America* (New York, 1992), 49.

5. John Winthrop, "A Modell of Christian Charity," *Collections of the Massachusetts Historical Society*, 3d ser., vol. 7 (Boston, 1838), 47.

6. Carol Berkin, *First Generations: Women in Colonial America* (New York, 1996), 37–38.

7. William Perkins, *A Commentarie or Exposition, Upon the Five First Chapters of the Epistle to the Galatians* (Cambridge, 1604), 90.

8. David Underdown, *Fire from Heaven: Life in an English Town in the Seventeenth Century* (New Haven, Conn., 1992), 113–15.

9. Alden T. Vaughan, *The Puritan Tradition in America, 1620–1730* (Hanover, N.H., 1972), 51; McKenzie, *First Thanksgiving*, 34–35, 137–38.

10. The Massachusetts Body of Liberties (1641), at http://history.hanover.edu/texts/masslib.html [accessed Feb. 25, 2014].

11. John Winthrop, "A Little Speech on Liberty," (1645), in David D. Hall, ed., *Puritans in the New World: A Critical Anthology* (Princeton, N.J., 2004), 178–79.

12. David D. Hall, ed., *The Antinomian Controversy, 1636–1638: A Documentary History* (Durham, N.C., 1990), 337; Hall, ed., *Puritans in the New World*, 218.

13. David D. Hall, *Worlds of Wonder, Days of Judgment: Popular Religious Belief in Early New England* (New York, 1989), 15–16; Harry S. Stout, *The New England Soul: Preaching and Religious Culture in Colonial New England* (New York, 1986), 3; Alan Taylor, *American Colonies* (New York, 2001), 179.

14. Mary Rhinelander McCarl, ed., "Thomas Shepard's Record of Relations of Religious Experience, 1648–1649," *William and Mary Quarterly*, 3d ser., 48, no. 3 (July 1991): 465–66.

15. Nicholas Guyatt, *Providence and the Invention of the United States, 1607–1876* (New York, 2007), 27.

16. Taylor, *American Colonies*, 194–95.

17. Andrew Lipman, "'A Meanes to Knitt Them Togeather': The Exchange of Body Parts in the Pequot War," *William and Mary Quarterly*, 3d ser., 65, no. 1 (Jan. 2008): 16–17, 23.

18. Nathaniel Morton, *New England's Memorial* (Boston, 1855), 128; Charles Orr, ed., *History of the Pequot War* (Cleveland, Ohio, 1897), 30, 81.

19. Ira Berlin, *Many Thousands Gone: The First Two Centuries of Slavery in North America* (Cambridge, Mass., 1998), 58; Bremer, *Puritan Experiment*, 206.

20. Richard W. Cogley, *John Eliot's Mission to the Indians Before King Philip's War* (Cambridge, Mass., 1999), 50.

21. Thomas Mayhew and John Eliot, *Tears of Repentance* (London, 1653), A2–A3; Richard W. Cogley, "John Eliot and the Millennium," *Religion and American Culture* 1, no. 2 (Summer 1991): 234.

22. Edward Winslow, *The Glorious Progress of the Gospel Amongst the Indians in New England* (London, 1649), n.p.

23. *Glorious Progress of the Gospel*, n.p.

24. David J. Silverman, "Indians, Missionaries, and Religious Translation: Creating Wampanoag Christianity in Seventeenth-Century Martha's Vineyard," *William and Mary Quarterly*, 3d ser., 62, no. 2 (Apr. 2005): 146.

25. Len Travers, ed., "The Missionary Journal of John Cotton, Jr., 1666–1678," *Proceedings of the Massachusetts Historical Society*, 3d ser., 109 (1997): 63–65; Silverman, "Indians, Missionaries," 161, 163.

26. "Metacom's Grievances," in Camilla Townshend, ed., *American Indian History: A Documentary Reader* (Malden, Mass., 2009), 55–56.

27. *A Farther Brief and True Narration of the Wars Risen in New England* (London, 1676), 10.

28. Jill Lepore, *The Name of War: King Philip's War and the Origins of American Identity* (New York, 1998), 98, 105; Mary Rowlandson, *True History of the Captivity and Restoration of Mrs. Mary Rowlandson* (London, 1682), 3.

29. Lepore, *Name of War*, 138–41.

30. Lepore, *Name of War*, 173–75.

CHAPTER SIX. THE MIDDLE COLONIES

1. Russell Shorto, *The Island at the Center of the World: The Epic Story of Dutch Manhattan and the Forgotten Colony That Shaped America* (New York, 2004), 55.

2. Hugh Hastings, ed., *Ecclesiastical Records of the State of New York* (Albany, N.Y., 1901), 1: 56–57; J. Megapolensis and S. Drisius to the Classis of Amsterdam, Aug. 5, 1657, in *Documents of the Senate of the State of New York* 14, no. 32, part 6 (Albany, N.Y., 1902), 398–99.

3. Evan Haefeli, *New Netherland and the Dutch Origins of American Religious Liberty* (Philadelphia, 2012), 54–56; Jaap Jacobs, *The Colony of New Netherland: A Dutch Settlement in Seventeenth-Century America* (Ithaca, N.Y., 2009), 144.

4. "Indian Tradition of the First Arrival of the Dutch, at Manhattan Island," *Collections of the New-York Historical Society* (New York, 1841), 1: 71–72; Evan Haefeli, "On First Contact and Apotheosis: Manitou and Men in North America," *Ethnohistory* 54, no. 3 (Summer 2007): 420.

5. "Remonstrance of the West India Company Against a Peace with Spain," in E. B. O'Callaghan, *Documents Relative to the Colonial History of the State of New-York* (Albany, 1856), 1: 96.

6. Corwin, ed., *Ecclesiastical Records*, 1: 57–59.

7. Corwin, ed., *Ecclesiastical Records*, 1: 62–63.

8. Bernard Bailyn, *The Barbarous Years: The Conflict of Civilizations, 1600–1675* (New York, 2012), 219–21.

9. Berthold Fernow, ed., *The Records of New Amsterdam*, vol. 1: *Minutes of the Court of Burgomasters and Schepens, 1653–1655* (New York, 1897), 31; Bailyn, *Barbarous Years*, 231.

10. "Father Jogues' Description of New Netherland," Aug. 3, 1646, in *Collections of the New-York Historical Society* 3, part 1 (New York, 1857), 215–16; Haefeli, *New Netherland*, 91.

11. J. Megapolensis and S. Drisius to the Classis of Amsterdam, Aug. 5, 1657, in *Documents of the Senate of the State of New York*, 395–96.

12. Johannes Megapolensis to the Classis of Amsterdam, Mar. 18, 1655, in J. Franklin Jameson, ed., *Narratives of New Netherland, 1609–1664* (New York, 1909), 392–93; Bailyn, *Barbarous Years*, 254; "Ordinance against Practicing any Religion other than the Reformed," in Charles T. Gehring, ed., *Council Minutes, 1655–1656* (Syracuse, N.Y., 1995), 209–10; Haefeli, *New Netherland*, 116–17, 141.

13. Haefeli, *New Netherland*, 162–63; Bailyn, *Barbarous Years*, 255–56; George Rosen, "Psychopathology in the Social Process: Dance Frenzies, Demonic Possession, Revival Movements and Similar So-Called Psychic Epidemics: An Interpretation," in Brian P. Levack, ed., *Articles on Witchcraft, Magic and Demonology* 9 (New York, 1992), 233.

14. "Remonstrance of the Inhabitants of Flushing, L.I.," Dec. 27, 1657, and "Sentence of Tobias Feakx," Jan. 28, 1658, in B. Fernow, ed., *Documents Relating to the History of the Early Colonial Settlements* (Albany, N.Y., 1883), 403, 409.

15. Pieter Plockhoy, *The Way to the Peace and Settlement of These Nations* (London, 1659), 8, 17; Bailyn, *Barbarous Years*, 313–14.

16. Bailyn, *Barbarous Years*, 317–18; "all eccentric persons" quote from Frank L. Greenagel, *The New Jersey Churchscape: Encountering Eighteenth- and Nineteenth-Century Churches* (New Brunswick, N.J., 2001), 8.

17. Bailyn, *Barbarous Years*, 319–20.
18. William Penn, *The Great Case of Liberty of Conscience Once More Briefly Debated and Defended* ([London], 1670), 11; "free colony" in William Penn to Roger Mompesson, "17th of 12th mo., 1704–05," in "Mrs. Hughs," *The Life of William Penn* (Philadelphia, 1828), 205.
19. "Laws Agreed Upon in England, &c., 1682," in Daniel L. Dreisbach and Mark David Hall, eds., *The Sacred Rights of Conscience* (Indianapolis, 2009), 118–19.
20. Penn quoted in John Smolenski, *Friends and Strangers: The Making of a Creole Culture in Colonial Pennsylvania* (Philadelphia, 2010), 97, see also 121; Daniel K. Richter, *Trade, Land, Power: The Struggle for Eastern North America* (Philadelphia, 2013), 136.
21. James O'Neil Spady, "Colonialism and the Discursive Antecedents of Penn's Treaty with the Indians," in William A. Pencak and Daniel K. Richter, eds., *Friends and Enemies in Penn's Woods: Indians, Colonists, and the Racial Construction of Pennsylvania* (University Park, Pa., 2004), 31–32.
22. Richter, *Trade, Land, Power*, 136–37, 145–46.
23. George Keith, *The Presbyterian and Independent Visible Churches in New England* (Philadelphia, 1689), title page.
24. Jon Butler, "'Gospel Order Improved': The Keithian Schism and the Exercise of Quaker Ministerial Authority in Pennsylvania," *William and Mary Quarterly*, 3d. ser., 31, no. 3 (July 1974): 434, 445–46.
25. Butler, "Gospel Order Improved," 446–47.
26. Butler, "Gospel Order Improved," 448–50; Smolenski, *Friends and Strangers*, 160.
27. Butler, "Gospel Order Improved," 451.
28. [George Keith,] *An Exhortation and Caution to Friends Concerning Buying or Keeping of Negroes* ([New York, 1693]), 1–2; Travis Glasson, *Mastering Christianity: Missionary Anglicanism and Slavery in the Atlantic World* (New York, 2012), 52–53.
29. Thelma Willis Foote, *Black and White Manhattan: The History of Racial Formation in Colonial New York City* (New York, 2004), 104.

CHAPTER SEVEN. THE COLONIAL SOUTH AND CARIBBEAN

1. Fundamental Constitutions of Carolina (1669), at http://avalon.law.yale.edu/17th_century/nc05.asp#b3 [accessed Apr. 11, 2014].
2. Stephan Palmié, "Toward Sugar and Slavery," in Stephan Palmié and Francisco A. Scarano, eds., *The Caribbean: A History of the Region and Its Peoples* (Chicago, 2011), 143–45.
3. Linford D. Fisher, "'Dangerous Designes': The 1676 Barbados Act to Prohibit New England Slave Importation," *William and Mary Quarterly*, 3d ser., 71, no. 1 (Jan. 2014): 110, 112, 115–16.
4. Katharine Gerbner, "The Ultimate Sin: Christianising Slaves in Barbados in the Seventeenth Century," *Slavery and Abolition* 31, no. 1 (Mar. 2010): 59.
5. Gerbner, "Ultimate Sin," 66–67.
6. Virginia Bernhard, "Religion, Politics, and Witchcraft in Bermuda, 1651–1655," *William and Mary Quarterly*, 3d ser., 67, no. 4 (Oct. 2010): 679.

7. Bernhard, "Religion, Politics," 691–93, 706–7.
8. Karen Ordahl Kupperman, "Errand to the Indies: Puritan Colonization from Providence Island Through the Western Design," *William and Mary Quarterly*, 3d ser., 45, no. 1 (Jan. 1988): 80.
9. Kupperman, "Errand to the Indies," 80, 82.
10. Kupperman, "Errand to the Indies," 84.
11. Karen Ordahl Kupperman, *Providence Island, 1630–1641: The Other Puritan Colony* (New York, 1993), 337–38.
12. Richard S. Dunn, *Sugar and Slaves: The Rise of the Planter Class in the English West Indies, 1624–1713*, rev. ed. (Chapel Hill, N.C., 2000), 149, 151.
13. Dunn, *Sugar and Slaves*, 155–56.
14. Dunn, *Sugar and Slaves*, 183–84.
15. Dunn, *Sugar and Slaves*, 186–87; Matthew Mulcahy, "'That Fatall Spott': The Rise and Fall—and Rise and Fall Again—Of Port Royal, Jamaica," in Carole Shammas, ed., *Investing in the Early Modern Built Environment: Europeans, Asians, Settlers, and Indigenous Societies* (Boston, 2012), 191–92.
16. Dunn, *Sugar and Slaves*, 110–13.
17. John Archdale, "A New Description of that Fertile and Pleasant Province of Carolina," (1707), in Alexander S. Salley, Jr., *Narratives of Early Carolina, 1650–1708* (New York, 1911), 285, 308–9.
18. John Lawson, *The History of Carolina* (London, 1714), xv.
19. Kathryn E. Holland Braund, *Deerskins and Duffels: Creek Indian Trade with Anglo-America, 1685–1815* (Lincoln, Neb., 1993), 97–98.
20. David J. Weber, *The Spanish Frontier in North America* (New Haven, Conn., 1992), 142–43.
21. Weber, *Spanish Frontier*, 90.
22. Thomas J. Little, *The Origins of Southern Evangelicalism: Religious Revivalism in the South Carolina Lowcountry, 1670–1760* (Columbia, S.C., 2013), 26–28.
23. Little, *Southern Evangelicalism*, 29.
24. Anthony W. Parker, *Scottish Highlanders in Colonial Georgia: The Recruitment, Emigration, and Settlement at Darien, 1735–1748* (Athens, Ga., 1997), 11–12; Little, *Southern Evangelicalism*, 29–30.
25. Bertrand Van Ruymbeke, *From New Babylon to Eden: The Huguenots and Their Migration to Colonial South Carolina* (Columbia, S.C., 2006), 69, 97, 106.
26. Little, *Southern Evangelicalism*, 39, 42.
27. Little, *Southern Evangelicalism*, 32; Daniel Defoe, *The Case of the Dissenters in Carolina* (London, 1706), 4.
28. Johnston quoted in William Stevens Perry, *The History of the American Episcopal Church, 1587–1883* (Boston, 1885), 1: 379.
29. Fleetwood quoted in Little, *Southern Evangelicalism*, 72–73; Rebecca Anne Goetz, *The Baptism of Early Virginia: How Christianity Created Race* (Baltimore, 2012), 142.
30. Frank J. Klingberg, ed., *The Carolina Chronicle of Dr. Francis Le Jau, 1706–1717* (Berkeley, Calif., 1956), 37, 50, 52, 55; Travis Glasson, *Mastering Christianity: Missionary Anglicanism and Slavery in the Atlantic World* (New York, 2012), 6–7, 100, 103.

31. Denise I. Bossy, "Indian Slavery in Southeastern Indian and British Societies, 1670–1730," in Alan Gallay, ed., *Indian Slavery in Colonial America* (Lincoln, Neb., 2009), 224–26; Alan Gallay, *The Indian Slave Trade: The Rise of the English Empire in the American South, 1670–1717* (New Haven, Conn., 2002), 299.

32. Klingberg, ed., *Carolina Chronicle*, 69; Mark M. Smith, "Remembering Mary, Shaping Revolt: Reconsidering the Stono Rebellion," *Journal of Southern History* 67, no. 3 (Aug. 2001): 517, 527–30.

33. "Report of the Committee Appointed to Enquire into the Causes of the Disappointment of Success in the Late Expedition against St. Augustine," June 2, 1741, in *Collections of the South Carolina Historical Society*, vol. 4 (1887), 19.

CHAPTER EIGHT. AFRICANS AND ATLANTIC WORLD SLAVERY

1. Leslie M. Harris, *In the Shadow of Slavery: African Americans in New York City, 1626–1863* (Chicago, 2003), 14–15.

2. Randy J. Sparks, *Where the Negroes Are Masters: An African Port in the Era of the Slave Trade* (Cambridge, Mass., 2014), 8–9; Adrian Hastings, *The Church in Africa, 1450–1950* (Oxford, Eng., 1994), 71–72.

3. John K. Thornton, *The Kongolese Saint Anthony: Dona Beatriz Kimpa Vita and the Antonian Movement, 1684–1706* (Cambridge, Eng., 1998), 32–33; John K. Thornton, "Afro-Christian Syncretism in the Kingdom of Kongo," *Journal of African History* 54, no. 1 (Mar. 2013): 57–60.

4. John K. Thornton, *Africa and Africans in the Making of the Atlantic World, 1400–1800*, 2d ed. (New York, 1998), 246.

5. Jean Barbot in *A Collection of Voyages and Travels, Some Now First Printed from Original Manuscripts* (London, 1732), 5: 104, 134–35; Thornton, *Africa and Africans*, 236–37.

6. Ira Berlin, *Many Thousands Gone: The First Two Centuries of Slavery in North America* (Cambridge, Mass., 1998), 50–51.

7. Edward B. Rugemer, "The Development of Mastery and Race in the Comprehensive Slave Codes of the Greater Caribbean During the Seventeenth Century," *William and Mary Quarterly*, 3d ser., 70, no. 3 (July 2013): 438–39, 441.

8. Rugemer, "Development of Mastery and Race," 444–47, 450, 452.

9. Rugemer, "Development of Mastery and Race," 454–56.

10. Rugemer, "Development of Mastery and Race," 456; William G. McLoughlin and Winthrop D. Jordan, "Baptists Face the Barbarities of Slavery in 1710," *Journal of Southern History* 29, no. 4 (Nov. 1963): 497–98; L. H. Roper, "The 1701 'Act for the Better Ordering of Slaves': Reconsidering the History of Slavery in Proprietary South Carolina," *William and Mary Quarterly*, 3d ser., 64, no. 2 (Apr. 2007): 403.

11. John C. Coombs, "The Phases of Conversion: A New Chronology for the Rise of Slavery in Early Virginia," *William and Mary Quarterly*, 3d ser., 68, no. 3 (July 2011): 347, 350, 359.

12. Rebecca Anne Goetz, *The Baptism of Early Virginia: How Christianity Created Race* (Baltimore, 2012), 86–87, 106–7.

13. Goetz, *Baptism of Early Virginia*, 83, 137.

14. Berlin, *Many Thousands Gone*, 101.

15. David Richardson, "Shipboard Revolts, African Authority, and the Atlantic Slave Trade," *William and Mary Quarterly*, 3d ser., 58, no. 1 (Jan. 2001): 72, 74–75.

16. Stephanie E. Smallwood, "African Guardians, European Slave Ships, and the Changing Dynamics of Power in the Early Modern Atlantic," *William and Mary Quarterly*, 3d ser., 64, no. 4 (Oct. 2007): 683–84, 695–96, 713, 715.

17. Estimates from Emory University's *Voyages: The Trans-atlantic Slave Trade Database*, at http://www.slavevoyages.org/tast/assessment/estimates.faces.

18. Vincent Brown, *The Reaper's Garden: Death and Power in the World of Atlantic Slavery* (Cambridge, Mass., 2008), 15, 49–50.

19. Brown, *Reaper's Garden*, 52, 54.

20. Brown, *Reaper's Garden*, 53.

21. Trevor Burnard, *Mastery, Tyranny, and Desire: Thomas Thistlewood and His Slaves in the Anglo-Jamaican World* (Chapel Hill, N.C., 2004), 31.

22. Russell R. Menard, "Slave Demography in the Lowcountry, 1670–1740: From Frontier Society to Plantation Regime," *South Carolina Historical Magazine* 101, no. 3 (July 2000): 193; Berlin, *Many Thousands Gone*, 143.

23. Berlin, *Many Thousands Gone*, 146–47.

24. Berlin, *Many Thousands Gone*, 152–53.

25. Berlin, *Many Thousands Gone*, 154–55.

26. *The South-Carolina Gazette*, Dec. 5, 1771; J. William Harris, *The Hanging of Thomas Jeremiah: A Free Black Man's Encounter with Liberty* (New Haven, Conn., 2009), 29–30; Berlin, *Many Thousands Gone*, 157–58.

27. Berlin, *Many Thousands Gone*, 110–11.

28. Russell Menard, "Making a 'Popular Slave Society' in Colonial British America," *Journal of Interdisciplinary History* 43, no. 3 (Winter 2013): 384–86, 394.

29. Philip D. Morgan and Michael L. Nicholls, "Slavery in Piedmont Virginia, 1720–1790," *William and Mary Quarterly*, 3d ser., 46, no. 2 (Apr. 1989): 211–15, 217.

30. Berlin, *Many Thousands Gone*, 116; Edmund S. Morgan, *American Slavery, American Freedom: The Ordeal of Colonial Virginia* (New York, 1975), 313.

31. Travis Glasson, *Mastering Christianity: Missionary Anglicanism and Slavery in the Atlantic World* (New York, 2012), 76–80.

32. New York State Library, *83rd Annual Report* (Albany, N.Y., 1901), 264–65; Carl H. Nightingale, "Before Race Mattered: Geographies of the Color Line in Early Colonial Madras and New York," *American Historical Review* 113, no. 1 (Feb. 2008): 69; Glasson, *Mastering Christianity*, 81–84.

33. Nightingale, "Before Race Mattered," 59.

34. Harris, *In the Shadow of Slavery*, 43

35. Harris, *In the Shadow of Slavery*, 44–46.

36. Harris, *In the Shadow of Slavery*, 46–47.

37. Berlin, *Many Thousands Gone*, 369–370; Robin Blackburn, *The Making of New World Slavery: From the Baroque to the Modern* (London, 1997), 404.

38. Osnabrig was a coarse fabric named from Osnaburg, Germany, where it was originally produced. It was often used for sacks as well as slaves' clothing.

CHAPTER NINE. THE GLORIOUS REVOLUTION AND THE LINKS
OF EMPIRE IN ENGLISH AMERICA

1. *The Declaration of the Gentlemen, Merchants, and Inhabitants of Boston* (Boston, 1689), 1–3.
2. Richard S. Dunn, "The Glorious Revolution and America," in Nicholas Canny, ed., *The Oxford History of the British Empire: The Origins of Empire* (New York, 1998), 457.
3. Owen Stanwood, *The Empire Reformed: English America in the Age of the Glorious Revolution* (Philadelphia, 2011), 86–88.
4. Stanwood, *Empire Reformed*, 88–89.
5. Stanwood, *Empire Reformed*, 90–91; David William Vorhees, "'To assert our Right before it be quite lost': The Leisler Rebellion in the Delaware River Valley," *Pennsylvania History* 64, no. 1 (Winter 1997): 15.
6. Beverly McAnear, ed., "Mariland's Grevances Wiy the Have Taken Op Arms," *Journal of Southern History* 8, no. 3 (Aug. 1942): 401.
7. McAnear, "Mariland's Grevances," 404.
8. Stanwood, *Empire Reformed*, 107–9.
9. David S. Lovejoy, *The Glorious Revolution in America* (New York, 1972), 85.
10. Stanwood, *Empire Reformed*, 110–12.
11. Guy Chet, *Conquering the American Wilderness: The Triumph of European Warfare in the Colonial Northeast* (Amherst, Mass., 2003), 79–80.
12. Stanwood, *Empire Reformed*, 98–99.
13. Cotton Mather, *A Pillar of Gratitude* (Boston, 1700), 19; Thomas Hutchinson, *The History of Massachusetts* (Boston, 1795), 1: 332.
14. Hutchinson, *History of Massachusetts*, 1: 332; Charles M. Andrews, ed., *Narratives of the Insurrections, 1675–1690* (New York, 1915), 197; Stanwood, *Empire Reformed*, 100–101.
15. Stanwood, *Empire Reformed*, 102–6.
16. Stanwood, *Empire Reformed*, 151–52.
17. John R. Brodhead, *Documents Relative to the Colonial History of the State of New York* (Albany, N.Y., 1853), 696–98; Stanwood, *Empire Reformed*, 153–54.
18. Stanwood, *Empire Reformed*, 157–61, 170.
19. Thomas S. Kidd, *The Protestant Interest: New England After Puritanism* (New Haven, Conn., 2004), 10; Stanwood, *Empire Reformed*, 164–67.
20. Stanwood, *Empire Reformed*, 202; Kidd, *Protestant Interest*, 107–8.
21. Kidd, *Protestant Interest*, 41.
22. Richard Lyman Bushman, "Markets and Composite Farms in Early America," *William and Mary Quarterly*, 3d ser., 55, no. 3 (July 1998): 361.
23. Jacob M. Price, "The Imperial Economy, 1700–1776," in P. J. Marshall, ed., *The Oxford History of the British Empire: The Eighteenth Century* (New York, 1998), 81–86, 90.
24. Laurel Thatcher Ulrich, "Wheels, Looms, and the Gender Division of Labor in Eighteenth-Century New England," *William and Mary Quarterly*, 3d ser., 55, no. 1 (Jan. 1998): 6; Bushman, "Markets and Farms," 367.

25. T. H. Breen, "An Empire of Goods: The Anglicization of Colonial America, 1690–1776," *Journal of British Studies* 25, no. 4 (Oct. 1986): 467, 477, 485.

26. Laura E. Johnson, "'Goods to clothe themselves': Native Consumers and Native Images on the Pennsylvania Trading Frontier, 1712–1760," *Winterthur Portfolio* 43, no. 1 (Spring 2009): 118–21; James Axtell, *Beyond 1492: Encounters in Colonial North America* (New York, 1992), 129, 138.

27. Breen, "Empire of Goods," 488–89; Cary Carson, "The Consumer Revolution in Colonial British America: Why Demand?" in Cary Carson, Ronald Hoffman, and Peter J. Albert, eds., *Of Consuming Interests: The Style of Life in the Eighteenth Century* (Charlottesville, Va., 1994), 522–24.

28. Ann Smart Martin, "Commercial Space as Consumption Area: Retail Stores in Early Virginia," *Vernacular Architecture Forum* 8 (2000): 204; Breen, "Empire of Goods," 492.

29. Chris Evans, "The Plantation Hoe: The Rise and Fall of an Atlantic Commodity, 1650–1850," *William and Mary Quarterly*, 3d ser., 69, no. 1 (Jan. 2012): 79, 83.

30. Jennifer L. Anderson, "Nature's Currency: The Atlantic Mahogany Trade and the Commodification of Nature in the Eighteenth Century," *Early American Studies* 2, no. 1 (Spring 2004): 52, 54, 73.

31. Dunn, "Glorious Revolution," 465.

CHAPTER TEN. THE GREAT AWAKENING

1. Linford D. Fisher, *The Indian Great Awakening: Religion and the Shaping of Native Cultures in Early America* (New York, 2012), 113–15.

2. When used in the eighteenth century, the term "evangelical" was typically an adjective rather than a noun, as in an "evangelical book" or an "evangelical doctrine."

3. Thomas S. Kidd, ed., *The Great Awakening: A Brief History with Documents* (Boston, 2007), 68–70.

4. Mary Beth Norton, *In the Devil's Snare: The Salem Witchcraft Crisis of 1692* (New York, 2002), 179–80.

5. Thomas S. Kidd, *The Great Awakening: The Roots of Evangelical Christianity in Colonial America* (New Haven, Conn., 2007), 6–7.

6. Leonard W. Labaree et al., eds., *The Autobiography of Benjamin Franklin*, 2d ed. (New Haven, Conn., 2003), 178; Kidd, *Brief History with Documents*, 55.

7. George Whitefield, *A Continuation of the Rev. Mr. Whitefield's Journal, From a Few Days after His Return to Georgia* (London, 1741), 25.

8. Whitefield, *Continuation*, 31–32.

9. Whitefield, *Continuation*, 29, 38.

10. Kidd, *Brief History with Documents*, 71.

11. Catherine A. Brekus, *Strangers and Pilgrims: Female Preaching in America, 1740–1845* (Chapel Hill, N.C., 1998), 23–26.

12. Kidd, *Great Awakening*, 285.

13. Kidd, *Great Awakening*, 182–83.

14. Kidd, *Brief History with Documents*, 120–21.

15. Kidd, *Brief History with Documents*, 133.

16. Kidd, *Brief History with Documents*, 113.

17. Jon F. Sensbach, *Rebecca's Revival: Creating Black Christianity in the Atlantic World* (Cambridge, Mass., 2005), 188; David Hempton, *The Church in the Long Eighteenth Century* (London, 2011), 83–85.

18. Phillis Wheatley to Samson Occom, Feb. 11, 1774, *Boston Post-Boy*, Mar. 14, 1774, p. 3.

19. William Stevens Perry, ed., *Historical Collections Relating to the American Colonial Church* (Hartford, Conn., 1873), 348–50; Frank Lambert, "'Pedlar in Divinity': George Whitefield and the Great Awakening, 1737–1745," *Journal of American History* 77, no. 3 (Dec. 1990): 814.

20. Samuel Davies, *The State of Religion among the Protestant Dissenters in Virginia* (Boston, 1751), 10–11; Lambert, "Pedlar in Divinity," 823–24.

21. Lambert, "Pedlar in Divinity," 836.

22. Timothy E. W. Gloege, "The Trouble with *Christian History:* Thomas Prince's 'Great Awakening,'" *Church History* 82, no. 1 (Mar. 2013): 149.

23. Kidd, *Brief History with Documents*, 1.

24. Gloege, "Trouble with *Christian History*," 149–50.

25. Kidd, *Great Awakening*, 190–92; Fisher, *Indian Great Awakening*, 76–79.

26. Gerald R. McDermott, "Jonathan Edwards and American Indians: The Devil Sucks Their Blood," *New England Quarterly* 72, no. 4 (Dec. 1999): 540, 542, 545.

27. McDermott, "Devil Sucks Their Blood," 552, 554.

28. Fisher, *Indian Great Awakening*, 66–67, 75–76.

29. Fisher, *Indian Great Awakening*, 124–25.

30. Kidd, *Great Awakening*, 208.

31. Kidd, *Great Awakening*, 210–11; Fisher, *Indian Great Awakening*, 158, 183.

CHAPTER ELEVEN. THE ANGLO-AMERICAN BACKCOUNTRY

1. Ray Allen Billington and Martin Ridge, *Westward Expansion: A History of the American Frontier* (Albuquerque, N.M., 2001), 24.

2. Emory University, *Voyages: The Trans-Atlantic Slave Trade Database*, http://www.slavevoyages.org/tast/database/search.faces; James Horn, "British Diaspora: Emigration from Britain, 1680–1815," in P. J. Marshall, ed., *The Oxford History of the British Empire: The Eighteenth Century* (New York, 1998), 31–32; Christopher Tomlins, *Freedom Bound: Law, Labor, and Civic Identity in Colonizing English America, 1580–1865* (New York, 2010), 576–77.

3. Aaron S. Fogleman, "From Slaves, Convicts, and Servants to Free Passengers: The Transformation of Immigration in the Era of the American Revolution," *Journal of American History* 85, no. 1 (Jun. 1998): 49.

4. Fogleman, "From Slaves," 54.

5. Fogleman, "From Slaves," 55–57.

6. Thomas S. Kidd, *Patrick Henry: First Among Patriots* (New York, 2011), 7–9.

7. Bernard Bailyn, *The Peopling of British North America: An Introduction* (New York, 1986), 32.

8. Patrick Griffin, *The People with No Name: Ireland's Ulster Scots, America's Scots Irish, and the Creation of a British Atlantic World, 1689–1764* (Princeton, N.J., 2001), 70–71, 80.

9. Griffin, *People with No Name*, 88–89.

10. Griffin, *People with No Name*, 108–109.

11. Marie Basile McDaniel, "Divergent Paths: Processes of Identity Formation Among German Speakers, 1730–1760," in Jan Stievermann and Oliver Scheiding, eds., *A Peculiar Mixture: German-Language Cultures and Identities in Eighteenth-Century North America* (University Park, Pa., 2013), 190.

12. Jan Stievermann, "A 'Plain, Rejected Little Flock': The Politics of Martyrological Self-Fashioning Among Pennsylvania's German Peace Churches, 1739–65," *William and Mary Quarterly*, 3d ser., 66, no. 2 (Apr. 2009): 299.

13. Patrick M. Erben, *A Harmony of the Spirits: Translation and the Language of Community in Early Pennsylvania* (Chapel Hill, N.C., 2012), 221–23.

14. Robert P. Sutton, *Communal Utopias and the American Experience: Religious Communities, 1732–2000* (Westport, Conn., 2003), 3, 8.

15. Thomas S. Kidd, *The Great Awakening: The Roots of Evangelical Christianity in Colonial America* (New Haven, Conn., 2007), 260–62.

16. Kidd, *Great Awakening*, 262.

17. James H. Merrell, "Shamokin, 'the very seat of the Prince of darkness': Unsettling the Early American Frontier," in Andrew R. L. Cayton and Fredrika J. Teute, eds., *Contact Points: American Frontiers from the Mohawk Valley to the Mississippi, 1750–1830* (Chapel Hill, N.C., 1998), 16–18; Kidd, *Great Awakening*, 198–99.

18. Kidd, *Great Awakening*, 199.

19. Warren R. Hofstra, "'The Extention of His Majesties Dominions': The Virginia Backcountry and the Reconfiguration of Imperial Frontiers," *Journal of American History* 84, no. 4 (Mar. 1998): 1298–99.

20. Warren R. Hofstra, *The Planting of New Virginia: Settlement and Landscape in the Shenandoah Valley* (Baltimore, 2004), 34–35, 39, 42.

21. Kenneth Coleman, "The Founding of Georgia," in Harvey H. Jackson and Phinizy Spalding, eds., *Forty Years of Diversity: Essays on Colonial Georgia* (Athens, Ga., 1984), 16–17.

22. Turk McCleskey, *The Road to Black Ned's Forge : A Story of Race, Sex, and Trade on the Colonial American Frontier* (Charlottesville, Va., 2014), 3.

23. McCleskey, *Road to Black Ned's Forge*, 5, 75–76, 89–90.

24. McCleskey, *Road to Black Ned's Forge*, 110–14.

25. Thomas S. Kidd, *The Protestant Interest: New England After Puritanism* (New Haven, Conn., 2004), 96, 107–8.

26. Ian K. Steele, *Warpaths: Invasions of North America* (New York, 1994), 168–69.

27. Steele, *Warpaths*, 170; Harriet Cornelia Cooper, *James Oglethorpe: The Founder of Georgia* (New York, 1904), 175.

28. Steele, *Warpaths*, 162, 170; N. E. S. Griffiths, *From Migrant to Acadian: A North American Border People, 1604–1755* (Montreal, 2005), 350.

29. Steele, *Warpaths*, 170–71; Jonathan Edwards to a correspondent in Scotland, Nov.

1745, in George Claghorn, ed., *Letters and Personal Writings*, vol. 16 of *The Works of Jonathan Edwards* (New Haven, Conn., 1998), 197.

30. Steele, *Warpaths*, 173.

CHAPTER TWELVE. THE EARLY AMERICAN WEST

1. Lawrence N. Powell, *The Accidental City: Improvising New Orleans* (Cambridge, Mass., 2012), 42, 54–55.

2. Peter H. Wood, "From Atlantic History to a Continental Approach," in Jack P. Greene and Philip D. Morgan, eds., *Atlantic History: A Critical Appraisal* (New York, 2009), 285–86.

3. George B. Grinnell, "Pawnee Mythology," in *Journal of American Folk-Lore* 5 (1892): 120–21.

4. Kathleen DuVal, "'A Good Relationship, & Commerce': The Native Political Economy of the Arkansas River Valley," *Early American Studies* 1, no. 1 (Spring 2003): 75–76.

5. Tracy Neal Leavelle, "'Bad Things' and 'Good Hearts': Mediation, Meaning, and the Language of Illinois Christianity," *Church History* 76, no. 2 (June 2007): 363, 367, 374–75, 378–79.

6. Colin G. Calloway, *One Vast Winter Count: The Native American West Before Lewis and Clark* (Lincoln, Neb., 2003), 322–24; Brett Rushforth, *Bonds of Alliance: Indigenous and Atlantic Slaveries in New France* (Chapel Hill, N.C., 2012), 202–3.

7. Le Page du Pratz, *History of Louisiana* (London, 1774), 76–77; Calloway, *Vast Winter Count*, 319–20; Ira Berlin, *Many Thousands Gone: The First Two Centuries of Slavery in North America* (Cambridge, Mass., 1998), 89.

8. Berlin, *Many Thousands Gone*, 81–84.

9. Dunbar Rowland, *Mississippi Provincial Archives, 1701–1729* (Jackson, Miss., 1929), 2: 482; Berlin, *Many Thousands Gone*, 87.

10. Jennifer M. Spear, "Colonial Intimacies: Legislating Sex in French Louisiana," *William and Mary Quarterly*, 3d ser., 60, no. 1 (Jan. 2003): 85–86.

11. Juliana Barr, "A Diplomacy of Gender: Rituals of First Contact in the 'Land of the Tejas,'" *William and Mary Quarterly*, 3d ser., 61, no. 3 (July 2004): 408, 412.

12. Jesús F. de la Teja, "A Spanish Borderlands Community: San Antonio," *OAH Magazine of History* (Summer 2000): 26.

13. Pekka Hämäläinen, *The Comanche Empire* (New Haven, Conn., 2008), 59–61.

14. Pekka Hämäläinen, "The Rise and Fall of Plains Indian Horse Cultures," *Journal of American History* 90, no. 3 (Dec. 2003): 838.

15. Hämäläinen, *Comanche Empire*, 45; Gutiérrez, *When Jesus Came*, 152.

16. Pekka Hämäläinen, "The Western Comanche Trade Center: Rethinking the Plains Indian Trade System," *Western Historical Quarterly* 29, no. 4 (Winter 1998): 490–91, 501–4.

17. Rushforth, *Bonds of Alliance*, 229–32.

18. Elizabeth A. Fenn, "Whither the Rest of the Continent?" *Journal of the Early Republic* 24, no. 2 (Summer 2004): 168–69.

19. Paul W. Mapp, *The Elusive West and the Contest for Empire, 1713–1763* (Chapel Hill, N.C., 2011), 4–5, 292–304.

20. Claudio Saunt, *West of the Revolution: An Uncommon History of 1776* (New York, 2014), 40–41; Gwenn A. Miller, *Kodiak Kreol: Communities of Empire in Early Russian America* (Ithaca, N.Y., 2010), 69; Robert Nichols and Robert Croskey, "The Condition of the Orthodox Church in Russian America: Innokentii Veniaminov's History of the Russian Church in Alaska," *Pacific Northwest Quarterly* 63, no. 2 (Apr. 1972): 42.

21. Weber, *Spanish Frontier in North America*, 238, 242–43.

22. Steven W. Hackel, "The Staff of Leadership: Indian Authority in the Missions of Alta California," *William and Mary Quarterly*, 3d ser., 54, no. 2 (Apr. 1997): 350; Saunt, *West of the Revolution*, 62–69.

23. Weber, *Spanish Frontier*, 246; Kent G. Lightfoot, *Indians, Missionaries, and Merchants: The Legacy of Colonial Encounters on the California Frontier* (Berkeley, Calif., 2005), 68; Frank Soule et al., *The Annals of San Francisco* (New York, 1855), 51.

24. James A. Sandos, *Converting California: Indians and Franciscans in the Missions* (New Haven, Conn., 2004), 49–54.

25. Steven W. Hackel, *Children of Coyote, Missionaries of Saint Francis: Indian-Spanish Relations in Colonial California, 1769–1850* (Chapel Hill, N.C., 2005), 114–16, 127.

26. Hackel, *Children of Coyote*, 133–34.

27. Hackel, *Children of Coyote*, 148–51.

28. Hackel, *Children of Coyote*, 162.

29. Hackel, *Children of Coyote*, 262–66.

30. Powell, *Accidental City*, 113.

31. Powell, *Accidental City*, 123–24.

32. Emily Clark and Virginia Meacham Gould, "The Feminine Face of Afro-Catholicism in New Orleans, 1727–1852," *William and Mary Quarterly*, 3d ser., 59, no. 2 (Apr. 2002): 415, 417–20, 424.

33. Daniel H. Usner, Jr., *Indians, Settlers, and Slaves in a Frontier Exchange Economy: The Lower Mississippi Valley Before 1783* (Chapel Hill, N.C., 1992), 116–18.

CHAPTER THIRTEEN. THE SEVEN YEARS' WAR

1. William J. Eccles, *The Canadian Frontier, 1534–1760*, rev. ed. (Albuquerque, N.M., 1983), 160, 162.

2. George Washington, "Journey to the French Commandant: Narrative," 1753, in *Papers of George Washington, Digital Edition*, Edward Lengel, Director, at http://rotunda.upress.virginia.edu/founders/default.xqy?keys=GEWN-print-01-01-02-0003-0002 [accessed 8/8/14]; Eccles, *Canadian Frontier*, 162–63.

3. Fred Anderson, *Crucible of War: The Seven Years' War and the Fate of Empire in British North America, 1754–1766* (New York, 2000), 49.

4. Anderson, *Crucible of War*, 6, 55.

5. Anderson, *Crucible of War*, 63–64.

6. Benjamin Franklin, *Autobiography*, part 15, and "Advertisement about Wagons," Apr. 26, 1755, at http://franklinpapers.org/ [accessed Aug. 8, 2014].

7. Anderson, *Crucible of War*, 99–104.

8. Alan Taylor, *American Colonies* (New York, 2001), 424.

9. Jon Parmenter, "After the Mourning Wars: The Iroquois as Allies in Colonial North American Campaigns, 1676–1760," *William and Mary Quarterly*, 3d ser., 64, no. 1 (Jan. 2007): 42–43, 57; Onondaga quote on 59.

10. Parmenter, "After the Mourning Wars," 63–64.

11. William R. Nester, *The Great Frontier War: Britain, France, and the Imperial Struggle for North America, 1607–1755* (Westport, Conn., 2000), 158–59.

12. Benjamin Franklin to Robert Hunter Morris, Jan. 14, 1756, at http://franklinpapers.org/franklin//framedVolumes.jsp [accessed Aug. 12, 2014]; Anderson, *Crucible of War*, 108–9; Parmenter, "After the Mourning Wars," 68.

13. Samuel Davies, *Religion and Patriotism the Constituents of a Good Soldier* (Philadelphia, 1755), 3–5, 14.

14. Anderson, *Crucible of War*, 185–90.

15. Anderson, *Crucible of War*, 195–99.

16. Steele, *Warpaths*, 208–9; Paul Kelton, "The British and Indian War: Cherokee Power and the Fate of Empire in North America," *William and Mary Quarterly*, 69, no. 4 (Oct. 2012): 778.

17. Eliga H. Gould, *Among the Powers of the Earth: The American Revolution and the Making of a New World Empire* (Cambridge, Mass., 2012), 43–44; Steele, *Warpaths*, 227–28.

18. Thomas S. Kidd, *God of Liberty: A Religious History of the American Revolution* (New York, 2010), 28–29; Steele, *Warpaths*, 217–19.

19. *Canada Subjected* [1760?], broadside.

20. Kidd, *God of Liberty*, 30; Sherry Johnson, *Climate and Catastrophe in Cuba and the Atlantic World in the Age of Revolution* (Chapel Hill, N.C., 2011), 50–54.

21. Steele, *Warpaths*, 224–25.

22. David Dixon, "'We Speak as One People': Native Unity and the Pontiac Indian Uprising," in Daniel P. Barr, ed., *The Boundaries Between Us: Natives and Newcomers Along the Frontiers of the Old Northwest Territory, 1750–1850* (Kent, Ohio, 2006), 59–60.

23. Peter Silver, *Our Savage Neighbors: How Indian War Transformed Early America* (New York, 2008), 66–67, 78.

24. Silver, *Savage Neighbors*, 178–80, 203; Benjamin Franklin, *A Narrative of the Late Massacres* (Philadelphia, 1764), 27.

25. Elizabeth A. Fenn, "Biological Warfare in Eighteenth-Century North America: Beyond Jeffery Amherst," *Journal of American History* 86, no. 4 (Mar. 2000): 1553–58.

26. Fintan O'Toole, *White Savage: William Johnson and the Invention of America* (New York, 2005), 252, 256.

27. "Croghan's Official Journal, 1765," in Clarence W. Alvord and Clarence E. Carter, eds., *The New Régime, 1765–1767* (Springfield, Ill., 1916), 47–48; Gregory Evans Dowd, *War Under Heaven: Pontiac, the Indian Nations, and the British Empire* (Baltimore, 2002), 260–62.

CONCLUSION

1. Thomas S. Kidd, *George Whitefield: America's Spiritual Founding Father* (New Haven, Conn., 2014), 243–44.
2. Benjamin Franklin, "Examination before the Committee of the Whole of the House of Commons," (1766), in Papers of Benjamin Franklin, at http://franklinpapers.org/franklin//framedVolumes.jsp [accessed Sept. 3, 2014]; Gordon S. Wood, *The Americanization of Benjamin Franklin* (New York, 2004), 119–20.
3. Robert V. Wells, "Population and Family in Early America," in Jack P. Greene and J. R. Pole, eds., *A Companion to the American Revolution* (Malden, Mass., 2000), 42–44.
4. Thomas P. Slaughter, *Independence: The Tangled Roots of the American Revolution* (New York, 2014), 98; Fred Anderson, *Crucible of War: The Seven Years' War and the Fate of Empire in British North America, 1754–1766* (New York, 2000), 286–89.
5. Thomas S. Kidd, *Patrick Henry: First Among Patriots* (New York, 2011), 27–28.
6. Wood, *Americanization*, 105–6.
7. Wood, *Americanization*, 107; *Considerations Upon the Act of Parliament* (Boston, 1764), 7; Kidd, *Patrick Henry*, 55.
8. Edmund S. Morgan, ed., *Prologue to Revolution: Sources and Documents on the Stamp Act Crisis, 1764–1766* (Chapel Hill, N.C., 1959), 93–94.
9. Kidd, *Patrick Henry*, 51–52, 58–59.
10. Morgan, ed., *Prologue to Revolution*, 51, 110, 112.
11. Morgan, ed., *Prologue to Revolution*, 116–17; Thomas S. Kidd, *God of Liberty: A Religious History of the American Revolution* (New York, 2010), 15.
12. Morgan ed., *Prologue to Revolution*, 155.
13. Patricia Cleary, *The World, The Flesh, and The Devil: A History of Colonial St. Louis* (Columbia, Mo., 2011), 132–36.
14. Cleary, *The World, The Flesh*, 137–40.
15. Claudio Saunt, *West of the Revolution: An Uncommon History of 1776* (New York, 2014), 74–79.
16. H. E. Bolton, ed., *Anza's California Expeditions*, vol. 3 (Berkeley, Calif., 1930), 401; Saunt, *West of the Revolution*, 81.

INDEX

Printed and bound by CPI Group (UK) Ltd, Croydon, CR0 4YY

13/04/2025

14656468-0002